Within these walls

Roman and medieval defences north of
Newgate at the Merrill Lynch Financial Centre,
City of London

MoLAS Monograph Series

For more information about these titles and other MoLAS publications visit the publications page at www.molas.org.uk

1 Excavations at the priory and hospital of St Mary Spital, London

2 The National Roman Fabric Reference Collection: a handbook

3 The Cross Bones burial ground, Redcross Way, Southwark, London: archaeological excavations (1991–8) for the London Underground Limited Jubilee Line Extension Project

4 The eastern cemetery of Roman London: excavations 1983–90

5 The Holocene evolution of the London Thames: archaeological excavations (1991–8) for the London Underground Limited Jubilee Line Extension Project

6 The Limehouse porcelain manufactory: excavations at 108–116 Narrow Street, London, 1990

7 Roman defences and medieval industry: excavations at Baltic House, City of London

8 London bridge: 2000 years of a river crossing

9 Roman and medieval townhouses on the London waterfront: excavations at Governor's House, City of London

10 The London Charterhouse

11 Medieval 'Westminster' floor tiles

12 Settlement in Roman Southwark: archaeological excavations (1991–8) for the London Underground Limited Jubilee Line Extension Project

13 Aspects of medieval and later Southwark: archaeological excavations (1991–8) for the London Underground Limited Jubilee Line Extension Project

14 The prehistory and topography of Southwark and Lambeth

15 Middle Saxon London: excavations at the Royal Opera House 1989–99

16 Urban development in north-west Roman Southwark: excavations 1974–90

17 Industry in north-west Roman Southwark: excavations 1984–8

18 The Cistercian abbey of St Mary Stratford Langthorne, Essex: archaeological excavations for the London Underground Limited Jubilee Line Extension Project

19 Material culture in London in an age of transition: Tudor and Stuart period finds c 1450–c 1700 from excavations at riverside sites in Southwark

20 Excavations at the priory of the Order of the Hospital of St John of Jerusalem, Clerkenwell, London

21 Roman and medieval Cripplegate, City of London: archaeological excavations 1992–8

22 The royal palace, abbey and town of Westminster on Thorney Island: archaeological excavations (1991–8) for the London Underground Limited Jubilee Line Extension Project

23 A prestigious Roman building complex on the Southwark waterfront: excavations at Winchester Palace, London, 1983–90

24 Holy Trinity Priory, Aldgate, City of London: an archaeological reconstruction and history

25 Roman pottery production in the Walbrook valley: excavations at 20–28 Moorgate, City of London, 1998–2000

26 Prehistoric landscape to Roman villa: excavations at Beddington, Surrey, 1981–7

27 Saxon, medieval and post-medieval settlement at Sol Central, Marefair, Northampton: archaeological excavations, 1998–2002

28 John Baker's late 17th-century glasshouse at Vauxhall

29 The medieval postern gate by the Tower of London

30 Roman and later development east of the forum and Cornhill: excavations at Lloyd's Register, 71 Fenchurch Street, City of London

31 Winchester Palace: excavations at the Southwark residence of the bishops of Winchester

32 Development on Roman London's western hill: excavations at Paternoster Square, City of London

33 Within these walls: Roman and medieval defences north of Newgate at the Merrill Lynch Financial Centre, City of London

Within these walls

Roman and medieval defences north of Newgate at the Merrill Lynch Financial Centre, City of London

Jo Lyon

MoLAS Monograph 33

MUSEUM OF LONDON ARCHAEOLOGY SERVICE

Published by the Museum of London Archaeology Service
Copyright © Museum of London 2007

All rights reserved. No part of this publication may be reproduced, stored in a retrieval system or transmitted, in any form or by any means, electronic, mechanical, photocopying, recording or otherwise, without prior permission of the copyright owner.

The Ordnance Survey mapping included in this publication is provided by the City of London under licence from the Ordnance Survey © Crown copyright. Unauthorised reproduction infringes Crown copyright and may lead to prosecution or civil proceedings.
City of London 100023243-2007

A CIP catalogue record for this book is available from the British Library

Production and series design by Tracy Wellman
Typesetting and design by Sue Cawood
Reprographics by Andy Chopping
Copy editing by Katy Carter
Series editing by Sue Hirst/Susan M Wright
Post-excavation and series management by Peter Rowsome

Printed by the Lavenham Press

Front cover: Roman pipe clay figurine of Minerva <S1>; heraldic decoration on a medieval sheath-like leather object <S91>; delftware tile-lined water cistern from a post-Great Fire building

Back cover: Bastion 18 in 1912; detail of the floral pattern on a Dutch tile <T28> from the water cistern; artist's reconstruction of medieval Newgate

CONTRIBUTORS

Principal author	Jo Lyon
Building material	Ian Betts
Roman pottery	Rupert Featherby
Medieval and post-medieval pottery	Lucy Whittingham
Roman accessioned finds	Angela Wardle
Medieval accessioned finds	Jackie Keily
Animal bone	Jane Liddle
Plant remains	Anne Davis
Graphics	Neville Constantine and Peter Hart-Allison (plans), Faith Vardy (finds)
Photography	Andy Chopping, Maggie Cox, Edwin Baker
Academic adviser	Peter Rowsome
Project managers	Richard Malt, Angus Stephenson
Editors	Richard Malt, David Bowsher

CONTENTS

List of figures ix

List of tables xii

Summary xiii

Acknowledgements xiv

Foreword xv

Introduction **1**
- 1.1 Circumstances of the fieldwork 1
- 1.2 Previous archaeological investigations 4
- 1.3 Documentary sources 5
- 1.4 Organisation of the report 6
- 1.5 Textual and graphical conventions 7

Pre-Roman natural topography **2**
- 2.1 Introduction 9
- 2.2 Pleistocene geology (period 1) 9
  - Gravel terraces and palaeochannels 9
- 2.3 Holocene geology (period 1) 9
  - Brickearth ground surface 9
  - Palaeochannels 10
- 2.4 Discussion (period 1) 13

The Roman archaeological sequence **3**
- 3.1 Early Roman settlement, AD 43–late 2nd century (period 2) 14
  - Pre-Boudican development, c AD 43–70 (period 2, phase 1) 14
  - Post-Boudican development, c AD 70–120 (period 2, phase 2) 16
  - The Hadrianic fire and its aftermath, c AD 120–late 2nd century (period 2, phase 3) 29
- 3.2 Later Roman activity, late 2nd century–late 4th century AD (period 3) 35
  - Late Roman external activity (period 3, unphased) . . . 35
  - Construction of the Roman city defences, c late 2nd century–mid 3rd century AD (period 3, phase 1) . . . 37
  - Late Roman additions to the defences, c mid 3rd century–late 4th century AD (period 3, phase 2) . . . 46

The medieval archaeological sequence **4**
- 4.1 Introduction 53
- 4.2 Late Saxon settlement, c AD 880–1100 (period 4) . . . 54
- 4.3 Medieval settlement, c 1100–1300 (period 5) 57
  - The medieval city defences 59
  - The foundation of Greyfriars in 1225 63
  - Discussion of the earlier medieval settlement 64
- 4.4 Later medieval settlement, c 1300–1500 (period 5) . . . 65

			The rise and fall of Greyfriars, 1306–1538 65
			The later medieval city defences 72
			Finds, animal bones and plant remains from the medieval city ditch 75
			Discussion of the infilling of the medieval city ditch . 114
The post-medieval archaeological sequence	**5**	5.1	Introduction 116
		5.2	Pre-Great Fire settlement, c 1500–1666 (period 6) . . 117
			The demise of the city defences 117
			Christ Church and Christ's Hospital 121
			Discussion (period 6) 124
		5.3	Post-Great Fire redevelopment (period 7) 125
			Residential redevelopment 125
			Christ Church and Christ's Hospital rebuilt 126
			The Giltspur Street Compter (1787–1854) 133
			The General Post Office and the Merrill Lynch Financial Centre 142
			Discussion (period 7) 144
Conclusions	**6**	6.1	The Roman period 147
		6.2	The medieval period 148
		6.3	The post-medieval period 149
		6.4	Informing future research 149
Specialist appendices	**7**	7.1	The tin-glazed wall tiles 150
			Blue on white (or pale blue) designs 150
			Purple on white designs 154
			Blue and purple on white designs 154
			Purple and pale bluish-purple on white design . . . 154
			Polychrome designs 154
			Edging tiles 155
			'Marble' tiles 155
			Tile pictures 155
			Woodblock print design 155
			Copper plate designs 155
		7.2	The Roman pottery 163
			Methodology 163
			Quantification 163
		7.3	The medieval and post-medieval pottery 165
			Methodology 165
			Quantification 165
			Sources 165
		7.4	Roman accessioned finds 167

	Introduction	167
	Selected catalogue of accessioned finds from the well north of Building 8 (OA7, period 2)	167
	Selected catalogue of other Roman accessioned finds	168
7.5	Medieval accessioned finds	169
	Methodology	169
	Selected catalogue	170
7.6	Animal bone	175
	Summary statistics and methodology	175
7.7	Plant remains	176
	Introduction	176
	Methodology	177
	Results	177
	Conclusions	177

French and German summaries 181

Bibliography 184

Index 190

FIGURES

Fig 1	The study area in relation to the adjacent Roman city wall and Scheduled Ancient Monuments	2
Fig 2	Location of archaeological investigations 1992–2001	2
Fig 3	View from the east across the double basement of the GPO building after demolition	3
Fig 4	View from the west across the double basement of the GPO building after demolition	3
Fig 5	View of the west yard with a pile shaft trench in the foreground	4
Fig 6	View showing typical depth of a 1998 excavation trench in the west yard	4
Fig 7	The site during 1907–9 redevelopment, looking west, showing Bastion 19 excavated	5
Fig 8	Bastion 19 chamber, as preserved by Norman and Reader	6
Fig 9	Graphical conventions used in this report	8
Fig 10	East–west section through London's geology, from Holborn to the City	10
Fig 11	Pre-Roman topography showing the underlying geological deposits	11
Fig 12	Projected course of Marsden's 'western stream'	12
Fig 13	Panoramic view of Roman London in c AD 60	15
Fig 14	The study area in relation to the conjectured extent of the early Roman city, the London to Silchester road, local watercourses and local quarrying, c AD 43–70	15
Fig 15	Section through laying-out or roadside ditch (OA6) on the north side of Road 1	16
Fig 16	Post-Boudican development, c AD 70–120	18
Fig 17	Bone hairpin <S15> and spatula <S21> from Open Area 8	20
Fig 18	Brickearth sill beam and associated floors in Building 1	20
Fig 19	Detail of Building 2 and associated yard Open Area 9	21
Fig 20	Facet-cut colourless glass beaker <S30>	21
Fig 21	Copper-alloy brooch <S11>	21
Fig 22	Pottery assemblage from the well backfill adjacent to Building 6 <P27>–<P53>	22
Fig 23	Wall of Building 3 and associated internal and external surfaces	23
Fig 24	Section through the floors of Building 5	24
Fig 25	Section through internal deposits of Building 8	24
Fig 26	Finds associated with Building 8 <S13>–<S14>, <S24>	25
Fig 27	Pipe clay figurine of Minerva <S1> from a well (OA7)	26
Fig 28	Selected pottery from the well in Open Area 7 <P1>–<P26>	26
Fig 29	Selected finds from the well in Open Area 7 <S2>–<S10>	28
Fig 30	Wall plaster from Open Area 11	30
Fig 31	Post-Hadrianic fire redevelopment, showing Buildings 9–11 and the pre-city wall boundary ditch	32
Fig 32	Section through internal surfaces of Building 11 and earlier Hadrianic fire dumps	34
Fig 33	Stakeholes cut through floor surface of Building 11	34
Fig 34	Section through base of pre-wall boundary ditch (S1)	35
Fig 35	Excavating dark earth in spits	37
Fig 36	Bone pins <S16>–<S17> from the dark earth deposits	37
Fig 37	Rare, slip decorated, tegula roofing tile <T1> from the dark earth deposits	37
Fig 38	Panoramic view of Roman London in the early 3rd century AD	38
Fig 39	Plan of first phase of city defensive circuit c AD 185–250	38
Fig 40	Remains of Roman wall, Newgate, 1903	39
Fig 41	Section through city defences	39
Fig 42	Later Roman settlement c AD 150–250 and the first phase of Roman city defences as found at the MLFC site	40
Fig 43	Section through city wall with probable remains of internal bank	42
Fig 44	Plan of Roman Newgate, showing later medieval rebuilding	43
Fig 45	Reconstruction of Roman Newgate	43
Fig 46	Recording part of the Roman city wall	44
Fig 47	Part of the Roman city wall exposed in 1992	44
Fig 48	Detail of the internal face of the Roman city wall	44
Fig 49	Plan of second phase of city defensive circuit c AD 250–450	46
Fig 50	Late Roman settlement, c AD 250–450, showing second phase of the Roman city defences	48
Fig 51	Section through the first and second Roman ditches	49
Fig 52	Section through city wall, Bastion 17, and the first Roman ditch	50
Fig 53	Bastion 18, looking north-west	50
Fig 54	Bastion 18, looking south-west	51
Fig 55	Location of Lundenwic in relation to the old walled settlement of Londinium	54
Fig 56	Late Saxon town showing what may have been the initial settlement	55
Fig 57	The city defences crossing the study area in the Saxo-Norman period, c AD 880–1100	56
Fig 58	Saxo-Norman wattle-lined pit, looking west	57
Fig 59	Saxo-Norman wattle-lined pit, looking north-west	57
Fig 60	Shelly-sandy ware cooking pot <P54>	57
Fig 61	The city defences and the Greyfriars precinct in the study area, c 1100–1300	58

Fig 62	Junction of Bastion 19 with the Roman city wall . . 59		Fig 100	Wooden vessels with marks <S43>, <S45>–<S46>, <S48>–<S49>, <S52> 90
Fig 63	The study area in relation to the medieval defensive circuit of c 1300 60		Fig 101	Wooden comb <S33> and wooden implements <S54>–<S56> 91
Fig 64	Bastion 19 as recorded in 1906 61		Fig 102	Forepart of shoe sole <S98> and child-sized leather shoe <S99> 94
Fig 65	Conducting a survey of Bastion 19 in 1999 62		Fig 103	Engraved knife sheaths <S75>, <S80> 95
Fig 66	Detail of the base of Bastion 19 recorded in 1999 . 62		Fig 104	Knife sheaths and sheath-like objects <S78>–<S79>, <S81>, <S83>, <S85>, <S89>–<S91> . . 96
Fig 67	Recording the base of the medieval city ditch (S3) . 63		Fig 105	Knife sheaths with stamped motifs <S74>, <S77>, <S82>, <S86>–<S87> 99
Fig 68	Detail from Lobel's reconstruction map of London in 1520 64		Fig 106	Knife sheaths with embossed decoration <S76>, <S84> 101
Fig 69	The study area in later medieval times, c 1300–1500, in relation to the city defences and the Greyfriars precinct 66		Fig 107	Leather straps <S111>–<S114> 102
			Fig 108	Thong with knot terminal <S102> 103
Fig 70	Ralph Treswell's 'Plat of ye Graye Friers', compiled in 1617 68		Fig 109	Large thick leather sheet <S92> 103
			Fig 110	Sheet leather <S94>, <S96>, <S101>, <S104>, <S107> 104
Fig 71	Honeybourne's reconstructed map of the precinct of Greyfriars 70		Fig 111	Stamped leather waste <S95> 106
Fig 72	Foundations of the nave of Greyfriars church 70		Fig 112	Leather items <S93>, <S100>, <S103>, <S105>–<S106>, <S108>–<S110> 107
Fig 73	Foundations of Bridge House Rents (B17) 71		Fig 113	Decorated floor tiles from backfilling of the city ditch <T2>–<T5> 108
Fig 74	Detail of the 'Agas' woodcut view, redrawn 1561–70 72		Fig 114	Reigate stone moulding <1780> from Open Area 17 109
Fig 75	Reconstruction of part of the study area in the medieval period 73		Fig 115	Decorated floor tiles from Structure 6 <T6>–<T8> 109
Fig 76	Human bone in the backfill of an 18th-century cellar (B22) 74		Fig 116	Distal humerus and ulna from a golden eagle from [3799] 111
Fig 77	Detail of the study area, from Braun and Hogenberg's map of 1572 74		Fig 117	Dog skulls from [3553] and [3051] 112
			Fig 118	Copper-alloy tomb inscription letter <S63> . . . 114
Fig 78	Distinctive drinking vessels from the city ditch <P55>–<P57> 76		Fig 119	Bone pens <S65>–<S66> and stylus <S64> . . . 114
			Fig 120	Detail from Ogilby and Morgan's map of 1676 . . 117
Fig 79	Baluster jug <P58> 77		Fig 121	Plan of St Bartholomew's Hospital, showing the 1552 postern and a segment of the backfilled city ditch, drawn 1610 119
Fig 80	Highly decorated jugs from the city ditch backfill in London-type wares <P59>–<P61> 78			
Fig 81	Highly decorated jugs from the city ditch backfill in Kingston-type wares <P62>–<P70> 78		Fig 122	Plan of Christ's Hospital precinct dated 1652–60 120
Fig 82	Conical drinking jug <P71> and thumbed handle from large pitcher <P72> 79		Fig 123	Detail from the Faithorne and Newcourt map of 1658 121
Fig 83	Cooking vessels from the backfill of the city ditch <P73>–<P84> 80		Fig 124	Pre-Great Fire of London settlement, c 1500–1666 122
Fig 84	Pottery from the city ditch <P85>–<P92> 81		Fig 125	Chalk-built foundations of Building 18 123
Fig 85	Small dish <P93> 82		Fig 126	Southernmost buttress on north–south wall of Building 18 123
Fig 86	Gold finger-ring <S31> 82			
Fig 87	Fragments from stone mortars <S34>–<S36> . . . 83		Fig 127	View of Christ's Hospital and vicinity, 1940 . . . 124
Fig 88	Stone lamps <S38>–<S39> 83		Fig 128	Interior view of Christ's Hospital in 1798 125
Fig 89	Colourless glass stemmed drinking vessel <S41> . 84		Fig 129	Detail from Leake's post-fire survey of 1667 . . . 126
Fig 90	Tools from the city ditch backfill <S57>–<S60> . . 84		Fig 130	Detail from Rocque's map of 1746 126
Fig 91	Copper-alloy mounts <S71>–<S72> 85		Fig 131	Post-Great Fire of London settlement, c 1666–1787 127
Fig 92	Copper-alloy cosmetic tool <S32> 86			
Fig 93	Household utensils from Structure 6 <S37>, <S40>, <S42> 86		Fig 132	Decorated stove tile <T9> from Building 22 . . . 128
			Fig 133	Cellar floor of Building 27 128
Fig 94	Copper-alloy dagger hilt <S61>, iron spur rowel <S62> and cap or ferrule <S70> from Structure 6 . 87		Fig 134	Rear wall of Building 27 128
			Fig 135	Cleaning the cellar floor of Building 26 129
Fig 95	Bone bead-making waste <S69> 87		Fig 136	Tudor brick chimney fragment <T10> 129
Fig 96	Fragment of tinned sheet iron <S73> 87			
Fig 97	Bone tuning pegs <S67>–<S68> 88			
Fig 98	Wooden platters and bowls <S43>–<S45>, <S47>, <S51> 88			
Fig 99	Flat wooden platter <S50> and bowl <S44> . . . 89			

Fig 137	Building 28 showing the position of the tile-lined tank 130
Fig 138	The tile-lined tank in Building 28 130
Fig 139	Entrances of Christ's Hospital and Christ Church, 1895 131
Fig 140	West view of Christ Church with part of Christ's Hospital in 1830 131
Fig 141	Interior view of Christ Church in 1896 132
Fig 142	Watercolour of Christ Church after the Blitz in 1941 133
Fig 143	The Great Hall of Christ's Hospital c 1825 . . . 134
Fig 144	Foundation of a stairwell in the Great Hall of Christ's Hospital 134
Fig 145	George Dance's approved plan of the Compter, 16 June 1787 135
Fig 146	Facade of the Compter, 1812 136
Fig 147	Giltspur Street facade in 1813 136
Fig 148	George Dance's revised plan of the Giltspur Street Compter, 22 September 1787 137
Fig 149	Foundations of the front range of the Compter . . 138
Fig 150	Water tank and other foundations of the Compter 139
Fig 151	Brick-built culvert, cut through backfilled city ditch 139
Fig 152	a – George Dance's 1787 elevation through foundations of the Compter; b and c – the stepped brickwork as found during excavation . . 140
Fig 153	The remains of the Giltspur Street Compter and the Great Hall of Christ's Hospital as found 1992–2000, with Dance's original plan superimposed 141
Fig 154	Detail from Ordnance Survey map of 1894–6 . . . 142
Fig 155	Blue on white delftware floor tile <T11> from a drain in the Compter 142
Fig 156	Residual medieval louvers <T12>–<T13> from a robber trench of the Compter 143
Fig 157	The site during the 1907–9 redevelopment 143
Fig 158	Plan of Christ's Hospital and the General Post Office building in 1957 144
Fig 159	West yard of Royal Mail sorting office with Post Office vans 145
Fig 160	The line of the city wall marked in paving slabs . . 145
Fig 161	The new bastion chamber in the MLFC building . 146
Fig 162	Cleaning and removal of tiles 151
Fig 163	Detail of tiles in situ, looking east 152
Fig 164	Reused 18th-century tin-glazed wall tiles <T14>–<T62> from Building 28 155
Fig 165	Stone lamps <S37>–<S39> 171

TABLES

Table 1	Nearby archaeological sites referred to in text	7
Table 2	Comparison of pottery assemblages from Buildings 1 and 2	21
Table 3	Distribution of pottery forms from the well in Open Area 7	26
Table 4	Distribution of pottery dates from Open Area 11	30
Table 5	Estimated number of jugs in various form types from ditch deposits (OA17) dated 1340–1400	77
Table 6	Details of illustrated tile and brick <T1>–<T13>	151
Table 7	Expansion of Roman pottery fabric codes used, with date ranges	163
Table 8	Details of illustrated Roman pottery <P1>–<P53>	164
Table 9	Expansion of medieval and post-medieval pottery fabric codes used, with date ranges	165
Table 10	Illustrated medieval and post-medieval pottery <P54>–<P93>	166
Table 11	Finds tabulated by functional category and period	167
Table 12	Summary of Roman vessel glass by colour	169
Table 13	Summary of Roman vessel glass by function	169
Table 14	Hand-collected animal bone from selected land uses	176
Table 15	Wet-sieved animal bone from selected land uses	176
Table 16	Plant remains from fills of the medieval ditch	177

SUMMARY

Archaeological excavations at the Merrill Lynch Financial Centre between 1992 and 2001 have provided important new information on Roman and later activity in the north-western part of the City of London. The archaeological evidence from the site has been supplemented by documentary research as well as antiquarian work and findings from nearby excavations.

The natural topography of the site was complicated by stream channels located on the eastern side of the Fleet valley. Early Roman settlement took place along the main east–west road, which lay immediately to the south of the site along Newgate Street and led westwards towards Silchester. Occupation expanded in the late 1st and early 2nd centuries as the area was landscaped and roadside buildings were established. Properties along the street included shops and taverns which took advantage of passing trade.

Construction of the city's landward defences around the end of the 2nd century AD had a significant impact on land use at Newgate, and may have prompted the disuse and backfilling of at least two stream channels. The route of the city defences was determined by topographical factors as well as the size of the existing settlement, and at the Merrill Lynch Financial Centre site the position of the wall was influenced by the location of the Fleet valley and the localised extent of the terrace gravels and overlying natural brickearth, with the wall line following the edge of this higher and drier ground. The foundations of the defensive wall and its later bastions north of Newgate were not of uniform construction but of varying design to suit the local topographical conditions.

The Roman city defences continued to form the City's boundary through much of the medieval and early post-medieval periods. The layout and location of the Merrill Lynch Financial Centre site, sandwiched between Newgate Street to the south and the curve of the city wall to the west and north, had a profound influence on the evolving use of the land from the late Roman period onwards. Study of documentary, cartographic and archaeological information for the medieval period demonstrates that the site's size and shape led to its identification as a suitable place to build the Greyfriars Friary in 1225. The precinct of the friary occupied most of the site area throughout the medieval period.

The defensive ditch north of Newgate was redug in the Late Saxon and medieval periods. At the Merrill Lynch Financial Centre site backfilling of the medieval ditch reduced it to a small channel after only about 100 years of use. The expanding 16th-century city's demand for land to build on was a cause of further encroachment on the ditch. By the mid 16th century the ditch had been completely backfilled in the Newgate area and the land rented or sold off for new building. The friary was suppressed during the dissolution of the monasteries of 1536–40 and converted into a school for orphaned children known as Christ's Hospital. Parts of the site not occupied by the school precinct became residential properties. The choir of the friary church continued in use as a parish church, known as Christ Church; this was destroyed in the Great Fire of 1666, and rebuilt by Christopher Wren in 1674–87. The site of the nave was used as a parish burial ground until the 1850s.

By the mid 18th century it was no longer feasible to keep the city wall intact and it was gradually demolished. Historic maps show that by 1746 the wall no longer existed above ground on the Merrill Lynch Financial Centre site. Cellared buildings were built across the line of the wall by the end of the 18th century. The western part of the wall and Bastion 19 were also demolished, and construction of the Compter prison in Giltspur Street by the architect George Dance the younger took place on the site in 1787–91. The rest of the wall was lost to building projects initiated by St Bartholomew's and Christ's hospitals in the 19th century. The Compter was demolished in 1854. Christ's Hospital bought the land but never redeveloped it, and by the early 20th century the school had moved out of London.

For the majority of the 20th century the site was occupied by the General Post Office building, whose deep basements had destroyed most of the archaeological strata on the site. The new Merrill Lynch Financial Centre building was designed to preserve the majority of the remaining archaeological deposits in situ. Wren's Christ Church was gutted during the Blitz and never rebuilt, but the steeple and vestry house have both been restored. Today the area of the post-medieval church and adjoining disused burial ground are laid out as a public garden, and are part of the London Greyfriars Scheduled Ancient Monument.

The power of the relict urban landscape of the site was reaffirmed in the 2005 Award for Building in Context, given to the Merrill Lynch Financial Centre by the Royal Town Planning Institute. The judges commented:

> Great care has been taken to protect the Scheduled Ancient Monuments, particularly the remains of Roman and medieval walls. Through the creation of a viewing chamber, the public may see some of these impressive old structures. The Merrill Lynch Financial Centre is a perfect example of so-called constraints being turned to creative challenges. A thorough understanding of the individual characteristics and potential of the site has resulted in opportunities being taken which lesser designers would have missed. Fine and well-mannered old buildings have been brought back to life. Even previously hidden archaeological remains have been used to add interest to a reception area. New buildings have been constructed whose restraint and dignity do not seek to compete with, nor dominate, their sensitive surroundings.

ACKNOWLEDGEMENTS

The excavation, analysis and publication of this project have been funded by Merrill Lynch, to whom the author, on behalf of MoLAS, would like to extend grateful thanks. Particular thanks go to Dan Donohoe of Merrill Lynch, Adam Glover and Ed Tucker of Gardiner and Theobald, and Richard Hughes and Paul Nuttall of Ove Arup and Partners who worked closely with the MoLAS team throughout the project.

Invaluable site assistance was provided by site managers MACE, especially Roy Stobart, Tim Malone and John Kennedy, and by contractors Expanded Piling, especially Steve Leak, as well as members of the Swift project team, members of the Controlled Demolition project team, Sharon Wigfull of LEB (EDF Energy) and Roger Webber of Necropolis. Thanks also go to Ian Gregory and Helen Peters of Merrill Lynch for help in the completion of the signage for the Bastion Chamber; to Kathryn Stubbs, Senior Planning and Archaeology Officer of the City of London; and to Ellen Barnes and later Steven Brindle in their role as Inspector of Ancient Monuments for English Heritage London Region, for all their advice and support.

The excavations were supervised by Bruce Watson, Ken Pitt and Jo Lyon. Special thanks are extended to the MoLAS field team and specialists who worked on the various stages of archaeological investigation between 1992 and 2001: Joe Abrams, Portia Askew, Julian Ayre, Ryszard Bartkowiak, Michaela Basford, Yvonne Bates, Jeremy Bell, Ian Blair, Richard Bluer, Tim Bradley, Trevor Brigham, Mark Burch, Damian Carr, Lindy Casson, Laurie Coleman, Jane Corcoran, Gill Cruise, Toby Cuthbertson, Will Davies, James Drummond-Murray, Lesley Dunwoodie, Imogen Duthie, Nick Elsden, Antony Francis, Kieron Heard, Luis Huscroft, Mark Ingram, David Jamieson, Nigel Jefferies, Marie Leverett, Tony Mackinder, Malcolm McKenzie, Patrick McNulty, Richard Macphail, Gordon Malcolm, Alison Nailer, Blaze O'Connor, Ricky Patten, Chris Rees, Allan Roy, Norena Shopland, Gemma Smith, Simon Stevens, Dan Swift, Jez Taylor, Al Telfer, Chris Tripp, Dan Waterfall, Oliver Webb-Carter, Marion White and Mark Wiggins. On-site pottery scanning was provided by Lyn Blackmore, Louise Rayner, Fiona Seeley and Roberta Tomber. Jackie Keily would like to thank Quita Mould who commented on the leather and Alison Nailer who wrote the leather assessment.

Surveying, graphics and photographic work, particularly the recording of the city wall and Bastion 19, was carried out by Steve Every, Duncan Lees, Sarah Jones, Kate Pollard, Nick Soothill, Edwin Baker, Andy Chopping, Maggie Cox, Jeannette McLeish and Tracy Wellman. The digital archive for the site was created by Sarah Jones, Johanna Vuolteenaho and Sadie Watson.

Angus Stephenson project managed the early field stages of the work, with Dick Malt managing the later stages of fieldwork and post-excavation. Project programming was provided by Gordon Malcolm. The summary was translated into French by Elisabeth Lorans and into German by Manuela Struck. The index was compiled by Susanne Atkin.

The author would also like to thank Ken Pitt and Sadie Watson for taking the time to discuss the overall development of the Newgate area and the evidence from sites they excavated to the south, including the latest theories on the early streams and channels which crossed the area during the Roman period.

Foreword

As Merrill Lynch prepared to build its European headquarters in 1998, it was both exhilarating and humbling to discover this very same space was once occupied by the Romans back in the 1st century.

Archaeological analysis has shown just how rich in cultural value the Merrill Lynch Financial Centre site is. It was home to early Roman clay and timber buildings pre-dating AD 100 and contains later sections of the third-century Roman City defensive wall. The site also features important threads of London's history through Saxon, Norman and medieval times, right up to the 17th and 18th centuries.

It is incumbent upon leading global businesses like Merrill Lynch to play an active part in our local communities, so protecting the legacy of the site where our regional headquarters now stand was paramount. Our company, and our peers in other firms across London, have a responsibility to preserve the unique heritage of this great and ancient city.

It has been an honour for Merrill Lynch to play a role in a project of such historical scope and significance. In constructing a headquarters for the 21st century we wanted a building that reflects the aspirations of our firm. At the same time, we wanted to safeguard the site's archaeological riches to ensure we remember our past.

Bob Wigley
Chairman,
Merrill Lynch Europe, Middle East & Africa

1
Introduction

1.1 Circumstances of the fieldwork

This publication is based on the results of archaeological investigations carried out at 2 King Edward Street, City of London EC1A 1HQ between 1992 and 2001. The national grid reference for the centre of the site is 531900 181430. The site is bounded to the north by St Bartholomew's Hospital, to the east by King Edward Street, to the west by Giltspur Street and to the south by Newgate Street (Fig 1). During the excavation and post-excavation assessment stages of the archaeological project, the site was known as King Edward Buildings, after the General Post Office (GPO) building which had occupied the site. Since the construction of the Merrill Lynch building the postal address for the site has changed and King Edward Buildings no longer exists. For the purposes of this publication the site is called the Merrill Lynch Financial Centre (MLFC) site.

The programme of archaeological work was carried out as a condition of planning consent for redevelopment. The archaeological policy was complicated by the existence of three Scheduled Ancient Monuments (SAM) on and around the site (Fig 1): the Roman city wall and bastion beneath Postman's Park and King Edward Street (SAM 26T); the Roman city wall and medieval bastion within the Merrill Lynch development, along with the Roman and medieval gatehouse (SAM 26U); and London Greyfriars/Christ Church Greyfriars (SAM 129).

Field investigation first took place on the site in 1992, prior to the demolition of the GPO building, in order to evaluate the extent, nature and condition of the archaeological remains, including SAM 26U (Fig 1). The results of the evaluation were used to inform the new foundation design for the Merrill Lynch building. Further archaeological fieldwork, in the form of excavation and watching brief work, then took place on site, between 1998 and 2001 (Fig 2), during the demolition of the GPO building and the initial construction of the Merrill Lynch building (Fig 3; Fig 4). The results of these investigations have been integrated into the publication text where appropriate, but separate post-excavation assessment reports also exist.

In 1998–9 a series of pile shafts and caps was excavated (KEW98) in advance of the piling programme (Fig 5; Fig 6). A number of other piles were also monitored under watching brief conditions during 1998–9 (Watson 2000a).

In 1999–2000 further archaeological excavations took place on the sites of King Edward Buildings (KEW98) and Christ Church Greyfriars (GCC98). On the King Edward Buildings site a large open area excavation was carried out in the western extent of the site. A number of groundbeam trenches were also excavated in the central area, pile caps/shafts were excavated in the basements of buildings fronting onto Newgate Street and four sewer-heading trenches were excavated under Giltspur Street, Newgate Street and King Edward Street.

The bastion chamber was infilled with sand and the chamber roof was removed, to prepare for renovation (Lyon 2002). On the Christ Church Greyfriars site three small trenches were excavated in the central area of the monument, in advance of the installation of street lamps (Lyon 2002).

Introduction

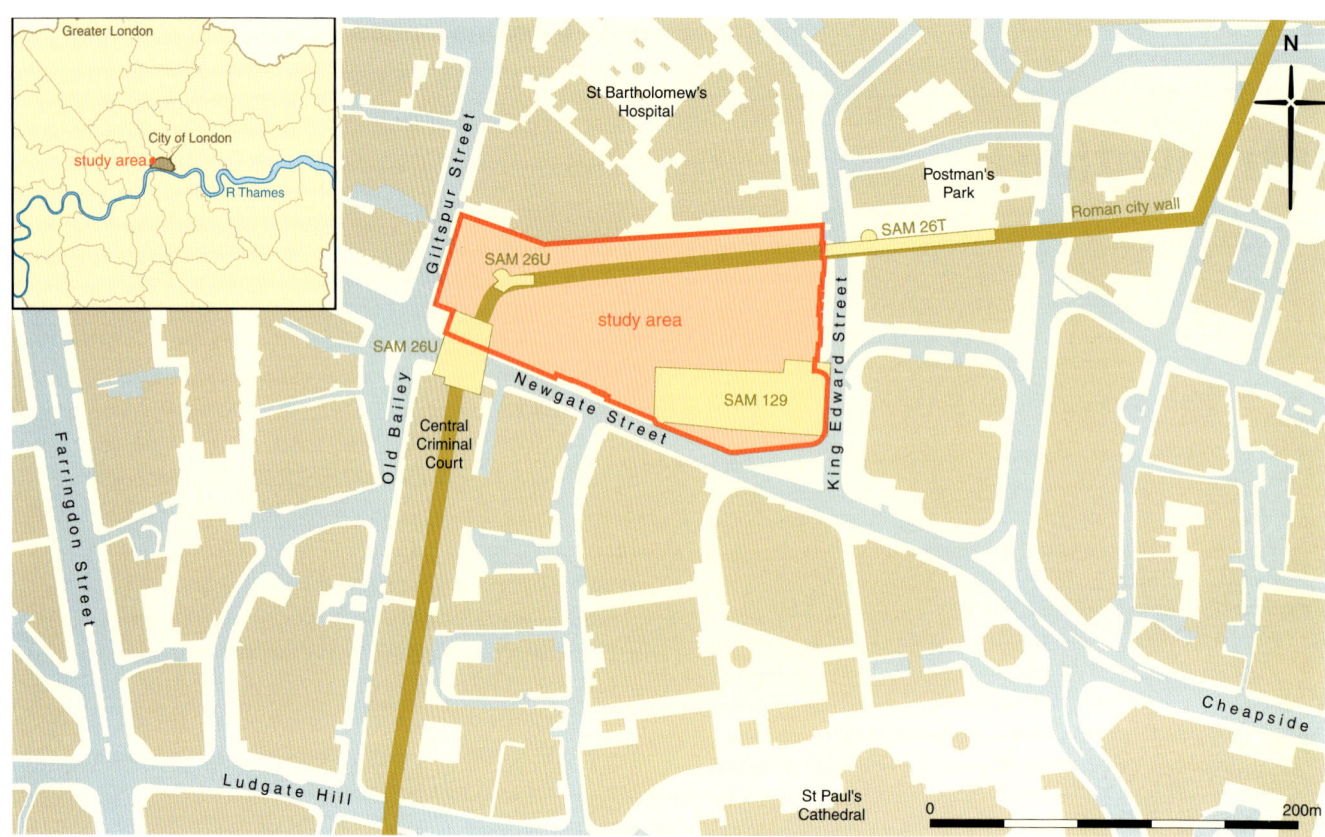

Fig 1 The study area in relation to the adjacent Roman city wall and Scheduled Ancient Monuments (SAM) in the study area (scale 1:4000)

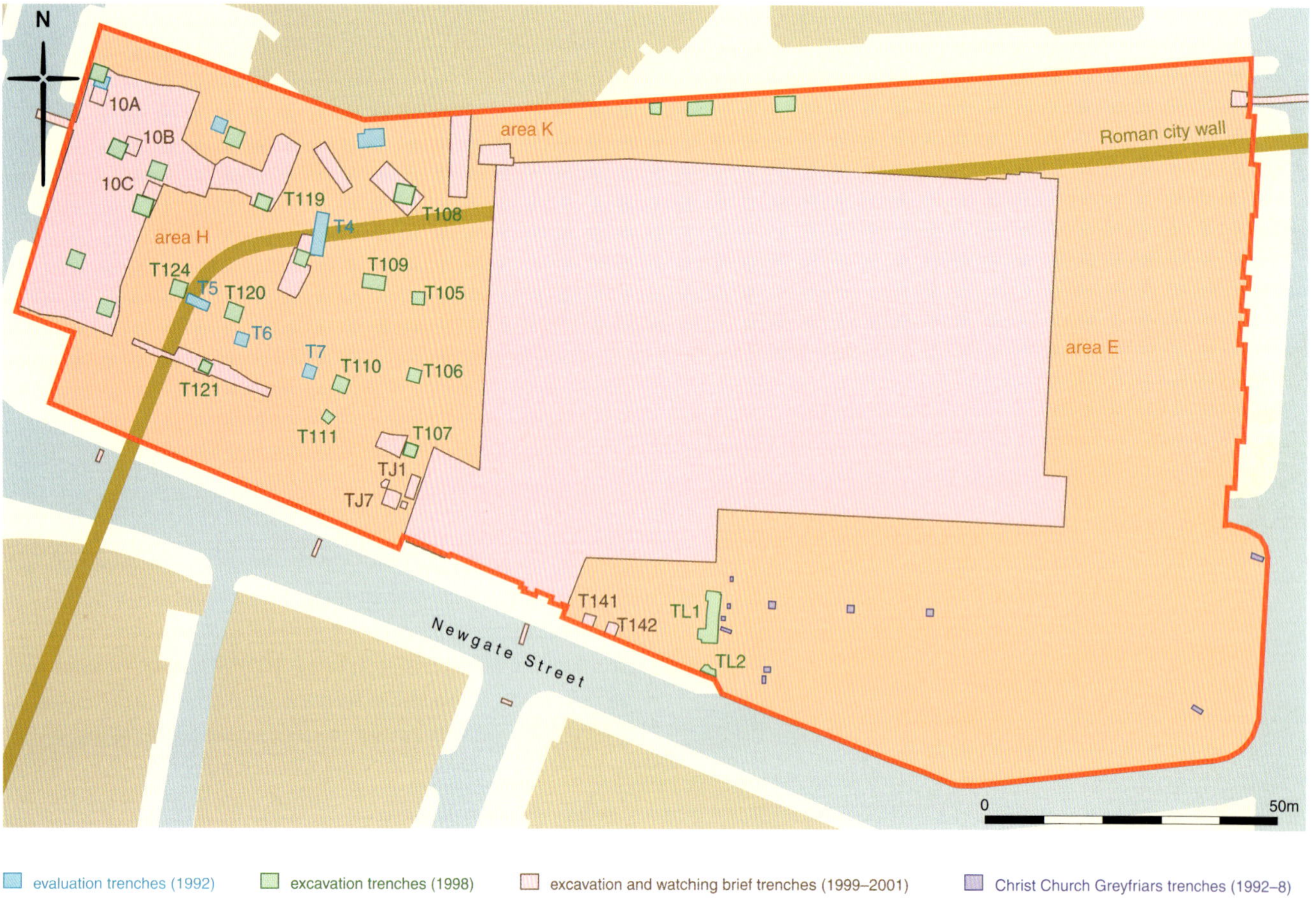

Fig 2 Location of archaeological investigations (1992–2001) (scale 1:1250)

Fig 3 View from the east across the double basement of the GPO building after demolition, during 1998 excavation

Fig 4 View from the west across the double basement of the GPO building after demolition, during 1998 excavation, with Wren's Christ Church to the top right

Fig 5 View of the west yard with a pile shaft trench in the foreground, looking west

Fig 6 View showing typical depth of a 1998 excavation trench in the west yard

In 1999, seven test pits were dug through the road surfaces of King Edward Street, Newgate Street and Warwick Lane (GCC98). These were excavated to assess the status of the Scheduled Ancient Monuments on Newgate Street (SAM 26U) and King Edward Street (SAM 26T), in advance of electricity cable laying (Watson 2000b).

In 2001 a further lift pit was excavated in the basement of 114 Newgate Street (KEW98). Ground reduction over the area of the preserved segment of Roman wall was carried out at this time and monitored (Lyon 2002). Also in 2001 four trenches were excavated, and monitored under watching brief conditions, in the area of the Greyfriars Scheduled Ancient Monument (SAM 129). This was done in order to facilitate the planting of trees (Lyon 2002).

1.2 Previous archaeological investigations

The MLFC site was first investigated during the early 20th century by Phillip Norman and Francis Reader, who were already aware of the great archaeological potential of the site as a result of their work in the surrounding area. Norman and Reader were antiquaries and artists, whose particular interest was in recording historic remains in the City of London that were on the brink of destruction. The information they recorded was not just of standing buildings prior to demolition, but also of archaeological remains exposed during redevelopment work. They were able to use their influence to gain access to a great many of the large city developments that took place at the turn of the last century, and even to interrupt the work programme in order that they might make sketches and notes of what they saw. The records that they made on these sites are invaluable, as the archaeology often went on to be destroyed by the redevelopment process.

Before the development of the GPO site in 1907–9, the area was largely occupied by the ancient precinct of Christ's Hospital school, the buildings of which had been inherited from Greyfriars Friary following the suppression of the monasteries in the 1530s. The western part of the site was open at this time and used as a playground for the school. The construction of the GPO building with a double basement, in the eastern part of the site, resulted in the destruction of Christ's Hospital and most of the underlying archaeological deposits in this area. Norman and Reader visited the site regularly throughout this process and, despite chaotic site conditions, were able to make detailed archaeological records, which were published in *Archaeologia* 63 in 1912 (Norman and Reader 1912, 277–344).

Norman and Reader also succeeded in persuading Parliament to allow them to conduct a research excavation in the western part of the site. They were aware that the line of the Roman and medieval defences crossed the site and had already observed the foundations of the city wall and Bastions 17 and 18 (as numbered by Merrifield 1965) in the eastern part of the site. They knew that the city wall turned a tight angle in the western part of the site, in order to meet the Roman and medieval gatehouse on Newgate Street, and that a further bastion (Bastion 19) had been situated at this point. They hoped that their excavation would reveal information on the nature and date of Bastion 19 (Fig 7). The funding for the

Fig 7 *The site during 1907–9 redevelopment, looking west, showing the angle bastion (Bastion 19) excavated (from a drawing by P Norman, in Norman and Reader 1912, pl L, 1)*

excavation was provided by the Society of Antiquaries.

Norman and Reader were unique at this time in their practice of making detailed records of archaeological remains, including scale drawings and descriptions, and in their belief in the value of preservation of archaeological remains *in situ*. It is a measure of their eloquence and vision that they were able to convince the government to preserve the excavated segment of city wall and Bastion 19, at a time when the preservation of archaeological remains in this country was not considered a priority. 'We hope that for all time it [Bastion 19] may be accessible to the student of London antiquities' (Norman and Reader 1912, 293). The remains they fought so hard to protect are still preserved today, within the modern Merrill Lynch building (Fig 8).

1.3 Documentary sources

Historic documents from a number of different sources have been used to supplement the archaeological evidence from the site in the medieval and post-medieval periods (Chapters 4 and 5). Documentary sources only become common in the City of London from the 12th century onwards, and in the area of the site many of the relevant records relate to the upkeep of the city defences. The records used fall into four main categories: royal, civic, private and literary. The royal (or government) records contain little information that is relevant to the site area. This is because the crown had made the City responsible for upkeep of the defences by the 13th century (Dyson 1993). For this reason, civic (Commonalty, later the Corporation, now the City) records contain the most information relating to the defences, and date mostly to the post-medieval period. Evidence was obtained from Letter Books (both published and unpublished, dating from the late 13th to the late 15th century), Repertories and Journals (15th and 16th centuries), City Lands Grant Books (from 1589) and City Lands Deeds (from the 17th century onwards). Private records belonging to Christ's Hospital were also consulted.

Of the ancient literary sources available, the main document used was John Stow's *Survey of London*, first published in 1598 and revised by the author in 1603. The volume was expanded and the language modernised in a number of later editions. The version referred to in this publication is Henry Morley's edition of 1902.

Fig 8 Bastion 19 chamber, as preserved by Norman and Reader, photographed during survey work in 1999

1.4 Organisation of the report

This volume forms part of the MoLAS Monograph Series. The presentation of the archaeological data is organised into dated periods to form a chronological narrative, with the associated specialist information integrated wherever possible. The archaeological periods are supported by plans showing major land-use features and individual finds are illustrated as part of the integrated text where appropriate.

The introduction (Chapter 1) is followed by a discussion of the geology and topography of the area and its influence on subsequent land use (Chapter 2). Chapter 3 looks at the Roman site sequence and the layout, appearance and role of the Roman city defences. Chapter 4 considers aspects of the medieval development of the area, including the use of the defensive circuit and the construction of Greyfriars monastery. The wealth of finds and environmental material recovered from the backfills of the city ditch is presented in this chapter. Chapter 5 looks at how the dissolution of the monasteries and the expansion of the City in the post-medieval period radically changed the nature of land use, culminating in the construction of the Giltspur Street Compter in the late 18th century. A summary of modern developments, up to the most recent rebuilding in the 1990s, is also provided here. Chapter 6 contains conclusions based upon the work. Specialist supporting data which is not suitable for integration with the main text is summarised as a series of appendices in Chapter 7. Methodological information and cross-referenced data are described here, in the form of tables and catalogues, to support the chronological and thematic discussions.

Because of the complicated mitigation strategy adopted for the site, interpretation and analysis of the archaeological material have relied heavily on the antiquarian evidence of Norman and Reader, and comparison with nearby archaeological sites. Relevant archaeological sites are referred to throughout this volume by address and/or site code, and are located on figures in relation to the MLFC site, where appropriate. The nearby sites are listed in Table 1.

As with most archaeological excavation and publication, the quantity of data recovered from the site was too great for full publication in traditional book form to be practical. In accordance with the principles laid out in *Management of archaeological projects* (MAP2, English Heritage 1991), post-excavation assessment of the data established a programme of analytical work designed to meet a series of original and modified research aims (Lyon 2002). This has meant that detailed material which is not of direct relevance to the main research aims has been omitted, providing more space for the discussion of the major themes. As a result, much of the detail relating to the specialist assemblages and categories of material, such as the post-medieval artefacts, is not presented here. All the material is included in a series of research archives, referred to in the specialist appendices as appropriate and listed as normal

Table 1 *Nearby archaeological sites referred to in text*

Site code	Site address
AES96	Alder Castle and Falcon House, 1–6 Aldersgate Street, EC1
ALG84	7–12 Aldersgate Street, EC1
ASQ87	12–16 America Square, 15–17 Crosswall and 15 Cooper's Row, EC3
BAR79	Medical School, St Bartholomew's Hospital, EC1
BHO86	Bible House, 146 Queen Victoria Street, EC4
BLM87	Blomfield House, 85–86 London Wall, 53 New Broad Street, EC2
CHR76	Christ Church Greyfriars, Newgate Street, EC1
DUK77	St James Passage subway, 2–7 Dukes Place, EC3
GF73	Christ Church Greyfriars, Newgate Street, EC1
GM131	Central Criminal Court, Old Bailey/Warwick Square, EC4
GM136	Paternoster Square development, EC4
GM146	Bastion 19, General Post Office Yard, Giltspur Street, EC1
GM242	Site of Bastion 7, Duke's Place, EC3
GM247	Roman Wall House, Crutched Friars, EC3
GM55	Site of Bastion 6, Duke's Place, EC3
GPO75	81 Newgate Street, EC1
HOU78	Chatsworth House, 48–56 Houndsditch, 66–70, St Mary Axe, EC3
LON82	57 London Wall, EC2
LBT86	Little Britain, 14–14a Bartholomew Close, EC1
LUD82	1–6 Old Bailey, 42–46 Ludgate Hill, EC4
MIL72	7–10 Milk Street, EC2
NEG98	3–9 Newgate Street, EC4
NGT00	Paternoster Square, Paternoster Row, EC4
ONE94	1 Poultry, EC2/EC4
PCH85	1–3 St Paul's Churchyard, EC4
SHN97	Sudbury House (former), Christchurch Court, 10–15 Newgate Street, EC1
SLY00	Juxon House, St Paul's Churchyard, EC4
WAP88	Wardrobe Court, 5A–10 Wardrobe Place, 146A Wardrobe Chambers, Wardrobe Court, 53–57 Carter Lane, 1–11 Addle Hill, EC4
WDC97	Wardrobe Court, 53–57 Carter Lane, 6–10 Wardrobe Place & 1–5 Addle Hill, EC4
WFG17	Fore Street/St Alphege Garden, EC2
WFG1A	Bastion 11a, Barbican Lakeside, EC2
WFG3	Windsor Court, Barber-Surgeons' Hall garden, EC2
WFG4	Bastion 14, Barber-Surgeons' Hall garden, EC2
WFG8	Bastion 15, Noble Street, EC2
XWL79	8–10 Crosswall, EC3

entries in the bibliography. The archive is lodged with the Museum of London under the individual site codes and may be consulted by prior arrangement with the Archive Manager at the London Archaeological Archive and Research Centre (LAARC), Mortimer Wheeler House, 46 Eagle Wharf Road, London N1 7ED.

1.5 Textual and graphical conventions

The basic unit of cross-reference used throughout the archive that supports this project is the context number. This is a unique number given to each archaeological event on site (such as a layer, wall, pit cut or fill, road surface and so forth). Context numbers are shown in square brackets thus: [200], and are used only where very specific reference is required. All context, accession and sample numbers used in this report are associated with the site code KEW98.

The analytical process involved allocating the contexts to subgroups and groups, but context numbers are sometimes referred to directly in the text, and especially in the discussion of the backfilled city ditch in Chapter 4, where key groups of contexts were analysed to publication level. The archaeological sequence is expressed in terms of periods and land uses. The periods (periods 1–7) are specific to this site and represent defined spans of time based on the finds, and on stratigraphic and documentary evidence. Divisions between periods are defined by major topographic change, such as the effects of a widespread fire or the construction of the city defences. The land uses are described as Buildings (B), Structures (S), Open Areas (OA) and Roads (R) throughout the document. Land-use numbers were assigned during analysis and the numbering does not run consecutively in this text.

All phases of the city wall and bastions, from the Roman period onwards, are identified as parts of Structure 2, as they represent an initial structure and later modifications and additions. Similarly, the late Roman and medieval phases of defensive ditch are all referred to as Structure 3, as in terms of land use they represent an original feature and its recuts. It should also be noted that individual external areas have generally not been assigned Open Area numbers from the medieval period onwards due to the incomplete nature of the evidence. Many features from the medieval period onwards are also simply referred to by their common name rather than by a land-use number.

Several categories of finds have been numbered in the research archive. To indicate clearly which catalogue is being referred to, a prefix denoting the category appears inside angled brackets with the artefact number. For example:

<S1> refers to (S)mall find no. 1
<P1> refers to illustrated (P)ottery or ceramics no. 1
<T1> refers to illustrated (T)ile or brick no. 1.

Pottery is described using fabric, form and decoration codes, to which keys are provided in Table 7 and Table 9; the date ranges assigned to pottery types are approximate. Only illustrated pottery has been given catalogue numbers in this publication (Table 8; Table 10). Selected accessioned finds and tin-glazed tiles have been catalogued in Chapter 7. All of the datable material is listed in the research archive. Scales of reproduction are given in the figure captions where appropriate. Where small finds are not catalogued, the original accession number is shown in angled brackets: <100>; environmental sample numbers are shown thus: {100}.

The bastion numbers used in this report were originally assigned by the Royal Commission survey of Roman London (RCHME 1928, 99–106). Excavations by the Roman and Mediaeval London Excavation Council mentioned in this report are indicated by a site reference such as WFG3, based on the system used in Shepherd (1998); Guildhall Museum sites are referred to, for example, as GM4, as used in Schofield (1998).

Introduction

The graphical conventions used in the period plans in this report are shown in Fig 9.

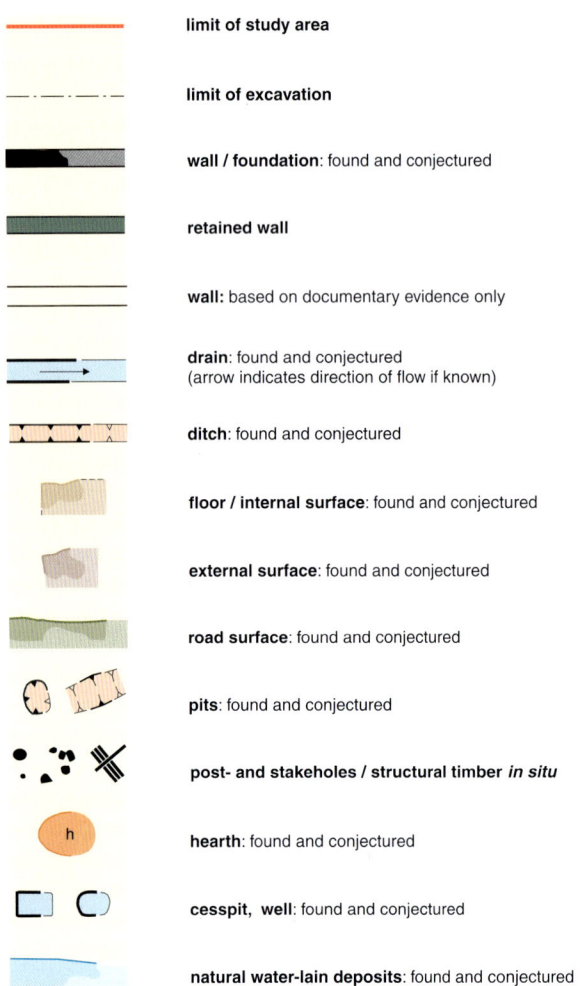

Fig 9 *Graphical conventions used in this report*

2 Pre-Roman natural topography

2.1 Introduction

The ground to the west of the site, beyond the line of the Roman and medieval city boundary, slopes steeply downwards to the River Fleet (now contained in a culvert). To the south-east the ground slopes down towards the Walbrook valley.

The geology of the study area consists of Eocene London Clay overlaid by Pleistocene River Terrace Gravels (British Geological Survey 1982). These gravel terraces were laid down by the precursor to the modern River Thames during the glacial periods of the Pleistocene. The gravel terraces are overlain in places by a sandy, silty clay known as the Langley Silt Complex (brickearth), a formation which dates to the end of the last Ice Age some 12,000–14,000 years ago, at the beginning of the Holocene epoch (Bridgland 1994, 155–6). The Walbrook and Fleet incised deep valleys through the brickearth during the Holocene period, resulting in the formation of the city's two plateau-like hills: Cornhill and Ludgate Hill (Jamieson 2002). The site is situated on the far north-western edge of Ludgate Hill, and as a result is directly underlain in places by the Mucking/Taplow and Corbets Tey/Lynch Hill/Hackney Gravels, and elsewhere primarily by brickearth (Fig 10).

2.2 Pleistocene geology (period 1)

Gravel terraces and palaeochannels

GRAVEL TERRACES (OA1) AND STREAM CHANNELS (OA13)
During the last Ice Age the River Thames existed as a fast-flowing braided river. At this time the area of the present City of London was characterised by floodplains formed of gravel terraces (OA1), cut through by small stream channels (Jamieson 2002).

A number of intercutting east–west channels of probable Pleistocene date (OA13) ran along the interface between the Taplow and Hackney gravel terraces and were observed during a watching brief in the eastern, double-basemented area of the site (area E, Fig 2). Large portions of the gravel terraces had been cut away by the palaeochannels. Another channel was found to the south, capped by brickearth deposited in the Holocene epoch.

2.3 Holocene geology (period 1)

Brickearth ground surface

BRICKEARTH DEPOSITS (OA3)
The brickearth deposits (OA3), which formed at the end of the last Ice Age, sealed large areas of the gravel terraces. The

Pre-Roman natural topography

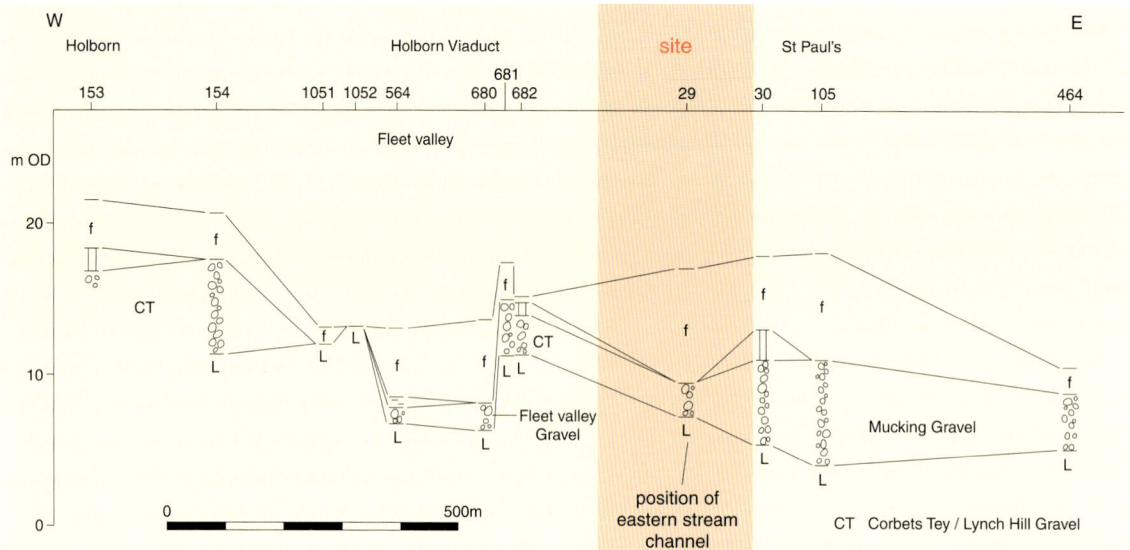

Fig 10 East–west section through London's geology, from Holborn to the City, showing main topographical and geological features on the MLFC site (after Gibbard 1994, 57) (horizontal scale 1:2500; vertical scale 1:500)

northern perimeter of the site follows the curve of the underlying brickearth plateau (Fig 11). It is not known exactly how far brickearth extended across the site, as much of this information was lost with the digging of the medieval city ditch and the construction of the General Post Office double basement. However, the approximate area of original coverage can be estimated using data from the recent excavations and the observations of Norman and Reader.

Brickearth deposits were recorded in all the 1992–8 excavation trenches inside the line of the city wall (Fig 2). The surface of the brickearth was located between 12.82m OD and 13.00m OD, c 4.0m below the present ground surface, and was found to slope down to the west, towards the Fleet valley. Brickearth deposits of variable thickness have been found across the study area, ranging from c 4.0m thick to the east to only a few centimetres elsewhere. It was only possible to measure the depth of brickearth on the MLFC site in area E (Fig 2), where it was found to be c 1.0m thick.

Norman and Reader observed brickearth at many points on the site in 1907–9. For instance, they noted that the city wall and Bastion 17 close to King Edward Street 'had been built on the natural surface of the brick-earth' (1912, 276). They also recorded that the fills of the V-shaped Roman city ditch were 'sufficiently dark to show in strong contrast with the bright colour of the brick-earth in which it was dug' (ibid, 278). This comment indicates that the deposit extended at least this far north on the eastern part of the site (Fig 11). Brickearth was also present in the area around Bastion 18, into which the bastion foundations were cut. It was also observed at the western angle of the city wall, although it seems to have been weathered and eroded here. The base of the city wall was found to rest on deposits of made-earth at this point, rather than resting on the brickearth surface as it does elsewhere on the site (Chapter 3.2). Norman and Reader (ibid, 288) state that 'the surface, which was found to be partly of gravel and brick-earth, appeared to have been subjected to frequent flooding, and was furrowed and worn by runnels, like land close to a stream'. It is possible that this part of the wall was very close to the edge of the brickearth cap, and that the area was levelled up to provide extra stability.

It is not known exactly how far the brickearth extended beyond the line of the city defences, but it was not present on the St Bartholomew's Hospital site (BAR79) to the north, where banded gravels and sands were observed (Bentley and Pritchard 1982, 135). The significance of the city wall's location in relation to the surrounding topography and underlying geology is discussed in Chapter 3.

Palaeochannels

A number of palaeochannels of Holocene date were discovered on site, cutting into the Open Area 3 brickearth deposits (Fig 11). The channels were first recognised by Norman and Reader during their archaeological investigations on the site in 1907–9. Circumstantial evidence for a stream channel was uncovered during the excavation of Bastion 19 in the extreme north-west of the site area. The orientation and full extent of the channel is not known, as Norman and Reader (1912, 289) had little chance to investigate it, but it appears to have run underneath Bastion 19, and was 21ft (6.4m) deep in the north-west. According to their observations, the stream may have begun to silt up by the time the bastion was built in the late Roman period, when the area was probably marshland. Norman and Reader noted (ibid) that the stream 'contained Roman pottery only' and the sloping side of the stream 'was followed by the bastion builders, who carried their wall down until the original gravel was reached. In consequence, the external face of the bastion is there deeper by 2ft [0.60m] than the interior, showing the steepness of the bank of this stream.'

No evidence for the feature was discovered during the 1998

Holocene geology (period 1)

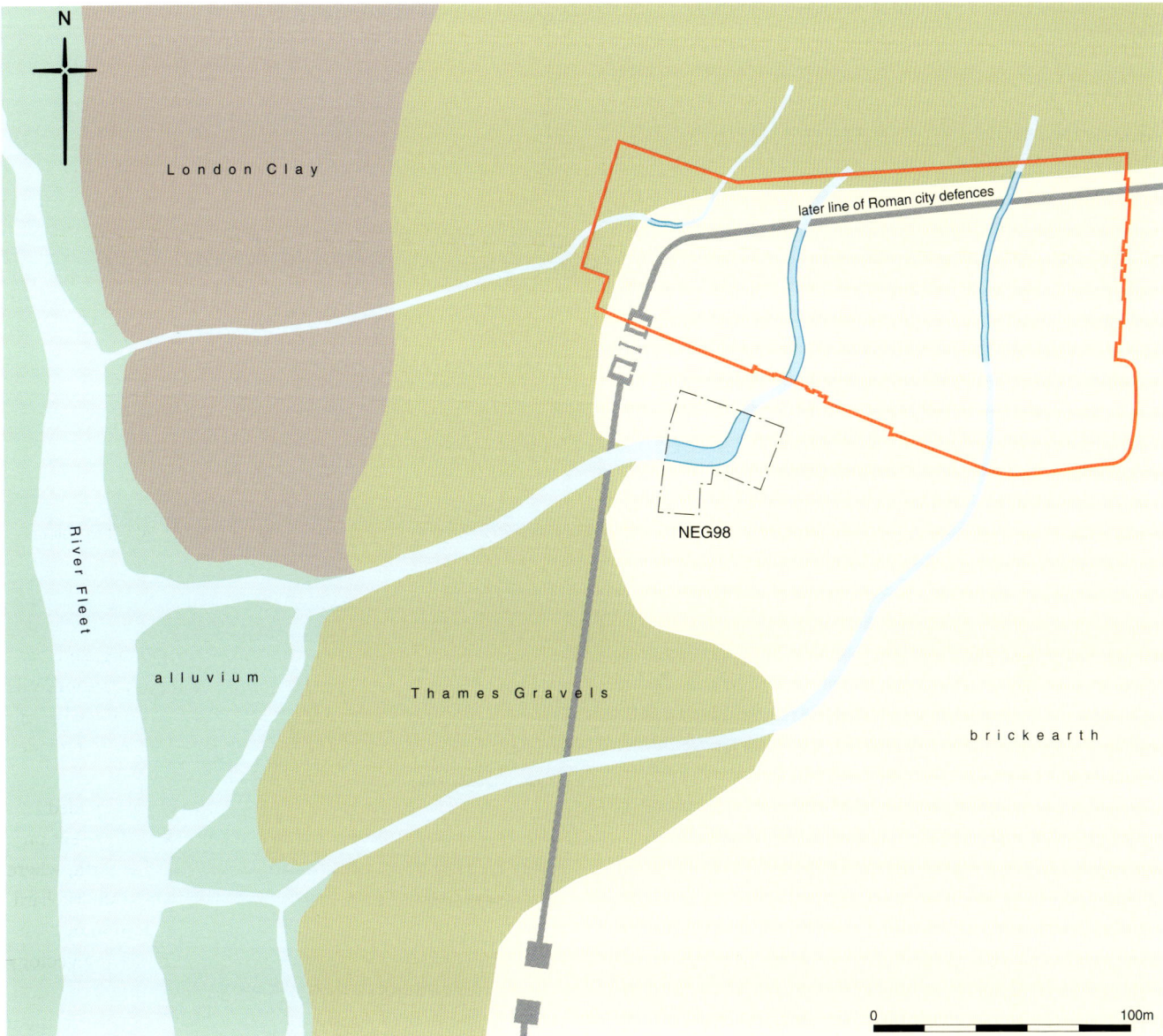

Fig 11 Pre-Roman topography showing the underlying geological deposits: note the extent of natural brickearth in relation to the later line of the Roman city wall and the projected course of palaeochannels (scale 1:2500)

excavation of area H (Fig 2), which was situated a few metres to the west of the bastion chamber. This may be because the stream channel turned westwards and did not pass through the main part of area H. Norman and Reader note (1912, 289) that 'from the way in which its sides rose, both towards the bastion and in the direction of the wall, it appeared that here the stream turned abruptly'. Evidence gained from excavations in the Fleet valley suggests that a stream may have flowed west-south-west to the River Fleet (McCann 1993) (Fig 11). If the stream did pass through area H, the medieval city ditch may have removed all evidence for it. Alternatively, Norman and Reader (1912, 289) could have been mistaken, and the feature that they thought was a stream channel may have been one of the Roman defensive ditches or even the medieval city ditch. They do say of this area, 'At this point there were indications which looked more like those usually found in the city ditch than at any other point nearer the wall.'

1st-century AD stream channels

Holocene stream channels were discovered on the central and eastern parts of the site in the early 20th century, during preparatory ground clearance for the construction of the GPO building. Deep excavation revealed two parallel, north–south aligned infilled stream channels, c 64m apart (Fig 11) (Norman and Reader 1912, 275, 282–3). The western of these channels was described as being 15.24m wide and 4.8m deep, while the eastern was 12.2m wide and 5.3m deep. The lower portion of the channel fills consisted of 'black mud with reeds and rushes'. The base of the eastern stream contained a massive Kentish ragstone wall set into the natural gravels (see Chapter 3.1). Only Roman finds were discovered in the deep silts and peats within both stream channels, suggesting that they silted up or were backfilled and fell out of use during the Roman period.

Most of the evidence of the stream channels was truncated

by the construction of the double basement of the GPO building, but ground reduction took place at such a pace that Norman and Reader were unable to record the features in any great detail. A surviving fragment of the western channel was discovered during the 1998 excavation (not illustrated). Only the basal deposits had escaped truncation and no further interpretation could be made. The rediscovery of this channel allowed its location to be more firmly fixed and the height of the base identified as being 7.5m OD.

The same stream channels have been identified at several other archaeological sites to the south of the MLFC site. During the redevelopment of Paternoster Square in 1961–2 (GM136), two dark linear stains in the natural, converging to form a single, much wider channel just south of Newgate Street, were interpreted as the continuation of the two stream channels discovered on the MLFC site (Marsden 1965, 137). Marsden described the main channel of his stream as having a deep V-shaped profile, with the two arms measuring c 9.45m across, and the base at 7.35m OD (Marsden 1968, 2). Deposits of silt and peat containing late 1st-century AD finds again suggest that the feature had silted up or been backfilled in the Roman period. Marsden interpreted the Paternoster Square evidence as a naturally formed, north–south aligned, forked stream channel flowing to the Thames but canalised and managed during the Roman period. The channel has sometimes been referred to as the 'western stream' (Bentley 1987, 328) (Fig 12).

More sightings of what was apparently the same feature have been made at sites further to the south. Evidence from sites south of St Paul's Cathedral suggests that the feature was medieval in date, contradicting Norman and Reader's and Marsden's findings (Corcoran 2002; Bentley 1987, 334; Tyler 2000, 35–6; Watson in prep).

More recent excavations at 3–9 Newgate Street (Pitt 2006) and Paternoster Square (Watson in prep) have produced important new evidence. This suggests that Marsden's 'western stream' was not a single, natural feature. Instead, the westernmost channel observed on the MLFC site ran south and west across 3–9 Newgate to flow towards the Fleet, while the eastern stream channel ran south and west across the northern part of the Paternoster Square site before also flowing into the Fleet. This would indicate that the converging channels and main north–south channel arrangement observed by Marsden were part of a ditch system probably dating to the 2nd century AD (Pitt 2006; Watson in prep). The existence of a managed drainage system for a time in the Roman period would be consistent with Norman and Reader's evidence that the eastern stream channel contained a stone foundation and may have been recut or straightened to some extent.

Excavations at Juxon House (SLY00, Fig 12) in 2000, at the south-western corner of the Paternoster Square site, revealed part of the north–south channel recorded by Marsden. The feature was recorded as a flat-bottomed, north–south aligned, 22m wide ditch, but radiocarbon dates obtained from the earliest silts at the base of the feature give a Saxon date (Watson in prep). The sides of the channel had been recut and its upper fills were homogeneous backfills dating to the 11th or 12th

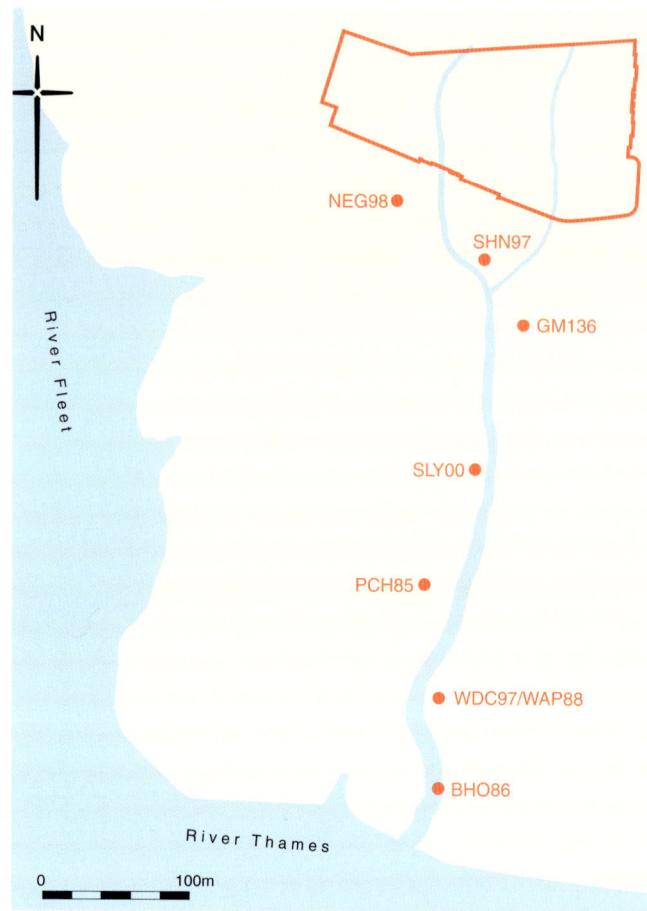

Fig 12 Projected course of Marsden's 'western stream' (after Bentley 1987), now identified as a system of Roman drains and later boundary ditches (for site details see Table 1) (scale 1:5000)

centuries. A north–south aligned drainage ditch may have been present in the Roman period but if so it had been entirely truncated by Saxon and Norman features, perhaps relating to a boundary or defensive system associated with St Paul's Cathedral precinct (Watson in prep; Schofield 1993, 38).

THE WESTERN STREAM CHANNEL AND ITS CONJECTURED COURSE (OA2)

The western of the two stream channels was traced across the MLFC site in 1907–9 by Norman and Reader (1912, 282), who recorded that it 'flowed with a bold curve to the south'. Norman and Reader (ibid, 283) did not record that this stream had been modified in antiquity, unlike the eastern channel. There were large amounts of reeds and rushes in its backfill, indicating that it had been open for a long period of time, but that 'its flow was checked for a considerable part of the Roman period'. All the finds they observed were of Roman date, but the upper portion had been disturbed by chalk wall foundations, and it was not possible to identify its final disuse date. Bastion 18 had been constructed over the backfill of the stream, and there was no evidence that the stream channel had been culverted where it crossed the line of the city defensive wall, indicating that the stream must have been infilled prior to the construction of the city wall at about the end of the 2nd century AD (Norman and Reader 1912, 284). This view has been corroborated by recent evidence from 3–9 Newgate Street (NEG98, Fig 11), where excavation of a further portion of the stream has indicated that it was backfilled in c AD 120–60 (Pitt 2006, 47).

The conjectured line of the western stream channel would have crossed the line of the city defences twice, so it seems logical that some attempt might have been made to divert the stream prior to construction of the walls and defensive ditches. Norman and Reader suggested that the stream was already largely silted up by the Flavian period (see Chapter 3.1), and only acted as a managed drainage channel after that date. This would have made its diversion or disuse in the late 2nd century a relatively straightforward matter.

THE EASTERN STREAM CHANNEL AND ITS CONJECTURED COURSE (OA2)

The precise form of the eastern stream channel discovered by Norman and Reader remains unclear, as they did not excavate it under controlled archaeological conditions. According to Norman and Reader (1912, 275) the stream lay directly beneath the foundations of Greyfriars cloisters and, similar to the western stream channel, was 'filled with very black peaty mud, in which were plentiful remains of reeds and rushes'. They state that the stream had clearly been modified in antiquity and that Roman artefacts alone were discovered in its backfill.

At the MLFC site the eastern stream channel appears to have originated as a natural feature. It now appears that it followed a similar course to the western stream channel as recorded at 3–9 Newgate Street, flowing south-west to the Fleet. The geological map of the area shows the natural brickearth to be much eroded in this area, perhaps suggesting the presence of a stream (Fig 11).

As discussed earlier, Marsden recorded what he believed to be part of the same stream channel at Paternoster Square, where it converged with another channel and then ran south to the Thames. This arrangement of channels is now believed to be a 2nd-century AD drainage system which diverted the western and eastern stream channels found at the MLFC site southwards, further complicated by possible recuts in the Saxon and Norman periods (Watson in prep).

2.4 Discussion (period 1)

The geology and topography of the study area influenced Roman and medieval land use, particularly in determining the line of the Roman city boundary. The interface between the Hackney and Taplow gravels runs along the northern perimeter of the MLFC site and has been repeatedly cut into by ancient stream channels. The brickearth which formed above the gravel terraces in this area was cut by tributary streams of the Fleet.

In the prehistoric period the MLFC study area would have been open grassland cut by two, or possibly three, streams (Fig 11). Two of the stream channels can be identified at other archaeological sites to the south, with a third channel at the extreme north-west of the site less well known. All of these streams must have flowed south-west to the Fleet.

The two main stream channels recorded on the MLFC site, described as the eastern and western stream channels above, were originally interpreted by Marsden as branches of a single stream which converged just south of Newgate Street to flow south to the Thames. This arrangement, which became known as the 'western stream', can now be identified as a Roman drainage system which incorporated parts of the natural streams but diverted them southwards. The southern section of this route was apparently recut in the Saxon and Norman periods.

3

The Roman archaeological sequence

3.1 Early Roman settlement, AD 43–late 2nd century (period 2)

Evidence recorded at the MLFC site for Roman activity up to the late 2nd century AD has been divided into three broad phases, based on the site findings and more general changes in the settlement.

Pre-Boudican development, c AD 43–70 (period 2, phase 1)

Introduction

London was founded by the Romans shortly after their invasion of Britain in AD 43. The Roman settlement did not supersede a significant prehistoric settlement. The nearest Late Iron Age settlements were located to the east and west of the city (Kent 1978, 53–8). The London area appears to have been politically neutral at the time of the invasion and this has been cited as a possible factor in the Romans' choice of location, as was the economic and strategic importance of establishing a Thames crossing and port facilities near present-day London Bridge.

The Roman town began as a small settlement centred on Cornhill, the eastern of the two low hills north of the Thames in what is now the City of London. The settlement grew rapidly during the 50s AD, with extensive radial development along the main roads out of the town (Fig 13) (Hill and Rowsome in prep). The majority of the roadside buildings were single-storey shops, with living quarters and small workshops to the rear (Perring and Roskams 1991, 102–3; Hill and Rowsome in prep), a pattern of development probably related to the trading opportunities presented. Radial development was particularly pronounced along the main east–west road leading from Cornhill westwards across the Walbrook in the 1st century AD (Hill and Rowsome in prep; Watson in prep) but seems to have stopped short of 3–9 Newgate (Pitt 2006, 49) and the MLFC site (Fig 14).

The London–Silchester road

ROAD GRAVELS (R1) AND A ROADSIDE DITCH (OA6); EARLY LANDSCAPING (OA5)

The London to Silchester road (R1, Fig 14) has been recorded at several archaeological sites along Cheapside and Newgate Street. It was first identified by Sir Christopher Wren during the construction of St Mary le Bow Church (Merrifield 1965, 120). The establishment of the road has been dated to AD 47/8 by dendrochronology of a timber drain at 1 Poultry (Hill and Rowsome in prep). At the MLFC site, compact road gravels associated with the road were observed in a sewer heading beneath Newgate Street during the 1999 excavations, although no dating evidence was obtained from the deposits.

Sites along the course of the road have produced evidence that a laying-out ditch may have preceded construction in places. At 72–75 Cheapside (CID90) a V-shaped ditch 0.90m

Early Roman settlement, AD 43–late 2nd century (period 2)

Fig 13 *Panoramic view of Roman London in c AD 60, looking south-east; the MLFC site is in the lower foreground outside the developed area (Peter Froste, 1996)*

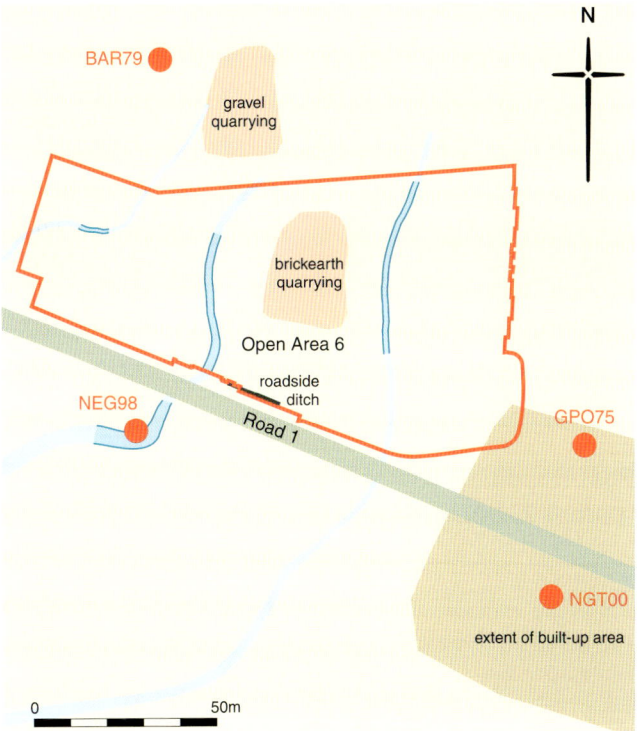

Fig 14 *The study area in relation to the conjectured extent of the early Roman city, the London to Silchester road (R1), local watercourses and local quarrying, c AD 43–70 (period 2) (scale 1:2000)*

wide and 1.85m deep lay c 8.50m to the south of the road (Hill and Woodger 1999). No northern equivalent of this ditch was found at the site. A portion of a laying-out ditch was also found at 3–9 Newgate Street (NEG98) c 6m south of the road (Pitt 2006, 5–6).

On the MLFC site, ditch fragments, which may have been part of the laying-out ditch, were discovered close to the street frontage (OA6, Fig 14; Fig 15). Part of the northern side of the ditch had survived and was situated c 6m from the projected northern edge of the road. A northern laying-out ditch for Road 1 has not been recorded elsewhere, and this may indicate that a single ditch to the south was used to survey the course of the road for much of its length. Alternatively, the feature recorded at the MLFC site may have been a roadside ditch contemporary with the early use of the road. Dating evidence indicates that the ditch was backfilled by c AD 50–100.

Areas of redeposited brickearth provide tentative evidence for early Roman landscaping which may have included the stripping of turf from the ground surface (OA5).

Discussion (period 2, phase 1)

There is no doubt over the location and early date of the Roman settlement's main east–west road, but the position of the western boundary of the town remains uncertain. It has been suggested that an early north–south boundary lay just east of the site of St Paul's (Bentley 1985, 124). Supporting evidence that has been cited includes a conjectured slight change in alignment of the main east–west road at this point (Merrifield 1965, 122), and the presence of early burials to the west of the suggested north–south line (Perring 1991, 14–15). More recent work has called both pieces of evidence into some doubt. Careful consideration of the evidence for the main east–west road shows that the Walbrook to Newgate section of the route was straight and did not vary in alignment (Perring 1991,

Fig 15 Section through laying-out or roadside ditch (OA6) on the north side of Road 1, looking west (scale 0.5m)

14–15; Hill and Rowsome in prep). The general area was used for burial in the early Roman period, with 1st-century AD cremations giving way to inhumations (Hall 1996, 58). However, while the eastern limit of the cemetery may have been near the eastern side of the Paternoster Square study area (Shepherd 1988, 11), this does not necessarily mean that the settlement had a precisely and physically defined western boundary (M Millett, pers comm).

The MLFC site lay to the west of the pre-Flavian built up area (Williams 1993, 33) and apparently west of any formal boundary to the settlement, if one existed. Pre-Boudican occupation to the east, at the General Post Office site (GPO75, Fig 14), included circular huts and a boundary ditch which was not aligned with the east–west road, suggesting that some occupation may even have pre-dated the round foundation (Perring and Roskams 1991, 3). Pre-Boudican occupation on the northern part of Paternoster Square (Fig 14, NGT00) (Watson in prep), directly south of the GPO site and just east of the MLFC site, included an early ditch on a different alignment from the road and roadside buildings, some of which were destroyed in the revolt.

No extant pre-Boudican occupation was found at 3–9 Newgate Street, on the south side of the main east–west road opposite the MLFC site; at this point early gravel quarries gave way to roadside building in the Flavian period (Pitt 2006, 49), although the presence of the western stream channel may have discouraged building. The recent work at the MLFC site involved only limited excavation along the street frontage, so the lack of evidence for pre-Boudican roadside properties does not make their absence certain. However, in 1907–9 Norman and Reader (1912, 285) observed the removal of deposits from the area between the two stream channels at the MLFC site and recorded that it did not appear to have been extensively built on. They found evidence that the area may have been used as a brickfield, and 'in places the surface had been burnt red to a depth of about 1ft [0.30m] where the clamps had stood'. No dating evidence was retrieved but the activity may have been early, perhaps associated with the production of building materials for the settlement to the east. Evidence recovered to the north of the MLFC site at St Bartholomew's Hospital (BAR79, Fig 14) consisted of 1st-century cultivation and gravel extraction, indicating a relative lack of development (Bentley and Pritchard 1982, 135).

Post-Boudican development, *c* AD 70–120 (period 2, phase 2)

Introduction

The Boudican revolt of AD 60–1 resulted in the destruction by fire of nearly all of the built up area of London (Perring 1991, 22), including the suburb south of the Thames. Archaeological evidence shows that commercial and residential rebuilding was slow, and did not begin in many areas until *c* AD 70. Much of the settlement may have lain empty for almost a decade (Perring and Roskams 1991, 119). There is evidence for the early re-establishment of elements of the infrastructure such as the main east–west road (Hill and Rowsome in prep), waterfront (Regis House, KWS94; Brigham and Watson in prep) and public water supply (30 Gresham Street, GHT00; Blair et al in prep). Recent work at Plantation Place, east of the Walbrook at Cornhill, has found important evidence of a fort or defended enclosure dating to the years immediately following the Boudican revolt (FER97; Dunwoodie et al in prep).

Properties in the core of the settlement and along the main roads may have been the first to be rebuilt, but during the 70s AD the settlement expanded rapidly, with an ambitious public building programme and new roads and buildings in areas not formerly built on. Roman Britain prospered as trade and commerce increased, with London benefiting through its role as both the capital and main entrepôt. The main east–west road leading from the Walbrook crossing towards Newgate experienced intense roadside property development (Hill and Rowsome in prep; Watson in prep; Hill and Woodger 1999).

Canalisation of stream channels and an enigmatic masonry structure

SILTING AND RECUTTING OF THE STREAM CHANNELS (OA4)

Roadside development at the MLFC site would have been hampered by the presence of the two north–south stream channels which crossed the site. Norman and Reader (1912, 275) observed that the western stream channel had largely silted up and may have been reduced to a small ditch in the early Roman period. It may have been carried beneath Road 1 in a culvert. The eastern stream was extensively modified in the Roman period, with Norman and Reader commenting: 'If this water-way was a natural stream, its banks had been a good deal modified, for they were cut very straight, and appeared to be artificial' (ibid). Roman finds were recovered from the basal and later fills of the eastern stream, suggesting that the modifications were associated with Roman landscaping and management, which may have begun at a relatively early date (Fig 16). Canalisation of the easternmost stream would have improved local drainage and might also have been intended to regulate and direct the flow of water southwards.

MASONRY STRUCTURE AT THE BASE OF THE EASTERN STREAM CHANNEL

Norman and Reader (1912, 275) recorded a massive Kentish ragstone wall, running north–south along the eastern edge of the stream's base (Fig 16). The wall was 2.45m thick and cut into natural gravel. The foundation followed the course of the stream for 45m. Near the southern edge of the MLFC site the wall appeared to stop abruptly, and Norman and Reader noted that there was a 'gap of 12ft [3.66m], after which it [the wall] occurred again'. It is not clear whether the gap was the result of the wall being breached or was part of the original construction, although Norman and Reader's plan and description of the wall suggest the latter.

The purpose of the masonry foundation is unclear and no trace of it had survived the early 20th-century basementing. Though it is tempting to conclude that the masonry was a relatively late feature coincidentally situated in the streambed, it closely followed the line of the channel. Norman and Reader state that 'there is little doubt that it was of Roman construction' (1912, 275). The stream was 12.2m wide and 5.3m deep, with the ragstone foundation reducing the channel to 7.9m wide. The structure is quite unlike any other known structure from Roman London. The foundation's thickness is similar to the Roman defensive wall, which was c 2.7m wide. The MLFC streambed foundation was situated c 5m below the contemporary ground surface, more than any other recorded Roman structure from London (Bentley 1987, 328). No evidence of the wall was found to the south of the main east–west road at Paternoster Square. If it was associated with the canalisation of the stream channel or some other purpose, it may have been specific to the area north of the main east–west road.

It is possible that the feature was never intended to reach the ground surface but was a buried structure of some kind, perhaps a water conduit. If so, it would make sense for the conduit to post-date the disuse and backfill of the stream, but no evidence of such a buried feature has been found at any of the nearby excavations. Another possibility is that the masonry structure and modified stream channel were part of an early boundary separating the settlement from its *territorium* (Morris 1982, 100), but if that were the case evidence might be expected at sites to the south of Newgate as well. It is not impossible that the wall was post-Roman, but it must pre-date the 1225 construction of the cloisters of Greyfriars. The depth, alignment and description of the wall make it even less likely to be medieval than Roman.

Roadside buildings

Truncated elements of early Roman buildings were recorded in limited areas of excavation north of the MLFC site's Newgate Street frontage. The piecemeal nature of the evidence made it difficult to reconstruct the extent of the buildings but eight have been identified (B1–B8, Fig 16; Fig 19; B3 not illustrated) with a date range of c AD 70–120. Most of these buildings were situated on the western part of the site (Fig 16) and appear to have been similar in layout to the strip buildings recorded along the north side of the main east–west road at the GPO site (Perring and Roskams 1991).

Observations indicated that some parts of the site area remained external throughout the Flavian period. Some areas were built on but reverted to external use later, though the limited extent of the excavation areas means that these may represent no more than yards in and around new building layouts. The complex structural sequence along the street frontage certainly demonstrates a period of intense occupation, though again the piecemeal nature of the excavation work limits interpretation.

OPEN AREA 8 AND BUILDINGS 1 AND 7

Quarry pits and drains were recorded in Open Area 8, an external area north of the main road (not illustrated). Notable artefacts included a bone hairpin (<S15>, Fig 17) and a bone spatula from a wattle-lined pit (<S21>, Fig 17).

Building 1, located near the western side of the MLFC site, survived as fragments of floor surfaces and clay wall lines

The Roman archaeological sequence

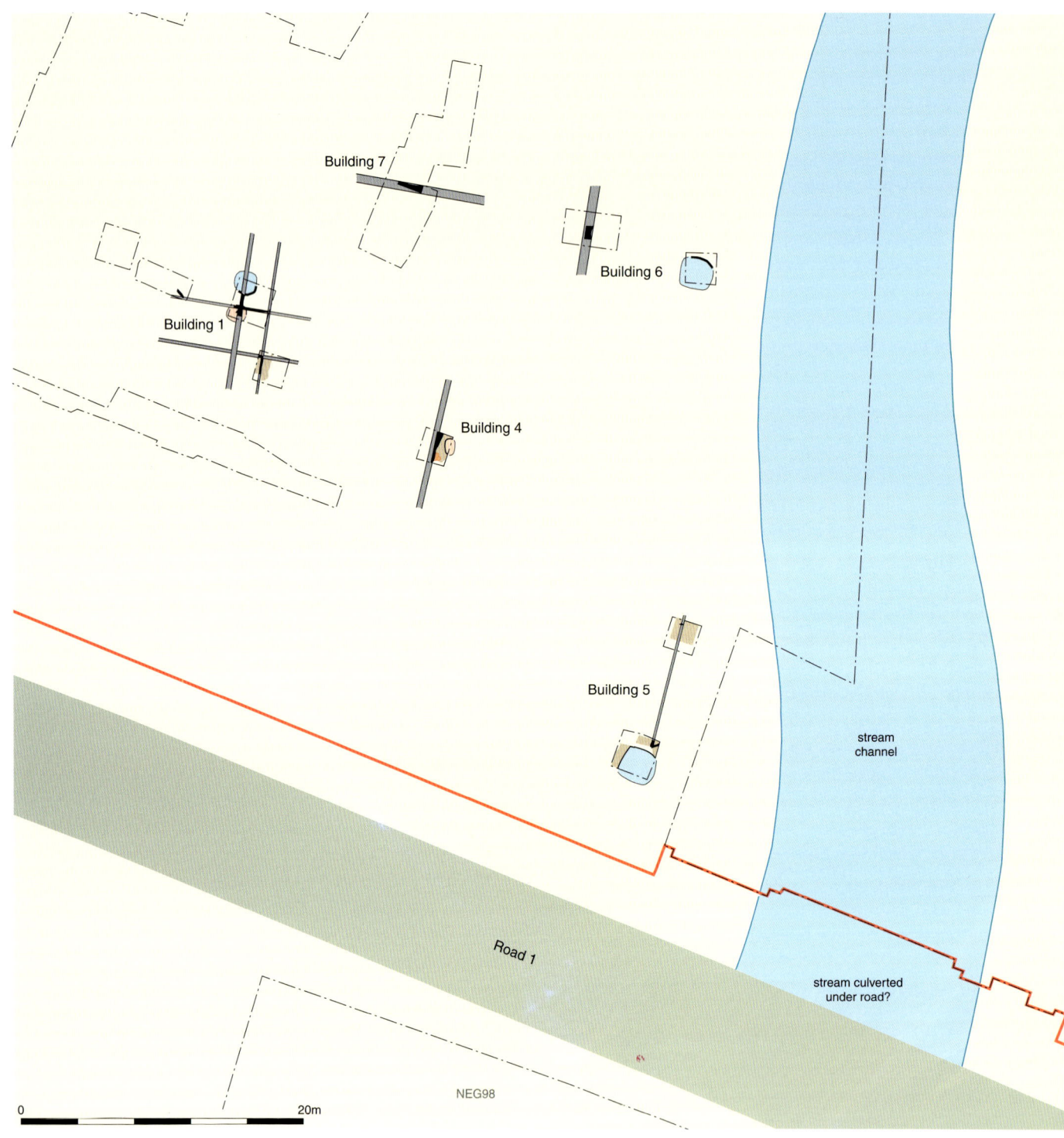

Fig 16 Post-Boudican development, c AD 70–120 (period 2, phase 2) (scale 1:400)

which overlay Open Area 8, c 25m north of the line of the main road (Fig 16). Internal wall divisions defined narrow rooms orientated roughly parallel to the road beneath Newgate Street (Fig 18), and these may have been store rooms situated in the rear of a roadside building. The internal areas of the building consisted of brickearth floors and levelling deposits, sealed by collapsed walls. Plain white plaster fragments may have been derived from the walls.

The pottery evidence indicates that Building 1 was probably constructed in c AD 90–100. The assemblage contained a small quantity of 1st-century fabrics and a relatively high number of Highgate Wood ware C (HWC) sherds, suggestive of a late 1st-century AD date (Groves 1993). The lack of early south Gaulish samian (SAMLG) forms and the identification of a mortarium stamp from Matugenus, who was producing mortaria in Verulamium during the period AD 80–125 (Hartley 1984, 286), support the AD 90–100 date. Glass fragments from bottles common during the Flavian period were also found, along with a coin dating from c AD 70–90.

Building 7, located north-east of Building 1, was

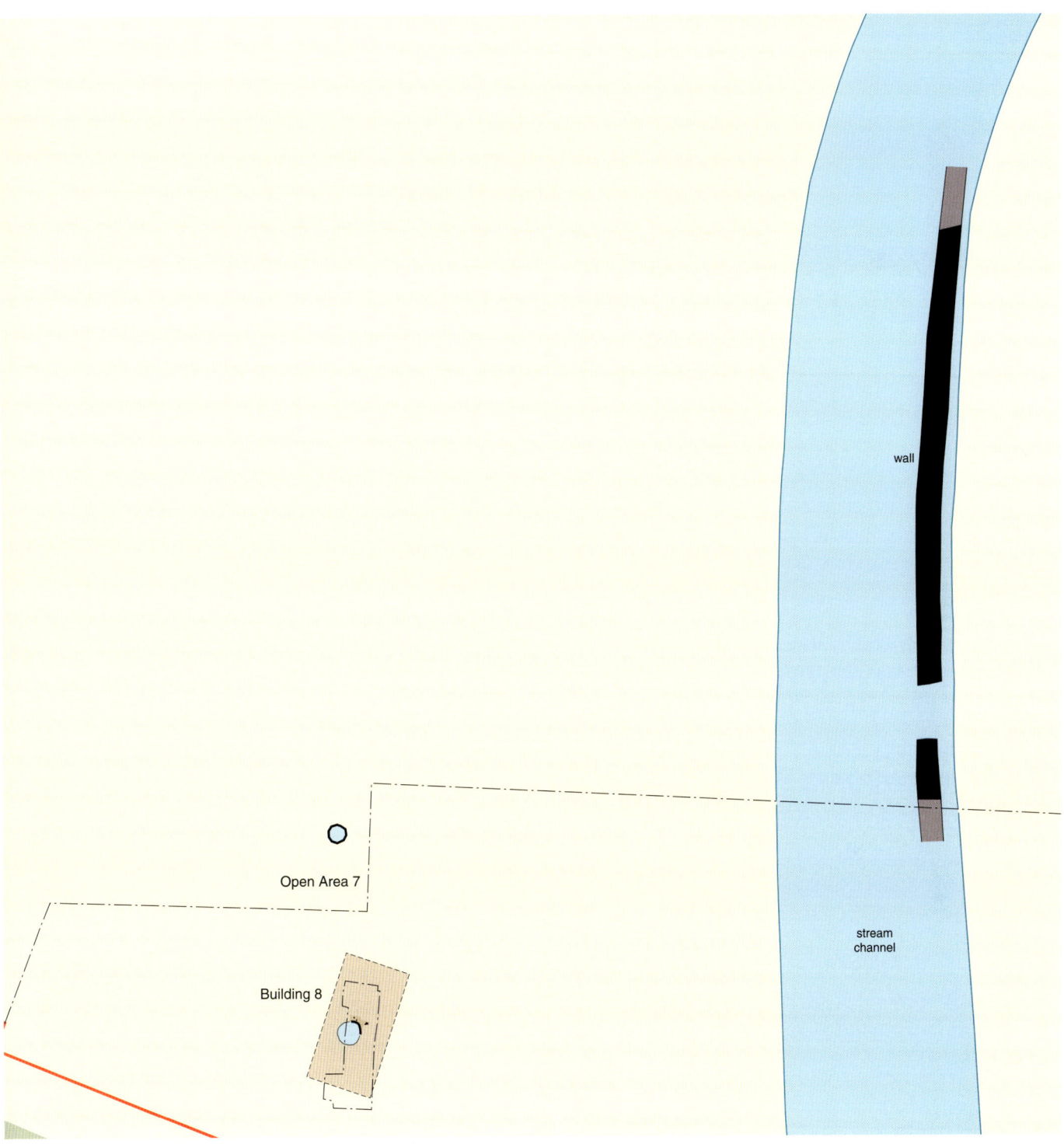

composed of a kiln, wall sill and floor surfaces (Fig 16). Most of the evidence was recorded in section, and as a result very few finds were recovered. The small amount of pottery suggests a date of AD 70–100, based on a jar/flagon in Hoo ware (HOO) dating from AD 50–100; two ovoid beakers in fine micaceous reduced ware (FMIC) and ring-and-dot beaker ware (RDBK) dating from AD 55–100; south Gaulish samian ware (SAMLG) dated AD 50–100; and a ring-necked flagon with flaring mouth in Verulamium region white ware (VRW) dated AD 70–120.

BUILDINGS 2 AND 3 AND ASSOCIATED YARD (OA9)

At the end of the 1st century AD, Building 1 was demolished and replaced by Building 2, with Open Area 9, a courtyard, to the rear (Fig 19). The only surviving structural evidence for Building 2 within the area investigated was the north-east corner of an external cob wall. The external gravel surfaces to the north overlay the area formerly occupied by the rooms of Building 1.

Dating evidence suggests that Building 2 was constructed in c AD 100–20, although the assemblages from Buildings 1 and

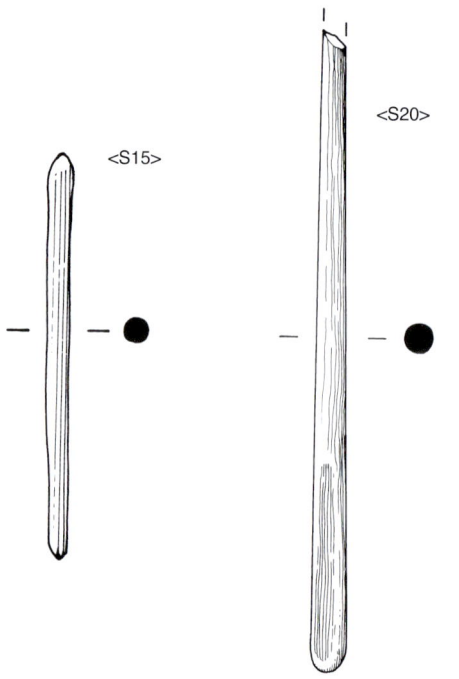

Fig 17 Bone hairpin <S15> and bone spatula <S21> from Open Area 8 (scale 1:1)

2 are not dramatically different. Both contain sherds of black-burnished wares dating to c AD 120 and varying quantities of Romano-British and reduced fine wares, some of which date to AD 120. The two assemblages appear to be very closely linked (Table 2). The finds from Building 2 were largely domestic in nature and included part of a bone needle <S22> and a good quality facet-cut colourless glass beaker dating from the late 1st or early 2nd century AD (<S30>, Fig 20).

The yard area to the north of the building contained a well (Fig 19). The pottery assemblage from the well indicates that it was backfilled in AD 120–60, suggesting that it was broadly contemporary with Building 2. The pottery consisted of sherds of a Dragendorff 27 cup in central Gaulish samian (SAMCG) dating to AD 120–60, Verulamium region white ware (VRW) dating to AD 50–160, and a flagon/jar in north French/south-east English oxidised ware (NFSE) also dating to AD 50–160. The well also contained a distinctive and very heavy brooch dating from the mid 1st century AD (<S11>, Fig 21) and a large number of painted wall plaster fragments which may be intrusive from the Hadrianic fire debris in Open Area 11.

Open Area 9 may have extended eastwards and a second well was recorded in the area to the east of Building 6 (Fig 16). A large amount of pottery was retrieved from the backfill of the well, with a date range of AD 70–5. The most common fabric types in the assemblage are Highgate Wood ware B (HWB) (<P41>–<P47>, Fig 22) and Verulamium region white ware (VRW) (<P53>, Fig 22). Early Roman micaceous sandy ware (ERMS) is also highly represented (<P32>–<P34>, Fig 22), and as a group the early Roman sandy wares (ERS) are the second most common ware (<P35>–<P36>, Fig 22). Alice Holt/Surrey ware (AHSU) (<P27>–<P30>, Fig 22) is more common than Highgate Wood ware C (HWC) (<P48>). South Gaulish samian (SAMLG) was the only samian identified from the well. The AD 75 date is provided by the identification of sherds from a carinated beaker with a tall upright plain rim in a black eggshell ware (BLEG), dated AD 45–75 (<P31>, Fig 22). One sherd from a dish with a simple inturned rim in terra nigra (TN), dated AD 40–80, was also identified (<P52>, Fig 22). Both these wares are uncommon and strongly suggest that the well was backfilled at an early date.

Other vessels of interest were three beakers in fine micaceous reduced ware (FMIC) (<P37>–<P39>, Fig 22),

Fig 18 Brickearth sill beam and associated floors in Building 1

Early Roman settlement, AD 43–late 2nd century (period 2)

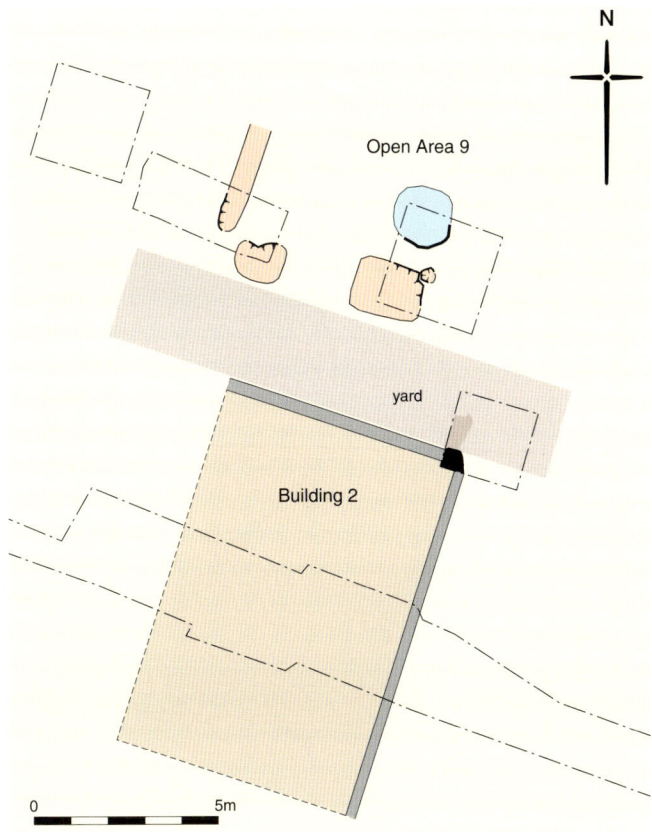

Fig 19 Detail of Building 2 and associated yard Open Area 9 (period 2, phase 2) (scale 1:200)

Table 2 Comparison of pottery assemblages from Buildings 1 and 2 (for expansion of fabric codes see Table 7)

Fabric	Building 1 No. sherds	%	Building 2 No. sherds	%
AMPH	1	0.6	4	1.0
BAETE	10	5.8	9	2.4
CADIZ	4	2.3	10	2.6
GAUL1	5	2.9	8	2.1
GAUL2	1	0.6		
SAMCG	1	0.6		
SAMLG	13	7.6	21	5.5
SAMMV2	1	0.6		
LOMI			4	1.0
RDBK	1	0.6	2	0.5
BB1			13	3.4
BB2	3	1.7		
FINE	3	1.7	4	1.0
FMIC	1	0.6	6	1.6
NKGW	1	0.6		
TN			1	0.3
WSEL	1	0.6		
AHSU	16	9.3	34	8.9
CCGW			5	1.3
ERMS	2	1.2	1	0.3
ERSB	3	1.7	10	2.6
HWC	19	11.0	78	20.5
SAND	14	8.1	26	6.8
VRG	1	0.6	0	0.0
GROG	1	0.6	0	0.0
HWB	4	2.3	6	1.6
NKSH	1	0.6		
SHEL			1	0.3
BHWS	1	0.6		
HOO	7	4.1	2	0.5
NFSE	1	0.6		
LOXI			5	1.3
OXID	5	2.9	12	3.1
OXIDF	1	0.6	2	0.5
RWS	4	2.3	5	1.3
VCWS	2	1.2	0	0.0
VRW	43	25.0	107	28.1
SEAL	2	1.2	5	1.3
Total	173	100.7	381	99.8

two beakers in unsourced oxidised ware (OXID) (<P49>–<P50>, Fig 22), a bowl in unsourced grog-tempered ware (GROG) (<P40>, Fig 22) and a beaker in ring-and-dot beaker fabric (RDBK) (<P51>, Fig 22).

The upper fill of the well adjacent to Building 6 contained 40 sherds of post-Flavian vessels, including fragments from two round-bodied jars with burnished decoration on the shoulder in Highgate Wood ware C (<P48>, Fig 22), which may be intrusive material associated with dumping prior to construction of the city defences. The fill also contained domestic material including glass vessel fragments, a handle of a copper-alloy implement that may have had a medical or surgical function <S20> and an iron double spiked loop fitting <1470>.

Building 3 (not illustrated) was represented by part of an external cob wall (Fig 23), situated close to Building 2 but set

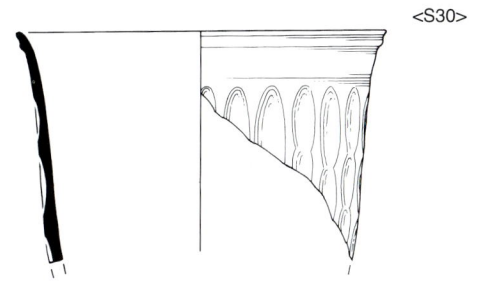

Fig 20 Facet-cut colourless glass beaker <S30> (scale 1:2)

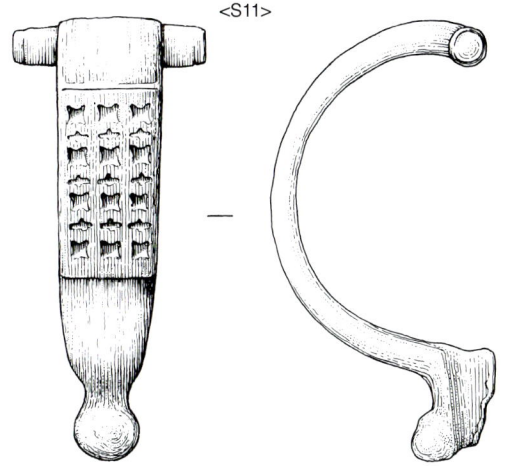

Fig 21 Copper-alloy brooch <S11> (scale 1:1)

21

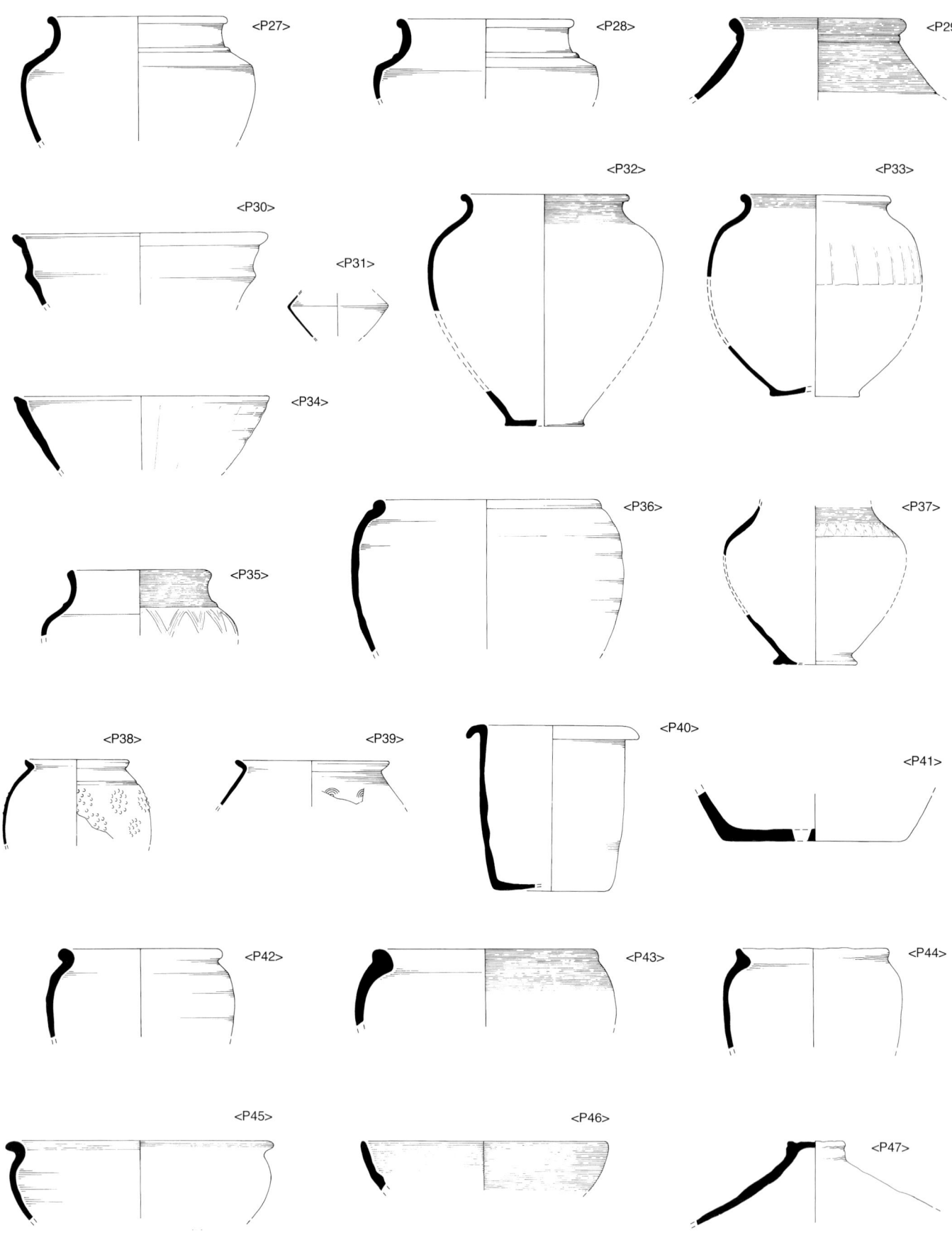

Fig 22 Pottery assemblage from the backfill of well adjacent to Building 6: Alice Holt/Surrey ware (AHSU) vessels <P27>–<P30>; black eggshell ware (BLEG) beaker <P31>; early Roman micaceous sandy ware (ERMS) vessels <P32>–<P34>; early Roman sandy ware vessels <P35>–<P36>; fine micaceous reduced ware (FMIC) vessels <P37>–<P39>; unsourced grog-tempered ware (GROG) bowl <P40>; Highgate Wood ware B (HWB) vessels <P41>–<P47>; Highgate Wood ware C (HWC) bowl <P48>; unsourced oxidised ware (OXID) vessels <P49>–<P50>; ring-and-dot beaker fabric (RDBK) beaker <P51>; terra nigra (TN) dish <P52>; and Verulamium region white ware (VRW) bowl <P53> (scale 1:4)

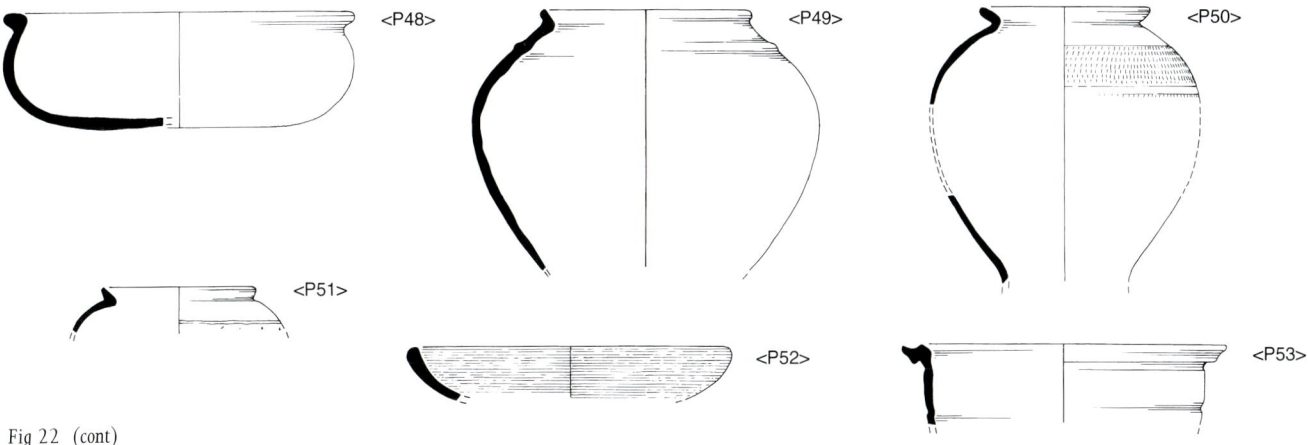

Fig 22 (cont)

Fig 23 Wall of Building 3 and associated internal and external surfaces, looking west (scale 0.5m)

on a slightly different alignment. Two sherds of pottery were recovered but do not provide a close date.

BUILDINGS 4, 5 AND 6 AND OPEN AREA 10

Building 4, located c 10m east of Buildings 1–3 (Fig 16), consisted of an internal north–south aligned wall and associated floors to the east. The building had been modified when the wall was demolished and sealed by new internal floors (not illustrated). The pottery assemblage gives an early date of AD 70–80, based on the presence of a few Flavian forms such as Highgate Wood ware C (HWC), dating to AD 70–160, a ring-neck flagon with flaring mouth in red- and white-slipped wares, dating to AD 70–120, a ring-necked flagon with vertical neck in Verulamium region white ware (VRW), dating to AD 70–100, and two south Gaulish samian (SAMLG) Dragendorff 37 bowls, dating to AD 70–100. Most importantly, a sherd from a terra nigra (TN) plate, dating to AD 50–80, was identified. Other finds were purely domestic in nature and consisted of a copper-alloy key <S28>, fragments of vessel glass, one fragment of window glass and an unidentified coin.

Building 6 survived only as internal surfaces and beam slots recorded in a small area c 10m to the north of Building 4. The pottery assemblage suggests a date range of AD 70–100 or possibly AD 70–80. The AD 70 date is provided by a sherd from a ring-necked flagon with flaring mouth in Verulamium region white ware (VRW), dating to AD 70–120, and a sherd from a decorated Dragendorff 37 bowl in south Gaulish samian (SAMLG), dated AD 70–100. Also of note are three sherds of Highgate Wood red-slipped ware B (HWBR), one from an imitation of a Pompeian red-slipped ware plate and two from a miscellaneous form but probably some sort of bowl. This fabric is not common in London and tends to indicate an early Flavian date. Eight sherds from a bead-rimmed jar in an unsourced sand-tempered ware (SAND) were identified, dated AD 50–100. Normally this type of vessel requires no special mention but the fabric of the vessel is very reminiscent of Rhineland granular grey ware (RGGW), dated AD 50–80. If it is RGGW then this is further evidence that the building is relatively early.

Building 5 lay c 20m to the south-east, nearer to the road frontage, and was represented by fragments of floors (Fig 24) and

Fig 24 *Section through the floors of Building 5, looking south (scale 0.5m)*

sill beams recorded in two physically separate trenches. The pottery evidence suggests that the building may have had a long life and was repaired or altered over a period of c 50 years. The identification of one sherd of Lyon ware (LYON), dating to AD 50–70, and one sherd of Sugar Loaf Court ware (SLOW), dating to AD 50–80, coupled with the absence of destruction debris, suggests a pre-Flavian but post-Boudican date. Two sherds of black-burnished ware may indicate an early 2nd-century AD disuse date.

A large, unlined well was located at the southern end of Building 5 in what may have been an external area (OA10, Fig 16). The well extended beyond the limits of excavation and the physical relationship between the well and building was truncated. Occupation levels from Building 5 or later buildings had slumped down the sides of the well, although it is also possible that the well post-dated some of the initial floor levels.

BUILDING 8 AND YARD AREA (OA7)

Building 8 was located c 50m to the east of Building 5, between the two stream channels which crossed the site (Fig 16). The surviving evidence consisted of fragments of floor surfaces, dumping and stakeholes (Fig 25). There were no extant wall lines to indicate the building's orientation. Its surfaces sealed an

Fig 25 *Section through internal deposits of Building 8, looking north (scale 0.5m)*

earlier well (OA7) into which many of its floor surfaces had slumped. The pottery assemblage from Building 8 dates to AD 70–100. Highgate Wood ware B (HWB), dating AD 40–100, is in greater quantities than Highgate Wood ware C (HWC), dating AD 70–160, and Alice Holt/Surrey ware (AHSU), dating AD 50–160, is also common. The samian present is all south Gaulish (SAMLG), dating AD 50–100. Two sherds of ring-and-dot beaker fabric (RDBK), dating AD 50–100, have also been identified. Other finds include a dark blue glass melon bead (<S13>, Fig 26), a turquoise faience bead (<S14>, Fig 26), a complete ceramic lamp, stamped with the maker's name FORTIS (<S24>, Fig 26), and a fragment of volute lamp <S25>, all dating to the 1st century AD.

Building 8 may have been associated with an external area to its north, part of Open Area 7 retained in use, which also contained a well (Fig 16). The well contained a near-complete pipe clay figurine of Minerva (Hall and Watson 2000, 5) as well as a large ceramic assemblage. The Minerva figurine is depicted standing on a pedestal with her right arm raised to her shoulder and her left arm holding an oval shield (<S1>, Fig 27). The right arm may originally have held a spear. She is clothed in an ankle length tunic with a breast-plate on which the aegis, the head of the gorgon Medusa, can be seen. The head of the figurine appears to have been deliberately snapped off before it was put in the well (see Chapter 7.4).

A total of 12,405 sherds of pottery, representing c 66% of the whole Roman ceramic assemblage from the site, were recovered from this well. A study of the pottery indicates that the lower fill of the well dates to AD 90–100 while the upper fill dates to AD 100–20. There are enough sherd links between vessels in the two groups to suggest that they were dumped in one episode during the period AD 100–20, possibly even AD 100–10. Flagons make up 23% of the assemblage (Table 3), the majority of which are ring-necked flagons with flaring mouths in Verulamium region white ware (VRW), dating to AD 70–120 (<P20>–<P24>, Fig 28). Other flagons were found in ring-

Fig 26 Finds associated with Building 8: melon bead in blue glass <S13>; turquoise faience bead <S14>; and a ceramic lamp <S24>, stamped with maker's name FORTIS (scale c 1:1)

The Roman archaeological sequence

Fig 27 Pipe clay figurine of Minerva <S1> from a well (OA7) (height 131mm)

Table 3 Distribution of pottery forms from the well in Open Area 7, period 2, by sherd count and ENV

Form	No. sherds	%	ENV	%	Weight (g)	%
Amphora	6	0.4	6	1.9	1880	5.1
Beaker	69	4.2	10	3.1	544	1.5
Bowl	20	1.2	13	4.1	533	1.4
Cup	16	1.0	11	3.4	172	0.5
Dish	20	1.2	12	3.8	251	0.7
Flagon	828	50.9	73	22.9	10974	29.7
Flagon/jar	430	26.4	129	40.4	15938	43.1
Jar	202	12.4	45	14.1	3488	9.4
Jar/beaker	14	0.9	8	2.5	527	1.4
Mortarium	11	0.7	4	1.3	2120	5.7
Lid	9	0.6	7	2.2	211	0.6
Tazza	1	0.1	1	0.3	342	0.9
Total	1626	100.0	319	100.0	36980	100.0

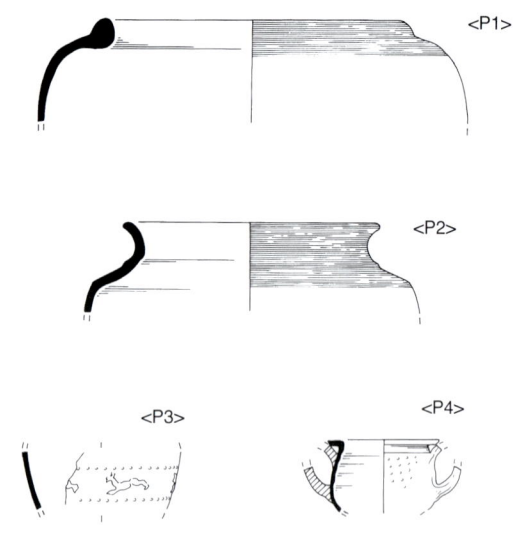

Fig 28 Selected pottery from the well in Open Area 7: Alice Holt/Surrey ware (AHSU) jars <P1>–<P2>; central Gaulish glazed ware (CGGW) vessels <P3>–<P4>; early Roman sandy ware B (ERSB) jar <P5>; unsourced fine reduced ware (FINE) beakers <P6>–<P7>; fine micaceous reduced ware (FMIC) bowl <P8>; Highgate Wood ware C (HWC) vessels <P9>–<P10>; London mica-dusted ware (LOMI) vessels <P11>–<P13>; Verulamium region white ware (VRW) tazza <P14>; north French/south-east English oxidised ware (NFSE) flagon <P15>; north Kent shell-tempered ware (NKSH) jar <P16>; unsourced fine oxidised fabric (OXIDF) jar <P17>; ring-and-dot beaker fabric (RDBK) flagon <P18>; unsourced white slip ware (RWS) flagon <P19>; VRW flagons <P20>–<P24>, jar <P25> and mortarium <P26> (scale 1:4)

and-dot beaker fabric (RDBK) and unsourced white slip ware (RWS) (<P18>–<P19>, Fig 28). Approximately 41% of the total assemblage is made up of bases that could be either flagons or jars. Interestingly 73 flagon rims, either complete or partial, were identified, as opposed to 129 bases, amounting to at least another 56 vessels. Seven more vessels could be accounted for by two-handled 'honey pot' jars in VRW, dated AD 50–150 (<P25>, Fig 28), leaving 49 bases. By including

Early Roman settlement, AD 43–late 2nd century (period 2)

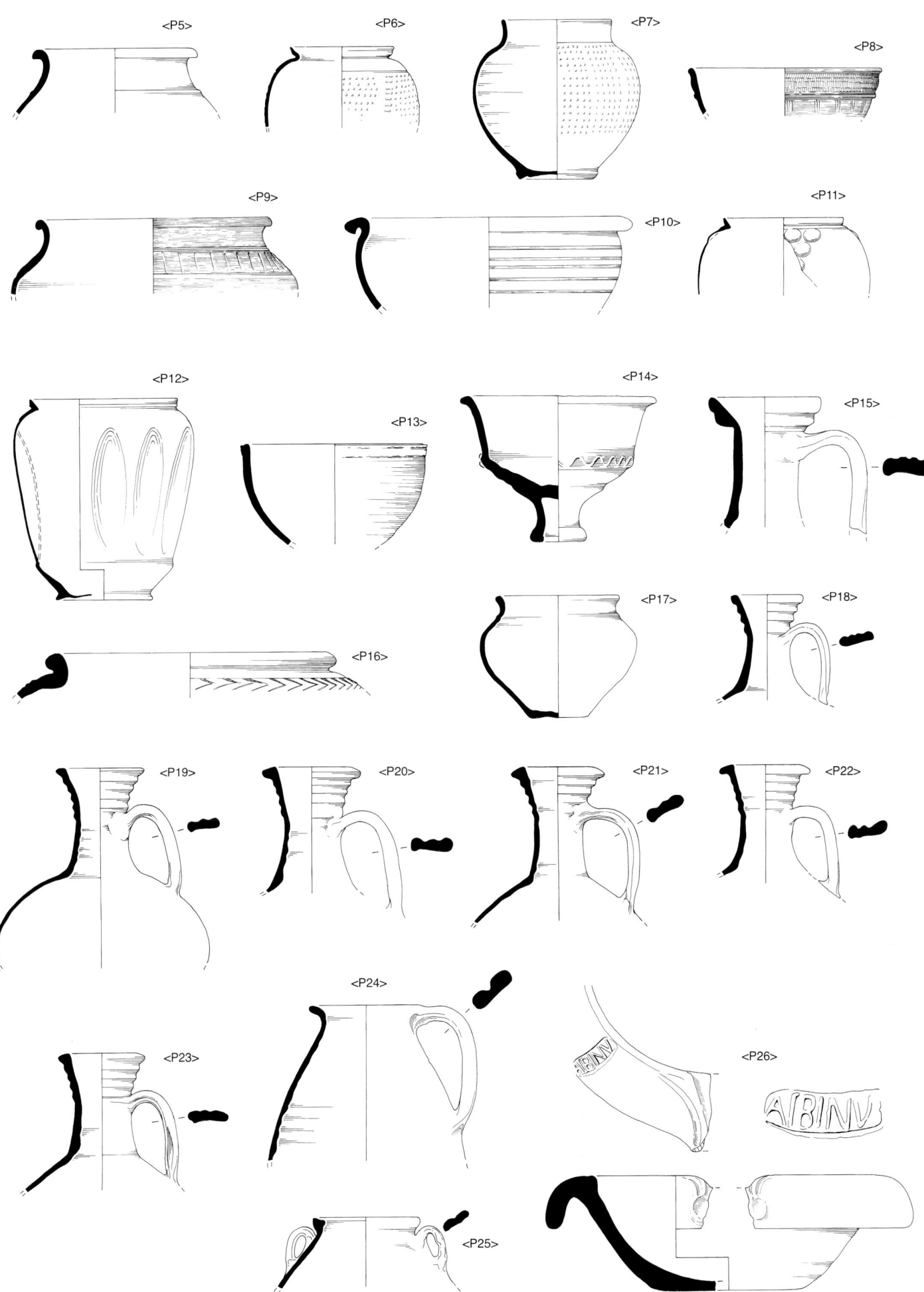

The Roman archaeological sequence

the 73 flagons and 7 jars in the figure for bases we can estimate that the well contained a total of 239 vessels. This large assemblage includes cups, beakers and plates, jars and flagons (<P1>– <P17>, Fig 28), three mortarium sherds (<P26>, Fig 28), six amphorae sherds and a tazza (<P14>, Fig 28).

Glass fragments recovered from this well come from vessels used at table or for food storage and should be considered in relation to the ceramic vessels. The fragments represent a small assemblage of 11 fragments from a minimum of five vessels but include two drinking cups (<S6>–<S7>, Fig 29), one jug handle (<S8>, Fig 29), a different jug base (<S9>, Fig 29) and a bottle (<S10>, Fig 29). All are from vessels used for drinking, serving or storing liquids. The two drinking cups date from the mid 1st century AD and are likely to be residual.

Other material from the well includes a poorly preserved copper-alloy vessel (<S2>, Fig 29) and an unusual form of copper-alloy mount or strap fastener which may have been used on a harness or a vehicle (<S3>, Fig 29). A bone counter and simple bone knife handle were similar to many others from London (<S4> and <S5>, Fig 29).

The ceramic assemblage from the well probably came from a tavern, as it is extremely unlikely that any household

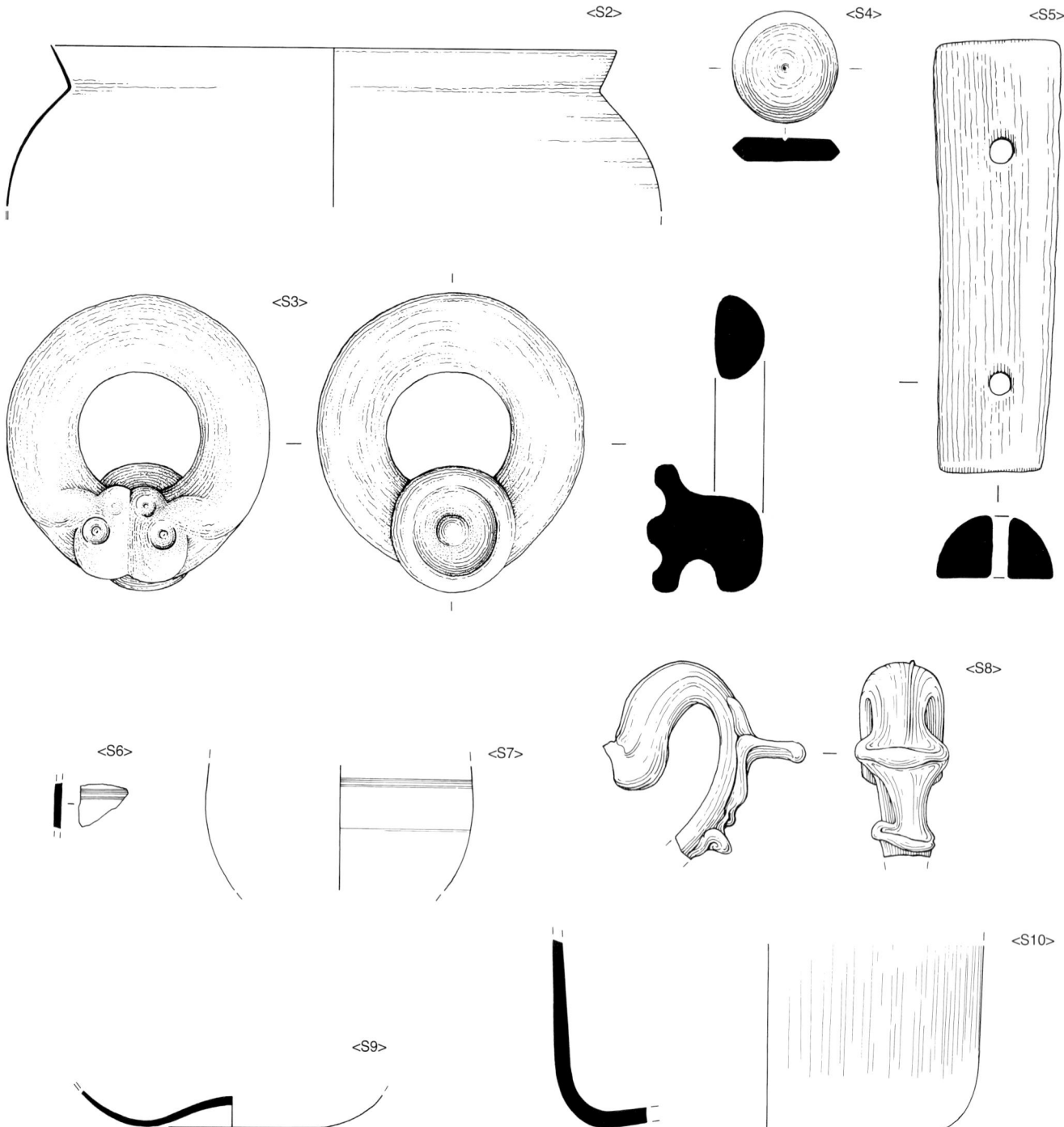

Fig 29 Selected finds from the well in Open Area 7: copper-alloy vessel <S2> and mount <S3>; bone counter <S4> and handle <S5>; vessel glass <S6>–<S10> (scale 1:2 except <S3>–<S5> and <S8> 1:1)

would have possessed so many flagons. The vessels all show signs of use and many contained residues. Food waste was also present in the backfill of the well (Table 14; Table 15), including a range of domesticates, fish and some game (woodcock and swan). Swan is not common from Roman deposits in London and is generally found on sites thought to have a high status, such as the Roman buildings at Winchester Palace in Southwark (Rielly 2005, 166). Small quantities of swan were recovered from a possible tavern well deposit at Fish Street Hill (MFI87) which also contained many bird and fish bones (Davis and Rielly in prep). The well also produced some oysters, which may have been farmed stock, as the shells are of similar size.

Discussion (period 2, phase 2)

In the latter part of the 1st century AD the area near Newgate progressed from being peripheral to the settlement to become densely built up with roadside properties. Initial landscaping of the area must have involved some management of the two stream channels that crossed the site, making more land suitable for building development. Building 5 lay very near the west side of the western stream channel, which may have been silted up by this time. Botanical evidence suggests that the stream area may have been prone to seasonal flooding. External areas may have been used for small-scale horticultural activities.

The western extent of the early Roman settlement is uncertain but it is noteworthy that Flavian building remains were found sealed under the bank of the later city wall and further to the north on the St Bartholomew's Hospital site (Bentley and Pritchard 1982, 136–7). The extent of the built up area suggests that the settlement extended some way beyond the limits set by the city wall at the end of the 2nd century AD, although it is not known whether these 1st- and 2nd-century buildings would have been considered part of the town proper or suburban development.

Very little can be said about the function and layout of the buildings, due to the piecemeal nature of the archaeological evidence. Most of the early buildings (B1–B8) were built between c AD 70 and the end of the 1st century. The buildings appear to have been in use for at least a decade and possibly 20 to 30 years before being replaced. It is likely that the buildings served a mixture of residential and commercial functions, similar to other examples of roadside strip buildings recorded along the east–west road (Hill and Rowsome in prep; Watson in prep; Perring and Roskams 1991). Flavian buildings recorded at the GPO site had relatively short life spans and appear to have been used as shops or taverns, with large rooms and hearths to the rear possibly producing goods for sale at the road frontage (Perring and Roskams 1991, 102–3).

Excavations at 3–9 Newgate Street (NEG98) found evidence of roadside buildings along the south side of the main east–west road. These buildings did not appear to conform to the usual strip-building layout, and were either square or rectangular with their long sides facing the road in some cases (Pitt 2006, 49). Their arrangement may have been influenced by the presence of the stream channel to the east and south (ibid).

The majority of the MLFC site, with its stream channels, would not have been an ideal location for residential buildings, and the development of the area can be seen as further evidence for the importance of commercial activity along the main east–west road. Evidence of industry was found in association with Flavian roadside buildings at the GPO site, where large quantities of burnt bone, slag and charcoal were recorded. Possible evidence for copper working was found at 3–9 Newgate Street (Pitt 2006, 65). The only indications of industrial activity from the MLFC site are a single fragment of crucible from Building 8, a kiln from Building 7, and areas of burnt brickearth recorded by Norman and Reader in 1907–9 (1912, 285).

Nearly all the finds from the Flavian buildings recorded at the MLFC site are domestic in nature. The largest assemblage came from the backfilled well in Open Area 7, which may have been associated with a tavern fronting onto the main road. The Minerva figurine found in the well may have been an offering to water deities when the well was blocked (Hall and Watson 2000, 4–5), with its decapitation symbolising the release of the goddess's spirit. Most figurines from London have been found deliberately broken up, often headless (ibid, 5). Ritual activities were an integral part of Roman life and figurines were often purchased as gifts for the deity depicted, intended to win favour from the god or goddess (ibid, 4). The MLFC Minerva may have been used at a temple or perhaps in a small shrine in Building 8. Association with a ritual feast, with the well acting as a *favissa*, cannot be proven. Although the pottery vessels appear to have been deposited over a short period of time, the figurine may not have been directly associated with the ceramic assemblage. It may have been placed in the well in an act of termination or purification, and Minerva is associated with water in other parts of the country. More simply, if the contents of a house were being cleared, a disused well may have been a suitable place for the burial of a household shrine, its head removed and its spirit free.

The Hadrianic fire and its aftermath, *c* AD 120– late 2nd century (period 2, phase 3)

Introduction

The Roman city was in its prime by the early 2nd century AD. The principal public buildings were in place by this time, including the forum-basilica on Cornhill, and the amphitheatre and Huggin Hill public baths west of the Walbrook. The road system and port facilities had also been extensively developed. It was at this point that London suffered the second major setback that can be identified archaeologically, as a fire swept through the densely built up settlement destroying most of the buildings. The fire can be dated to c AD 120–5 from samian assemblages found at waterfront warehouses at Regis House (Marsh 1981, 173–238; Brigham and Watson in prep). Recovery from the fire was prompt in central areas and along major roads but hesitant elsewhere, as changing economic

The Roman archaeological sequence

conditions in the mid 2nd century AD may have contributed to London's diminishing commercial importance (Hill and Rowsome in prep).

The Hadrianic fire

HADRIANIC FIRE DEBRIS (OA11)

Fire debris dating to c AD 120–30 was recorded in some areas of the MLFC site, while in other areas where there was no direct evidence of debris, earlier buildings appear to have gone out of use and been cleared at a similar date. The fire debris was not directly associated with particular buildings but had been redeposited as levelling dumps before post-Hadrianic redevelopment.

Some individual items of building material were identifiable among the burnt daub and other dumping. Waster tiles may have been associated with Roman tile manufacture and were similar to those found at Paternoster Square (Watson in prep). Wall plaster from the debris was identical to that found in a well in Open Area 9 and shows evidence of two phases of decoration. The first comprises a backing layer covered by a crudely smoothed, plain white surface layer (intonaco), while the second decoration comprises a red panel area bordered by a white band, followed by an area of green. There are also border areas in grey followed by white, and in green and yellow, separated by a white band. Three decorative areas are present: a floral decoration in pink, white, green and bluish-grey on a black background; a small garland in dark red on a green (or discoloured bluish-green) background; and two parts of a human figure, one of which shows the top of a shoulder and part of the torso painted above a red background ([1493], Fig 30).

The pottery assemblage from Open Area 11 is mixed, containing fabrics from the 1st and 2nd centuries AD as well as late Roman intrusive material (Table 4). The mixed nature and dating of the assemblage is a good indication of the extent to which the area was reworked after the fire. The fire debris

Table 4 Distribution of pottery dates (approximate) from Open Area 11

Earliest date (AD)	Latest date (AD)										
	80	100	120	140	150	160	170	200	250	300	400
40		1									
50	1	4	2	1	2	7	1	1	3		1
60		1				1					
70	1	5				3					
90		2									
100			3	1	1	1					
120				4	2	12					1
140						1					
150						1					
200									1		
250											3
350											1

Fig 30 Wall plaster from Open Area 11 [1493] showing shoulder area of figure (scale 1:1)

also contained a mix of domestic objects such as fragmentary domestic glassware and window glass, iron nails and an iron key <S27>. Personal items included copper-alloy tweezers <S18>, a ligula <S19> and an enigmatic fragment of pipe clay figurine, possibly from a shrine or aedicula <S29>.

It may be noteworthy that the area appeared to remain external along the line of the later city wall until the wall's construction in AD 185–225, but in other areas new residential buildings were established directly over the Hadrianic fire debris by the mid 2nd century.

Post-Hadrianic buildings

Rebuilding along the east–west road leading to Newgate was relatively common compared to more peripheral areas of the settlement (Perring and Roskams 1991, 119–20; Williams 1993, 35). Evidence for post-Hadrianic rebuilding along the road has been recorded at several nearby sites, particularly the GPO site to the east (Perring and Roskams 1991), and Paternoster Square (Watson in prep) and 3–9 Newgate Street (Pitt 2006, 53) to the south of the road. At the MLFC site, evidence for post-Hadrianic rebuilding was sparse, consisting of the fragmentary remnants of three buildings (B9–B11, Fig 31). Although interpretation is hampered by the very limited extent of excavation work, much of the site appears to have remained external after the fire.

BUILDINGS 9–11

Building 9, which was built directly above dumps of fire debris, was represented by a small internal area of floor surfaces and postholes. The limited excavation area meant that the layout and orientation of the building could not be established. Its location, set back c 25m from the line of the main east–west road, suggests that it was either part of the rear of a roadside strip building or a property set back from the main road and reached by an alley. There are no early Roman fabrics within the associated pottery assemblage, which indicates a date range of c AD 140–60. Other finds include fragments of 2nd-century vessel glass, one the rim of a jar.

Building 10 lay c 10m to the west of Building 9 and was also built on top of levelled Hadrianic fire debris and the remains of demolished buildings. Beam slots recorded in two separate excavation areas provide some evidence for the east–west and north–south aligned walls of the building. Evidence from within the building included floor surfaces and a series of tile-lined hearths and bowl hearths. The building evidence was situated c 30m north of the main east–west road, and it may have been part of the rear of a long strip building or a property set back from the road and reached by an alley.

The Building 10 pottery assemblage consisted largely of fabrics which date either to before AD 120, for example London mica-dusted ware (LOMI) dating to AD 70–120, or from AD 120 onwards, for example black-burnished ware 1 (BB1) dating to AD 120–400. Other finds included fragments of window glass dated broadly to the late 1st/2nd century AD. The building contained mainly domestic finds, although the presence of hearths may be suggestive of other activities. One environmental sample contained charred cereal grains and weed seeds, mainly from grasses.

Building 11, located 20m east of Building 9, was also constructed directly on top of levelled Hadrianic fire dumping (Fig 31; Fig 32). Evidence for the building survived as a series of brickearth floors, some cut by stakeholes, set back about 15m from the road frontage (Fig 33). The pottery from the building suggests an overall date range of AD 120–70, based on a sherd of Baetican amphora (BAETE) dating to AD 50–170, and one sherd of a Dragendorff 33 cup in central Gaulish samian (SAMCG), dated AD 120–200.

Buildings 9–11 were demolished in the later 2nd century, prior to construction of the city defences. Demolition may have been in preparation for that work, with the buildings possibly falling into disuse at the same time, but the limited amount of excavation makes this uncertain.

External activity in the late 2nd century AD

OPEN AREA 14/15

There is little evidence of Roman buildings on the MLFC site following the demolition of Buildings 9–11, or after about AD 160. A large external area (Open Area 14/15) was established across much of the site at about this time, perhaps in preparation for the construction of the city wall at the end of the 2nd century AD. The external activity continued beyond the end of the 2nd century and is discussed in more detail as part of period 3 (Chapter 3.2).

The settlement's early boundary

The northern boundary of the early Roman town is thought to have been located slightly to the south of the late 2nd-century AD defensive wall between Aldgate and Cripplegate (Perring 1991, 67). Several sites have produced evidence that the early boundary was marked by a ditch, or perhaps several successive ditches. At Duke's Place (DUK77) a shallow 2nd-century AD ditch was located close to the line of the later city wall (Maloney 1983, 97). Other traces of a pre-wall ditch have been found at 8–10 Crosswall (XWL79; Egan et al 1981), Crutched Friars (GM247; Merrifield 1965, 291), Baltic Exchange (Howe 2002, 7), 57 London Wall (LON82; Pye 1985), 85 London Wall (BLM87; Sankey and Stephenson 1991, 118) and 1–6 Aldersgate Street (AES96). Dating evidence from the latter site indicated that the ditch had been dug in c AD 100 (Butler 2001, 46). Evidence of a possible late 1st-century AD east–west boundary ditch, or *pomerium*, was found during excavations at 100 Wood Street in 1997 and coincided with the line of the south wall of the later Cripplegate fort (Howe and Lakin 2004, 18–19). The masonry defences of other Romano-British towns, such as Verulamium and Silchester, were also preceded by a ditch and rampart (Wacher 1995, 71).

The Roman archaeological sequence

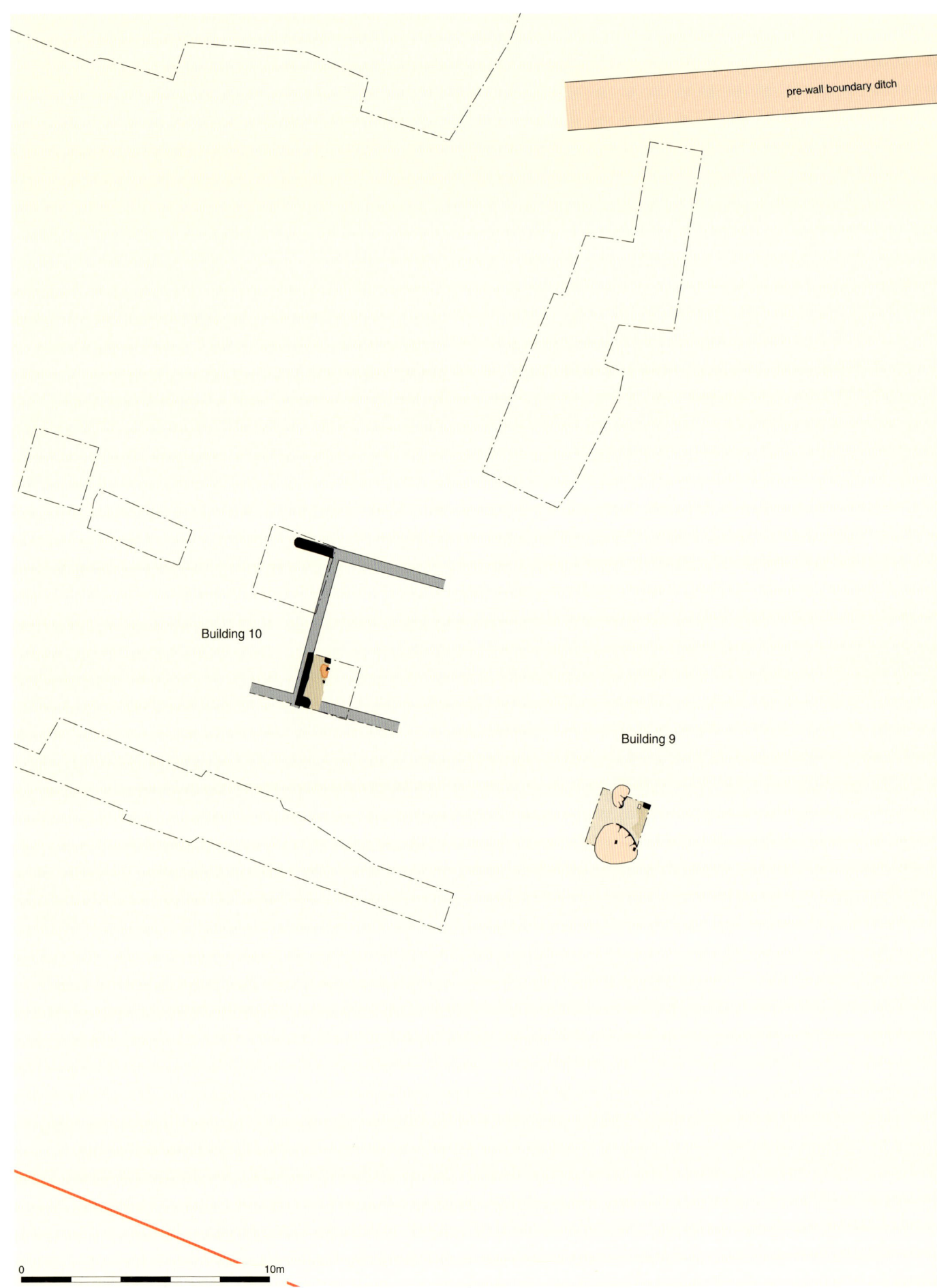

Fig 31 Post-Hadrianic fire redevelopment, showing Buildings 9–11 and the pre-city wall boundary ditch (S1) (period 2, phase 3) (scale 1:200)

Early Roman settlement, AD 43–late 2nd century (period 2)

LATE 2ND-CENTURY AD BOUNDARY DITCH (S1)

As discussed earlier, the location of the settlement's early western boundary is not known, though it was probably some distance to the east of the MLFC site (Maloney 1983, 97). Interestingly, the mid 2nd–early 3rd century AD cremations recorded at St Bartholomew's Hospital (BAR79) appear to respect the line of the later wall, suggesting that some form of boundary was in place from an earlier date (Bentley and Pritchard 1982, 161).

An east–west aligned ditch (S1) was recorded on the northern part of the MLFC site, on a similar orientation to the later city wall and very close to its location (Fig 31). This feature may have served a similar purpose to the boundary ditches found at Duke's Place and elsewhere. The ditch contained only three sherds of pottery, making it difficult to gain a secure date, but it can be tentatively dated AD 150–300 on the basis of the presence of a sherd of east Gaulish samian (SAMEG). The feature was not found in any of the other excavation trenches and it was not possible to trace its original route or extent (Fig 34).

Discussion (period 2, phase 3)

The Hadrianic fire of c AD 120–5 destroyed the earlier period 2 roadside buildings identified at the MLFC site along the north side of the main east–west road. The area was cleared and rebuilding along the road seems to have been prompt, although the overall extent and density of occupation was less than before the fire, with many areas remaining external. Only three post-Hadrianic buildings were recorded at the site, and these had a date range of c AD 120–60. There was evidence that repairs and alterations had been made to Building 10 but the sequence was much less complex than that from before the fire. The same pattern of reduced building activity has been recorded at nearby sites such as GPO Newgate Street.

The overall evidence implies that the MLFC area was not extensively reoccupied after the Hadrianic fire. Evidence from many sites nearer the core of the settlement, particularly in areas set back from main roads, suggests that the settlement began to contract from the mid 2nd century AD onwards.

Evidence of a possible mid 2nd-century AD boundary was discovered on the northern part of the MLFC site, following the same alignment as the later city wall. If this was an early boundary it may indicate that the buildings to the south-east lay within the formalised 2nd-century AD area of the city.

The archaeological sequence dated to the second half of the 2nd century and recorded at the MLFC site, although based on very limited excavation data, appears to follow a broadly similar pattern to that found at other sites in the area. At GPO Newgate Street the latest extant building phase ended in c AD 160 and was sealed by dark earth (Perring and Roskams 1991, 120) although soil formation processes may have destroyed evidence of later building activity. At St Bartholomew's Hospital, to the north of the MLFC site, there is evidence that mid to late 2nd-century AD buildings were dismantled (Bentley and Pritchard 1982, 137). South of the main east–west road at 3–9 Newgate Street, the last

The Roman archaeological sequence

Fig 32 Section through internal surfaces of Building 11 and earlier Hadrianic fire dumps, looking west (scale 0.5m)

Fig 33 Stakeholes cut through floor surface of Building 11, looking north (scale 0.5m)

Fig 34 *Section through base of pre-wall boundary ditch (S1), looking east (scale 0.5m)*

extant phase of roadside buildings was demolished c AD 160, possibly to make way for a large roadside masonry structure (Pitt 2006, 50–3). The evidence from Paternoster Square also shows that properties south of Road 1 were abandoned in the late 2nd century and secondary roads to the south may also have gone out of use, with pitting and dumping becoming the primary land use (Watson in prep).

3.2 Later Roman activity, late 2nd century –late 4th century AD (period 3)

Evidence of activity between the late 2nd and the late 4th centuries AD is presented here in terms of broad land uses and has been divided into two phases where possible, but external activities on some parts of the site, such as dark earth formation, may extend through the entire period and cannot be assigned to a more precise chronology.

Late Roman external activity (period 3, unphased)

Introduction

Evidence from many London sites suggests that there was a decline in building density and economic activity from about the 2nd century AD onwards, although this was less pronounced along the main roads and in the Walbrook valley and eastern hill (Hill and Rowsome in prep). These changes were probably related to more widespread economic change in Roman Britain and the Empire, and also to the establishment of a stable Roman frontier in the north of England (Perring 1991, 88–9). These and other factors meant that less trade passed directly through London.

Changes in the nature of occupation have been recorded at many locations in the Roman town, including the MLFC site, where there is little evidence of buildings after c AD 160 but external activity which included the formation of dark earth. At most sites there seems to be a marked decline in new building and building density from about this date, although this was apparently less pronounced in the centre of the settlement, the Walbrook valley and at some locations along the main east–west road (Hill and Rowsome in prep). The greater amount of truncation of late Roman deposits, including that which may have been caused by subtle soil formation processes, requires that we exercise a degree of caution when interpreting the evidence (P Rowsome, pers comm).

External activity in the 3rd century AD

PITS, GULLIES AND OTHER EXTERNAL ACTIVITY (OA14/15)
After Buildings 9–11 (period 2, phase 3) had gone out of use, the land reverted to an open area where the main activity was pitting (OA14/15, Fig 42). A gravelled surface and a number of gullies were also recorded, one associated with a bank. It is probable that the levelling of Buildings 9–11 and the activities defined in Open Area 14/15 were precursors to, or associated with, the building of the city wall. The gravel surface could be evidence for an internal road, running along the inside of the bank relating to the city defences.

There is little dating evidence associated with Open Area 14/15 deposits. Aside from residual pottery, a copper-alloy penannular brooch <S12> and a melon bead <473> could both date from the 1st to the 3rd centuries AD. The dumps also produced a fragment of lava quern <S26> and a ceramic spindle whorl <S23>. Ten fragments of glass comprised two bottles, a bowl and miscellaneous body sherds, all dating from the 1st/2nd century AD. The latest recorded feature in Open Area 14/15 was a gully and associated cobbled surface which appeared to have been in use at the beginning of the 3rd century AD, while the city wall was under construction. A number of uncommon late Roman fabrics were also identified in the gully, including Argonne ware (ARGO), dated AD 250–400, and central Gaulish/Lezoux black colour-coated ware (CGBL), dated AD 150–250.

Late Roman dark earth deposits

EXTERNAL DEPOSITS (OA12)

Dark earth is the name given to a homogeneous silty garden soil-like deposit which has been found on many archaeological sites in Roman London. The deposit seems to have accumulated or been dumped after c AD 150, though in some places it appears to date from much later in the Roman period. Opinion is divided on the nature of the deposit and the process by which it accumulated. There is evidence to suggest that it may have been deliberately dumped on some sites, perhaps introduced for gardening and other small-scale horticultural activities (Perring 1991, 89). At Milk Street (MIL72, Fig 39) and GPO Newgate Street (GPO75, Fig 39) tip lines were said to be visible. However, a review of London dark earth has suggested that the deposit may be the product of biological reworking of late Roman deposits, and that it should not be viewed as a single phenomenon (Yule 1990, 620–8). Dark earth certainly differs in composition and date range from site to site, although this has often been interpreted as the result of digging-over and root action. It may be more likely that dark earth resulted from a combination of dumping, soil formation and accumulative processes, and that additional evidence of late Roman buildings has been lost in antiquity as a result of truncation associated with the deposition or formation of dark earth. At Milk Street and GPO Newgate Street many of the late Roman coins were found either within the dark earth or the post-Roman deposits, divorced from the latest surviving Roman buildings (ibid, 620–8). At some sites, such as 1 Poultry, there is clear evidence that the roadside timber building sequence on at least some properties continued into the 4th century, and this evidence is best on lower terraces where the strata may have been better protected from later truncation or bioturbation (Hill and Rowsome in prep).

Extensive dumping of dark earth to create a horticultural soil would have required a sustained effort, and it seems unlikely that there would have been sufficient demand for urban market gardens to prompt such work. The town was surrounded by farm land and in any case must have continued to require grain and other agricultural goods from its hinterland and beyond. On the other hand, abandoned areas would have made convenient rubbish tips, which would eventually have provided poor quality grazing (Watson 1998, 103). Micromorphological study of dark earth at several London sites has identified two distinct horizons: a lower horizon representing an initial build-up of biologically reworked Roman strata mixed with dumped material such as ash and cess, and an upper, more uniform, horizon resulting from soil formation, dumping and reworking. Pollen extracted from London dark earth has identified the presence of plants characteristic of grassland or urban wasteland and little clear evidence for cultivation (Watson 1998, 105).

The MLFC site dark earth deposits may date from the late 2nd century AD. Dark earth was identified in eight of the excavation trenches located inside the line of the city wall and was probably present across most of the site before it was lost to truncation (Fig 35). It was not possible to define any tip lines or layers within the deposits, even though a complete, untruncated soil profile survived in part of the area (Watson 1998, 105).

The dark earth deposits were mixed and contained mainly residual materials, such as a 1st-century AD Colchester brooch. Several hairpins (<S16>–<S17>, Fig 36) which date to after AD 150/200, were also recovered. A wide range of building materials was present, some with 4th-century dates, including stone roofing and fine sandstone paving. Residual building material included a rare, slip decorated, tegula in fabric group 2815 (<T1>, Fig 37). In most of the trenches the dark earth had a date range of c AD 300–400. In trench T6, however, rubbish dumps and dark earth deposits were dated to c AD 120–200. The deposits in this trench were preceded by a truncation horizon, which may imply that the area was levelled prior to the deliberate laying of dark earth. In all other trenches dark earth sealed the remains of amorphous pitting and dumping activities, or post-Hadrianic building remains.

In one trench (T7) a layer of dumping was sealed by a complete dark earth profile 1.2m thick. The dark earth was derived from two sources: firstly, the dumping of ash, cess and rubbish, and secondly, the weathering and biological reworking of the underlying Roman deposits and natural soil build-up (Macphail and Cruise 1993). The deposit was excavated in a series of 200mm thick spits, and pottery dating to AD 250–400 was recovered from both the top and bottom spits, suggesting extensive reworking. Pollen confirms that the area was urban wasteland, not garden or woodland. The dark earth was sealed by a Saxo-Norman ground surface (Watson 1998, 105).

Although dark earth may have been deliberately dumped on some parts of the MLFC site before the end of the 2nd century AD, other areas which became external at about the same time were apparently left unused until sealed by dark earth at the beginning of the ?4th century AD. It is not clear whether early Roman buildings were demolished or simply left to fall into ruin before being covered over.

The soil profile at the MLFC site is indicative of an area used at least intermittently as a rubbish tip in the 3rd and 4th centuries AD by people still living nearby, perhaps along the main street to the south. This soil horizon continued to develop through biological processes for another 500 years before the area experienced any significant reoccupation (Watson 1998, 106).

Later Roman activity, late 2nd century–late 4th century AD (period 3)

Fig 35 Excavating dark earth in spits

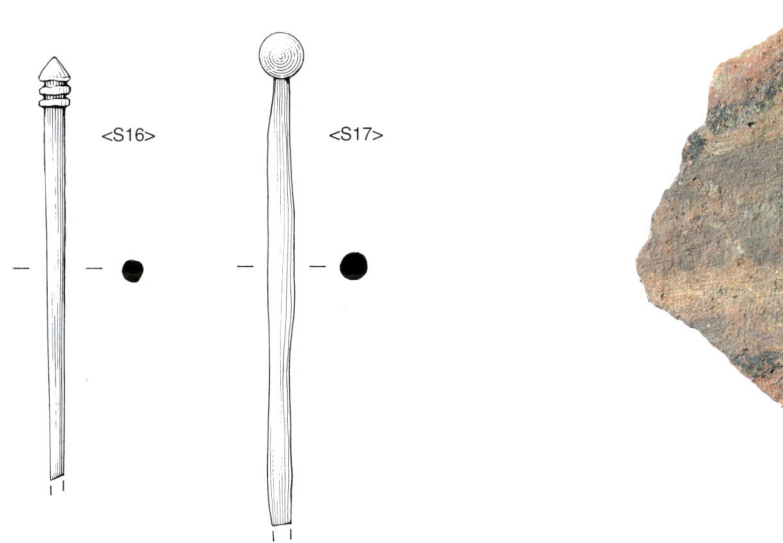

Fig 36 Bone pins <S16>–<S17> from the dark earth deposits (OA12) (scale 1:1)

Fig 37 Rare, slip decorated, tegula roofing tile <T1> from the dark earth deposits (OA12) (scale 1:1)

Construction of the Roman city defences, c late 2nd century–mid 3rd century AD (period 3, phase 1)

Introduction

The landward side of Roman London was provided with a defensive circuit between c AD 185 and 225 which enclosed an area of 133 hectares (Fig 38). The wall and its bastions, ditches and banks have been recorded on many sites and the wall's route is well documented. What is less certain is its construction date and whether it was intended to function as a genuinely defensive structure.

The city boundary, first defined by the Romans, was reused in the medieval and post-medieval periods. As a consequence, the wall and its ditches have been subject to many alterations

The Roman archaeological sequence

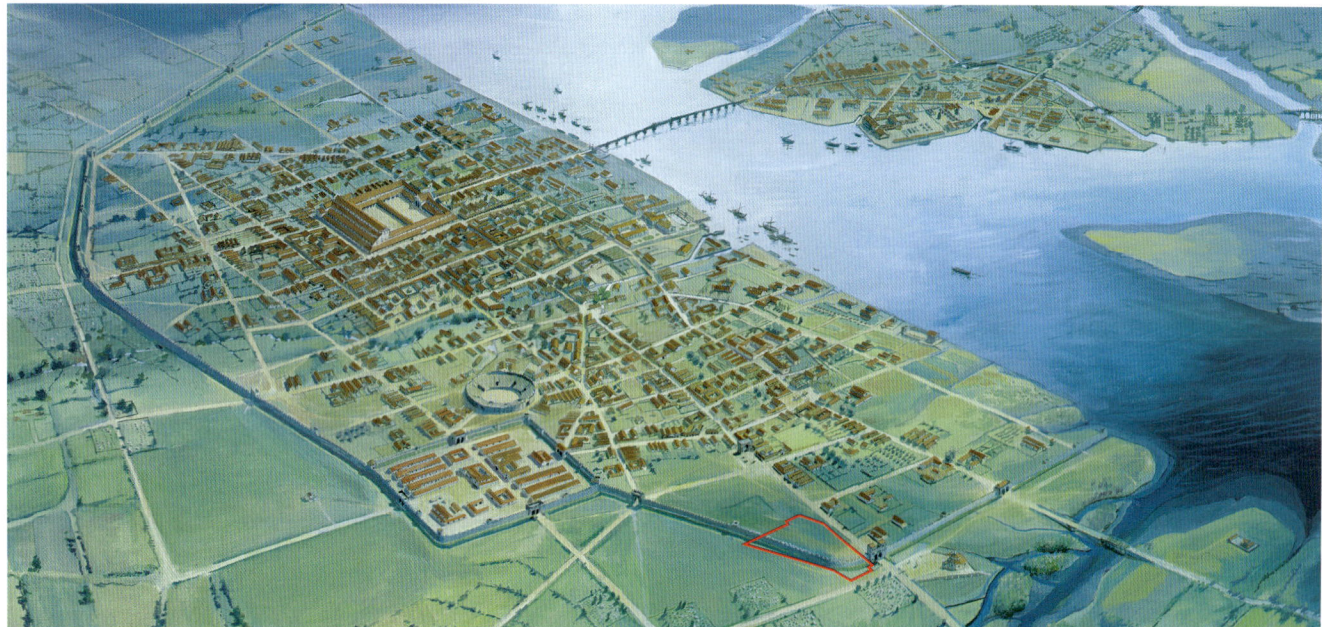

Fig 38 Panoramic view of Roman London in the early 3rd century AD, looking south-east; the MLFC site is in the lower foreground straddling the city wall (Peter Froste, 1996)

and additions throughout their lifespan. Although the later reuse of the city wall has resulted in the preservation of some of the Roman foundations and lower wall courses, redevelopment has also destroyed many associated deposits, which may have contained important dating evidence. As a result, dating evidence for the construction, use and disuse of the defences is scarce.

Description of the defences

It is now generally accepted that the first phase of the city defences consisted of a masonry wall, with an unknown number of internal towers, an internal bank, and an external ditch (Fig 38; Fig 39). The wall also had gatehouses where the major roads crossed its line at Aldgate, Bishopsgate, Newgate and Ludgate.

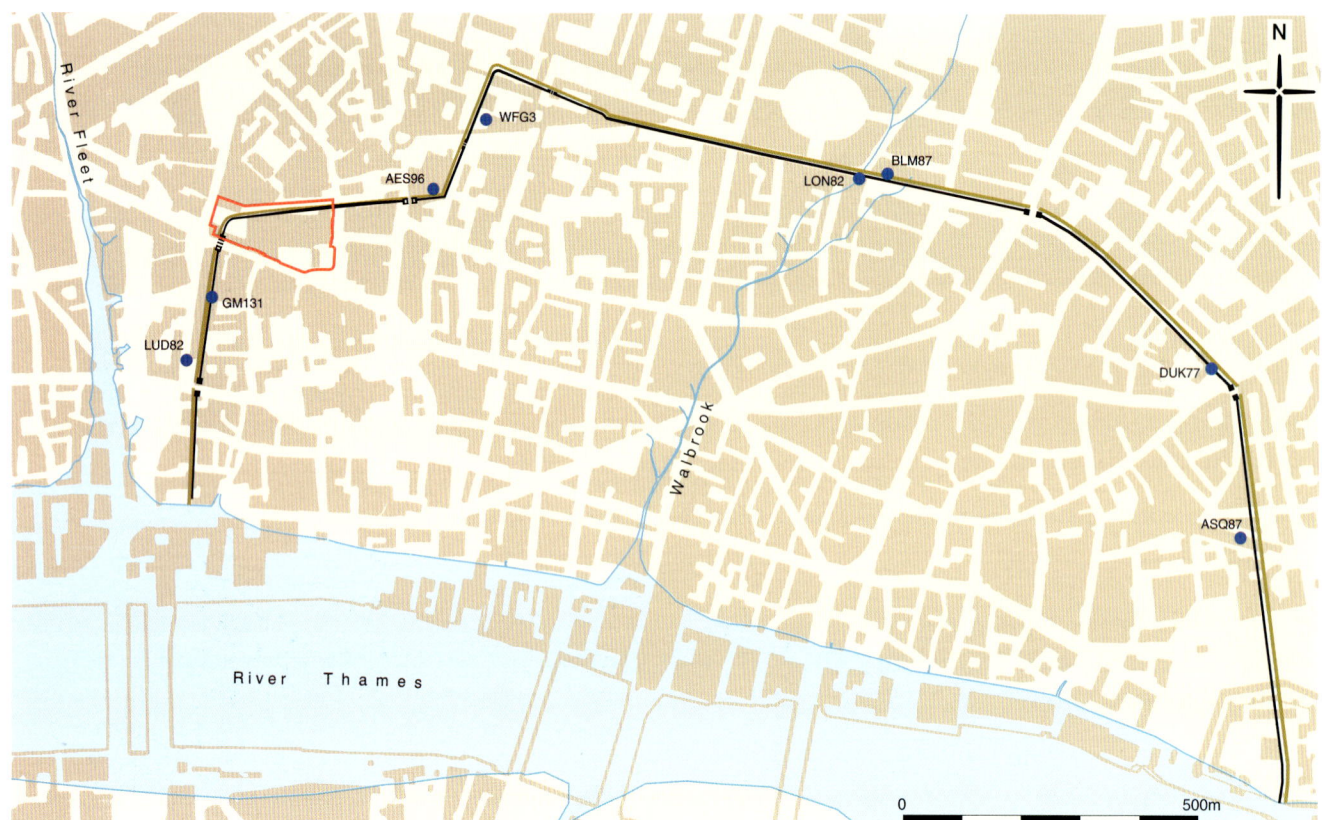

Fig 39 Plan of first phase of city defensive circuit c AD 185–250, showing relevant sites (key to site codes in Table 1) (scale 1:12,500)

Aldersgate was a later insertion, perhaps replacing the blocked west gate of Cripplegate fort. Postern gates may have existed at Aldermanbury, Moorgate and Tower Hill to provide access about every 300m between the main gates. Some of the major gatehouses are thought to have been free-standing monuments which pre-dated the wall and were later incorporated into the circuit (Maloney 1983, 97). There is some evidence that the internal bank may have been bordered on its inside edge by a road (Grimes 1968, 51), which may not have been continuous (Marsden 1965, 135). More recently, evidence that the outer berm may have been lined with metalling was discovered at America Square (ASQ87, Fig 39) and 85 London Wall (BLM87, Fig 39). This might indicate that an extramural road also ran along parts of the wall (Sankey and Stephenson 1991, 122), although no similar evidence has been found at other London sites. Canterbury's town wall is known to have been constructed with an extramural road (Bennett 1989, 127).

London's city wall was constructed on trench-built foundations of puddled clay, packed with flints, capped by a layer of ragstone rubble. External ground level was marked by a chamfered sandstone plinth and internal ground level was marked by a triple course of horizontally bedded tiles. Above plinth level the width of the wall varied between 2.05m and 2.63m (RCHME 1928, 72); above this point it narrowed successively at each tile level, of which there are a further four (Maloney 1983, 98–101). The internal and external faces were constructed from regular courses of small squared blocks of Kentish ragstone and the intervening space filled with rubble and poured mortar (Fig 40).

The original height of the city wall is not known, due to extensive truncation and later rebuilding. The wall has only been recorded in two places as surviving up to the fourth band of tiles, 4.0–4.42m above the plinth (RCHME 1928, 86, 91). Above the fourth band of tiles it is believed that there was a parapet walkway fronted by crenellated breastwork (Fig 41). In Canterbury a stretch of the Roman town wall had survived to the top of the crenellation level, and measured 7m tall. If London's town wall was of a similar height, then the highest surviving segments may have been at parapet level (Maloney 1983, 101).

The ditch and bank do not seem to have been constructed with as much regularity. For example, the ditch has generally been found to be V-shaped, 3.05–4.88m wide and 1.17–2m deep (Maloney 1983, 101), and may have operated as little more than a drain (Norman and Reader 1912, 278). On the site at 85 London Wall (BLM87, Fig 39), however, the ditch contemporary with the wall was not V-shaped but broad and

Fig 40 Remains of Roman wall, Newgate, 1903 (watercolour by P Norman, in Norman 1905, 114, pl 28)

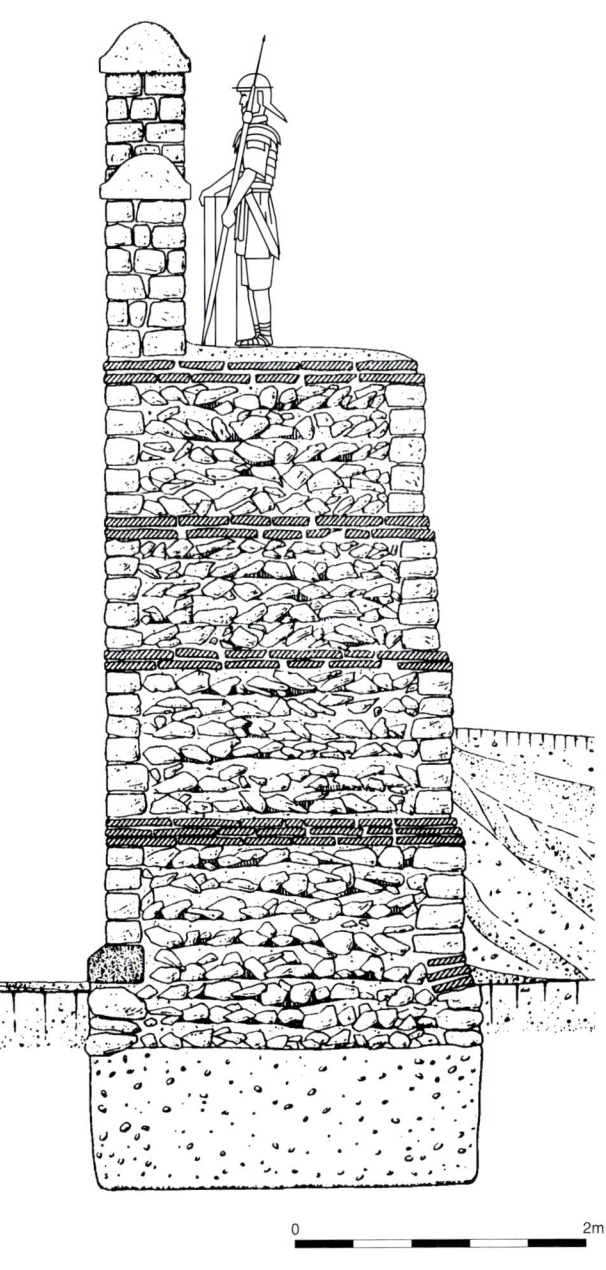

Fig 41 Section through city defences (drawing by C Green, in Maloney 1983, 99, fig 94) (scale 1:50)

flat bottomed. The feature seems to have channelled water into the nearby Walbrook (Sankey and Stephenson 1991, 117).

The ditch was separated from the wall by a berm, whose width has been recorded as varying considerably between 2.7m and 5.2m (Maloney 1983, 101). The internal bank has also been recorded on many archaeological sites and was c 2.0m tall and between 4.0m and 9.0m wide (Marsden 1970, 3–4; Maloney 1983, 101).

The variability in these observations demonstrates that the defences were not totally uniform across London, and that the design was regularly altered in response to the local natural topography. In fact, it could be argued that the entire defensive circuit owes its placement, size and shape more to topography than to the extent of the settlement.

Dating evidence for the defences

Wheeler believed that the city wall was constructed 'in the half century following the Boudican rebellion' (RCHME 1928, 73–9), a view since disproven by archaeological excavations. Historical sources suggest that the instruction to build the wall was given by Clodius Albinus, governor of Britain AD 193–7, in preparation for his clash with Septimus Severus (Corder 1955, 22–4). This date brings London into line with many other Romano-British towns, which were fortified at a similar time (ibid, 20–42).

The most convincing piece of dating evidence for the wall came from Grimes's excavation at Windsor Court (WFG3, Fig 39), where a worn coin of Commodus was found, dating to AD 183–4, underneath the city thickening on the west wall of the fort (Grimes 1968, 50–1). The late 2nd-century AD construction date has been confirmed by evidence from various sites, including the Central Criminal Court (GM131, Fig 39), excavated in the 1960s, and Duke's Place, excavated in the 1970s (DUK77, Fig 39), where pottery dated to AD 180 was found in deposits sealed by the wall and in the bank (Marsden 1970, 2–6; Maloney 1983, 104). This date has also been supported by more recent excavations at 1–6 Aldersgate Street (AES96, Fig 39), which found that the earlier boundary ditch, sealed under the city wall, had been backfilled by the second half of the 2nd century AD (Butler 2001, 48).

The later end of the date range for the construction period was provided by the discovery of forger's coins and pottery, dated AD 220–5, in the floor of one of the wall's interval turrets at the Central Criminal Court (GM131, Fig 39) (Marsden 1970, 5–6). A much larger group of forger's coins

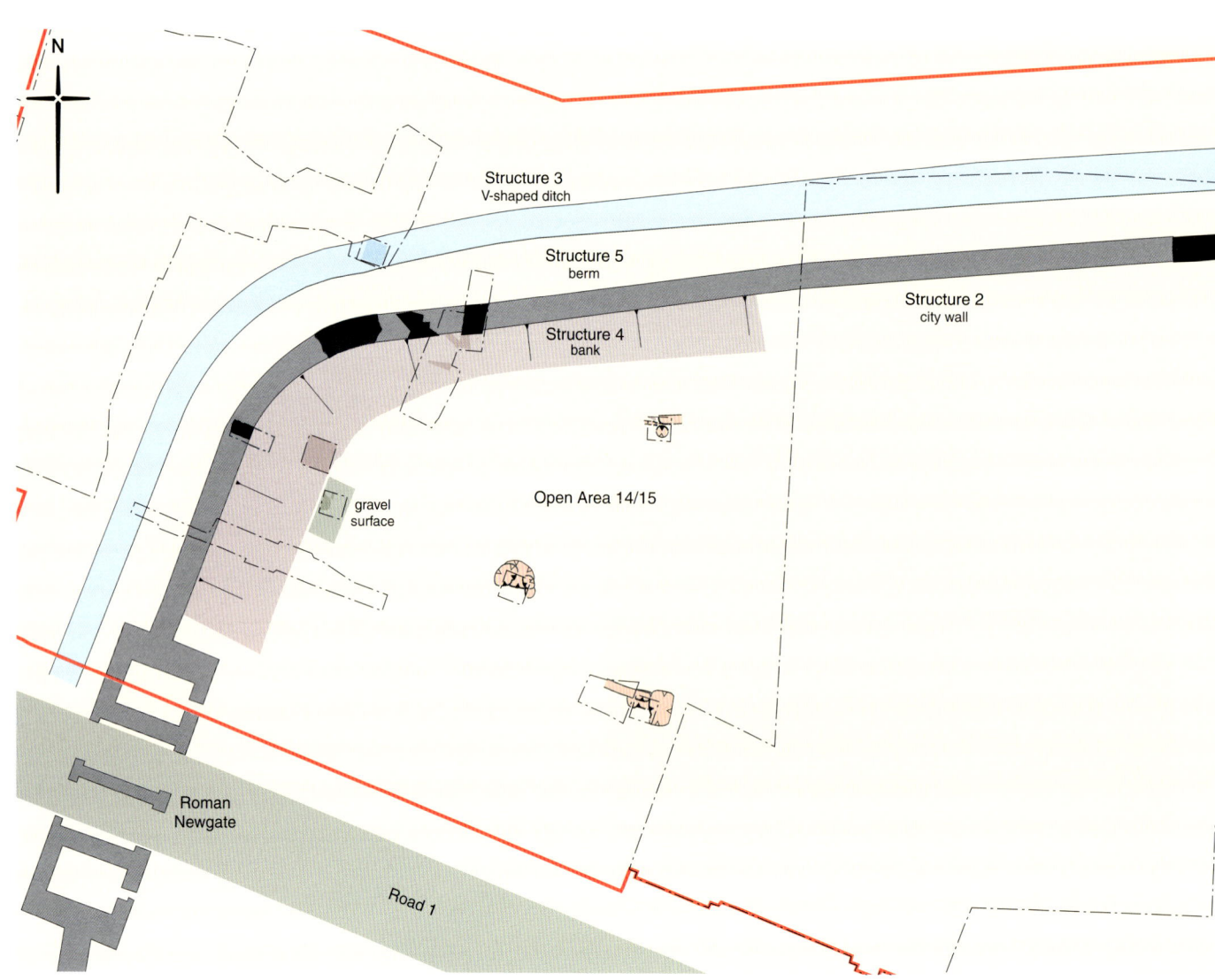

has since been discovered at Blomfield House, on New Broad Street (BLM87, Fig 39). These have a longer date range and could suggest that the wall was constructed at a later date (Sankey and Stephenson 1991, 120). There is no recent publication that draws together all the information relating to the city defences, and the last time such a study was carried out was before World War II (Bell et al 1937). Until a new study is carried out the accepted date range for the construction of the defensive circuit remains AD 185–225.

The MLFC evidence

THE CITY WALL (S2)

The line of the city defences crosses the northern and western parts of the MLFC site for a total length of c 220m (S2), as observed by Norman and Reader (1912, 274) (Fig 42), who probably observed and recorded more sections of the city defences than anyone else.

The record made of the defences by Norman and Reader is the primary source of information for the western corner of the Roman city wall. The first stretch of wall they encountered at the MLFC site was situated close to King Edward Street. This was traced for a distance of 12.20m, and survived to a height of 3.12m (Fig 42). The wall was built on natural brickearth and rested on ragstone/flint and clay-puddling foundations. Built up against the first segment of wall were the foundations of Bastion 17. Running parallel to the wall was the external V-shaped ditch, which was situated c 3.5m away from the external face of the wall and measured c 3.7m wide and 2m deep (Fig 42). The internal bank was also recorded in this area, measuring 1.52m high and c 5.03m wide (Norman and Reader 1912, 276) (Fig 43).

A longer section of the wall, measuring c 20m, was found further to the west (Fig 42). According to Norman and Reader (1912, 280), this section of wall 'displayed all the usual features', and continued on its course (surviving to varying heights) unbroken, until it reached the foundations of the Great Hall of Christ's Hospital (Chapter 5.3), at which point it had been destroyed. Running parallel to the wall for c 25m was the V-shaped ditch, which had been largely cut away by the second later Roman ditch. Another isolated segment of the wall, c 9m in length, was found c 9.0m to the west of the longest section; no description was provided (Fig 42).

The final section of wall recorded by Norman and Reader was still further west, at the point at which the wall turned south to meet Newgate (Fig 42). This part of the site was

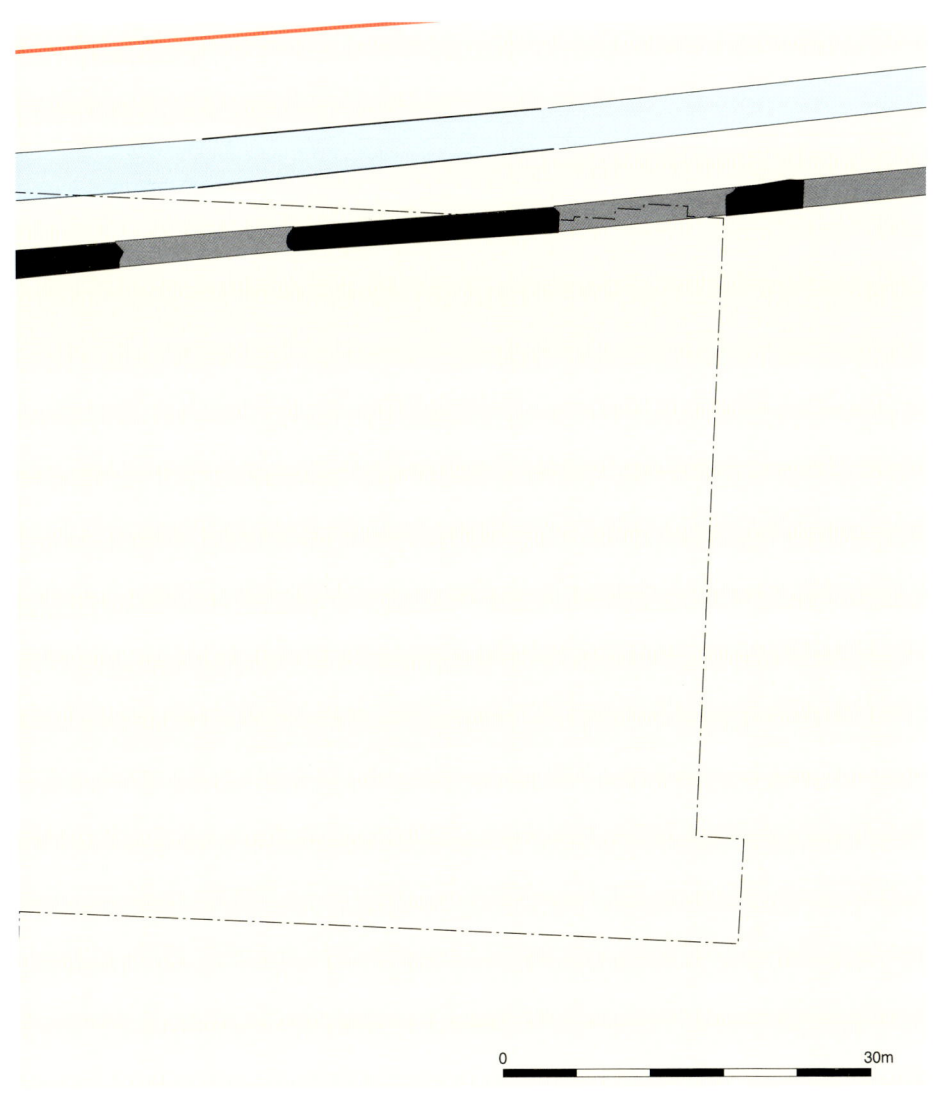

Fig 42 Later Roman settlement c AD 150–250 (period 3, phase 1) and the first phase of Roman city defences as found at the MLFC site (scale 1:600)

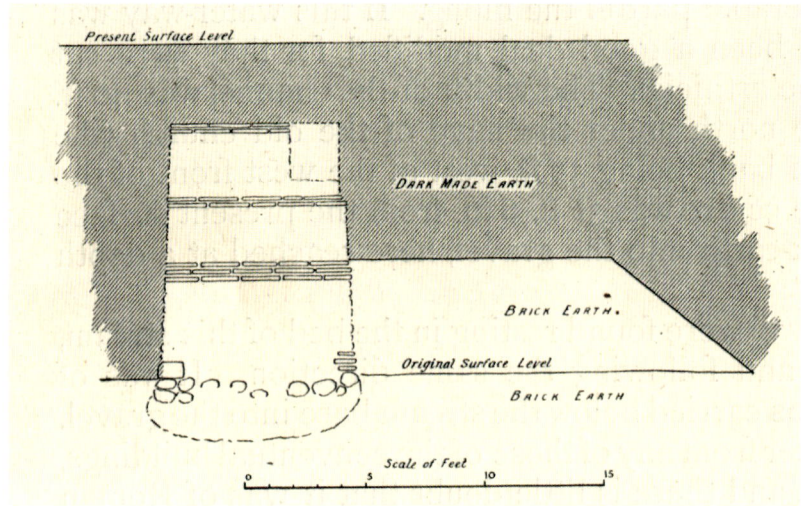

Fig 43 Section through city wall with probable remains of internal bank (Norman and Reader, 1912, 276, fig 9) (scale c 1:90)

outside the GPO building footprint and was not intended for redevelopment. Norman and Reader obtained permission from HM Government and funding from the Society of Antiquaries to conduct a small research excavation in this area in order to study the remains of the wall and bastion (Bastion 19) they knew to be situated there. The stretch of wall they discovered here was c 3.0m long and survived up to the third tile course. The character of the wall was the same as recorded elsewhere, but the foundations were not. The sandstone plinth did not rest on natural brickearth but on deposits of made-earth dumped in order to consolidate the ground before construction. The foundation trench was unusually deep and had been excavated through the levelling deposits into the natural gravel to a depth of more than c 1.8m. The foundations were composed of ragstone packed tightly with clay.

Norman and Reader observed that the natural ground underneath the wall here was very wet and uneven, like land close to a stream (Chapter 2.3). The natural brickearth in the internal area of Bastion 19, adjacent to the wall, appears to have been very irregular and contained hollows in which water had collected. An attempt had been made to solve this by laying down a series of fresh brickearth surfaces, but hollows had also formed in these. This indicates that water was a real problem in this part of the site. The made-earth used to level up the area beneath the city wall was composed mainly of rubbish, and seems to have done little to remedy the marshy conditions. Norman and Reader (1912, 288) noted that the outer face of the wall was coated with iron deposits, as if water had been standing against it for a long period of time. Underneath this iron coating, they found that the wall had been pointed with pink mortar, which, they note, was normally only used in the construction of water tunnels (ibid). It is probable, therefore, that this facing was a deliberate waterproofing layer to combat the wet conditions.

Despite these extra measures the wall eventually began to subside. Norman and Reader concluded that all the structural damage to the wall had occurred in the Roman period and that Bastion 19 had been constructed to prevent it from subsiding any further. This bastion is now known to have been built in the medieval period (Chapter 4.3). Water damage had probably begun to affect the wall in the Roman period, hence the addition of pink mortar, but the wall must have been intact when the defensive circuit was renovated in the late Roman period, otherwise further measures would surely have been taken to stabilise it.

Norman and Reader found no sign of the V-shaped ditch in this area, and thought its absence was due to the fact that a stream channel flowed very close to the wall (Chapter 2.3). The presence of a stream may have removed the need to construct a ditch in this area, and the V-shaped ditch recorded further to the east could have flowed into this stream as it approached the angle of the wall. However, no evidence for a stream channel was found during the nearby 1998 excavation (Chapter 2.3). If there was a stream here, following the curve of the brickearth plateau, this may have influenced the wall builders' decision to turn southward at this point. The position of the north–south wall line may therefore have been determined by a desire to avoid crossing yet another stream as much as the need to incorporate an existing gatehouse at Newgate.

The foundations of the Newgate gatehouse were discovered by Norman and Reader just to the south of the MLFC site. The gate was 10.5m wide, with a double carriageway flanked by two towers (Fig 44; Fig 45). Newgate appears not to have been contemporary with the wall and may have been an earlier, free-standing arch (Marsden 1980, 124). In Colchester and Verulamium triumphal arches were reused as town gates (Hill 1958; Frere 1983).

The wall and Bastion 19 were consolidated and preserved in a viewing chamber under the GPO yard, and were surveyed once again during the recent excavations. During the 1992 evaluation of the site a further fragment of the wall was located (Fig 42; Fig 48). This was found to be in excellent condition, with the top of the masonry standing at 17.01m OD (Fig 46). The wall core stood almost to the third tile course, but the ragstone facing blocks had been truncated to a slightly lower level (Fig 47). The base of the plinth stood at 13.92 to 13.98m OD (Fig 48). The pattern of internal offsets differed from that observed in the masonry adjoining Bastion 19. Subsidence in

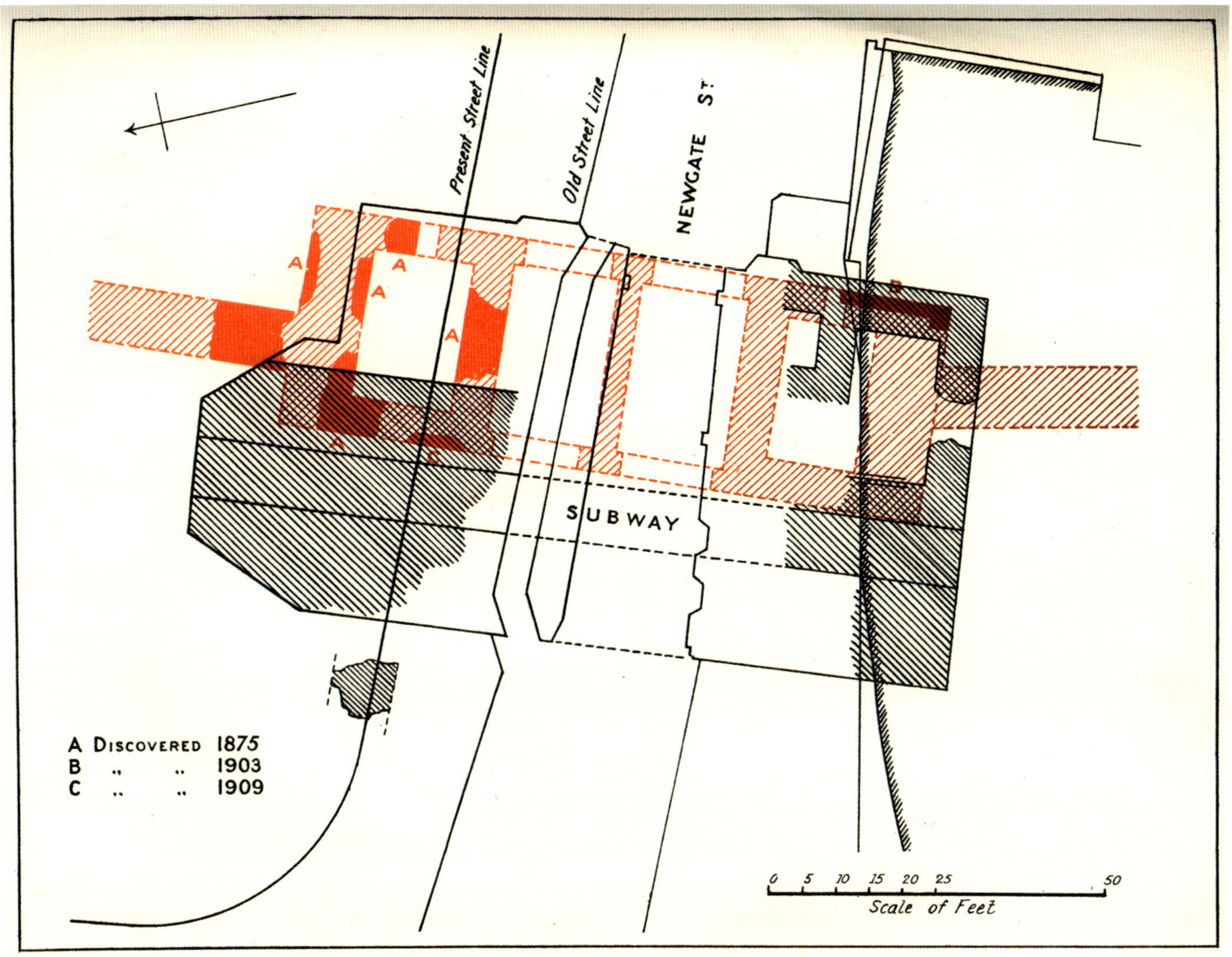

Later Roman activity, late 2nd century–late 4th century AD (period 3)

Fig 44 Plan of Roman Newgate (showing later medieval rebuilding, in black) (Norman and Reader 1912, pl LVI) (scale 1:300)

Fig 45 Reconstruction of Roman Newgate (Jeannette McLeish) (scale 1:300)

antiquity had caused this part of the wall to lean slightly towards the north, presumably due to the same unstable ground conditions recorded by Norman and Reader in the area of Bastion 19. The good level of survival of the wall in the bastion chamber and the wall recorded in 1992 implies that the intervening masonry wall (still preserved under the concrete slab) may be equally well preserved. The construction of the viewing chamber in 1912 entailed a slight truncation of the masonry to just below the second tile course (top 16.10m OD).

The foundations of the city wall were also located further west, where the wall had been truncated to below plinth level by the construction and destruction of the 18th-century Compter prison (Fig 42). The discovery of this fragment of the foundations indicated that the wall followed a slightly more

The Roman archaeological sequence

Fig 46 Recording part of the Roman city wall, looking north

Fig 47 Part of the Roman city wall exposed in the 1992 investigations, looking north

Fig 48 Detail of the internal face of the Roman city wall, looking north (scale 0.2m)

westerly curving alignment than originally projected by Norman and Reader.

THE DEFENSIVE DITCH (S3), BANK (S4) AND BERM (S5)

Other features relating to the city defences were discovered during the 1992–9 excavations, including a small portion of the bank (S4, Fig 42), dumping thought to be part of the berm (S5, Fig 42), and a fragment of the V-shaped ditch (S3, Fig 42). In addition, the remains of the gravel surface (OA14/15, Fig 42) could be evidence for an internal road, running along the inside of the bank, although insufficient evidence was found to be certain.

Discussion (period 3, phase 1)

The roadside buildings on the southern part of the MLFC site may have fallen out of use in c AD 160; external dumping of dark earth was present in many areas by the end of the 2nd century. This suggests that there was little activity on the site in the three or more decades pre-dating construction of the wall, although late Roman buildings may have been truncated or located outside the limited areas of excavation.

The deposition of dark earth at many sites across the settlement has been interpreted as evidence for wholesale changes in land use in the late Roman period. By the time the wall was built the city may have been characterised by large town houses with gardens, similar to the rural villas known from the areas outside London (Perring 1991, 100). Despite these changes the settlement remained important and the decision to construct the wall may have been more to do with the assertion and display of status and wealth than with defence.

It is clear from the MLFC investigations that the route of the wall depended on a number of factors and not just the extent of the town. In the north-west part of the city the route was influenced by the presence of the earlier Cripplegate fort, whose north and west walls were thickened and incorporated into the wall circuit. The route would have also had to take into account any pre-existing structures that were planned to be incorporated into the wall. The Newgate gatehouse in particular does not appear to have been part of the wall's original structure and may have been an earlier monument that was integrated into the defensive circuit.

Another factor that would have influenced the route chosen for the city wall was the local topography. The precise line of the wall on the MLFC site probably owes its route to the underlying geological deposits and the location of nearby topographic features. The boundary line seems to have followed the interface between different geological deposits, with the wall following the northern edge of the brickearth plateau. This was probably no accident, as it would have been extremely difficult to construct the wall any further to the north due to boggy conditions. The tight turning angle of the wall north of Newgate is probably due to the proximity of the edge of the Fleet valley, whose topography may also have enhanced the wall's defensive capability.

The wall line also crossed two north–south aligned stream channels on the MLFC site. The natural stream channels are now known to have turned westwards south of Newgate to flow into the Fleet (Pitt 2006, 46–7). There is evidence that both stream channels were backfilled prior to the wall's construction, at least in the north and west where they crossed the planned line of the defences, and that drainage was provided by a ditch which ran south across Paternoster Square towards the Thames (Watson in prep; Pitt 2006, 47–8).

The Roman engineers were obviously aware that constructing their wall so close to unstable gravel terraces, boggy ground and deep stream channels could lead to subsidence problems. The ground was levelled up under the wall angle, foundations built much deeper, and the wall's external face pointed with waterproof pink mortar. The wall was also reinforced in similar ways at other points along the circuit where unstable ground conditions were encountered. At 1–6 Aldersgate Street to the east, the wall foundations were unusually thick at 3.23m wide (AES96; Butler 2001, 48) and had been reinforced with large ragstone blocks and timber piles (Merrifield 1965, 103). This seems to have been carried out because of the presence of a stream or hollow which extended to a depth of 'at least 18ft [5.48m] below street level' (Butler 2001, 48). Similarly, at 57 London Wall the ground under the city wall had been levelled up, and the foundations were unusually deep at 1.6m due to the proximity of the Walbrook stream (LON82, Pye 1985). It is possible that the stretch of wall on the MLFC site had similarly robust foundations where it crossed the two backfilled stream channels, but any evidence has not survived later truncation.

The line of the city wall did not enclose all the land which had been built on in the early Roman period. Norman and Reader (1912, 280) found that the wall had cut through a tiled floor surface at the MLFC site, interpreted as part of an earlier building. Building 7, recorded during the recent excavations, was sealed under the internal bank to the city wall. The excavation at St Bartholomew's Hospital in the 1980s, well to the north of the city wall, also encountered Roman buildings. Similar examples have been found on other sites. At 85 London Wall (BLM87) timber building remains were preserved under the early Roman flat-bottomed ditch (Sankey and Stephenson 1991, 117), and at 1–6 Old Bailey (LUD82, Fig 39) building material found dumped in the base of the wall construction trench may have belonged to a building that was demolished to make way for the defences (Rowsome 1984). It appears that the extent of the city at the end of the 2nd century AD did not define or determine the placement of the wall, but rather the wall itself was intended to define a new city limit.

It remains uncertain to what extent the walls were intended to be put to defensive use. One school of thought states that the walls were decorative and 'were certainly not built for military reasons' (Luttwack 1976, 168). It is unlikely, however, that such a massive project would have been undertaken for the sake of aesthetics alone. The wall could have been built a hundred years earlier if it was intended solely as a display of London's wealth (Maloney 1983, 104). Construction of the wall would have required immense resources and labour at a time when the settlement was apparently still in decline, suggesting that it was constructed in response to a direct threat (ibid). If defence was the priority, however, it is difficult to see why the river wall was built at a much later date. The absence of the river wall would have left the city vulnerable to an attack from the sea. It has also been suggested that the fortification of London was carried out on the order of Clodius Albinus, governor of Britain AD 193–7, in preparation for a war with Septimus Severus (Corder 1955, 22–4). It is more likely, however, that the walls were not constructed in response to an immediate threat, but that the work was carried out over a period of time (Merrifield 1965, 50–1).

The construction of the wall may have taken decades, perhaps interrupted by changes of administration or shortages of funds, but must have been carefully planned at least at inception. In building the wall, the authorities determined that the settlement would have a finite number of permanent entry and exit points, allowing better control over access and movement (Perring 1991, 98). This would have been important for security and perhaps also for the control of taxation (ibid). London's wall could have acted as a customs frontier, providing a source of income for the city (ibid).

Late Roman additions to the defences, *c* mid 3rd century–late 4th century AD (period 3, phase 2)

Introduction

There is extensive evidence from many sites in London that the defences were added to and generally improved during the late Roman period. The main addition was the construction of the river wall in AD 255–70, which completed the circuit (Hillam and Morgan 1986, 83–4). Bastions were added to parts of the landward and riverside walls in the mid 4th century. The same period also saw the addition of a wider, flat-bottomed ditch, U-shaped in profile, which replaced the smaller V-shaped ditch, and the internal bank was also bolstered (Fig 49). Other works such as renovation of the gatehouses probably also took place in the same period, but little evidence for these activities has survived (Maloney 1983, 110). The impetus for these additions and changes is not known but may first have been associated with the Saxon raids of the mid 3rd century AD, and later with unrest in the mid 4th century AD (Perring 1991, 124).

The city bastions

The presence of bastions on the landward side of the city wall has been well documented, but the chronology of these structures remains unclear. Previous work has suggested that the bastions form two groups. In general the eastern group are D-shaped, have solid bases and contain reused Roman monumental stone, whereas the western group are horseshoe-shaped, hollow and not known to contain reused Roman stone (Maloney 1983, 105–10). There is a gap of 230m, along the northern stretch of the wall, where no bastions are known. Apart from this gap the bastions appear to have been regularly spaced. The eastern bastions are widely regarded as late Roman, while the western ones are believed to be medieval (ibid; Merrifield 1965, 111;

Fig 49 Plan of second phase of city defensive circuit c AD 250–450, with the additions of the riverside wall, bastions (Bastions 1–19) and later U-shaped ditch, showing relevant sites (key to site codes in Table 1) (scale 1:12,500)

Perring 1991, 124), but recent work suggests that not all the bastions fit neatly into this classification system.

Many of the eastern group of bastions were investigated by Norman and Reader, and then later by Grimes. Based on the evidence found, they had no reason to suppose that the eastern group were anything but late Roman in date. Although many of the bastions had been observed to have random rubble cores and no tile courses (Norman and Reader 1912, 277), the excavation of eastern Bastions 6, 7, and 9 (GM55, GM242 and Bastion 9, Fig 49) revealed courses of bonding or facing tiles. It has been suggested that this characteristic could have originally been common to the whole group (Merrifield 1965, 70, 112). Although most of the eastern group had solid foundations, those of Bastions 1 and 11 were hollow (Fig 49). Bastion 11 was dated to the Roman period because it appeared to have been constructed while the V-shaped ditch was still open. The portion of ditch in front of the bastion had been backfilled with rubble to support the foundations which overlay it, but on either side of this it had 'clearly remained open for some time after the building of the bastion, accumulating mud and rubbish against the obstruction of the bastion footings' (Norman and Reader 1912, 274). The difference between the hollow and solid foundations has been interpreted as a reflection of the use of different weapons to defend the circuit. Heavy artillery was thought to have been used in the solid-based bastions and lighter artillery in the hollow ones (Merrifield 1965, 68). It has also been suggested that the solid-based bastions might have been built quickly, in response to an immediate threat. Many of these contained reused monumental stones, such as tombstones, which were not interpreted as being a building material of choice, but rather the only thing available at short notice (ibid).

A small number of the eastern group of bastions has been excavated under controlled conditions. The discovery of Bastion 4A at 8–10 Crosswall (XWL79, Fig 49) revealed that the bastions were regularly spaced at intervals of c 53m, rather than randomly placed, as previously thought (Maloney 1983, 108). The presence of a 3rd-century inscribed Roman tombstone within the foundations of Bastion 4A indicated that it was Roman in date, like the rest of the eastern group (Maloney 1980, 68–76). The foundations of the bastion had been stepped down to the base of the V-shaped city ditch, indicating that the builders were aware of its presence, as with Bastion 11. During the excavation of Bastion 6 at Duke's Place (DUK77, Fig 49) it was observed that the V-shaped ditch had been backfilled in order to facilitate the construction of the bastion. Dating evidence from Duke's Place suggests that Bastion 6 was constructed in AD 341–75, a date range which is now applied to all the eastern bastions (Maloney 1983, 108).

The western bastions were traditionally believed to be medieval, due to Stow's statement in his *Survey of London*, which claimed that in 1257 Henry III 'caused the walls of this city, which were sorely decayed and destitute of towers, to be repaired' (1598, 11). Norman and Reader's work on the city defences in the first decades of the 20th century seemed to indicate that this was not so, and that the western bastions were in fact Roman. Grimes's post-war excavation of the city, however, proved that at least some of the western bastions were medieval.

The excavation of Bastion 11A in 1965 (WFG1a, Fig 49) revealed that its foundations were dug through deposits containing 13th-century pottery (Grimes 1968, 75–6). As Bastions 14 and 15 (WFG4 and 8, Fig 49) were of similar construction to Bastion 11A, all three were believed to be medieval (Grimes 1968, 71–6). It should be noted, however, that during the excavation of Bastion 14 a coin of Constans dated AD 346–50 was found in the original gravel floor of the bastion. A bronze pendant of 9th-century date was also found in the floor, albeit higher up in the sequence. This cast doubt on the date of the bastion, but the pendant could have been intrusive (Merrifield 1965, 70). The medieval date of Bastion 15 has been confirmed by recent excavations at 1–6 Aldersgate Street (AES96, Fig 49), where a sherd of pot dated 1080–1350 and a fragment of tile dating to 1240/70–1270/1350 were found within the bastion foundations (Butler 2001, 53). Bastion 16 (not illustrated) is thought to have been medieval, because of antiquarian observations that it contained early medieval worked stone and had hollow foundations (Maloney 1983, 105; Norman and Reader 1912, 287, footnote 1).

Bastions 17, 18 and 19 (GM146, Fig 49) on the MLFC site were believed to be Roman by Norman and Reader (1912, 291–2), but it has since been confirmed that Bastion 19 was built in the medieval period (Watson and Jones 1999). A question still remains over the date of Bastions 17 and 18. The remains of Bastions 20 and 21 (not illustrated) have never been studied as they were completely destroyed by terracing along the Fleet valley in the 19th century (Rowsome 1984; Merrifield 1965, 325).

Although some of the western bastions are certainly medieval in date, the possibility remains that others are Roman. None of the bastions listed as being of probable medieval date in Maloney's study has been subject to controlled archaeological excavation. It is possible, as Maloney points out, that the situation is more complicated than previously thought.

The MLFC evidence

Three bastions (Bastions 17–19, Fig 49) were discovered and recorded by Norman and Reader during the 1907–9 redevelopment of the site. All were believed to have been constructed at the same time as a late Roman, U-shaped ditch. A study of Norman and Reader's records indicates that Roman dates for some of the western bastions are possible.

All the later phases of the city wall and bastions, from the Roman period onwards, are also identified as parts of Structure 2, as they represent modifications and additions to the original structure. Similarly, the late Roman and medieval phases of defensive ditch are all referred to as Structure 3, as they represent a series of recuts of the original feature in terms of its land use.

THE LATE ROMAN DITCH (S3)

It is believed that a large, wide, late Roman ditch, U-shaped in profile, was intended to replace the much smaller V-shaped

The Roman archaeological sequence

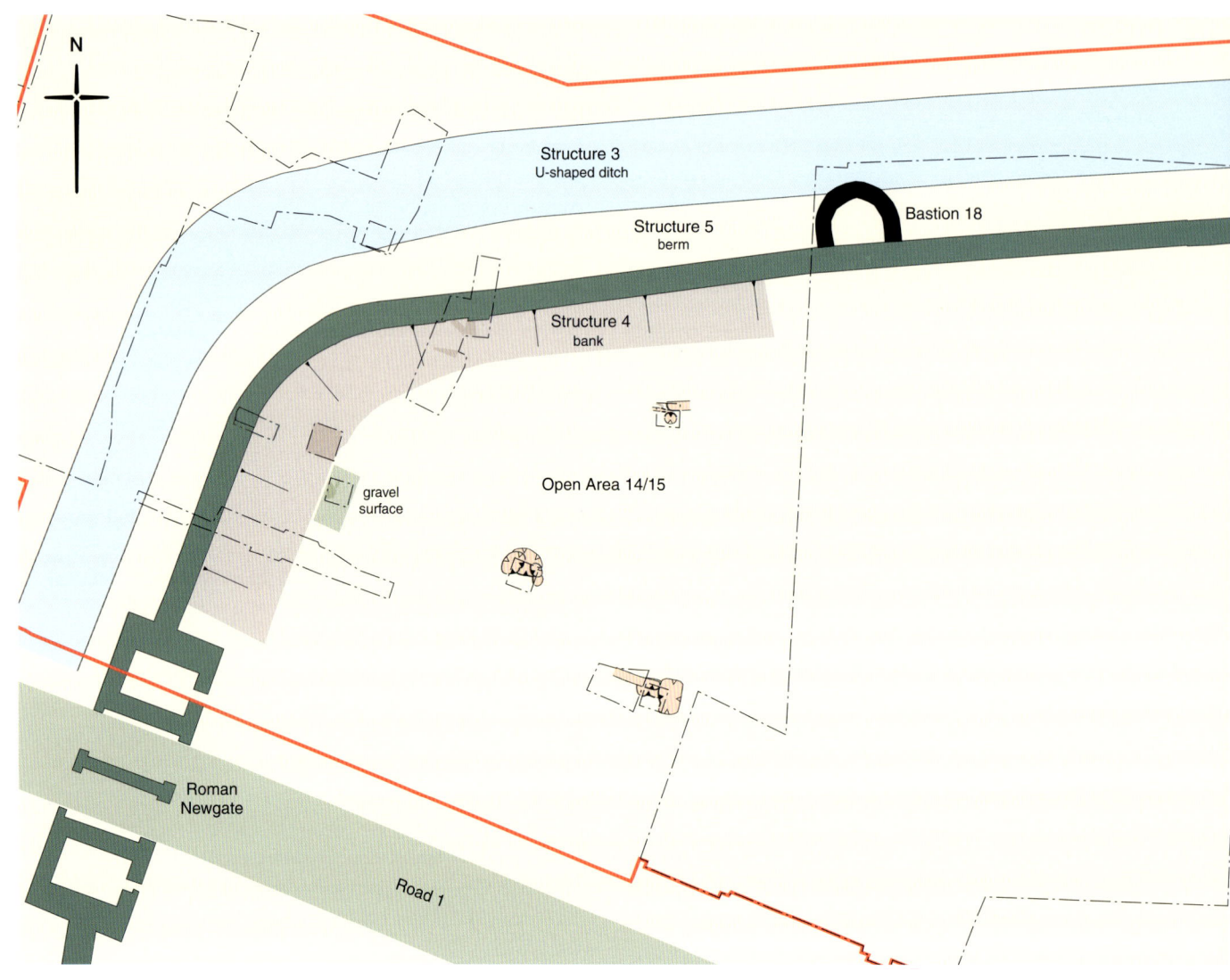

ditch and to complement the construction of bastions along the wall. The U-shaped ditch has been identified on many sites and clearly extended all the way around the defences. By contrast the bastions are believed to have been constructed only on the eastern side of the defences (Maloney 1983, 108). The U-shaped ditch was identified and recorded by Norman and Reader on the MLFC site (Fig 51; Fig 50). It was located to the north of Bastion 17 and measured 7.6m wide and 4.4m deep. The inner side cut through the base of the V-shaped ditch at this point, and the outer edge had in turn been cut away by the medieval city ditch. In every observed case around London, the outer edge of the late Roman ditch has been cut away by the medieval ditch, and its full extent is not known.

BASTIONS 17–19 (S2)

Bastion 17 was the first to be discovered by Norman and Reader (1912, 277) on the MLFC site. The bastion was located towards the eastern end of the site (Fig 50) and was associated with a segment of the city wall and the external V-shaped ditch:

> Owing to the resistance offered by this formidable obstacle, which defied the ordinary methods of excavation, the digging was carried on in the softer material adjoining it, leaving it isolated and disclosing clearly the piece of the city wall against which it was built, together with a section of the Roman ditch, in which the bastion partly obtruded itself. (ibid)

Norman and Reader also noted that the tower projected 16ft (4.87m) from the wall and that it was constructed of random ragstone flint and tile rubble, 'the whole being well grouted with mortar, and constructed solidly in the horse-shoe form'. The bastion had a solid base, unlike the other recorded western bastions, which are all hollow. The foundations extended 2.10m below the base of the city wall and rested on solid ground (RCHME 1928, 104) (Fig 52).

Norman and Reader (1912, 278) imply that the builders of this bastion were aware of the presence of the V-shaped ditch, as with Bastion 4A, Bastion 6 and Bastion 11 at All Hallows (Fig 49). They state:

> The bastion had been carried down 7ft [2.1m] below the base of the wall-plinth, by reason of which it rested firmly on undisturbed soil, and consequently the ditch was quite

Later Roman activity, late 2nd century–late 4th century AD (period 3)

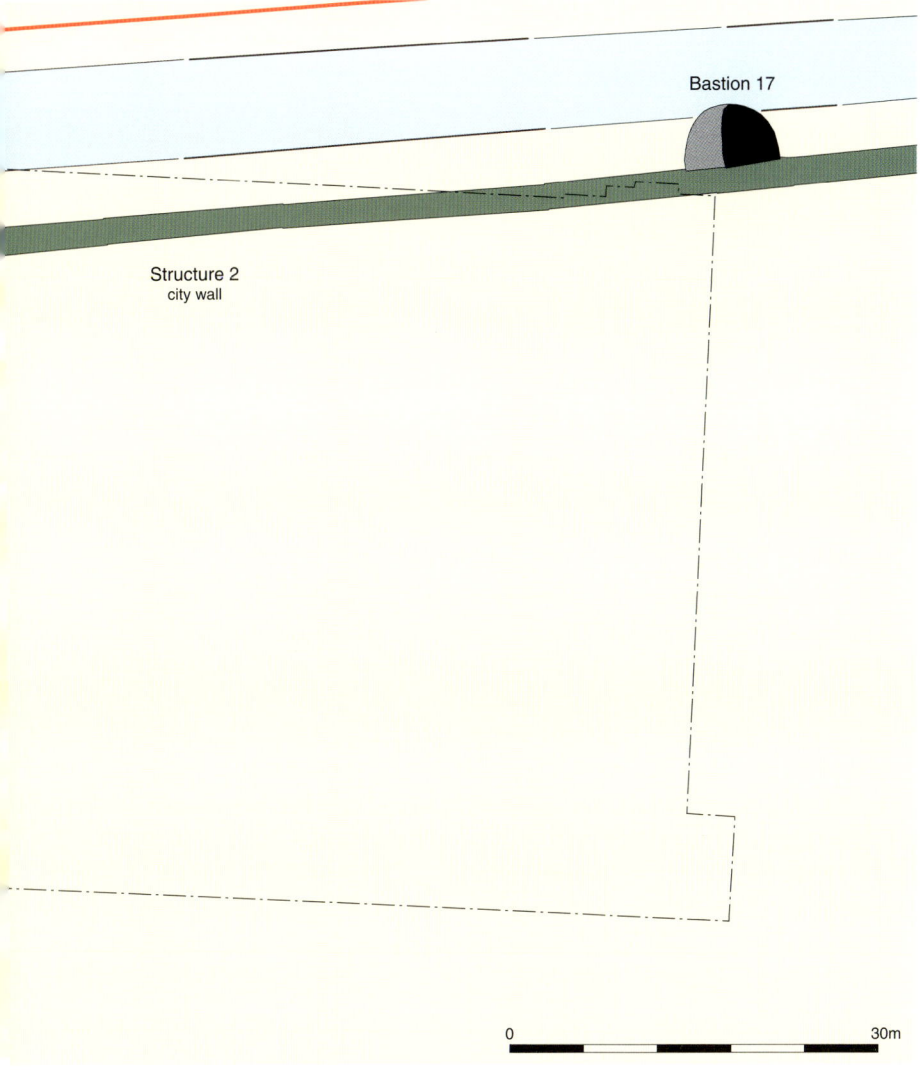

Fig 50 Late Roman settlement, c AD 250–450 (period 3), showing the second phase of the Roman city defences (scale 1:600)

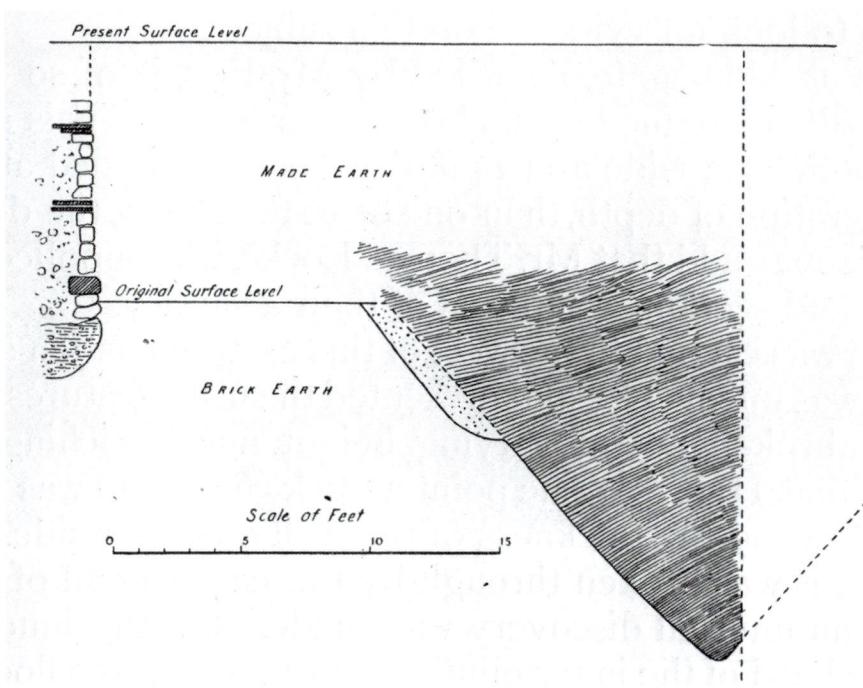

Fig 51 Section through the first and second Roman ditches (Norman and Reader 1912, 279, fig 11) (scale 1:90)

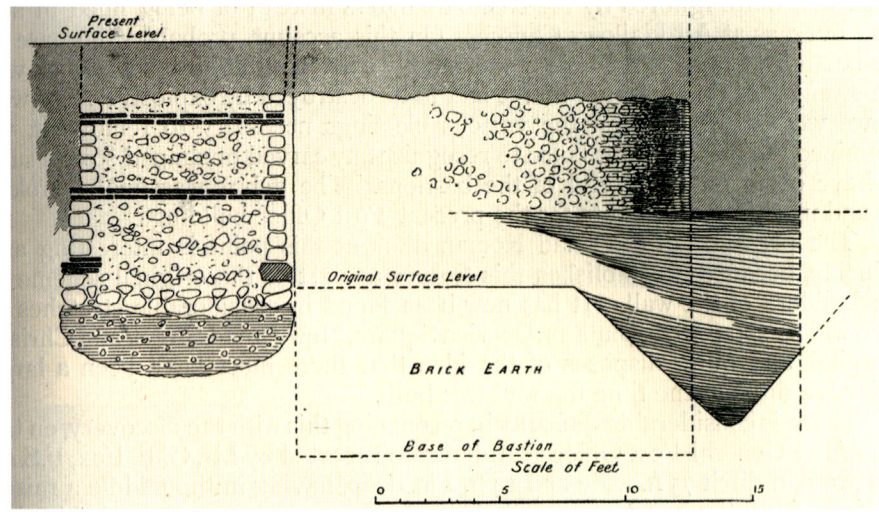

Fig 52 *Section through city wall, Bastion 17, and the first Roman ditch (Norman and Reader 1912, 277, fig 10) (scale 1:90)*

ignored by the bastion builders instead of being filled in and built over, as at All Hallows Church. On this account, probably, the base of the bastion was not extended; it was simply carried straight down. (ibid)

This implies that the ditch may have been open when the bastion was constructed, and that the builders extended the bastion's foundations down into the base of the ditch before backfilling it. It is highly improbable that bastion builders in the medieval period would have been aware of the first V-shaped ditch, which had long been backfilled and was mostly cut away by the flat-bottomed ditch. If Norman and Reader's account is to be believed, and the same dating criteria is applied to the east and west bastions, then the logical conclusion is that Bastion 17 may have been constructed in the Roman period, like the eastern bastions.

Bastion 18 was found further west (Fig 50), under the foundations of the Great Hall of Christ's Hospital (Chapter 5.3). The city wall had been totally destroyed in this area, so extensive were the hospital's foundations, and it was thought that no structures relating to the wall could have survived. The bastion had survived, however, and Norman and Reader (1912, 281) recorded that it was 'of horseshoe form, enclosing a hollow space 13ft [3.96m] wide' (Fig 53; Fig 54). It extended

Fig 53 *Bastion 18, looking north-west (Norman and Reader 1912, pl XLVIII, 2)*

Fig 54 Bastion 18, looking south-west
(Norman and Reader 1912, pl XLIX)

5.45m beyond the projected line of the city wall and c 3.10m below the wall plinth, where it ended 'abruptly, without any splayed footing, resting in the soft soil, of which there was another 3ft [0.91m] or 4ft [1.22m] before firm ground was reached' (ibid). The unusually deep foundations of Bastion 18 may be explained by the fact that it had been sited over the western of two backfilled stream channels, which ran north–south through this part of the site (Chapter 2.3).

Norman and Reader believed that the bastion was constructed in the Roman period. They thought that its builders did not realise there was an ancient stream bed here, and had eventually given up digging down to find solid ground 'and relied on the hollow form of construction for stability' instead. The stream was 15.25m wide (at brickearth surface) and c 9.2m deep, however, and it is unlikely that Roman engineers would have been unaware of such a massive natural feature, which may still have been visible even if backfilled. Significant planning and effort must have gone into diverting and backfilling the stream channel when the city wall was built over 100 years earlier, and

there could even have been records of the original work. If the bastion was built in the Roman period it seems likely that the engineers would have been aware of the backfilled stream and designed the bastion accordingly, its hollow structure perhaps intended to minimise subsidence in the poor ground conditions. Bastion 18 may also have helped to stabilise the adjacent city wall, which may have been subsiding at its western angle due to the poor ground conditions.

Bastion 18 could have also been built in the medieval period, at the same time as medieval Bastion 19, and for exactly the same reasons. However, Norman and Reader's photographic archive from the site contains pictures of the bastion, and the stonework appears very Roman in nature. The wall had been truncated down to a flat surface (Fig 53), perhaps indicating the level of a Roman tile course; some of the Roman bastions on the east side of the defensive circuit are known to have contained tile courses (for example Bastions 6, 7 and 9; Fig 49).

Bastion 19 was situated at the wall angle, just north of the gatehouse at Newgate. This bastion was preserved in situ by the efforts of Norman and Reader, along with the stretch of wall that it abutted. Norman and Reader originally thought that this bastion was Roman in date, due to the fact that only Roman finds were discovered in the deposits surrounding it. Modern archaeological survey of the bastion confirmed that the stonework and mortar of the bastion are in fact medieval (Watson and Jones 1999). Norman and Reader were not aware that the bastion had been trench-built, which would have explained the lack of medieval finds in the area. Bastion 19 is illustrated and discussed in more detail in Chapter 4.

Discussion (period 3, phase 2)

The construction of the river wall in the 3rd century (c AD 270) completed the city defensive circuit, at a time when Saxon shore raids were becoming more frequent (Parnell 1993, 13; Vince 1990, 6). The riverside wall was remodelled, in part, during the 4th century AD (ibid), when a series of bastions was also added to the landward wall. The eastern bastions are believed to have been built c AD 341–75, based on dating evidence from Bastion 4A. Historical sources indicate that two expeditions were made to the city to restore order in the 360s AD, and it is widely believed that the construction of the bastions was related to these events (Maloney 1983, 115). Other changes made to the city defences in the late 4th century included the digging of a larger city ditch and possibly the renovation of the gatehouses.

The known bastions along the wall circuit appear to fall into two main groups. It has been suggested that the eastern group was constructed in the late Roman period, and the western group in the medieval period. Apart from the dating evidence and the overall stylistic differences between the two groups, there may be a topographic argument for dating the eastern group alone to the late Roman period. It has been suggested that the eastern part of the wall would have been more vulnerable to attack from downriver and that the natural terrain in this area provided little advantage to the defender (Maloney 1983, 115). The absence of bastions along most of the northern stretch of the wall has been explained by the presence of marshes, which may have made bastions unnecessary (ibid). Similarly, bastions could have been deemed unnecessary on the western side of the settlement due to the proximity of the Fleet river and its tributaries. However, a complete absence of bastions along the western side of the settlement seems surprising, even if defence of the eastern circuit was considered to be the priority. The bastions would have been of little value if the circuit was not completed, and the defences could easily have been outflanked (Merrifield 1965, 72).

By this same logic, it could also be argued that if there were no bastions on the western side of the defensive circuit, the Romans would not have needed to construct the U-shaped ditch in this area. There is, however, plenty of evidence to show that the U-shaped ditch was constructed all the way around the circuit. If there were no bastions on the western side the Romans could have left the V-shaped ditch intact, as this would have been a more effective defence for a wall that was not protected by bastions.

It has been observed that all the (recorded) bastions differ greatly from one another in size, shape, and construction technique. The different design of each bastion seems to have been dictated to a certain extent by what raw materials were to hand, and the nature of the surrounding topography (Maloney 1983, 108). Two of the bastions on the MLFC site stand apart from the rest of the western group, and have more similarities with the eastern group. Bastion 17 was solid-based and may have been constructed while the first V-shaped ditch was still open. This was also the line of reasoning used to propose a Roman date for Bastions 4A, 6 and 11 on the east side. Bastion 18 was hollow in form, like many of the bastions on the western side of the city, but may have contained tile courses like some of the eastern bastions. This bastion was dug through the backfilled path of the western of the two stream channels which crossed the site (see Chapter 2.3). It is possible that the hollow form was used for structural reasons to cope with the poor ground conditions. While this does not necessarily prove Bastion 18 to be of Roman date, it does raise a question over the legitimacy of regarding the hollow form as an exclusively medieval style. Roman Bastions 1 and 11 on the east side were also hollow.

Although the eastern side of the city would have been more vulnerable to attack from the sea, the MLFC evidence suggests that bastions may not have been limited to the eastern side of the settlement during the late Roman period. The western angle of the wall may have already been suffering from water damage and subsidence by the late Roman period (Norman and Reader 1912, 288–9), and it is possible that Bastions 17 and 18 were added to provide stability as much as defence. It is unlikely that this part of the wall would have been left to deteriorate if it was in need of renovation, especially if the city was under threat of attack. Unless new evidence proves otherwise, the possibility that some of the western bastions were constructed during the late Roman period cannot be ruled out.

4 The medieval archaeological sequence

4.1 Introduction

The collapse of imperial rule at the end of the 4th century AD was accompanied by the convulsive events of AD 406–11 which included barbarian invasion, usurpation and revolt (Millett 1990, 217; Salway 1981, 415). The end result was that Britain was no longer a province of the Empire, although the process of painful disengagement and change began before AD 410 and probably continued for several decades afterwards. From some point in the early 5th century AD London was abandoned and its great walls slowly fell into decay.

The Saxon settlers who came to the south of England in the 7th century AD did not reoccupy the walled city, but instead created a settlement, Lundenwic, further to the east in the Aldwych area (Fig 55). The walled city established by the Romans was not reoccupied until c AD 890, in response to increased Viking attack (Vince 1990, 20). The re-established settlement expanded during the 10th and 11th centuries AD as trade increased and new wealth was gained, with property development prominent along the waterfront and main thoroughfares such as Cheapside and Lombard Street. Street and property boundaries were gradually formalised during this period, and wards and parishes established. These boundaries would persist long into the medieval period and in many cases up to modern times.

After the Norman Conquest of 1066 London's rate of growth increased. Over the next 200 years the city gained three castles and a new cathedral, together with monastic buildings, hospitals, priories and nunneries (Schofield 1993, 37). In the area of the MLFC site the monastic precincts of St Bartholomew's Priory and Greyfriars Friary were founded in 1123 and 1225 respectively. The city defences were repaired and strengthened, with parts of these rebuilds visible in upstanding fragments of the wall at Tower Hill, Cooper's Row and St Alphege churchyard. Several of the surviving Roman bastions were repaired and rebuilt, and new ones added to the circuit. The bastions were not simply treated as military buildings and appear to have had a range of functions, with many let as dwelling places and four regularly occupied by hermits (Bell et al 1937, 63–70). The gatehouses also had other functions, and Newgate and Ludgate were used as prisons from the 12th century onwards (Stow 1598, 65, 68). A much deeper and wider city ditch was dug in order to accommodate the new bastions, and perhaps to keep potential enemies within range of new weapons such as the crossbow (Schofield 1993, 70).

London's population and wealth grew throughout the 14th and 15th centuries, fuelled by the export trade in products such as wool. A successful war with France in 1324–7 also brought control of the lucrative wine trade (Schofield 1993, 81). Work continued on the city's religious buildings and other high status buildings were constructed by the livery companies, with Stow recording that there were 46 halls by 1598.

The medieval archaeological sequence

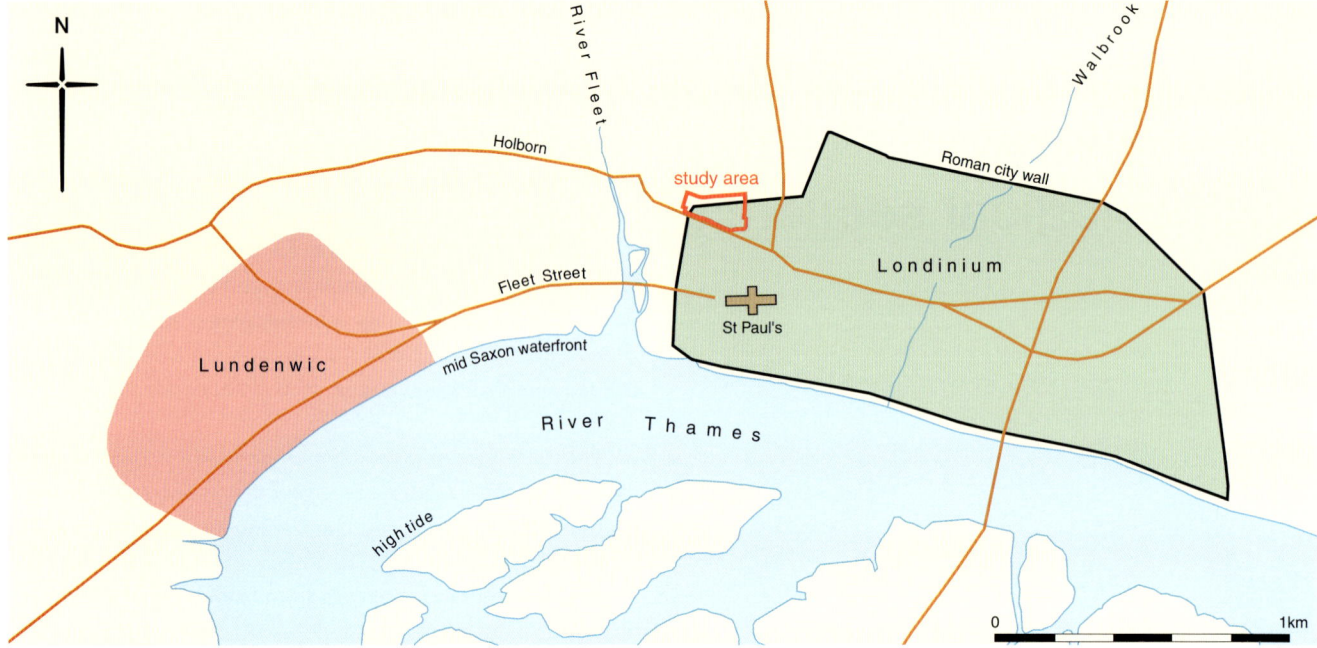

Fig 55 Map showing the location of Lundenwic in relation to the old walled settlement of Londinium (scale 1:25,000)

4.2 Late Saxon settlement, c AD 880–1100 (period 4)

The walled city was not occupied by a significant population between the 5th and 9th centuries AD. It is known that St Paul's was established in c AD 604 (Vince 1990, 16–18, 81) but there is very little evidence of domestic occupation anywhere within the walls for four centuries. The Anglo-Saxon Chronicle records that Saxon settlers may have taken refuge in the walled city during the Viking raids recorded in AD 842 and 851 (Whitelock 1955, 173), and that the Vikings may have gained control over London in AD 871–2, prior to King Alfred's reign (ibid, 178). Historical records suggest that London may have contained a Viking garrison between AD 872 and 886, although it is not certain where this might have been situated (Stenton 1971, 258). Alfred besieged the Vikings and captured the city in 886 (Whitelock 1955, 173) and it is implied that the walls may have been 'repaired' at this time, although no evidence for this has been found (Stenton 1971, 258). London is not listed in the Burghal Hidage, compiled in the late 9th or early 10th century AD, either because it was still in Viking hands at this time or because it lay outside the west Saxon burghal system (Vince 1990, 86–7). There is evidence that the city's first Saxon dock was situated at Queenhithe between AD 880 and 980 (Ayre and Wroe-Brown in prep).

The earliest Saxon settlement recorded within the city is characterised in the archaeological record by 'sunken-floored' houses and pitting. Tenth-century AD sunken buildings have been recorded at many sites near the waterfront and along Cheapside and other streets, where growing formalisation of roadside property use can be traced (Fig 56) (Hill and Woodger 1999; Burch and Treveil in prep). Later Saxon buildings are known from sites further to the north of Cheapside, such as the Guildhall (Bowsher et al in prep) and Cripplegate (Howe and Lakin 2004, 61). More substantial stone-cellared buildings began to appear by the 12th century, along with parish churches (Burch and Treveil in prep).

The city walls may have survived in fairly good condition until the Late Saxon period. There is no evidence of Late Saxon structural repairs to the walls but the defensive ditches may have been renovated. During the Late Saxon period, the city defences had been strong enough to keep attackers at bay, and were imposing enough to dissuade William the Conqueror from a direct assault on the city. Guy of Amiens reported in 'Song of the battle of Hastings' that the conquest of London would require siege engines and battering rams and that Londoners were 'a vast and fierce population' (Hobley 1981, 9).

Excavations in the western part of the city have produced evidence for a Late Saxon ditch parallel to the city wall at several sites. At 1–6 Aldersgate Street (AES96, Fig 63) a flat-bottomed ditch 6.6m wide is dated to the 11th–12th centuries (Butler 2001, 52). The probable continuation of this feature was recorded at 7–12 Aldersgate Street (ALG84, Fig 63), where the outer edge was located c 25m from the city wall (Egan 1985). At 71–76 Little Britain (LBT86, Fig 63) a large east–west ditch lined with stakes was dated to the mid 11th–mid 12th century (Gibson 1995). Similar evidence was discovered further west at 1–6 Old Bailey (LUD82, Fig 63), where a sequence of early ditches was seen and the late Roman U-shaped ditch was cut by a shallower ditch containing 9th- to 10th-century pottery. This in turn was cut by a narrower V-shaped ditch which contained 11th- to 12th-century pottery (Rowsome 1984). A similar sequence was recorded on the adjacent site at Ludgate Hill (Hill 1977, 45). A possible early ditch was also identified along the eastern side of the city at 47–56 Houndsditch (HOU78, Fig 63) (Vince 1990, 90).

Late Saxon settlement, c AD 880–1100 (period 4)

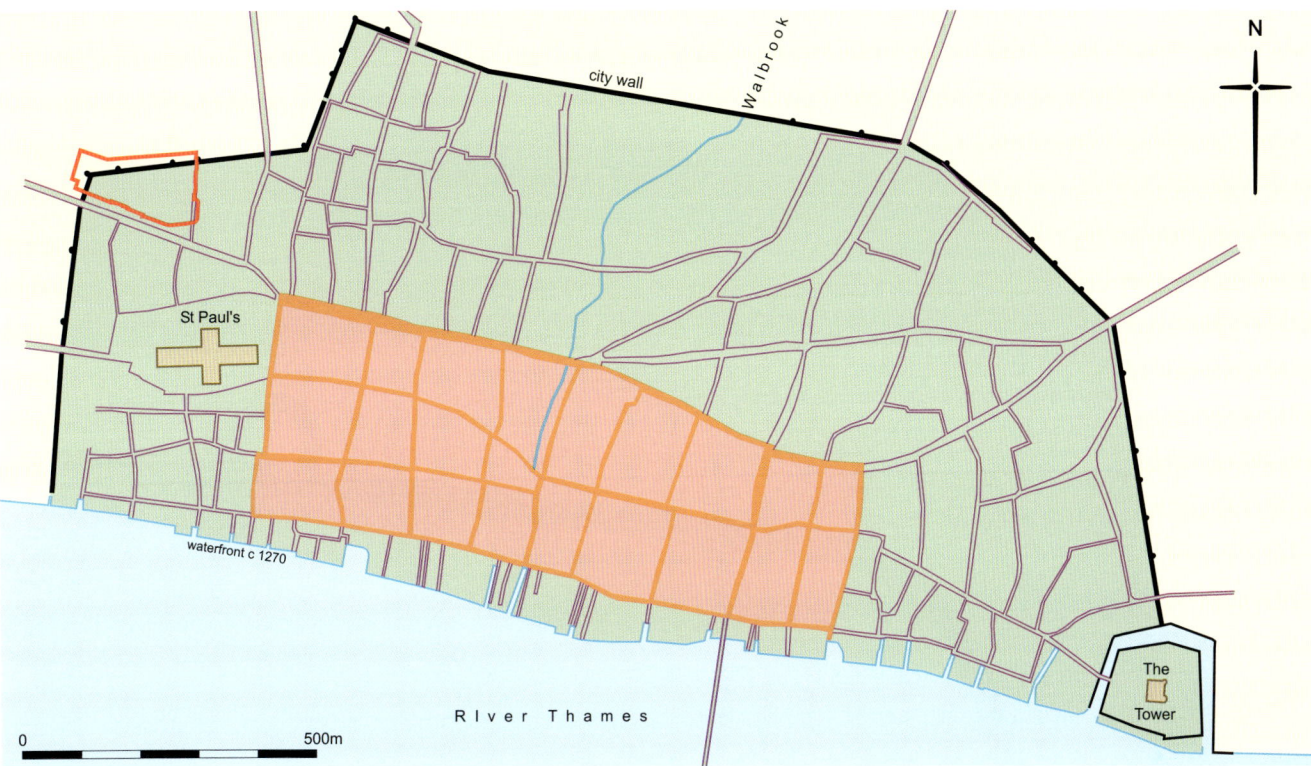

Fig 56 *Late Saxon town with what may have been the initial settlement shown in tone (scale 1:12,500)*

The MLFC evidence

SAXO-NORMAN DEFENSIVE DITCHES (S3)

A series of early medieval ditches was also detected on the MLFC site. The earliest ditch in the sequence was identified in the northern part of the study area (S3, Fig 57) as a recut of the original Roman ditch. It was not possible to define the original extent of the feature as the inner (southern) edge had been truncated by the later medieval city ditch and the outer edge lay beyond the limit of excavation. The feature appeared to be orientated east–west but was recorded in section only. The ditch had been backfilled with homogeneous dumps of largely sterile gravel. A small amount of pottery was retrieved, with a date range of 1000–1200. Two wattle-lined cess or rubbish pits, cut through the backfilled ditch, dated to 1140–1220 at the earliest (Figs 57–59). The substantial remains of a shelly-sandy ware (SSW) cooking pot were found in one of the pits. This large, rounded vessel, which has a rolled, flattened, everted flat rim (<P54>, Fig 60) and applied thumbed decoration on the body, is typical of its fabric type. The second pit contained London-type ware (LOND) jugs: one is painted with white slip in a lattice pattern, and another is highly decorated with applied coloured vertical strips, dated stylistically to between 1240 and 1350. The backfills of the pits also contained a large quantity of food plant remains and part of a child's leather shoe sole, dating to the 11th or 12th century.

A second length of ditch was recorded along the west side of Area H, running north–south parallel to Giltspur Street (not illustrated). Similar to the east–west ditch, this ditch was only recorded in section and had been truncated by the latest phase of city ditch. Pottery was retrieved from the backfill with a date range of 1150–1200, indicating that both ditches were virtually contemporaneous (S3, Fig 57). Both lengths of ditch were backfilled by 1200. The ditches appeared to lie further from the wall than the later medieval city ditch, similar to early medieval ditches found on other sites. It was not possible to reconstruct the full profile of these ditches, as was done at 1–6 Old Bailey (LUD82).

EXTERNAL ACTIVITY (OA12)

Surface drainage may have taken place along the line of the two former stream channels that crossed the site in the early Roman period, particularly if the backfill of the streams had subsided. A sequence of north–south gullies indicates that the area was low lying and prone to seasonal flooding. The gullies contained pottery dated to the 12th to 14th centuries, which dates their disuse.

There are few other features that date to this period. Saxo-Norman pottery was discovered in dumps above the dark earth (OA12, Fig 57). Pits cut into this deposit were concentrated near the Newgate Street frontage. Saxo-Norman pits and a well were dug through the internal bank of the city wall and one other deep well was recorded (not illustrated). Pottery from the features is dated 1050–1150. Evidence from a sewer heading beneath Newgate Street indicates that pits may have been dug through the Roman road, but no dating evidence was recovered from them.

SUNKEN-FLOORED BUILDING (B31)

Part of a possible Saxo-Norman sunken-floored building (B31, not illustrated) was recorded in section on the east side of

The medieval archaeological sequence

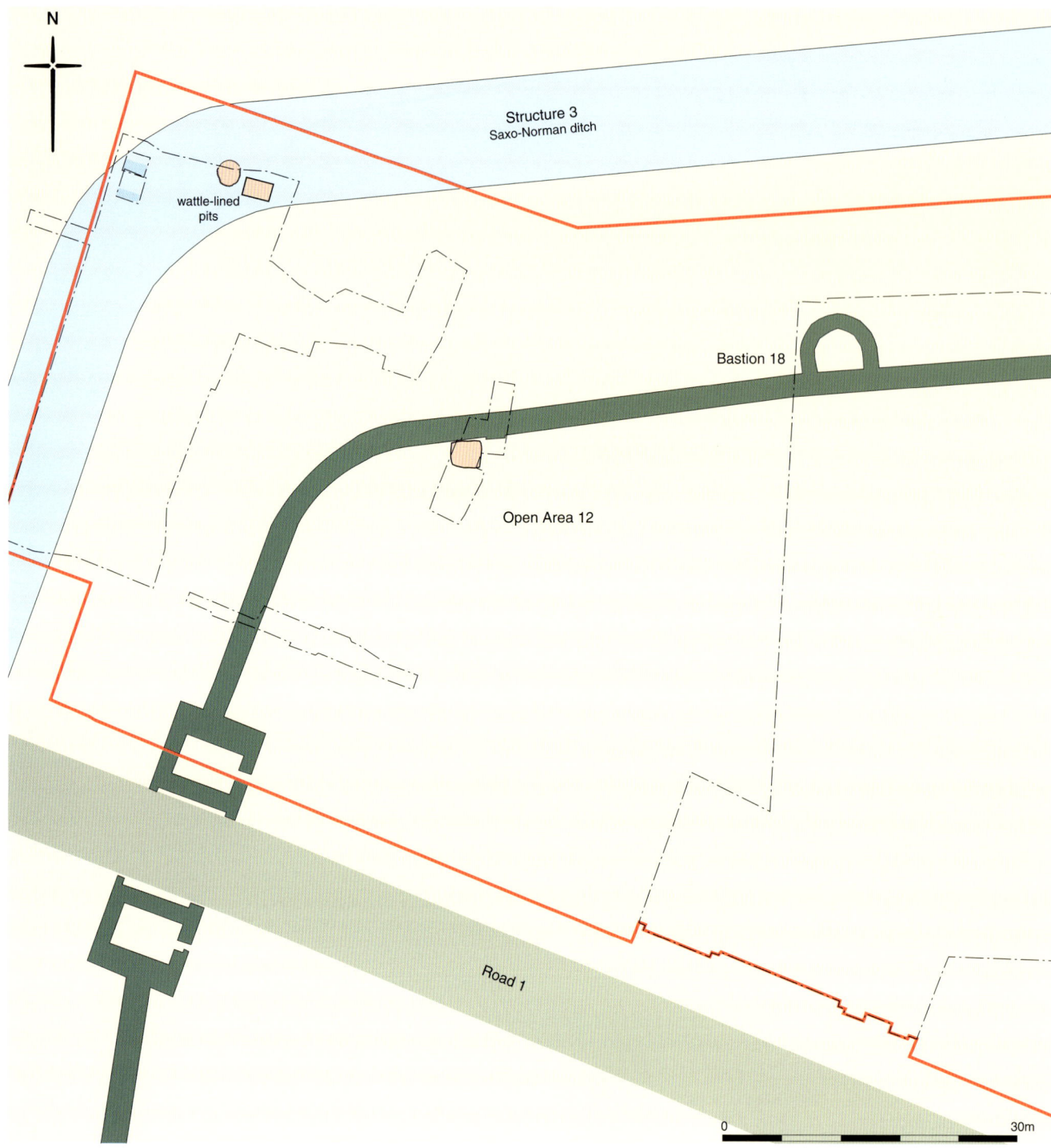

Fig 57 The city defences crossing the study area in the Saxo-Norman period, c AD 880–1100 (period 4) (scale 1:600)

Giltspur Street during a watching brief on a sewer heading. The structure consisted of make-up deposits and beaten earth floors and was backfilled with rubbish deposits. The walls of the structure were not observed and no direct dating evidence was retrieved, but the building appears to have cut through the backfilled Saxo-Norman ditch (S3).

Discussion (period 4)

Post-Roman ditches have been recorded at several sites along the defensive circuit, including the MLFC site. It is possible that renovation of the defensive circuit, including the city ditch, took place in the Saxon period and was intended to help defend the enclave of St Paul's from Viking attacks and the Alfredian settlement from the Danish attacks of AD 994, 1009 and 1013 (Bond 2002). Aside from some pitting and drainage gullies there was little evidence for activity at the MLFC site.

Archaeological evidence from the western part of the city for this period is also dominated by a series of large ditches, with little in the way of occupation. To the north of the city wall, a large ditch of Saxo-Norman date was recorded running east–west past Smithfield Market (Telfer 2003, 115). Near the

Fig 58 Saxo-Norman wattle-lined pit, looking west

Fig 59 Saxo-Norman wattle-lined pit, looking north-west

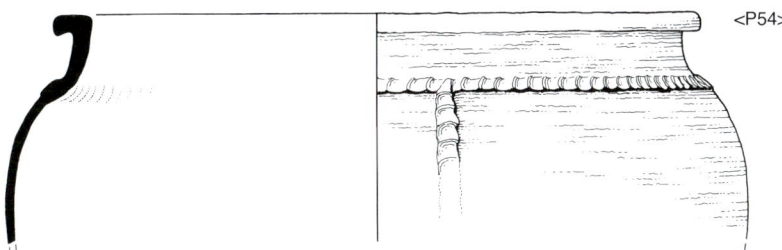

Fig 60 Shelly-sandy ware (SSW) cooking pot <P54> (scale 1:4)

crest of Ludgate Hill and just west of St Paul's, a north–south ditch followed the line of a Roman drainage system: this is sometimes referred to as the 'western stream', and may be a recut of the earlier feature. Radiocarbon dates from deposits found near the base of the recut suggest that it was open in the Saxon period (Watson in prep). The position and date of the ditch may indicate that it was an early boundary for the St Paul's precinct (ibid).

4.3 Medieval settlement, c 1100–1300 (period 5)

Religious buildings dominated the Newgate area in the medieval period, with three different religious orders settling nearby. The Augustinians were established just outside the city walls at St Bartholomew's Priory and Hospital by 1123. The first order to establish a permanent home within the city were the Franciscan Grey Friars, who built their friary in the area between the city wall and Newgate Street from 1225 onwards (Honeybourne 1932, 10). Further south, the Dominican priory of Blackfriars was built in 1275 over the area previously occupied by Baynard's Castle and Montfichet's Tower (Schofield 1993, 66–7).

The monasteries were generally constructed close to the city walls where unused land was often still available, although houses and streets were cleared where necessary (Tyler 1991). It is a measure of the importance of London's friars that the construction of the Blackfriars Friary saw the city wall breached and extended westwards to include the priory grounds (Schofield 1993, 66–7).

The MLFC site was probably largely unoccupied before the Greyfriars precinct was built. By the mid 13th century the site was the focus of two major building projects: the construction of the monastery and the renovation of the city defences (Fig 61).

The medieval archaeological sequence

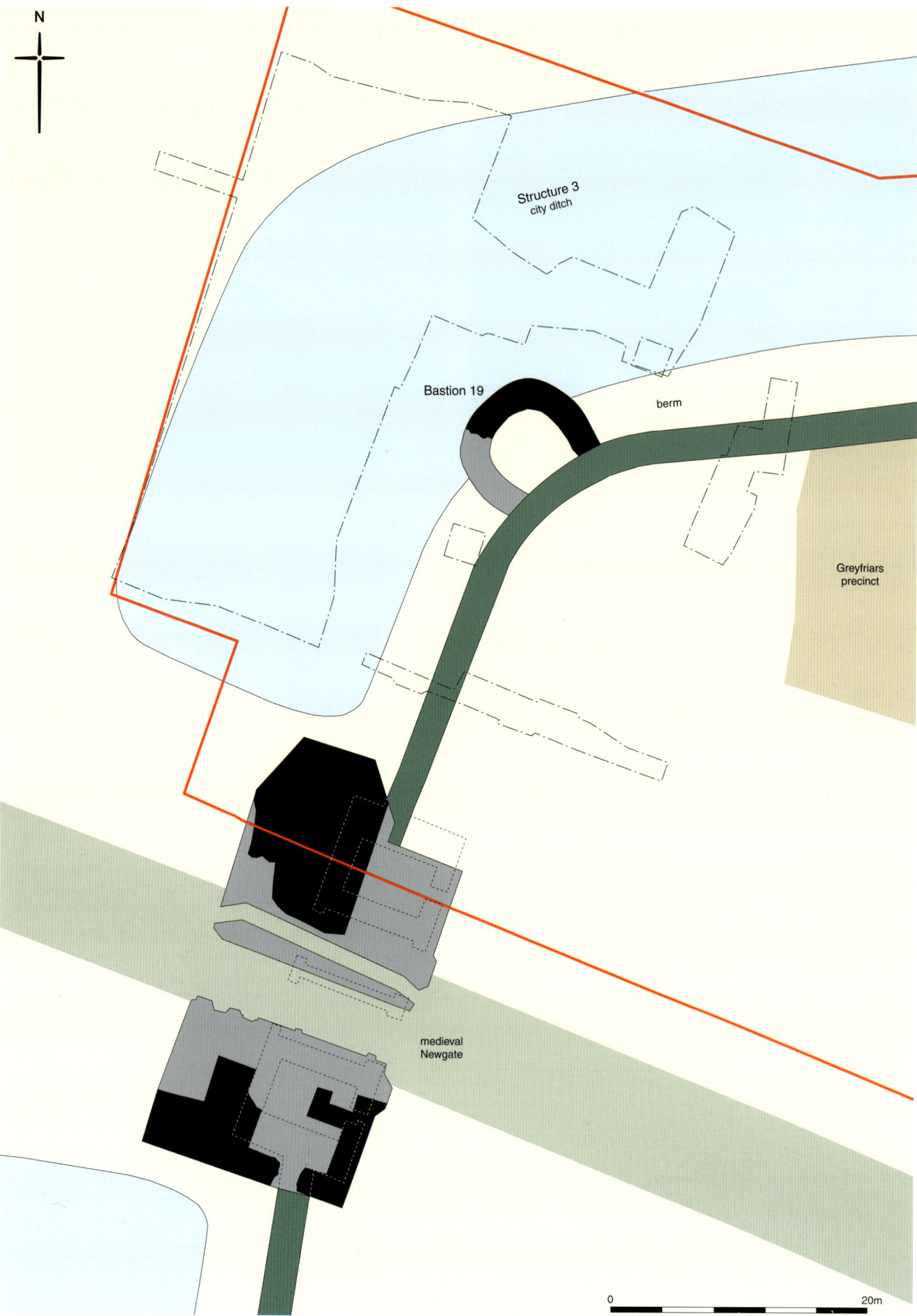

Fig 61 The city defences and the Greyfriars precinct in the study area, c 1100–1300 (period 5) (scale 1:400)

The medieval city defences

By the mid 13th century the city defences appear to have been in need of repair, as shown by the implementation of a rebuilding programme funded in part by King John himself (Schofield 1993, 67). Stow writes that in 1215 the king's army 'applied all diligence to repair the gates and walls of this city' (1598, 69). Murage tax was also introduced to build up funds for repairs to the wall. This was levied at the gates of the City between 1233 and 1236, and whenever was required after that (Sharpe 1899–1912, Cal. L. B).

Examples of medieval rebuilding of the upper portions of the wall can still be seen on many sites around London. At St Alphege churchyard the rebuild includes possible 12th-century round-headed embrasures and fragments of a stair to the parapet walkway (Westman 1987, 7–22). Norman and Reader recorded during their observations in 1906 that none of the medieval portion of the wall on the MLFC site had survived. Grimes noted that when Bastion 19 was exposed in 1907–9 'Its top as surviving appeared to be toppling over outwards – a fact which can be observed today. The end of the bastion, butting against the wall, fits the curve of its upper courses and there can be little doubt that when the bastion was built the wall could not have been standing to any appreciably greater height than it does now' (1968, 65). This may give a good indication of just how dilapidated the Roman defences had become by the mid 13th century (Fig 62).

The city gates were also rebuilt and strengthened during this period. William FitzStephen records that there were seven double gates through the city wall in the 1170s (Stow 1598, 58). Newgate, which was situated close to the MLFC site, is the best explored of all the gates. Stow believed that Newgate was built in the reign of Henry I or Stephen to ease traffic congestion in the city, caused by the cathedral precinct blocking the old route westward (ibid, 64–5). The excavation of Newgate in the early 20th century, however, indicated that the gatehouse had originally been constructed in the Roman period, and that the fabric of the Roman gatehouse had been incorporated into its larger medieval successor (Fig 44; Fig 61) (Norman 1904, 132; Merrifield 1965, 102). It is now thought that the gate had been blocked up at some unknown point in antiquity (possibly the late or post-Roman period), and that it was just the unblocking and reinstatement of the gate that took place in Henry I or Stephen's reign (Vince 1990, 79–80). The first known record of the name Newgate occurs in a grant of land dated 1162, from the Dean and Chapter of St Paul's to the Canons of St Mary in Southwark (Hist MSS Comm, 224). According to Leland (1715), Newgate was previously known as Chamberlain Gate (Bond 2002).

The gates are documented to have had several uses which were not directly related to defence of the City. Some gates were let for residential purposes, such as Aldgate, which was occupied by the poet Geoffrey Chaucer for 12 years (Bell et al 1937, 56). Both Ludgate and Newgate were used as prisons throughout the medieval period. The first record of Newgate as a prison can be found in a Pipe Roll dating to 1190 (Bond 2002). During Norman's excavations of Newgate in 1904, a north–south passageway or subway (2.4m wide) was discovered within the foundations of the gatehouse, which had connected the two portions of the medieval prison on opposite sides of the street (Norman 1904, 133). Part of the upstanding ashlar masonry of the medieval prison was found to survive c 0.90m below pavement level, on the south side of the street. A similar level of survival was discovered during the watching brief on the excavation of service trenches in 1999, where medieval masonry belonging to the prison was found to survive c 0.50m below modern pavement level, on the north side of the street.

Fig 62 Junction of the angle bastion (Bastion 19) with the Roman city wall (Norman and Reader 1912, pl LII, 2)

The bastions and evidence from the MLFC site

Some of the City's western bastions could have had a Roman origin, but Bastions 11A, 12, 13, 14, 15, 16 and 19 are almost certainly medieval additions (Fig 63). According to Stow the medieval bastions may have been constructed in 1257 (1598, 11), shortly after the redigging of the city ditch.

The bastions, like the city gates, were also used for a range of non-military purposes during the medieval period. In 1235 Bastion 21 was let as a dwelling to Alexander Swereford, the treasurer of St Paul's Cathedral, on the understanding that he would vacate it in times of war as 'it may be needful to munition the city wall with arms and men, the turret and even

The medieval archaeological sequence

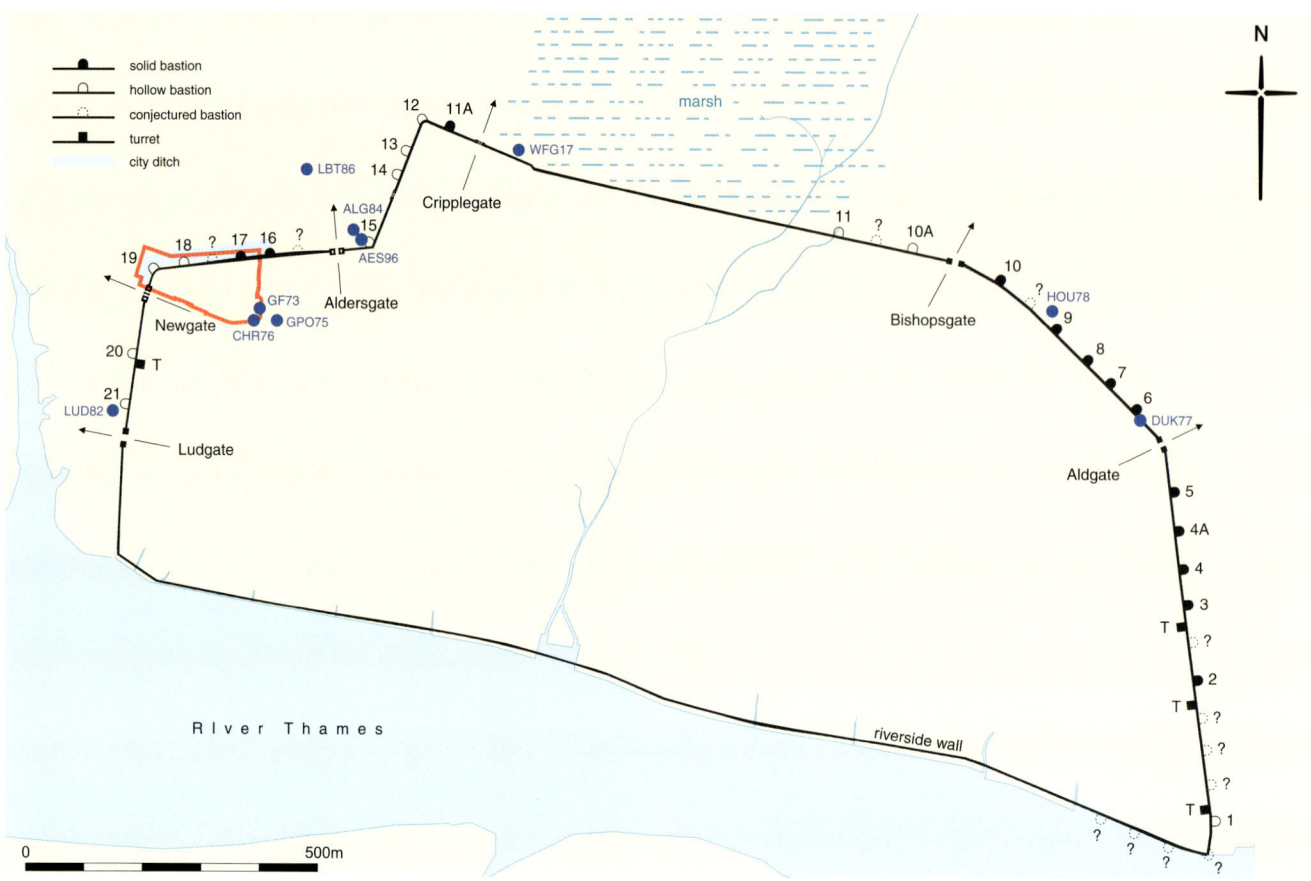

Fig 63 The study area in relation to the medieval defensive circuit of c 1300, showing all phases of the eastern and western bastions (Bastions 1–21) and relevant archaeological sites (see Table 1 for site details) (scale 1:12,500)

the buildings in it shall be exposed to receive the munitions of the city like the other turretts in the wall' (cited in Schofield 1993, 69). Other bastions were occupied by hermits or anchorites. Simon the Ankar (anchorite) is famously known to have lived in Bastion 11 (Bell et al 1937, 65). Prior to the dissolution, hermits were common in London and their living quarters were often found in association with religious houses and churches. They were 'visited by devout people, who regarded his sacrifice in excluding himself from the world and his life of prayer as giving him particular sanctity' (ibid, 66). As well as living in the City's bastions, they sometimes occupied 'cells' constructed against the foot of the city wall (ibid, 65). No records have been found which may suggest that hermits lived along the wall at the MLFC site, although the possibility cannot be ruled out. It is likely that Greyfriars Friary, which backed onto the city wall along the northern extent of the site, had the use of Bastions 17 to 19.

BASTION 19

Norman and Reader were able to obtain the permission and resources to conduct a small research excavation to study the angle bastion and city wall (see Chapter 3.2; Fig 64a–c). As a result of their endeavours Bastion 19 and the curving fragment of city wall against which it was built were preserved in a viewing chamber under the west yard.

Bastion 19 is the largest of the recorded bastions in the City of London. Its hollow, horseshoe-shaped structure extended 8.0m from the external face of the city wall, almost 3.0m further than the nearby Bastion 18 (Norman and Reader 1912, 287). The foundations extended to a depth of 2.10m from base of plinth, and the walls were c 2.0m thick at base. The base of the structure was irregular in order to conform to the uneven natural ground below (RCHME 1928, 104). The bastion was constructed of ragstone set into white mortar, and the external face was carefully pointed (Fig 65; Fig 66). No attempt had been made to key in the bastion and the earlier Roman wall (Fig 62).

Norman and Reader (1912, 290) believed Bastion 19 to be Roman for several reasons. Careful excavation of its interior had found only Roman artefacts: 'all the soil below a level of 10ft [3.05m] from the present surface was of one description, and contained only Roman objects'. Norman and Reader were not aware that the structure had been trench-built, a process which left the surrounding Roman deposits in situ. They noted that the upper part of the bastion was full of material presumably thrown up by the digging of the trench for the bastion. This material consisted of brickearth and gravel, along with 'masses of opus signinum' (ibid) and other Roman building materials. They thought that the bastion was constructed in the late Roman period to support the subsiding wall. Although the date of the bastion is now known to be medieval, it may have been intended to provide support for the toppling wall.

Medieval settlement, c 1100–1300 (period 5)

Fig 64 Angle bastion (Bastion 19) as recorded by Norman and Reader in 1906: a – exterior of city wall and angle bastion (1912, pl LIII, 2); b – angle bastion exterior, looking east (1912, pl LIII, 1); c – angle bastion interior (1912, pl LII, 2)

The construction of the city ditch and evidence from the MLFC site

A wider and deeper city ditch was dug in the mid 13th century. This ditch was generally closer to the wall than the previous ditches had been (Rowsome 1984; Maloney and Harding 1979, 350; Butler 2001, 53). Stow recorded that the ditch 'was begun to be made by the Londoners in the year 1211, and was finished in the year 1213, the 15th of King John' (1598, 50).

The medieval city ditch has been recorded on many archaeological sites around London. On some sites the main phase of ditch had been recut a number of times. Stow recorded its width at 200ft (c 61m), but archaeological investigations have indicated that its width was not constant and that its profile varied from site to site (Maloney and Harding 1979, 350–1). At 1–6 Old Bailey (LUD82, Fig 63) the ditch was 4.0m deep and 12–17m wide, and its profile varied, being wide and flat-bottomed in the north and south and V-shaped in the central area. This variation may have been due to the presence of Bastion 21 and the fact that further to the west the ditch terminated in a butt-end, just before Ludgate (Rowsome 1984). To the east at 1–6 Aldersgate Street (AES96, Fig 63), the medieval ditch was 17.50m wide and 4.0m deep with a flattish base. Similar to the site at Ludgate, the ditch is thought to have terminated to the west in a butt-end just before Aldersgate (Butler 2001, 54). The ditch has also been investigated on the eastern side of the city at Dukes Place (DUK77, Fig 63) and 47–56 Houndsditch (HOU78, Fig 63).

61

The medieval archaeological sequence

Fig 65 Conducting a survey of Bastion 19 in 1999

Fig 66 Detail of the base of Bastion 19 recorded during the survey in 1999 (scale 0.2m)

THE CITY DITCH (S3) AND PHASE 1 BACKFILLING (PRIMARY FILL)

The 13th-century city ditch was recorded at the MLFC site (S3 retained in use, Fig 61) during evaluation work and again in the main excavation, when the upper backfills of the ditch were investigated across a large open area (area H, Fig 2). A series of auger holes was subsequently driven through the base of the ditch and three extra trenches (10A–C, Fig 2) were excavated to gain further information on the ditch profile. Part of the north-east ditch area was selected for detailed analysis, as here it was possible to relate the evidence from the deeper trenches to that from the overlying open area excavation. A model sequence through the ditch has been reconstructed using this information and the associated deposits from this area fully analysed.

Despite these efforts very little information was recovered about the ditch profile and its primary fills (Fig 67). The small amount of pottery retrieved from the primary silts dated to c 1150–1200, which accords with Stow's documented construction date of 1211–13. The backfilled ditch occupied the whole area of excavation and neither the inner nor outer edges of the ditch were observed. Ditch deposits were not present in a small trench to the south of Bastion 19 but were seen in a small trench to the north-east c 4m from the face of the city wall (Fig 61). It is probable that the inside edge of the ditch was located just to the south, creating a berm of just under 4.0m (Fig 61). The ditch was observed to turn a tight corner at the northern extent of excavation and the base was recorded curving upwards at this point, making it likely that the ditch was c 25m wide (Fig 61).

The foundation of Greyfriars in 1225

The Newgate area was not particularly built up in the early 13th century, which was one of the key reasons for siting the Greyfriars precinct here (Fig 61; Fig 68), although there were properties along the main street frontage. Excavations at GPO Newgate Street (GPO75, Fig 63) revealed garden soil from Greyfriars sealing simple 13th-century buildings fronting onto Stinking Lane, now King Edward Street (Tyler 1991). A small excavation in the south aisle of the later Wren church (CHR76, Fig 63) revealed a similar sequence of buildings, some of which pre-dated the monastery (Herbert 1979, 327–8). These buildings may have been related to the Shambles meat market on Newgate Street, and there may have been similar buildings along Newgate Street to the west. The buildings were swept away as the friars began to construct their monastic precinct.

The Grey Friars were sent to England by St Francis of Assisi in 1224 (Honeybourne 1932, 9). A small number resided in London near Holborn until 1225 when 'John Iwyn, a wealthy mercer of London, bought for their use a plot of land in Stinking Lane near Newgate, and established them in the north-west corner of the city, which for three centuries was to be the home of the Grey friars' (Kingsford 1915, 16). It is possible that the location, just inside the city walls close to the filthy city ditch and equally malodorous Shambles meat market, was not regarded as a salubrious one (Honeybourne 1932, 28; Kingsford 1915, 16).

The initial donation made to the friars is likely to have been fairly small, consisting of a plot of one or two houses (Kingsford 1915, 28). But as their popularity grew, and notable patrons were attracted, the site expanded. In 1227–8 Joce Fitz Piers donated land in Stinking Lane which probably adjoined

Fig 67 Recording the base of the medieval city ditch (S3), looking west

The medieval archaeological sequence

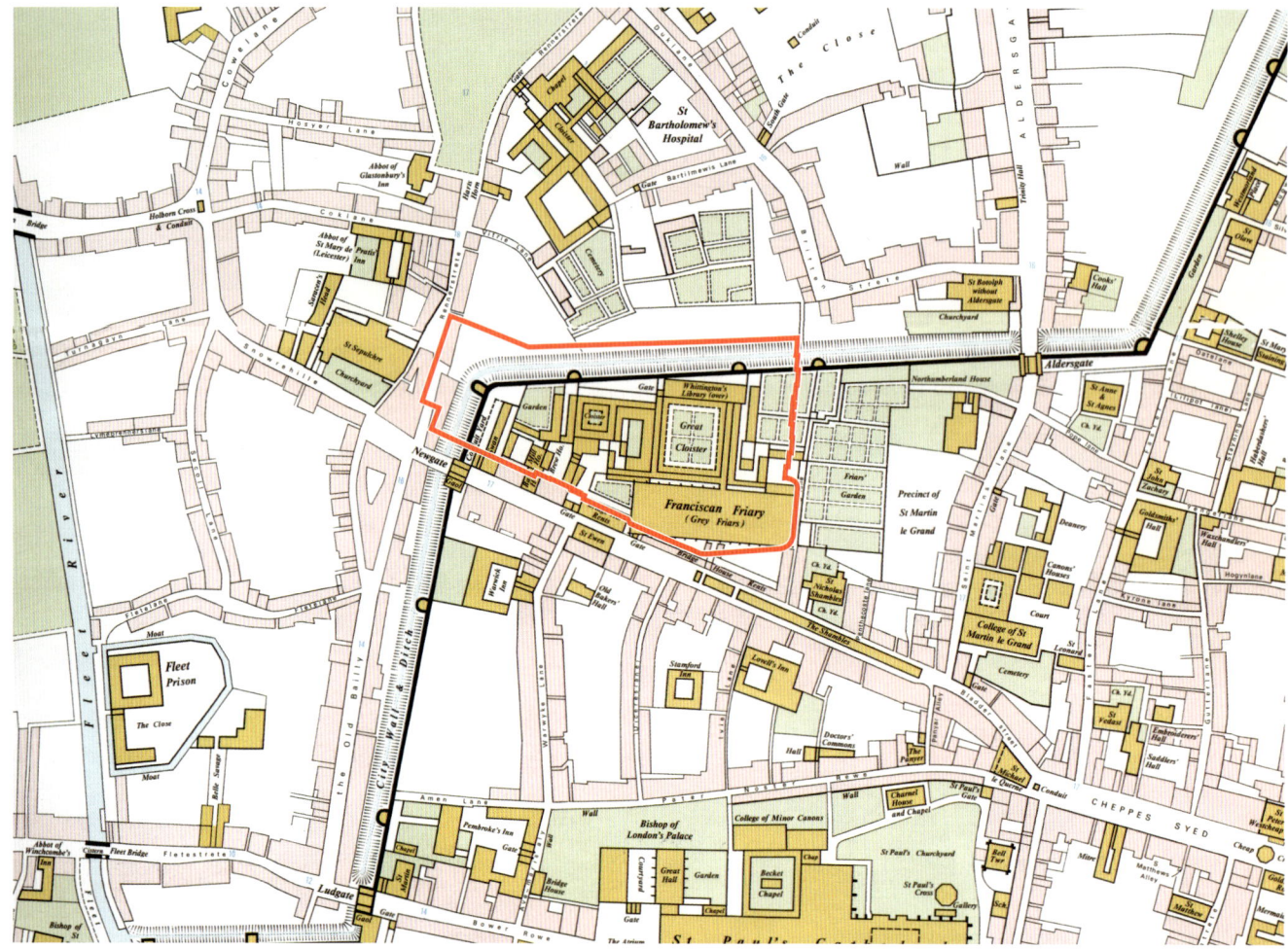

Fig 68 Detail from Lobel's reconstruction map of London in 1520 (Lobel 1989, map 2) (scale 1:4000)

John Iwyn's gift (ibid, 29). In 1229 the king donated oak for building purposes and William Joyner, mayor in 1239, covered the cost of building the first church and probably also donated more land between 1238 and 1243 (ibid). The numbers of friars residing in the precinct began to expand and Kingsford records that there were 80 friars present by 1243 (ibid, 16).

More purchases were made in the following years and by 1306 the limits of the Greyfriars precinct were largely set (Kingsford 1915, 32). The outline of the main buildings in the complex can be seen on Lobel's reconstruction map for 1520 (Fig 68). It is clear that by this time the monastery owned most of the land between the city wall, Newgate Street (including most of the Newgate Street frontage), and Stinking Lane (now King Edward Street) to the east. The monastery also owned a considerable area to the east, which is identified on maps as the friary garden. Development of the site is likely to have occurred in many stages, as the complicated system of holding property in medieval times would have made numerous payments and agreements necessary before the friars could take full possession of all areas in the precinct (Honeybourne 1932, 37). Following the construction of the first chapel, more land was purchased, and the first intensive construction period occurred between 1279 and 1290, during which time the cloister and other conventual buildings were constructed. These included the chapter house (built by Walter Potter, alderman 1269–89), the dormitory (Gregory de Rokesley, mayor 1274–81 and 1284–5), the refectory (built by Bartholomew de Castro) and the infirmary (built by Peter Helyland) (Kingsford 1915, 34–5).

At the beginning of the 14th century Queen Margaret acquired land on behalf of the priory in the parish of St Nicholas Shambles which was used as the site for a new church in 1306 (Kingsford 1915, 32). Queen Margaret died in 1318, before the construction of the church had been completed, and was buried in front of the high altar (ibid). The church was not completed until 1337, during the reign of Edward III, facilitated by Isabella de Valois and Queen Philippa who donated funds. The church was a grand building by all accounts. It was the largest building within the complex at c 91m long, c 27m wide and c 19.5m high, consisting of a nave and choir (both with twin aisles) topped by a spire. The church was the largest in the City of London after the cathedral of St Paul's (Stow 1598, 302).

Discussion of the earlier medieval settlement

The Newgate area was not densely built up in the early medieval period and it is not known if any buildings existed on the MLFC site, although nearby sites have produced evidence for roadside buildings fronting King Edward Street and it is probable that similar structures lined Newgate Street.

By the mid 13th century a number of major developments were under way. The subsiding city wall was rebuilt from 1215 onwards and Bastion 19 was added to the wall to strengthen its structure in 1257. Bastions 17 and 18 were also built or rebuilt at this time and the city ditch was widened and deepened in 1211–13. No evidence of medieval rebuilding of the wall survives at the MLFC site, but a significant portion of the infilled city ditch was investigated during the excavation, along with the medieval foundations of Bastion 19.

Not long after the renovations of the city defences began, a small plot of land fronting Newgate Street was donated to a small group of Franciscan Grey Friars, who made the site their permanent home. In the years leading up to the 14th century the popularity of the Grey Friars grew and they received further donations of land, property and money. By the beginning of the 14th century the friary owned most of the land within the present site boundary, and more further to the east, upon which the monastery and related buildings were constructed.

4.4 Later medieval settlement, *c* 1300–1500 (period 5)

The establishment of Greyfriars inevitably changed the topography of the Newgate area, although it was still constrained by the city defences and main road.

The rise and fall of Greyfriars, 1306–1538

The 14th century was a time of great prosperity for Greyfriars. The church, completed in 1327, had benefited from the patronage of two queens, making it popular as a place of burial for the rich and famous and as a place to attend mass. This great popularity can be seen in the list of noble people recorded by Stow as being buried in its church (Stow 1598, 303–6), and by the numerous requests for masses and pittances recorded in the friary register (Kingsford 1915, 18). Some of the friars seem to have been quite wealthy, suggesting that the rule of poverty may no longer have been strictly adhered to (ibid). Alterations and improvements were made to the buildings of the precinct throughout the 14th and 15th centuries. In 1398 the south-west porch was added to the church and the gatehouse in Newgate Street was erected (Kingsford 1915, 42–3). The friary was renowned as one of the primary conventual schools of the English province, and between 1370 and 1420 the 'Schools' or 'Studies' were rebuilt on a much larger scale on the east side of the Great Cloister. The Great Cloister itself was substantially modified at this time and the library was also rebuilt by Richard Whittington in 1420–1 (ibid, 21).

Greyfriars owned most of the Newgate Street frontage by the beginning of the 14th century. Much of the frontage was evidently considered to be of little value, as in 1368 the friary parted with a considerable strip directly to the south of the main church, which was acquired by the 'Mayor and Commonalty of the City, trustees of the [London] Bridge' (Honeybourne 1932, 12). Another strip further west was purchased for the same purpose in 1397, and as neither plot was large enough to build on, permission was given to take 6ft (1.8m) from the Newgate Street highway for building (Fig 69). The Bridge House Rents were subsequently constructed along the street frontage. The south gate to the precinct bisected the two plots and was built out to the same line as the Bridge House Rents.

The friary is shown on Ralph Treswell's 'Plat of ye Graye Friers', compiled in 1617 (Fig 70). Although this map shows the site in great detail it has some drawbacks. It appears to have been compiled using different sources, including some that were over 70 years old at the time of drafting, which has resulted in some inaccuracies (Honeybourne 1932, 11). The map also misses off much of the eastern part of the precinct and does not show the precinct boundary line. Not all the land between the city wall and Newgate Street to the west of King Edward Street belonged to the friary. Nevertheless, the map is useful in identifying most of the buildings on the site at the time. The probable extent of the precinct before the surrender of Greyfriars in 1538 has been reconstructed by Honeybourne (Fig 71).

Although the friary falls within the confines of the MLFC site, none of the precinct's burial grounds or main buildings lay within the area of the 1992–9 excavations in the west yard. The portion of the precinct that fell within the excavation area contained gardens and stables, as shown on Treswell's and Honeybourne's plans (Fig 70; Fig 71). The rest of the area within this part of the precinct was occupied by the friary millhouse, bakehouse and brewhouse (Fig 70; Fig 71). Buildings belonging to the Swan Inn on Newgate Street, including 'The Swan Yarde', are depicted to the west of the precinct on Treswell's 1617 map (Fig 70).

The MLFC evidence

Limited evidence for early medieval building remains, on similar alignments to those of the Greyfriars church and other buildings, was discovered during the excavation of the site in 1998.

THE GREAT CHURCH OF GREYFRIARS (B12)
A massive trench-built foundation of uncoursed chalk and ragstone rubble (Fig 69; Fig 72) was recorded and preserved *in situ*. No dating evidence was retrieved from the foundations, which are thought to represent the buttress of the west wall of the nave of the friary church. The foundations lay directly underneath what would have been the south-western corner of the church. The construction of the church began in 1306 but the nave may not have been completed until *c* 20 years after the completion of the choir (Kingsford 1915, 36).

The medieval archaeological sequence

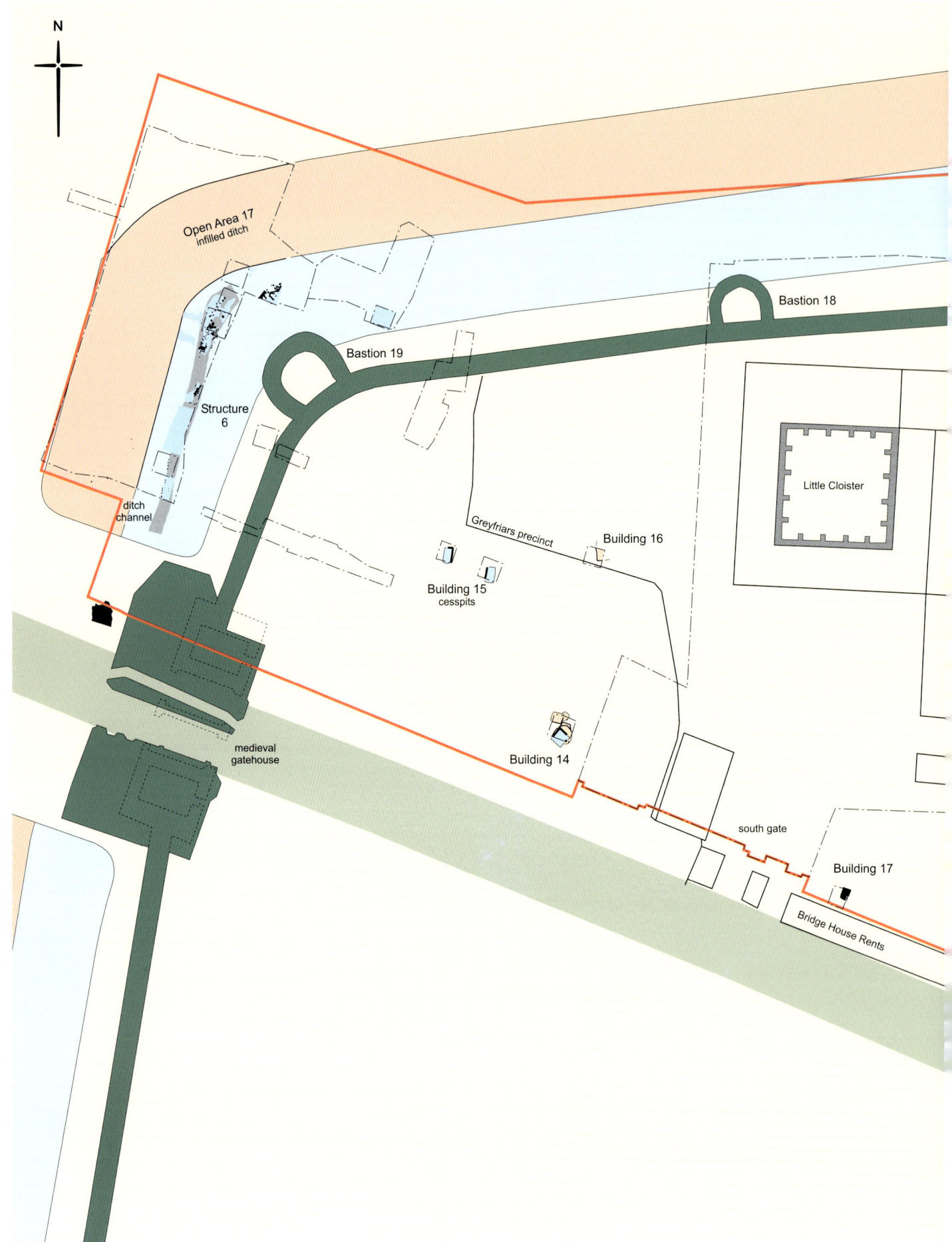

Fig 69 The study area in later medieval times, c 1300–1500 (period 5), in relation to the city defences and the Greyfriars precinct (scale 1:600)

Later medieval settlement, *c* 1300–1500 (period 5)

The medieval archaeological sequence

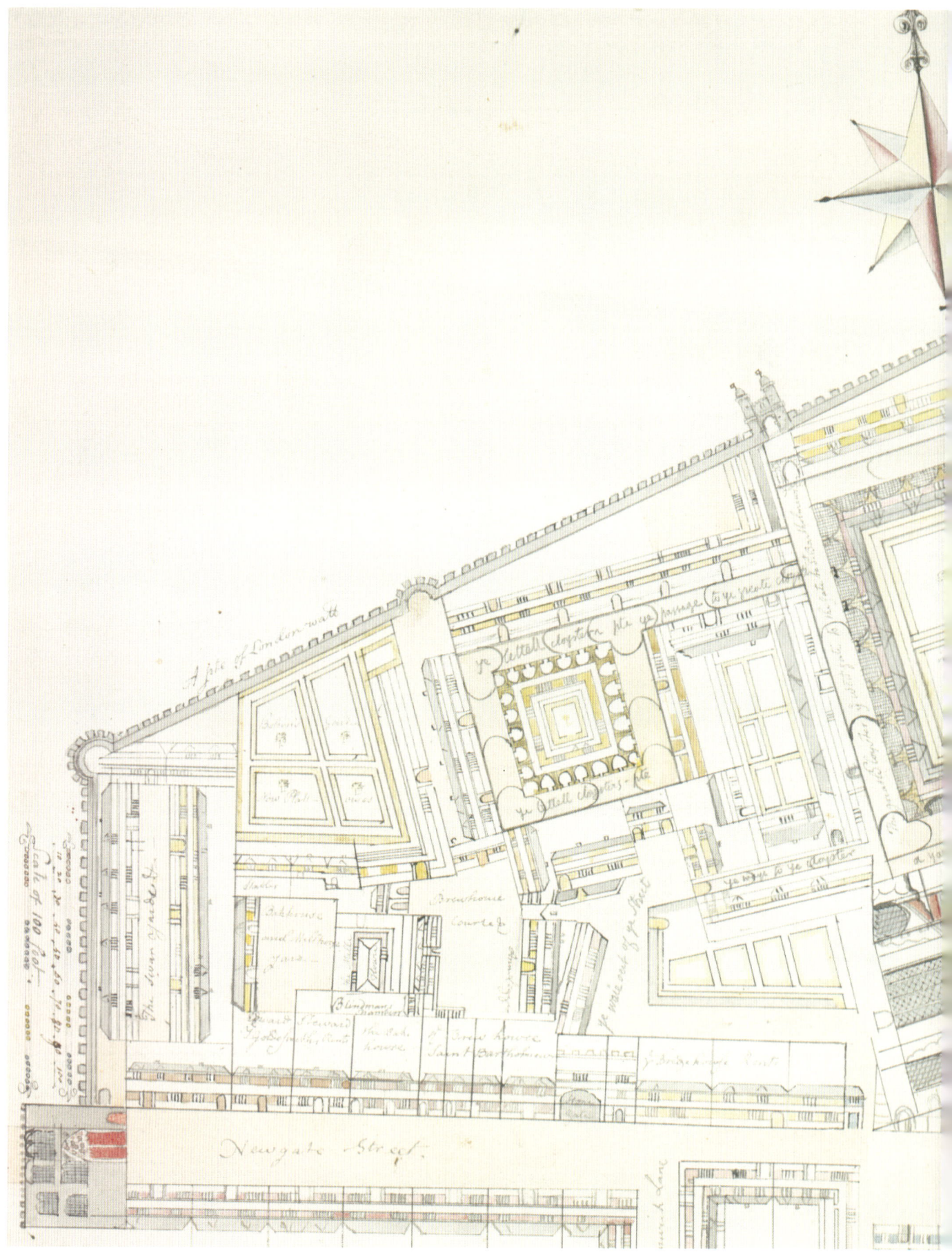

Fig 70　Ralph Treswell's 'Plat of ye Graye Friers', compiled in 1617 (reproduced courtesy of the British Library)

Later medieval settlement, *c* 1300–1500 (period 5)

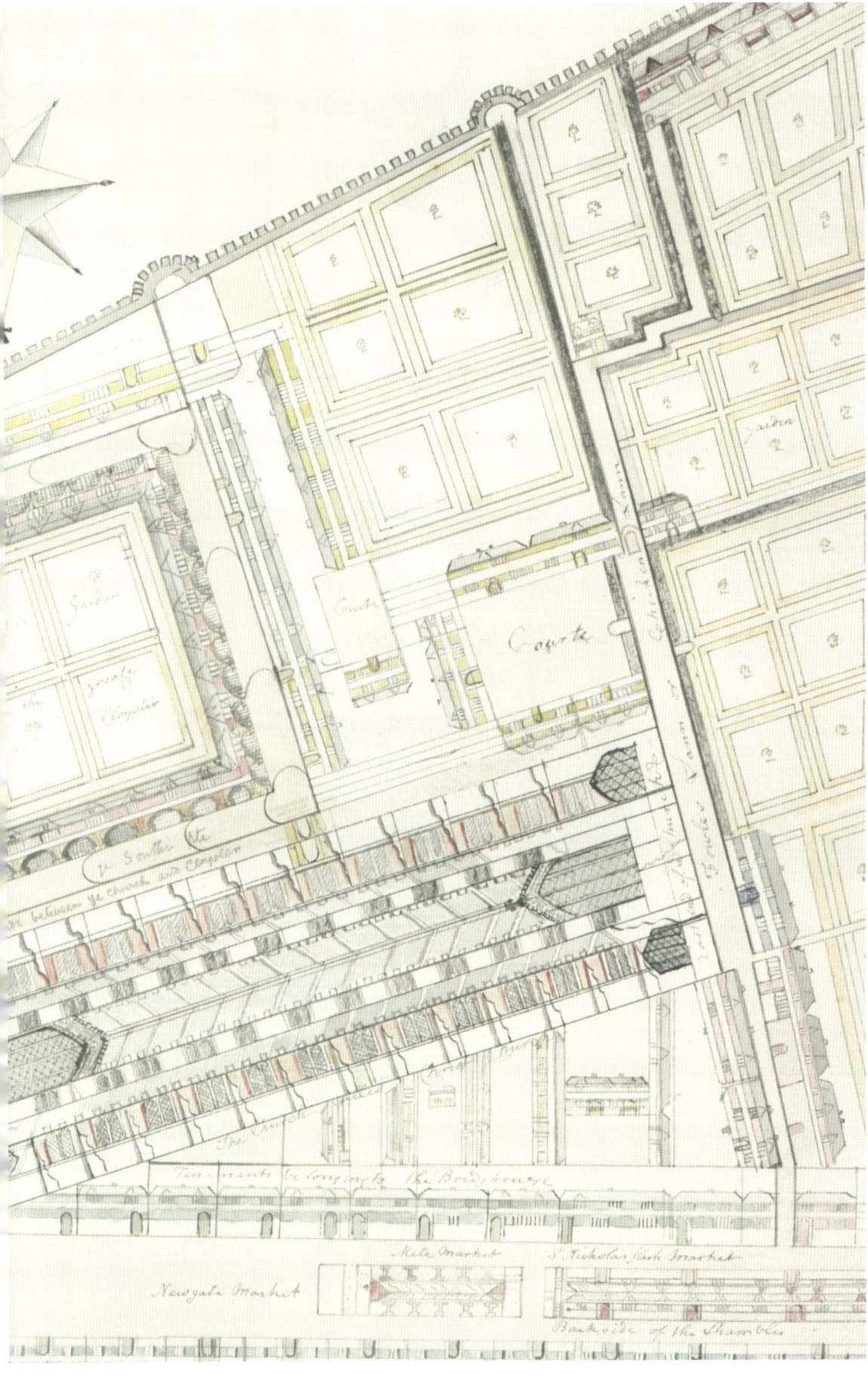

The medieval archaeological sequence

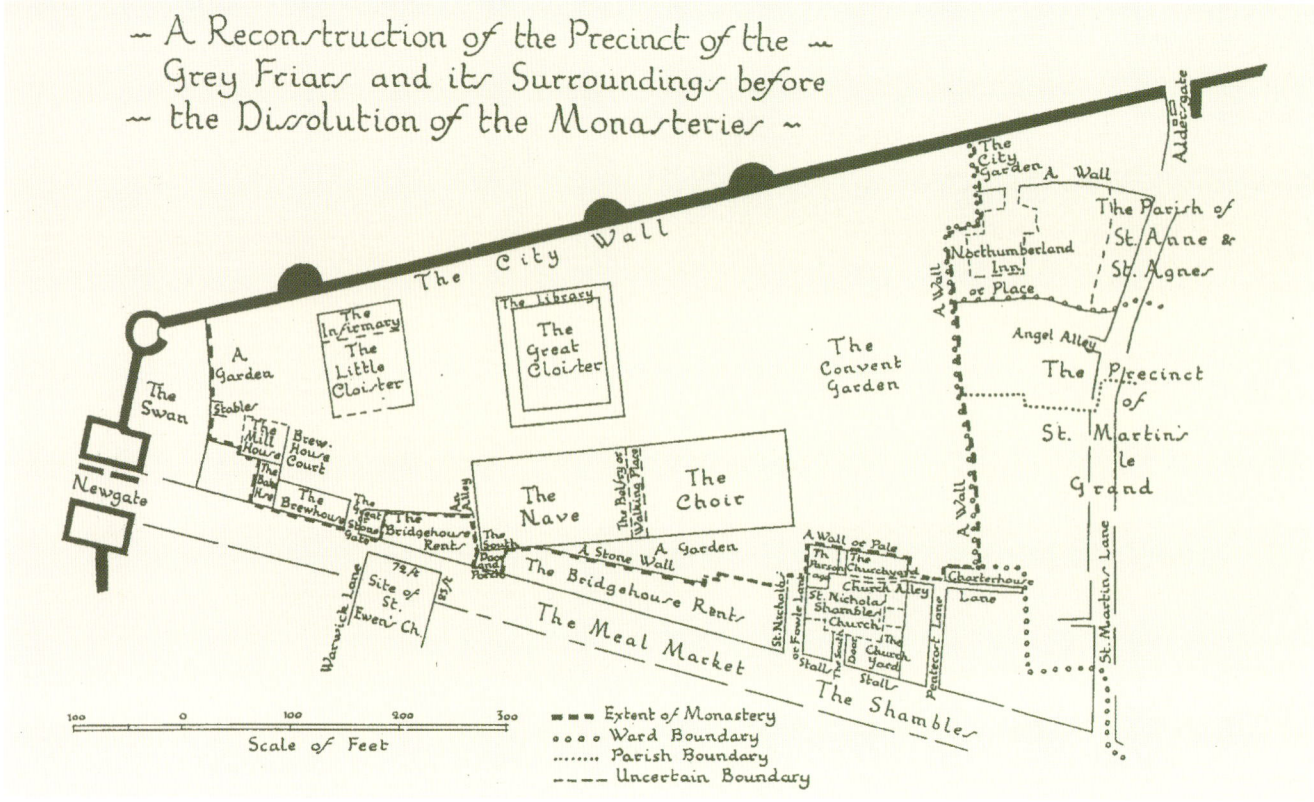

Fig 71 Honeybourne's reconstructed map of the precinct of Greyfriars before the dissolution of 1538 (Honeybourne 1932, pl II)

Fig 72 Foundations of the nave of Greyfriars church (B12), looking north (scale 0.5m)

BRIDGE HOUSE RENTS (B17)

A large, trench-built chalk medieval foundation was excavated along the Newgate Street frontage (Fig 69; Fig 73). The structure was probably part of the foundations of the Bridge House Rents buildings, constructed along the Newgate Street frontage by the City following the purchase of land from Greyfriars in 1397. The remains were badly truncated by 19th-century cellars and were mainly recorded in section. It is thought that the foundations represent the rear portion of the properties.

BUILDING FRONTING NEWGATE (B14)

A truncated chalk- and ragstone-lined cesspit was all that remained of a building that would once have fronted on to Newgate Street (Fig 69). The cesspit may have belonged either to the bakehouse or to the brewhouse of the friary, as pictured on Treswell's map of 1617 (Fig 70).

GOLDSMITHS RENTS (B15)

Two cesspits (B15, Fig 69) are likely to have belonged to buildings shown on Treswell's map, perhaps the buildings labelled as 'Goldsmiths Rents' or the structures immediately to the north (Fig 70). The two cesspits were chalk-lined, built of unmortared chalk blocks, and their backfills contained pottery dating to 1170–1200.

BUILDING 16

Building 16, situated within the Greyfriars precinct, survived as no more than a robust chalk-block foundation pier (Fig 69) of unknown extent but a minimum of 2m deep. The lower part of the structure had been trench-poured, with a securely packed and mortared cap laid on the top. The foundation was reused in a post-medieval cellared building.

Discussion of the friary in the later medieval period

Construction of the friary church was completed and many of the main conventual buildings were in place during the first half of the 14th century. Greyfriars was an important religious complex, attracting patronage from many of the City's key officials and the monarchs. The day-to-day business of the monastery, details of its patrons, and lists of the friars and their respective positions and burial records, are detailed in the friary register, which gives an invaluable insight into life at the friary. In contrast, there are very few detailed plans of the precinct which accurately show the different stages of its development over the medieval period.

The basic monastery plan is shown on historic maps of the area. The 'Agas' map of c 1562 (Fig 74) shows the cloisters, gardens and great church, with the latter clearly depicted as the dominant building in this part of the City (St Paul's is beyond the confines of this map). Treswell's map of 1617 (Fig 70) is the most detailed known plan of the Greyfriars precinct and most of the buildings shown are clearly labelled. The map post-dates the dissolution but was compiled using a combination of earlier and later sources (Honeybourne 1932, 11).

There is very little archaeological evidence from the MLFC site to add to the documentary and cartographic evidence which is reconstructed in Fig 75. Most of the buildings were destroyed

Fig 73 *Foundations of Bridge House Rents (B17), looking south (scale 0.5m)*

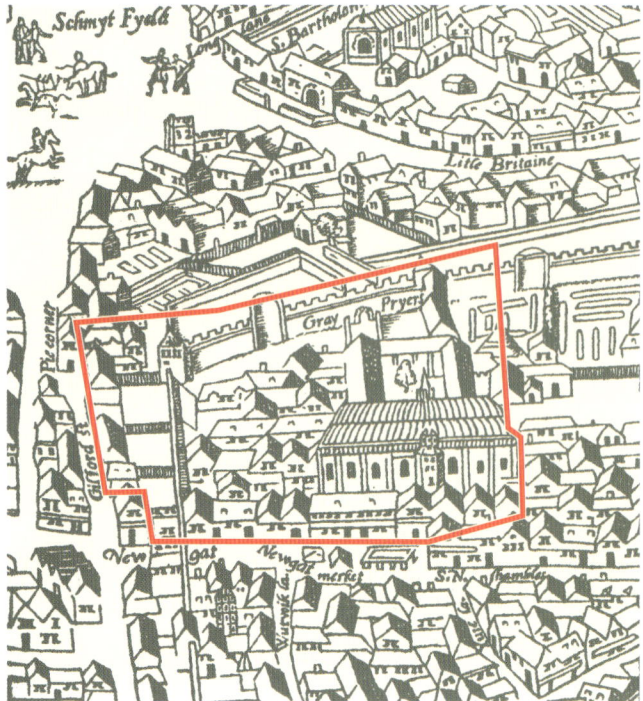

Fig 74 Detail of the 'Agas' woodcut view, based on the copperplate map of c 1559 redrawn and amended between 1561 and 1570 (Agas c 1562)

by the Great Fire in 1666, and the below-ground portions of these buildings were subsequently removed by the deep basement of the GPO building in 1907–9. Norman and Reader (1912, 274) were unable to make more than the most cursory of observations about the monastery foundations as they were removed during the ground clearance. They recorded simply that the chalk-built arched foundations of the cloisters were visible in the first trench, parallel to King Edward Street, and that 'many walls belonging to the Greyfriars period were disclosed, and as quickly destroyed'. The small trenches excavated on the site during the 1992–2001 excavations meant that very little information on the friary buildings was retrieved. A fragment of the west wall of the 14th-century church nave, the remains of cesspits which may have belonged to precinct buildings, and part of the foundations to the Bridge House Rents properties fronting Newgate Street, were identified. The remains discovered do not add significantly to the understanding of the layout of the precinct, beyond confirming the location of the church as that seen on historic maps.

Previous archaeological sites in the area add little more to the overall picture. Excavations in 1973 (GF73, Fig 63) and 1976 (CHR76, Fig 63) in the eastern end of the Wren church suggested that the external walls of the church had reused the arched foundations of the conventual church (Johnson 1974, 224–5; Herbert 1979, 330). Norman and Reader observed similar arched foundations under the cloisters (1912, 274). The internal deposits of the church were extensively disturbed by later burials and it was not possible to reconstruct the internal layout of the church from these excavations.

The area originally occupied by Greyfriars churchyard was largely cleared during the early 20th-century GPO redevelopment. Excavation of a trench in 1999 uncovered large amounts of redeposited human bone in the backfill of an 18th-century cellar (B22, Fig 76; Fig 131). The remains appeared to have been dumped there during the 1907–9 redevelopment of the site, when Greyfriars cemetery (further to the east) was cleared. These remains have been reburied on the site of the present Christ's Hospital in Horsham, Sussex.

The later medieval city defences

Historical and archaeological background

The city defences were reinstated and improved alongside the development of Greyfriars. Newgate had become well established as a gaol by the late medieval period and was notorious for its bad conditions. Despite the fact that a number of instances of relief were recorded, for example by William Walworth in 1385 who 'gave somewhat to relieve the prisoners in Newgate', the gaolers and 64 of Newgate's prisoners died of plague or fever in 1414 (Stow 1598, 66). The prison was rebuilt and improved in 1422, using funds donated by Richard Whittington (ibid).

The crenellated parapet of the wall and the appearance of the bastions are clearly visible on historic maps, for instance, on the 'Agas' map of c 1562 (Fig 74) and the Braun and Hogenberg map of 1572 (Fig 77) (Braun and Hogenberg 1572). Bastions 17–19 are visible on the latter map; Bastion 19 is depicted with a conical roof. In general, the bastions stood one storey higher than the wall and were equipped with arrow slits (Schofield 1993, 70).

The defences were regularly maintained and carefully policed to prevent any kind of unlawful encroachment, as demonstrated by this excerpt from the Letter Books of the City authorities, dating from October 1434:

Whereas every tenement situated near the walls or gates of the City should be distant from them by 16ft [4.8m] at least, according to the laws and customs of the City, the said intermediate space being the common soil of the City; and whereas Bartholomew Seman, late goldsmith, and Katharine his wife, now wife of Robert Oteley grocer, were seised of an ancient messuage called le Swan formerly belonging to Hugh Croydon, and situated within the gate of Newgate in the parish of St Sepulchre, near the common soil of the City, and the said Bartholomew had recently built a new tenement upon a portion of the soil of the ancient messuage, as set out by metres and bounds; and whereas the executurs of Richard Whittington, late mercer, similarly built a certain portion of the new gate of Newgate upon a part of the common soil lying between the said gate and the said new tenement of the said Bartholomew – in order to remove any doubt about the appropriation of the soil by the aforesaid buildings, it was proved and declared on 5 October 1435 that the said new tenement, now belonging to Robert Otterley and Katharine his wife, is built on private ground and that the 16ft [4.8m] of common soil intervenes between it and the City's wall, as is usual. (CLRO, CCPR, Lett Bk 5 Oct 1434)

Later medieval settlement, c 1300–1500 (period 5)

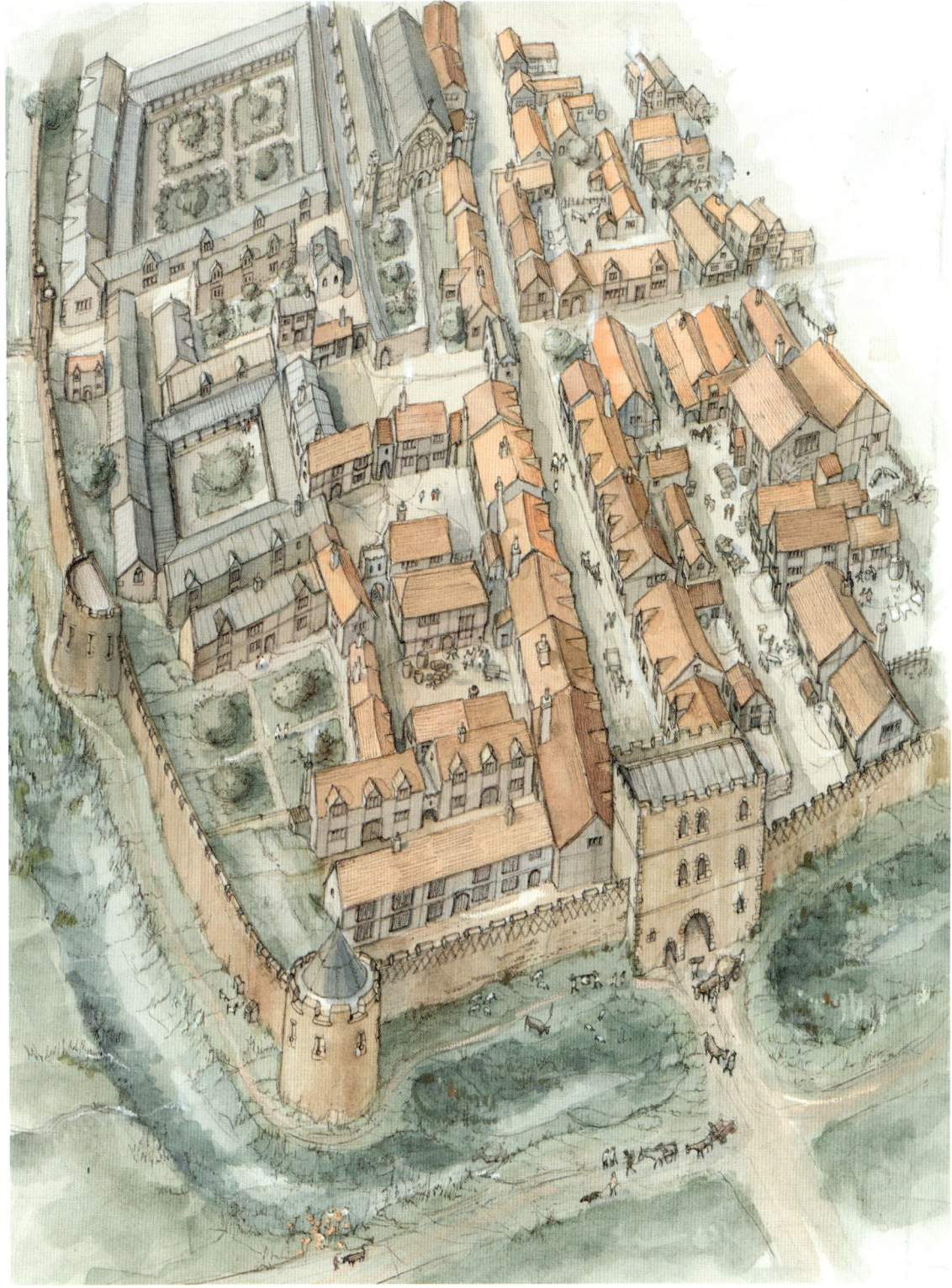

Fig 75 Reconstruction of part of the study area in the medieval period, looking down Newgate Street with Greyfriars to the left of the drawing (Judith Dobie)

The tenement 'le Swan' referred to in this record is almost certainly the messuage which lay just outside the Greyfriars precinct within the city walls.

In 1471 a foiled attack on the City by Kentish rebels inspired mayor Ralph Josselyn to order the most substantial repairs to be carried out to the city defences to date. Work began in 1477 on the ditch and wall, and this phase of rebuilding was carried out entirely in brick. This was one of the first major uses of brick on such a large scale in the City, and examples of it can still be seen around London (Schofield 1993, 129).

The defensive ditch of 1211–13 evidently began to silt up very rapidly following its construction. Stow writes that 'This ditch being originally made for the defence of the city, was also long together carefully cleansed and maintained, as need required' (1598, 50). There are records of the ditch being cleared out at different times during the 14th and 15th

Fig 76 Human bone in the backfill of an 18th-century cellar (B22), looking south

centuries, but it is not always clear if the entire circuit was recut, or whether particular sections alone were cleared. For instance, in 1354 King Edward III gave the order for the city ditch to be cleared out, as it had begun to overflow into the Tower ditch (ibid). In 1379 mayor John Philpot ordered a toll of fivepence to be collected from every householder in order to finance the cleaning of the ditch. In 1387 Richard II 'granted a toll to be taken of wares sold by water or by land, for ten years, towards repairing of the wall and cleansing of the ditch' (ibid).

Mayor Thomas Falconer arranged for the ditch to be cleared in 1414, and mayor Ralph Josselyn ordered the renovation of the entire defensive circuit in 1477, including the clearing of the ditch. Stow records that the ditch was also cleared out in 1519, 1549, 1569 and 1595 (ibid, 51).

As discussed earlier in this chapter, the city ditch has been investigated on a number of archaeological sites in London, and evidence for numerous episodes of clearing-out has been identified. It has not always been possible, however, to establish the date at which the recutting took place. Excavations at 1–6 Aldersgate Street (AES96, Fig 63) provided a good sequence through the different phases of the 13th-century ditch. The earliest phase contained waterlain silts, suggesting that it may initially have contained clean, flowing water. The ditch was recut in 1350–1400, 1400–1500 and from 1500 onwards indicating that it silted up at a fast rate. It is thought that this part of the ditch may have been particularly prone to tipping (as it was close to the road at Aldersgate) and that the authorities waged a constant war against offenders (Butler 2001, 59). A similarly dated ditch was excavated at 47–56 Houndsditch (HOU78, Fig 63), which also appears to have had a fresh water environment for the early part of its life (Maloney and Harding 1979, 351). Similar evidence has been retrieved from 1–6 Old Bailey (LUD82, Fig 63) where a number of medieval ditch recuts were recorded close to the road at Ludgate. This ditch had been cleared out during the first 100 years of its existence, but by the 14th century it had fallen into disuse and was completely clogged up (Rowsome 1984). The butt-end of the ditch at Ludgate was probably prone to tipping, like the ditch at Aldersgate. Stow described the ditch as a 'filthy channel' (1598, 50), and indeed the upper fills of the ditch from all three of the sites discussed above contained highly organic matter that was evidently stagnant (Butler 2001, 58; Maloney and Harding 1979, 351; Rowsome 1984).

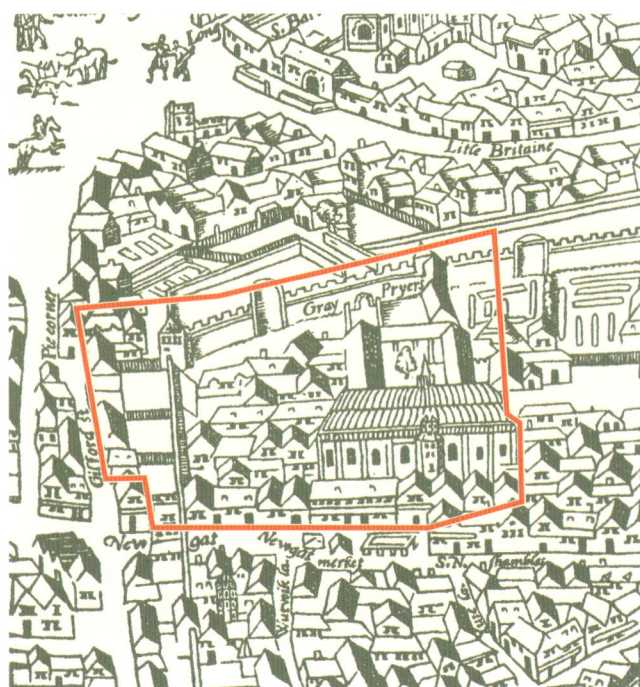

Fig 77 Detail of the study area, from Braun and Hogenberg's map of 1572 (Braun and Hogenberg 1572)

The infilling of the city ditch

Unlike other sites in the area, there was no evidence that the ditch was cleared out and recut to any great extent on the MLFC site, with a single phase of ditch apparently persisting through the medieval period. A full ditch sequence survived, but it was not possible to investigate all the episodes of its infilling due to the archaeological mitigation strategy, which only allowed a small number of 2m x 2m pile trenches to be excavated to the base of the ditch. By contrast, a large volume of the upper ditch was excavated. The majority of the finds and environmental material therefore came from the upper part of the ditch and very little information was retrieved about the primary fills (Chapter 4.3).

Detailed analysis of the north-eastern part of the ditch area has demonstrated that the second, or main, phase of infilling occurred over the period 1230–1450. Although many fills within the ditch appeared to be clearly stratified, finds dating to both the early and late medieval periods were discovered throughout the sequence. It is likely that, once the backfilling of the ditch began, it happened quickly, as at 1–6 Old Bailey (LUD82, Fig 63). Much of the material in the ditch may have been derived from both sanctioned and clandestine tipping. There may have been particular places where dumping happened, causing some sections to become infilled very quickly and others more gradually. The material within the dumps could have been brought from all over London, from both within and beyond the city walls. Some materials could have been derived from the waste of particular processes carried out in the vicinity and others from further afield. Analysis of the sequence is complicated by the presence of extensive pitting, gullies and redeposition material within the ditch. All the material in the ditch fills can be described as residual and redeposited, with any clear chronological sequence of dumping long since obscured.

CITY DITCH BACKFILLING PHASE 2 (OA17); A REVETMENT AND ASSOCIATED GULLY (S6)

The second, main phase of ditch infilling was characterised by large, organic deposits which formed as a result of standing water sedimentation, and refuse dumping activities over the period 1230–1450. There is no evidence that the city ditch was recut on any large scale in this area, but the inside edge of the ditch was reinforced with a timber revetment and an associated gully some time in the 14th or 15th century (S6, Fig 69). The revetment was traced for c 34m and the gully measured c 2.5m at its widest point, with its eastern edge lying beyond the limit of excavation. The revetment was repaired throughout the medieval period and after the disuse of the rest of the ditch. Some parts of the revetment were very substantial, with large vertical timbers, while in other areas it was flimsy. It is possible that the revetment was intended to provide further support to Bastion 19 and the city wall.

An enormous quantity of finds and environmental evidence was recovered from the ditch fills and may have come from across the settlement, providing an invaluable insight into everyday life in the City of London in the medieval period. Some of the material could have originated locally and this possibility is also explored in the following sections.

Finds, animal bones and plant remains from the medieval city ditch

Pottery

POTTERY FROM THE PHASE 2 BACKFILLING OF THE CITY DITCH

Lucy Whittingham

The secondary backfills of the medieval ditch contained 89% of the total pottery assemblage. Although the ditch fills appeared to be stratified during excavation, pottery of the same date was found throughout the sequence, indicating that the backfilling was rapid. The fills all fall within a date range of 1340–1400, although within these backfills there are subtle differences and some deposits can be dated more closely. The ditch fills contain large assemblages of well-preserved sherds, in total 4488 sherds from 1078 vessels (ENV). The most common fabric types are coarse Surrey-Hampshire border ware (CBW), London-type ware (LOND), Kingston-type ware (KING) and Mill Green ware (MG). All these fabrics produce a wide variety of vessel forms in tablewares, kitchen/food preparation vessels and serving vessels, but principally drinking vessels and jugs for serving liquid refreshments, most likely ale. Numerous types of jug are found in all four principal fabrics (Table 5) accounting for 67% of the vessels found in these groups. In addition to these four main fabric types there are also examples of imported Saintonge mottled green (SAIM) and polychrome jugs (SAIP), and the occasional Raeren and Siegburg drinking jugs (*tricterhalskrug*). A small group of distinctive drinking vessels has been identified, such as a highly decorated cup (<P57>, Fig 78) in KING, and a small drinking jug (<P55>, Fig 78) and bottle (<P56>, Fig 78), both in LOND.

The second largest category of vessels in this assemblage consists of food preparation and serving vessels, which constitute 28% of the vessels. These occur in a variety of forms: bowls, carinated bowls, spouted bowls and cauldrons in Kingston-type ware (KING), coarse Surrey-Hampshire border ware (CBW), south Hertfordshire-type greyware (SHER) and late London-type slipware (LLSL); skillets in LOND, KING and LLSL; cauldrons in CBW, KING, LOND and late medieval Hertfordshire glazed ware (LMHG); pipkins in LOND, KING and CBW; dripping dishes in CBW, LMHG and LOND; and frying pans in CBW, KING and LOND

Some vessels, such as the small dishes in coarse Surrey-Hampshire border ware (CBW) and Cheam whiteware (CHEA), probably had several functions and could have been used as drinking bowls, finger bowls or serving/condiment dishes. A small number of other vessel types have definitive functions, such as bunghole cisterns in CBW (as in Pearce and Vince 1988, fig 110.434), and a possible urinal and two money boxes, both in KING (as in Pearce and Vince 1988, fig 99.378–9).

Fig 78 Distinctive drinking vessels from the city ditch: small London-type ware (LOND) drinking jug <P55> and bottle <P56> (scale 1:4); Kingston-type ware (KING) cup <P57> (scale c 1:1)

CHRONOLOGICAL TRENDS

There are two identifiable trends visible within the phase 2 ditch backfilling, which show a different pattern of fabric association in relation to chronology. The London-type ware (LOND) and coarse Surrey-Hampshire border ware (CBW) show two trends in the proportions of each fabric type present. These reflect a chronological sequence, as indicated by the stratigraphy of the infilling of the ditch. London-type wares decrease as a percentage of the assemblage from the earlier to later fills, while CBW increases. LOND is dated 1080–1350 and CBW is dated 1270–1500, and usually there would be a natural replacement of the one by the other over a sequence of time. Unfortunately, this trend is not reflected in all the fabric types, which suggests that the infilling of the city ditch was a disorganised and random process, using material from a number of different locations around London. After the phase 1 silting of the ditch, all the pottery occurs in deposits dating from between 1340, 1350 or 1380 and 1400. The material is, therefore, discussed as one body of material and not detailed as a sequence of fabrics, which naturally replace one another over a period of time.

FABRIC AND FORM CHARACTERISTICS

Within the assemblages which date to 1340–1400, from the phase 2 filling of the ditch, there are four principal fabric components: Kingston-type (KING), coarse Surrey-Hampshire border ware (CBW), London-type ware (LOND) and Mill Green ware (MG). The primary component is LOND at 37%, followed by CBW at 26%, KING at 18% and MG at 13%. Within these four major industries there is a diverse range of vessel forms, 89% of which are drinking vessels or jugs and 28% cooking or serving vessels. Some of these particular vessel forms can be closely dated by parallel research and it is interesting to note the association of various form types within the city ditch.

Within the large assemblage of jugs there is a huge variety of forms, which can be closely dated (Table 5). Four divisions stand out within the jug forms as the principal types found: large, tulip-necked baluster jugs, highly decorated jugs, rounded jugs and drinking jugs. By far the most common of all the jugs in the assemblage are the various styles of baluster jug in London-type ware (LOND BAL) (for example <P58>, Fig 79), Mill Green ware (MG), Kingston-type ware (KING) and coarse Surrey-Hampshire border ware (CBW). All are classics of their type: the London-type ware baluster and tulip-necked baluster jugs with white slip and a splashed copper glaze on the exterior (as in Pearce et al 1985, figs 36.118 and 37.126); Kingston-type ware jugs, plain (as in Pearce and Vince 1988, fig 48.1) or with white slip-painted (KINGSL) decoration; MG jugs frequently with vertical combed lines in the slip (as in Pearce et al 1982, fig 3.3); and CBW vessels with large flared bases (as in Pearce et al 1985, fig 105.409/412). The large number of these basic and poorly decorated, but functional, vessels in London-type ware must represent the common use of a basic standard jug in the mid 14th century.

Highly decorated jugs form a smaller part of the assemblage, and include some well-preserved examples of what must have been exceptionally fine, well-thrown vessels. Four highly decorated London-type ware baluster jugs include polychrome decorated vessels with alternating sections of red and green applied vertical strips in the north French style (<P59>, Fig 80). One unusual London-type ware jug is decorated with a combination of pellets and applied vertical strips (<P60>, Fig 80). Each motif would usually be associated with either a Rouen-style (LOND ROU) jug (as in <P61>, Fig 80) or north French-style decoration (LOND NFR), but not usually both found on the same vessel. Highly decorated jugs are more common in the finer Kingston-type ware vessels,

Table 5 Estimated number of jugs in various form types from ditch deposits (OA17) dated 1340–1400

Jug form	Fabric					
	London-type ware	Mill Green ware	Kingston-type ware	Coarse Surrey-Hampshire border ware	Cheam whiteware	Saintonge wares
Early style	1					
Anthropomorphic or face			1			
Baluster	125	48	17	9		
Large baluster	2	10	1			
Cylindrical-necked baluster			1			
Flared baluster	1					
Tulip-shaped baluster	25					
Metal copy baluster			1			
Biconical	2				1	
Drinking	19		3	1		
Conical	3	18	4	2		
Highly decorated style/polychrome	4		13	2		5
North French style	3					
Rouen-style	3					
Stamped boss decoration			9			
Wheat-ear stamped boss decoration			6			
Barrel-shaped					1	
Rounded	5	2	23	11		
Large rounded	9			11		
Pear-shaped	2	1				
Small rounded	11	1	44	8		
Squat	1	7				
White slip decoration	1					
Miscellaneous	18	24	108	74		
Miniature				1		

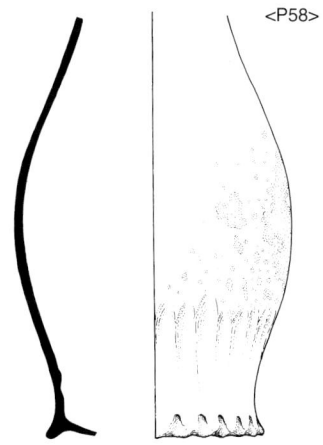

Fig 79 Baluster jug <P58> in London-type ware (LOND BAL) (scale 1:4)

which include at least seven metal copy baluster jugs with flared base and applied pellet decoration on the body (as in Pearce and Vince 1988, fig 57.33–36). At least 20 highly decorated jugs in Kingston-type ware have stamped bosses (KING SBOSS), applied vertical strip or anthropomorphic decoration (<P62>, Fig 81). Stamped bosses in the form of shields, ears of wheat, shells (<P68>, Fig 81), wheels (<P64>, Fig 81) and rosettes/flowers (<P65> and <P69>, Fig 81) or fleur-de-lis stamps are found on pear-shaped jugs (as in Pearce and Vince 1988, fig 66.86–87) and in cylindrical-necked baluster jugs (as in Pearce and Vince 1988, fig 53.15). Four examples of vessels with wheat-ear stamped bosses (KING WSBOSS) illustrate three different arrangements, one of which is a straight line of wheat-ear stamps around the upper part of the vessel (<P70>, Fig 81). Other wheat-ear decorations were spaced at larger intervals around the waist of the vessels or with an alternating arrangement of two rows of stamps. Some of these must have been exceptionally fine vessels, for example cylindrical-necked baluster jugs decorated with two shield stamps <P66> or with fleur-de-lis and shell bosses (<P67> and <P68>, Fig 81; similar examples in Pearce and Vince 1988, fig 53.14). One pear-shaped jug has anthropomorphic decoration in the form of applied arms and hands, as well as shell bosses (<P63>, Fig 81).

The third largest category of note within the jug forms are rounded jugs, both small and large. Small rounded jugs are particularly common in Kingston-type ware (KING), with smaller quantities in London-type ware (LOND) and coarse Surrey-Hampshire border ware (CBW). The fourth largest single category of jugs are conical drinking jugs (as in Pearce et al 1985, fig 66.323), found almost exclusively in LOND (<P71>, Fig 82), with three examples in KING and one in CBW. One example of a biconical jug (as in Pearce and Vince 1988, fig 122.546), is unusual in Cheam whiteware (CHEA) in this assemblage. Also associated with drinking are examples of bottles in LOND (<P56>, Fig 78). A small number of other jug forms occur in insignificant quantities. Their presence in an assemblage of this date should, however, be noted. These include conical jugs in all four principal fabrics, squat jugs in LOND and Mill Green ware (MG) and the thumbed handle from a large south Hertfordshire-type greyware (SHER) pitcher

The medieval archaeological sequence

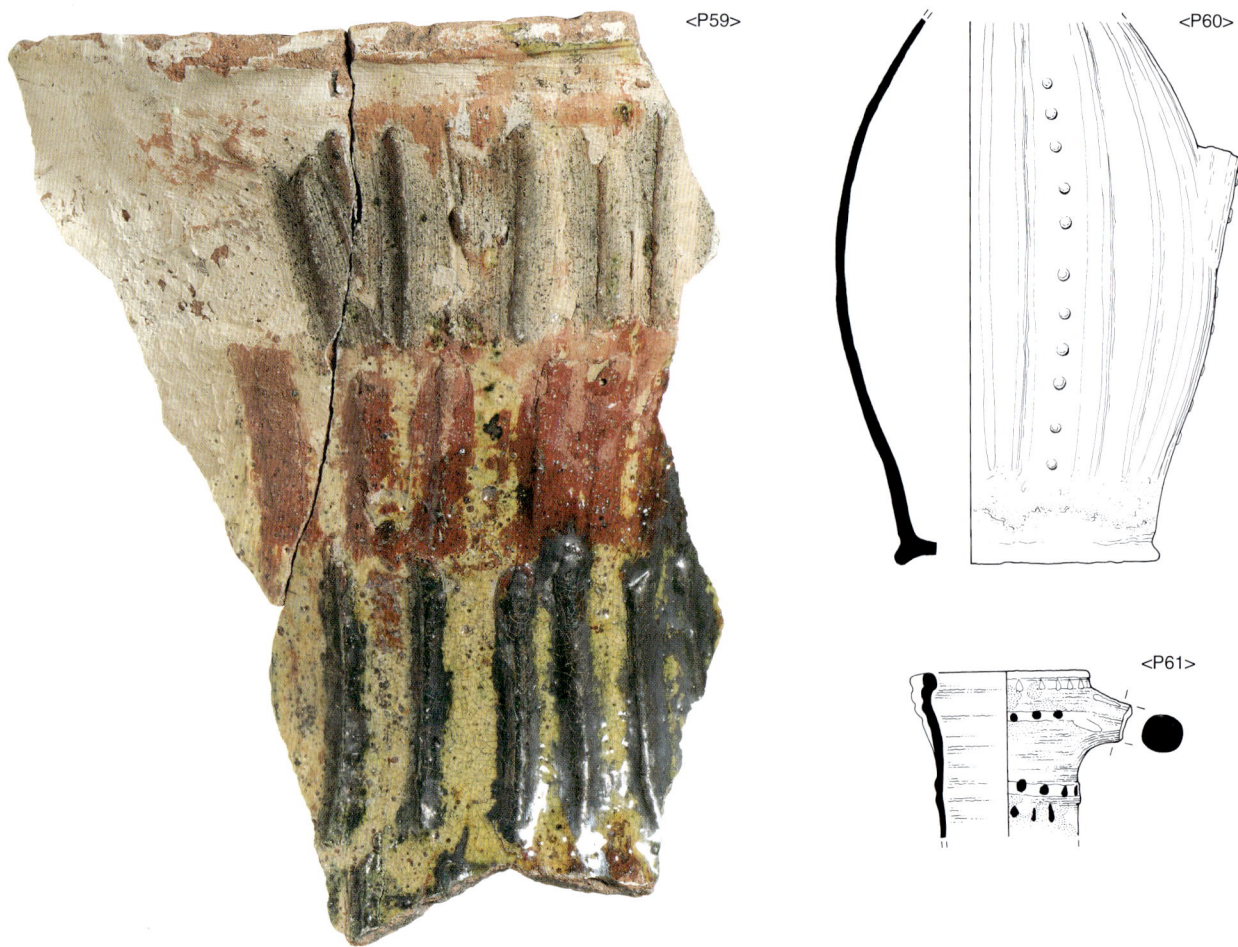

Fig 80 Highly decorated jugs from the city ditch backfill (OA17) in London-type wares (LOND): <P59> (scale c 1:1), <P60>–<P61> (scale 1:4)

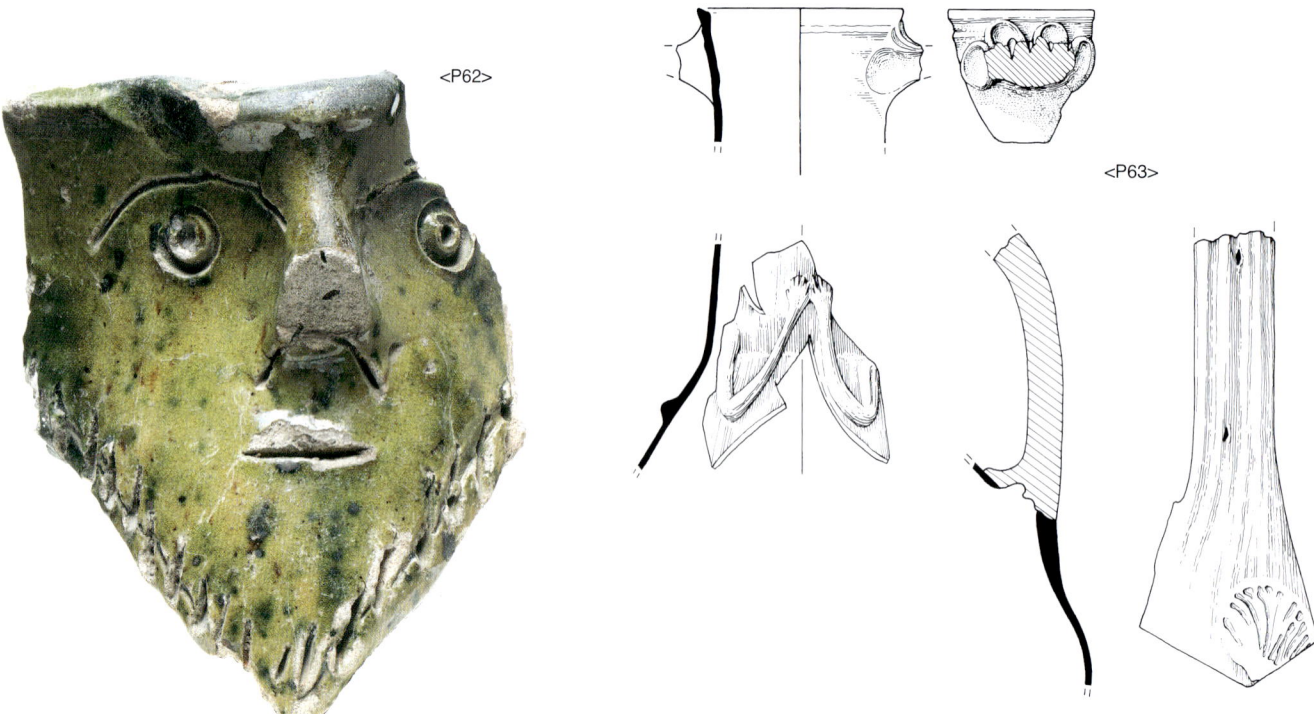

Fig 81 Highly decorated jugs from the city ditch backfill (OA17) in Kingston-type wares: with anthropomorphic decoration (KING ANT) <P62>–<P63>; with stamped bosses (KING SBOSS) <P64>–<P69>; and decorated with lines of wheat-ear stamps (KING WSBOSS) <P70> (scale c 1:1 except <P63> 1:4)

Later medieval settlement, *c* 1300–1500 (period 5)

Fig 81 (cont)

Fig 82 Conical drinking jug <P71> in London-type ware (LOND) and thumbed handle from large south Hertfordshire-type greyware (SHER) pitcher <P72> (scale 1:4)

(<P72>, Fig 82). The significance of these jug types is that they could all be contemporary, dating between 1270 and 1350. This demonstrates a demise of London-type and Kingston-type wares, overlapping with the introduction of coarse Surrey-Hampshire border ware in 1300/1350.

The cooking and serving vessels also display a diverse range of vessel forms: among them are Kingston-type ware (KING) cooking pots with flat-topped rims (as in Pearce and Vince 1988, fig 94.307) or thickened/lid seated forms (as in Pearce and Vince 1988, fig 94.296). Coarse Surrey-Hampshire border ware (CBW) cauldrons/cooking pots are the most common forms in the mid to late 13th-century assemblages. These occur with thickened bevelled rim forms (<P73> and <P74>, Fig 83; as in Pearce and Vince 1988, figs 114.465–468), flattened

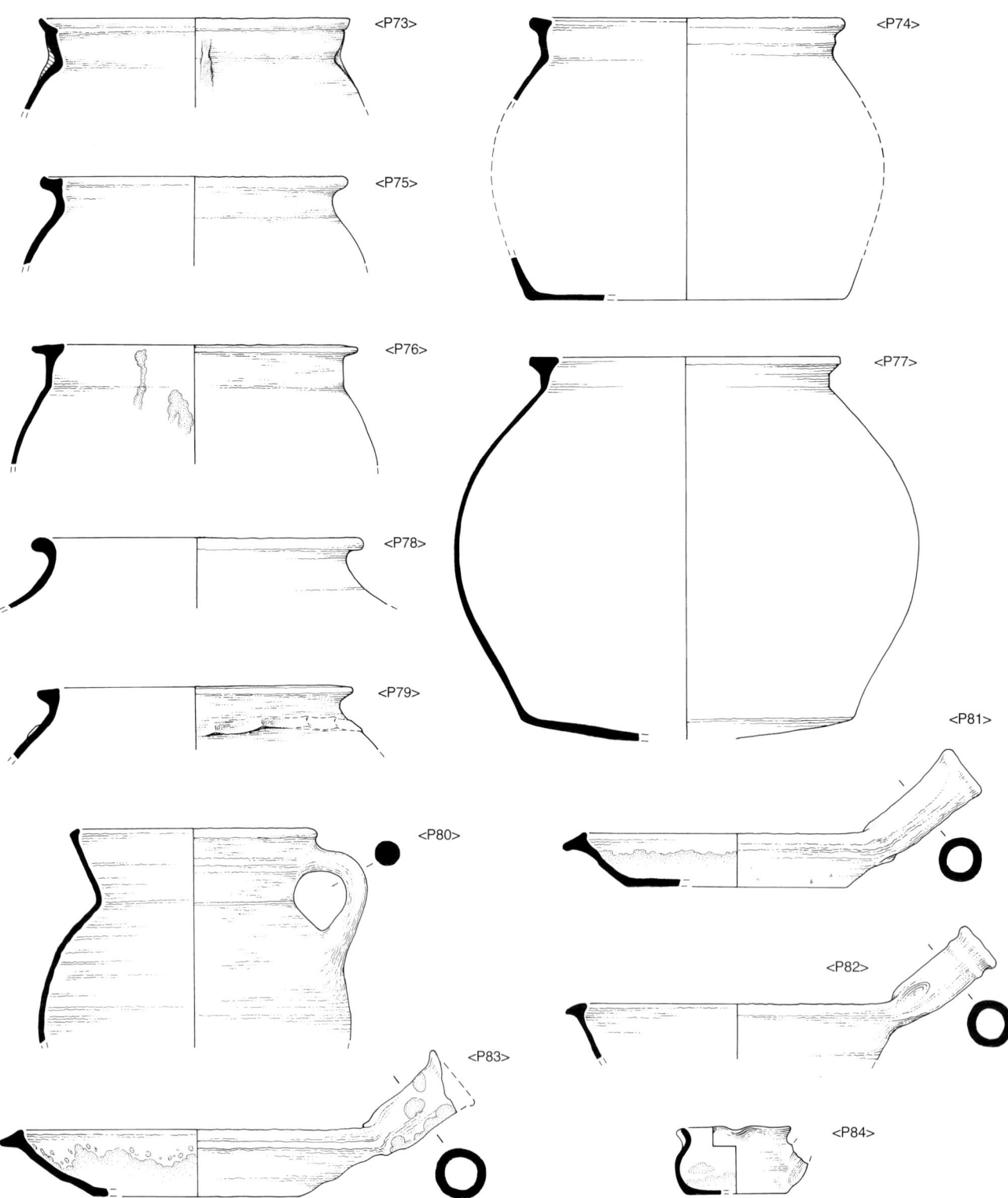

Fig 83 Cooking vessels from the backfill of the city ditch (OA17): coarse Surrey-Hampshire border ware (CBW) cauldrons/cooking pots <P73>–<P77>; south Hertfordshire-type greyware (SHER) cooking pots <P78>–<P79>; late medieval Hertfordshire glazed ware (LMHG) cooking pot <P80>; Kingston-type ware (KING) frying pan <P81>; coarse Surrey-Hampshire border ware (CBW) frying pans <P82>–<P83>; and miniature skillet <P84> in London-type ware (LOND) (scale 1:4)

lid seated rims (<P75>, Fig 83; as in Pearce and Vince 1988, fig 114.473), large plain everted rims (as in Pearce and Vince 1988, fig 116.488), and flat-topped rims (<P76> and <P77>, Fig 83; as in Pearce and Vince 1988, figs 114.469–471, 473–474). Note the lack of bifid lid-seated CBW cooking pots which are usually dated as a later form, being introduced after 1380.

Other cooking vessels include Kingston-type ware cooking pots (as in Pearce and Vince 1988, fig 94.297 and 309) and lid-seated (as in Pearce and Vince 1988, figs 94.308 and 96.321); and four types of south Hertfordshire-type greyware (SHER) cooking pots: flat-topped everted rim with applied thumbed strip around the shoulder (<P79>, Fig 83), angular rolled rims, rolled/rounded rims (<P78>, Fig 83) and squared/clubbed rims. An exceptionally well-preserved example of a double-handled late medieval Hertfordshire glazed ware (LMHG) cauldron (<P80>, Fig 83) also survives. Kingston-type ware (KING) frying pans with socketed handle and everted rim were present (<P81>, Fig 83), although coarse Surrey-Hampshire border ware (CBW) frying pans are more common (<P82> and <P83>, Fig 83). A small number of skillets/pipkins occur in CBW and London-type ware (LOND), one example of which is miniature (<P84>, Fig 83).

Other forms include small dishes/saucers in Kingston-type ware (KING) (<P85>, Fig 84; as in Pearce and Vince 1988, figs 98.357 and 364) and also as a spouted form in coarse Surrey-Hampshire border ware (CBW) (<P86>, Fig 84; similar to examples in Pearce and Vince 1988, fig 118.513). An unusual form of small London-type ware (LOND) dish was discovered (<P87>, Fig 84; as in Pearce et al 1985, fig 72.392), along with another example in Cheam whiteware (CHEA) (<P88>, Fig 84; as in Pearce and Vince 1988, fig 125.580–581). The assemblage also contained coarse Surrey-Hampshire border ware bowls, some with everted rims (<P89>–<P91>, Fig 84; as in Pearce and Vince 1988, fig 118.500–502, 504–505) and some spouted (<P92>, Fig 84).

POTTERY FROM THE REVETMENT (S6) WITHIN THE CITY DITCH

Lucy Whittingham

The assemblage of 503 sherds (293 ENV), weighing 13.4kg, from Structure 6 is similar in date and composition to that from the phase 2 backfilling of the city ditch (OA17). However, some differences are evident within certain ditch deposits. The majority of the assemblage, in Structure 6 dated 1350–1400, is similar to that from the surrounding phase 2 ditch backfill. For

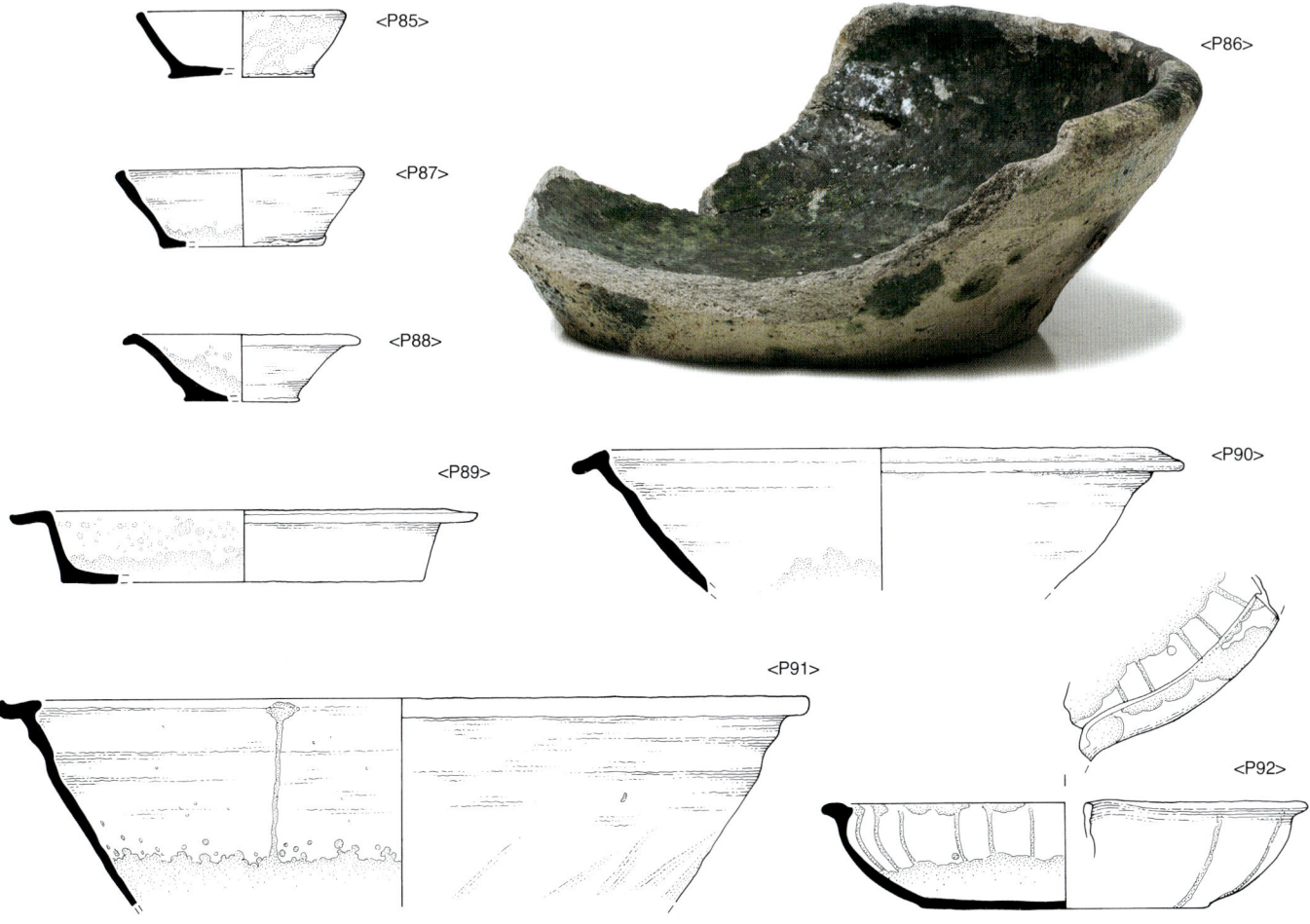

Fig 84 Kingston-type ware (KING) dish <P85>; small spouted dish <P86> in coarse Surrey-Hampshire border ware (CBW); an unusual form of small London-type ware (LOND) dish <P87> along with a similar example <P88> in Cheam whiteware (CHEA); Coarse Surrey-Hampshire border ware (CBW) bowls <P89>–<P92> (scale 1:4 except <P86> c 1:1)

instance, both assemblages primarily contain jugs of a baluster form in London-type ware (LOND), Mill Green ware (MG) and Kingston-type ware (KING). Other jug types are present in coarse Surrey-Hampshire border ware (CBW), Kingston-type ware (KING), Low Countries greyware (LCGR), Mill Green ware (MG), south Hertfordshire-type greyware (SHER) and imported Saintonge polychrome (SAIP). The Kingston vessels include highly decorated forms with applied scale decoration and rounded jugs with white slip decoration in lattice patterns. The majority of these jugs are common between 1270/1310 and 1350.

Cooking pots form a smaller part of this assemblage, in coarse Surrey-Hampshire border ware (CBW), Kingston-type ware (KING) and south Hertfordshire-type greyware (SHER); there is also a KING dish or possible lid. An imported Saintonge polychrome (SAIP) vessel might join with similar sherds in Open Area 17, indicating that the different fills within the city ditch might have come from a similar source. Alternatively, the action of cutting the revetment and gully through the underlying ditch deposits may have caused the pot fragments to be redeposited.

Another two assemblages from Structure 6 have the slightly later dates of 1380 and 1430 respectively. The later dating assemblages contain a wider variety of vessels than the earlier pottery but there are far fewer jugs present. The assemblage includes small dishes/saucers in coarse Surrey-Hampshire border ware (CBW) (<P93>, Fig 85); cauldrons, cooking pots with flat-topped and bifid rims and bunghole cisterns in CBW; and pipkins, skillets, dripping dishes and some cooking pots in Kingston-type ware (KING) and London-type ware (LOND). Jug forms include biconical drinking vessels and pitchers in late London-type ware (LLON), large rounded jugs in CBW, white slip decorated (LOND WSD) and north French style (LOND NFR) decorated jugs in London-type ware and a *tricterhalskrug* drinking jug in imported Siegburg stoneware (SIEG). These assemblages contain a mix of earlier vessel types, such as the London-type ware north French style (LOND NFR) jug dating from 1180 to 1270. However, both assemblages also contain a larger number of later vessels forms, such as CBW bifid rim cooking pots and bunghole cisterns, which became common after 1380. The assemblage in [3577] (OA17) in particular contains a greater proportion of later vessel types from after 1380. In addition there is also a barrel-shaped jug in Cheam whiteware (CHEA) (as in Pearce and Vince 1988, fig 121.536), dating from the 15th century, a Langerwehe (LANG) drinking jug and a 'Tudor green' ware (TUDG) lobed cup. The assemblages from the later fills may therefore date as late as the 14th or early 15th century.

Accessioned finds

ACCESSIONED FINDS FROM THE PHASE 2 BACKFILLING OF THE CITY DITCH (OA17)

Jackie Keily

The wet anaerobic conditions within the backfilled ditch ensured the preservation of a wide range of other types of artefact, aside from pottery vessels, including organics, such as wood and leather.

Few dress accessories were recovered from the selected ditch fills. They comprise two copper-alloy composite strap-ends, <1131> and <1151>, of a form found in London in the 14th century (Egan and Pritchard 1991, 148). The only other objects are two corroded copper-alloy pins with wound-wire heads <319>. A more interesting object, a thin gold finger-ring (<S31>, Fig 86), can be paralleled in London by finds from Bermondsey Abbey, Southwark (Geoff Egan, pers comm) and St Mary Stratford Langthorne Abbey, Newham (Keily 2004, 152). The only items associated with personal grooming are two wooden double-sided combs (<S33>, Fig 101 and <1022>). The former is the more complete and is of a form that probably dates to the 14th century. Two items associated with textile working were found: a copper-alloy thimble <1061> and a needle <414>.

Thirty-three objects were recovered that would have been used in a household and include a stone lamp, stone mortars, wooden bowls and platters, a fragment from a rotary quernstone, a wooden spatula and a small quantity of vessel glass. Fragments from up to four stone mortars were recovered (<S34>–<S36>, Fig 87). These vessels, used for grinding food, would have been associated with larger households but also had other uses such as in the preparation of medicines (Dunning 1977, 322–3).

Another object used in the preparation of foodstuffs was the fragmentary quern made from Mayen lava. The stone lamp

Fig 85 Small dish <P93> in coarse Surrey-Hampshire border ware (CBW) (scale c 1:1)

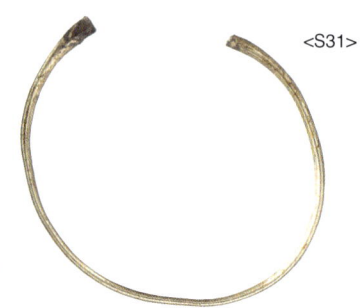

Fig 86 Gold finger-ring <S31> (scale 2:1)

(<S38>, Fig 88; Fig 165) is of interest as it is very similar to a multiple reservoir lamp from Bedern, York (Ottaway and Rogers 2002, 2858, fig 1435, no. 13475). The present example, however, is very fragmentary and it is impossible to identify its form fully. In addition, a circular stone lamp (<S39>, Fig 88; Fig 165) with a flat base was recovered, as well as the base of a glass lamp <1716>. Stone lamps have traditionally been associated with religious houses (Robins 1939, 90) and the presence of these examples and another from Structure 6 is of interest. It should be noted, however, that at York stone lamps were found in both religious and civilian areas (Ottaway and Rogers 2002, 2859–60).

The small vessel glass assemblage contained a urinal base and rim fragments from two wide-rimmed flasks or urinals, one of which may be part of the same urinal as the base fragment. Urinals were used for uroscopy – the analysis of urine to aid medical diagnosis – and the flask/urinal form is found in Europe from the 13th to the 15th centuries (Tyson 2000, 151). They are generally found in association with wealthier households, as well as religious houses and hospitals. Another glass vessel, which may have originated from a wealthy household, is a rim fragment of a stemmed drinking vessel (<S41>, Fig 89) decorated with applied opaque white trails. The vessel is probably French and of 14th- to 15th-century date.

The remains of up to 20 wooden vessels were also recovered from the selected contexts in the ditch fill and nine from other fills (for example Figs 98–100). These comprise fragmentary plain, shallow bowls and platters. The only decoration is in the form of incised grooves externally and sometimes also internally. The bowls are discussed further below, but it is of interest to note here the presence of marks either scratched or burnt into the surfaces of seven of the vessels. Although wood vessels would have been common in medieval life, it is unusual for so many to survive, due to problems of preservation. Other large groups include 18 wooden vessels from excavations at St Mary Spital, London (Thomas et al 1997, 108–9), and ten bowls and platters from Austin Friars, Leicester (Clay 1981, 139). The only other wooden object from the selected ditch fills is a small, incomplete spatula (<S54>, Fig 101). Similar examples have been recovered from elsewhere in London and it is thought they were used as cooking and possibly serving implements (Keys 1998a, 154). The ditch also produced the remains of a fine wooden spoon (<S55>, Fig 101), a lid and a vessel base or lid. The spoon is unusual as the form is more commonly found in metal.

A small number of tools were recovered from the phase 2 backfill, including two stone hones, both made from a mica-

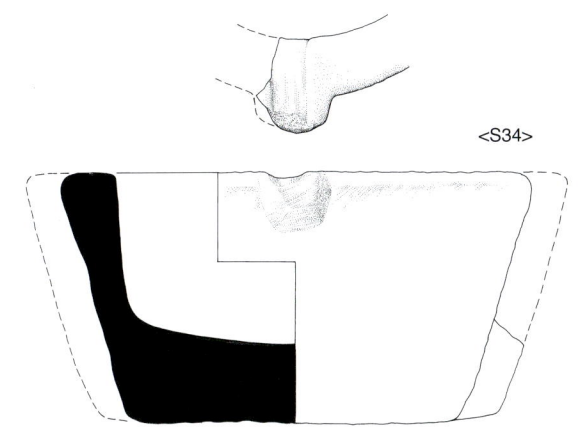

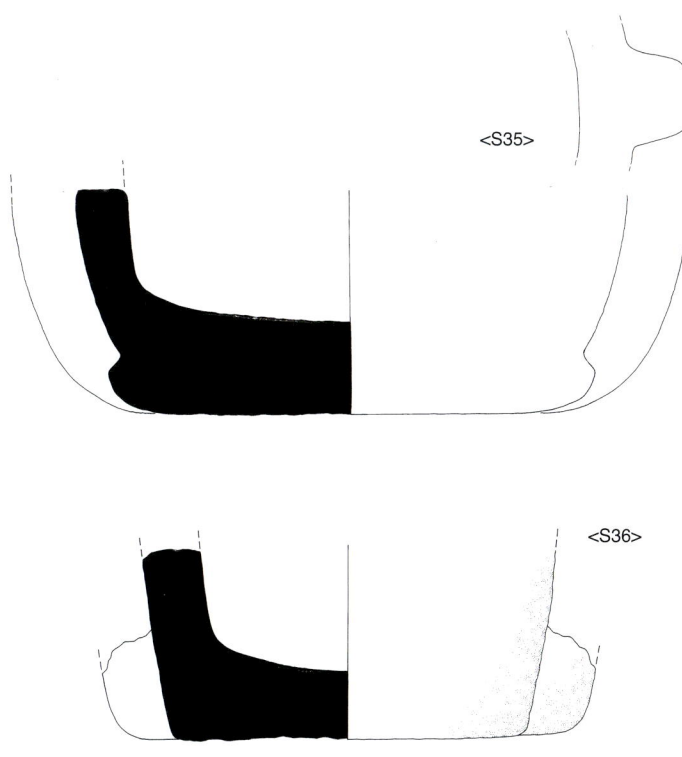

Fig 87 Fragments from stone mortars <S34>–<S36> (scale 1:4)

Fig 88 Stone lamps <S38>–<S39>
(<S39> H 95mm)

The medieval archaeological sequence

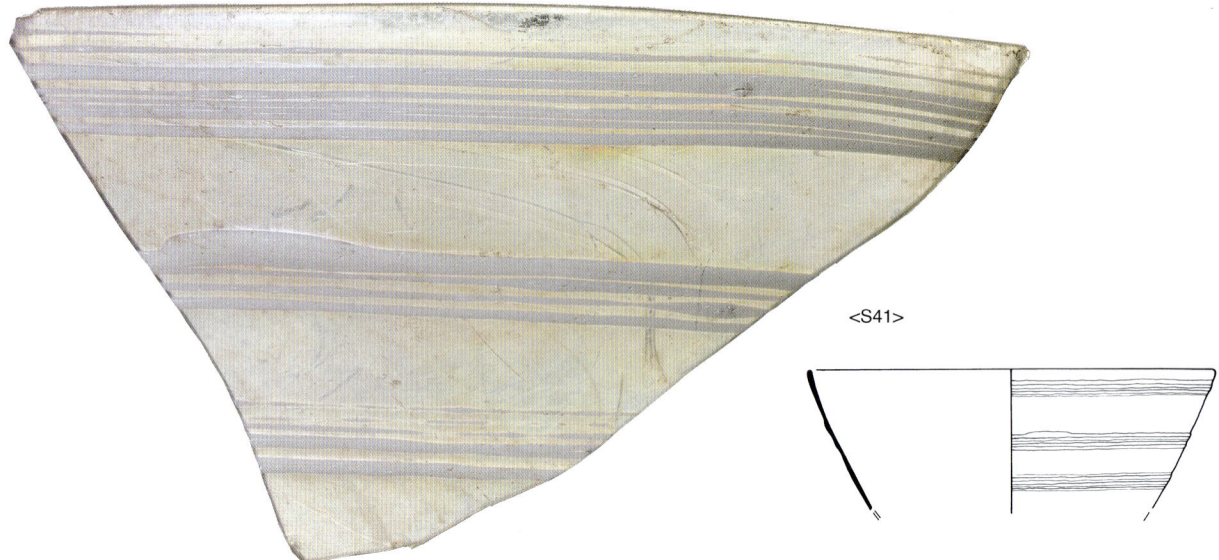

Fig 89 Colourless glass stemmed drinking vessel, decorated with applied opaque white trails <S41> (line drawing scale 1:2; detail at c 2:1)

schist. The stone was probably Norwegian ragstone, and the tools would have been used in the manufacture and sharpening of knives and other bladed implements. No knives were recovered from the selected contexts and only three were present in the non-selected groups: a whittle tang knife with a wooden handle <1103>; a scale tang knife with a wooden handle, copper-alloy fittings and a maker's mark (<S60>, Fig 90); and a blade fragment with a maker's mark (<S59>, Fig 90). Two

Fig 90 Tools from the city ditch backfill (OA17): one arm of small iron shears <S57> (scale 1:1); antler rake or tool <S58> (scale 1:2); iron knife blade fragment with a maker's mark <S59> (scale 1:1, detail c 4:1); iron scale tang knife with wooden handle and copper-alloy fittings <S60> (scale 1:1) and detail of maker's mark on blade (scale c 4:1)

bone handles may have come from whittle-tanged knives or other implements: one is quite large with a circular cross-section <1007>, while the other is smaller and has an elliptical cross-section <354>. One arm of a small shears (<S57>, Fig 90) was recovered and its small size may indicate that it was a domestic implement, used for cutting threads or possibly hair. The final tool from the selected contexts is a wooden rectangular blade or spade-type head, with the remains of a round-sectioned handle (<S56>, Fig 101). It may have been used in butter or cheese making or for some other function, but as yet, no parallels have been found for it. An antler rake or tool (<S58>, Fig 90) from the non-selected ditch contexts may be a residual earlier find, possibly Roman. The only items associated with religion and literacy from the ditch fills (OA17) were a copper-alloy tomb inscription letter of late 13th- to 14th-century date (<S63>, Fig 118) and two goose radii, possibly used as pens (<S65>–<S66>, Fig 119).

Little evidence for industrial activity was recovered from the ditch fills. A small number of red deer antler offcuts of uncertain date were found, <1757> and <1191>, amounting to 338g in weight. A fragment of bone bead-making waste <341> may be evidence for the production of rosary beads, which may be significant due to the proximity to Greyfriars. The only items providing evidence of metalworking are a small piece of ceramic crucible with copper-alloy working residues <1513>, a cut fragment of copper-alloy sheet waste <348> and three narrow D-sectioned strips <1503> – waste from bar mount manufacture. A small fragment of chalk <1488> with multiple linear cut marks may have been used as a stand or support in a manufacturing process. Fragments of wire were also recovered, some of which may be waste offcuts. One fragment <1138> changes from a circular section to a square section along its length and also tapers: this may be production waste. There was also evidence for the production of cast copper-alloy vessels in the form of 386g of ceramic mould fragments. Most of the fragments come from [2877] and include rim fragments and pieces that may come from vessel legs or possibly a spout. Another context [3128] produced part of a composite mould for a candlestick with a ring stem <1476>. The surviving fragment is for the ring and part of the stem; an example of this type of candlestick dating to the 15th century is illustrated in the London Museum medieval catalogue (Ward-Perkins 1940, 178, fig 55, no. 2). This may be some of the earliest evidence for the casting of candlesticks in London (Geoff Egan, pers comm). A much larger assemblage of bell and vessel casting waste was recovered from Baltic House (Egan 2002, 48–61), dating to c 1350–1500 or later. It is not possible to identify the source foundry for the present material and whether or not it was local to the ditch.

A series of small and flimsy fittings was recovered, including a copper-alloy sheet strip mount <1132>, a corroded copper-alloy split-pin or looped staple <349> and a small section of an iron strip mount <1541>. The latter has traces of tinning, a feature found on mounts from the late 13th century onwards (Brenan 1998, 64). The non-selected groups yielded part of a fine, moulded copper-alloy mount with silver plating

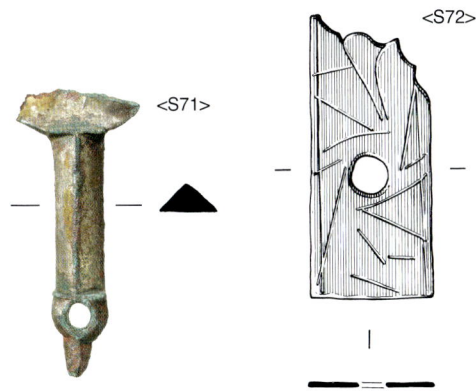

Fig 91 Moulded silver-plated copper-alloy mount <S71> and copper-alloy mount with engraved decoration <S72> (scale 1:1)

(<S71>, Fig 91), probably from a casket; a copper-alloy lobed sheet mount with central rivet <1735>; and a fragmentary copper-alloy strip mount with engraved decoration (<S72>, Fig 91). Other finds included a bone toggle <1744> made from a pig metapodial with a central hole, part of a small wooden pin <1417> and fragmentary wooden staves <1412> and <1729>, the latter presumably from stave-built vessels.

ACCESSIONED FINDS FROM THE REVETMENT (S6) WITHIN THE CITY DITCH

Jackie Keily

A large number of other finds also came from the revetment (S6) and gully. A total of 14 dress accessories were recovered from selected deposits in Structure 6, including seven copper-alloy pins. Six of the latter are small wire pins with wound wire heads <1085> and <1124>, but one has a hollow globular head formed from two sheet hemispheres <1109>. Other objects comprise a small bead in opaque green glass <1059>, two lacechapes <1013> and <1089> and the remains of only four buckles. The latter comprise two small circular iron shoe buckles <1501> and <1502>, dating to the late 14th to 15th centuries, a plain functional iron buckle frame <1536> and a cast copper-alloy buckle pin with a ridged grip <1035>, which was a form common in London and elsewhere in the medieval period (for example, Egan and Pritchard 1991, 115; Ottaway and Rogers 2002, 2895–6).

One of the finds was probably a cosmetic implement: it has a copper-alloy shaft with one pointed end, probably for use as a toothpick, and the other end flattened to form an incomplete spatula or scoop, probably for use as an earscoop (<S32>, Fig 92). Similar double-ended implements are known from London and elsewhere, largely from 14th- and 15th-century deposits (for example, Margeson 1993, 63–4; Egan and Pritchard 1991, 379; Ottaway and Rogers 2002, 2932). The sharp point on this example may indicate that it had seen little use by the time it was discarded or lost.

Five items that can be described as household utensils were recovered: a stone lamp (<S37>, Fig 93; Fig 165), a glass goblet lid (<S40>, Fig 93), a copper-alloy chafing dish handle

The medieval archaeological sequence

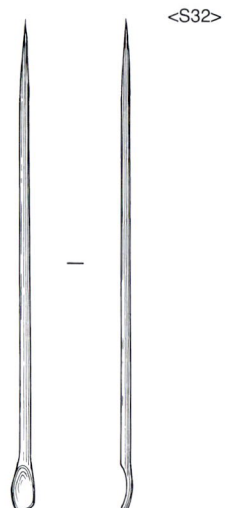

Fig 92 Copper-alloy cosmetic tool with spatula/scoop end and pointed end <S32> (scale 1:1)

(<S42>, Fig 93), the base or lid of a small wood vessel <1405> and a glass cup with vertical ribbing <1161>. Although this is a relatively small number, these types of artefacts would indicate a degree of wealth and status such as might be found in a religious household. The stone lamp is roughly square with a rounded flat base: it is similar in form to one found at Milk Street in the city (Pritchard 1991, 160, fig 3.44, no. 149) in a late 11th- to early 12th-century deposit, and is therefore probably a residual find. The glass lid is a relatively rare form: it is in colourless glass with colourless and blue glass trails and is probably a Venetian or French import dating to the 13th to 14th centuries (Tyson 2000, 70). Only

two examples in colourless glass with blue trails are known, both from London: one from St Swithin's Lane and the other from Threadneedle Street (ibid). Lids for goblets were high status objects: Tyson has described the lidded cup as 'a vessel of special distinction' (ibid, 26) as the lid enhanced the already high status of the goblet. Although the form may have been inspired by the religious chalice with lid, there is nothing to suggest that these are particularly religious vessels. They should be regarded rather as high status vessels which would have been associated with wealthy households, including religious ones, although it is interesting to note that a lid in opaque white glass was found during excavations at St Mary Stratford Langthorne Abbey, Newham (Keily and Shepherd 2004, 149 no. <G71>). The copper-alloy handle <S42> may be late medieval to early post-medieval in date and would have been used on a chafing dish. Two other household objects were recovered from non-selected groups in Structure 6, a stone mortar <356> and a small wood spatula <1463>.

The only tools recovered from Structure 6 were a stone hone, for sharpening and working bladed implements, and the remains of four knives, three whittle-tang and one scale tang. Two have the remains of wooden handles, one of which <1144> also has a maker's mark on the blade. One of the knives <1525> is quite large, probably part of a sword or dagger. The only other evidence for weaponry is part of a dagger hilt (<S61>, Fig 94). A small copper-alloy cap or ferrule (<S70>, Fig 94) probably comes from a knife, as does another ferrule <1181>. Two further iron knives came from non-selected contexts in Structure 6, one with a wood scale tang handle and copper-alloy fittings <350>. Three items of horse equipment were recovered: two fragmentary horseshoes <1141> and <1140> and a spur rowel (<S62>, Fig 94). The

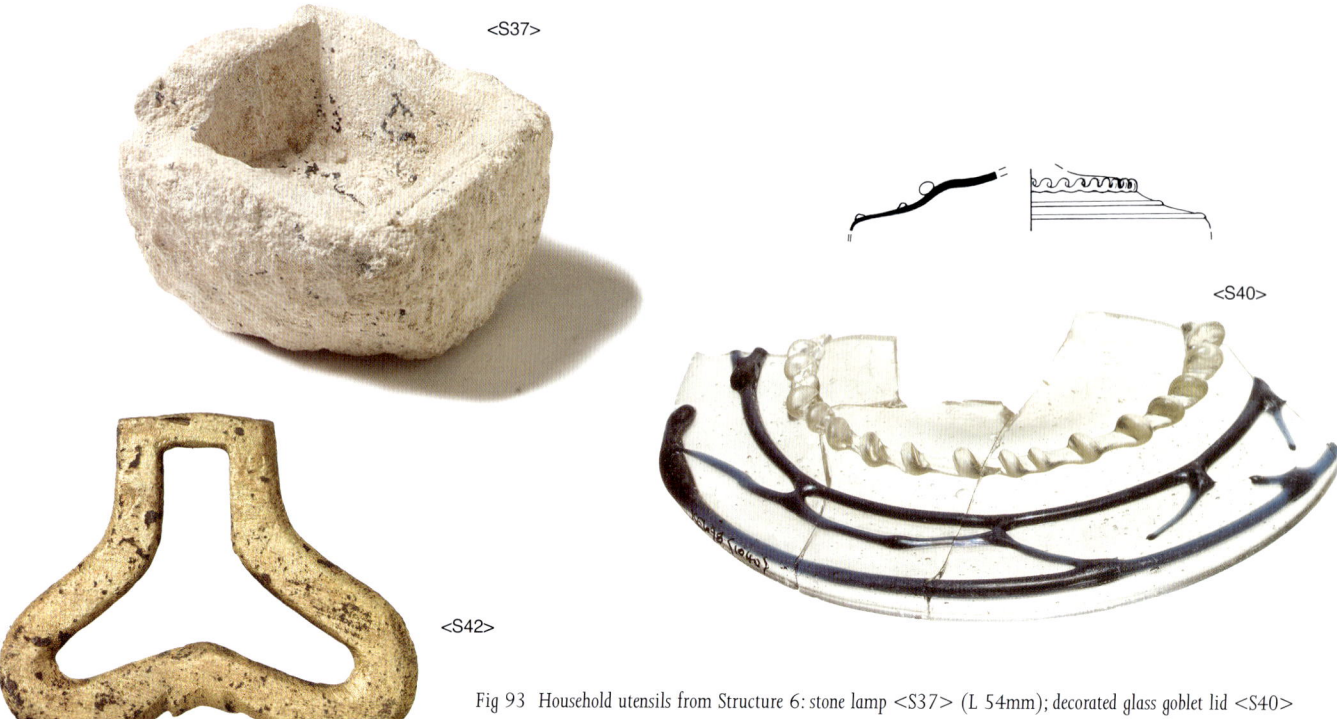

Fig 93 Household utensils from Structure 6: stone lamp <S37> (L 54mm); decorated glass goblet lid <S40> (line drawing scale 1:2); copper-alloy chafing dish handle <S42> (scale 1:1)

Later medieval settlement, c 1300–1500 (period 5)

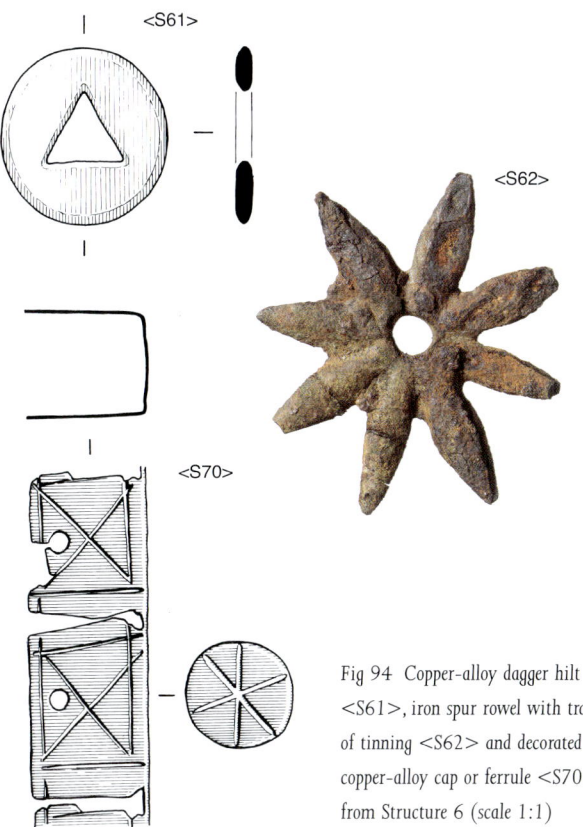

Fig 94 Copper-alloy dagger hilt <S61>, iron spur rowel with traces of tinning <S62> and decorated copper-alloy cap or ferrule <S70>, from Structure 6 (scale 1:1)

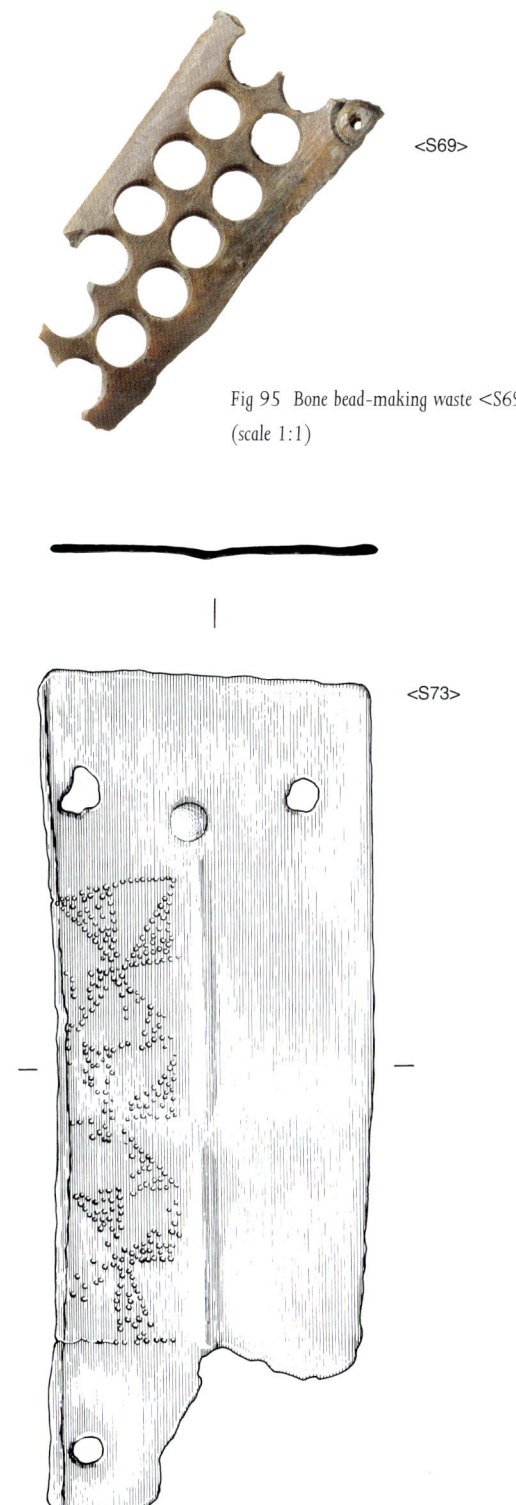

Fig 95 Bone bead-making waste <S69> (scale 1:1)

Fig 96 Fragment of tinned sheet iron with punched dot decoration and a rivet hole in each corner <S73> (scale 1:1)

horseshoes both probably date to the 14th to 15th centuries. The spur rowel has eight points, a central hole and traces of tinning.

Evidence for craft and industry was limited. Bone working is represented by a small number of offcuts (a fragment each of pig, cattle, sheep/goat and dog) and also waste from bead-making (<S69>, Fig 95 and <1770>). The latter may be from the production of rosary beads, given the proximity of the Greyfriars religious house. There was little evidence for metalworking: a copper-alloy rod, partly hammered flat <1088>, a cut fragment of sheet lead <1156> and a part-made iron object, possibly a horseshoe or fitting <1099>. The lead sheet may be waste from the manufacture of objects or from building work: lead sheet fittings were used on the roofs of high status buildings, such as churches and palaces – for example, Denny Abbey (Goodall et al 1980, 261, fig 55, no. 3) and Kennington Palace (Dawson 1976, 88, fig 15, nos 13–16). However, no identifiable lead-alloy structural fittings were recovered from the fills of the revetment. Two small fragments of ceramic mould also came from Structure 6. These, <1731> and <1113>, came from the production of copper-alloy cast vessels, although the remains are too small to identify the vessel forms.

Other finds from Structure 6 included fragments of copper-alloy wire <1086>, a plain incomplete wood peg <1406> and a small bone peg <1074>. One of the pieces of copper-alloy wire has a hooked end similar to that on a covered wire headdress frame from London (Egan and Pritchard, 1991, 295, fig 195, no. 1461). Also from Structure 6, but from a non-selected context, is a fragment of tinned sheet iron with punched dot decoration and a rivet hole in each corner (<S73>, Fig 96). Its function is uncertain but it appears to be too thin for use in armour.

An object that may have religious associations is a bone tuning peg (<S68>, Fig 97) for use with a stringed instrument; another contemporary tuning peg (<S67>, Fig 97) was found in the backfill of a 17th-century cellar (B27, Chapter 5.3).

Fig 97 Bone tuning pegs <S67>–<S68> (scale 1:1)

Wooden objects from the phase 2 backfilling of the city ditch (OA17) and the revetment (S6) within the ditch

Jackie Keily

The remains of up to 20 lathe-turned wooden vessels were recovered from the contexts selected for further study, with fragmentary remains of up to a further nine from the non-selected. In addition, a number of small stave fragments were also recovered which may have come from coopered vessels, such as buckets. A number of other implements were also found: a spoon, a tool, two combs, two spatulas, two lids and a possible vessel base. Wooden vessels and implements would have been extremely common during the medieval period but as they are only preserved in waterlogged, anaerobic conditions they frequently do not survive. The report on the medieval finds from Norwich (Margeson 1993, 73) highlights this point: only a relatively limited assemblage of one bowl, some casks, a peg, a spoon and a wooden container survived there. In London, many medieval excavations have failed to produce wooden artefacts while others, most notably those on the Thames waterfront, produce many (Keys 1998b, 196). Of particular note in recent years is a group of 18 wooden vessels recovered from a pit at St Mary Spital (Thomas et al 1997, 108–9) and thought to be associated with the hospital there.

TURNED BOWLS/PLATTERS

Of the 21 turned vessels that were studied in further detail, 13 were identified as bowls (although many of these are quite shallow), four as platters, three as bowl/platters and one as a small bowl or dish (for example <S43>–<S45>, <S47> and <S51>, Fig 98). All are face-turned, with the grain of the wood perpendicular to the axis of rotation during turning, a method used for making small to large bowls (Morris 2000, 2122). Seven of the vessels have had their wood species identified, comprising one alder (cf *Alnus glutinosa*) and six ash (*Fraxinus excelsior*). This reflects other medieval wood assemblages, where ash, an easily worked wood with a good grain pattern, becomes increasingly dominant from the 11th century on (Keys 1998b, 196; Morris 2000, 2196). Alder was the next most popular wood type used for turning but declines in use towards the later medieval period. The example in alder from the present site is a very thin vessel, perhaps suggesting that it was used at table rather than in food preparation and storage.

Where the rims survive, most (13) are plain and rounded, although two bowls, two platters, one bowl/platter and the bowl/dish had flattened, everted rims and one of the platters has an upright, squared rim. Overall the rim diameters range from 120mm to 260mm. It has been established that 80% of all surviving medieval and post-medieval bowls are between 90mm and 260mm in diameter (Morris 1993, 95) and were largely used for eating and drinking, with the larger examples

Fig 98 Wooden platters and bowls <S43>–<S45>, <S47> and <S51> (<S47> rim Diam c 160–170mm)

reserved for food preparation and presentation. The vessels from the MLFC site can be grouped as those with diameters of 120–130mm, which may have been used as drinking vessels, and those that are wider and were more likely to have been used for preparing, serving and eating from. Three vessels, bowl <1211>, bowl/dish <1725> and bowl/platter <S52> (Fig 100), may therefore be described as possible drinking vessels due to their size. Straight-sided or globular cups or beakers, as found in wood from earlier periods and in glass in the medieval period, appear to be unknown in wood in the later medieval period (Morris 2000, 2182) and it appears from manuscript and excavated evidence that small rounded bowls were used as 'cups' (ibid, 2182–4 and figs 1034–5). However, as all three also have flat everted rims it may be more likely that they were used as small containers in the kitchen or at table. Of the 14 remaining turned vessels with rims surviving, one has a diameter of 150–160mm, nine of 170–200mm, and four of 210–260mm, with both bowls and platters occurring in both of the larger sizes. Most of the bowls appear to be quite shallow but since all are fragmentary and most have become distorted during burial this may not be their true shape. It is interesting, however, to note that many of the complete examples illustrated from London (Keys 1998b, 200–10) are also quite shallow. Shallow bowls and platters must have been widely used for preparing and serving food but only one of the vessels (<S50>, Fig 99), a flat platter, has cut marks on its internal surface, indicating that it was used for cutting food on. Dark staining or blackening on the internal surface of a number of the bowls was also noted. This is likely to be the result of an accumulation of grease and stains and has been noted on vessels from Norwich, London and York (Morris 1993, 95; Keys 1998b, 198; Morris 2000, 2185).

The only visible forms of decoration on any of the vessels are lathe-turned grooves found externally on seven vessels and internally on two. One bowl (<S44>, Fig 99) has a row of fine 'stitch' holes near the rim edge, regularly spaced c 25mm apart. These appear to have been for the attachment of a rim, possibly of silver, although no staining or corrosion survives to indicate the material used. This bowl and a number of the others have a noticeably good grain pattern, which may also have been viewed as a form of decoration (Morris 2000, 2185). Bowl <S44> is also notable for having what appears to be a series of repair holes in the sides and base. These holes are round and much larger than the 'stitch' holes in the rim (4mm as opposed to 1mm). It is likely that they were intended for metal staples, although as no metal corrosion is visible around any of the holes it is also possible that the repairs were never completed. Three bowls from London also showed signs of repair, two with staples and the third with sewing, possibly with thin metal wire (Keys 1998b, 197).

Six of the vessels from Open Area 17 have marks. Some of these marks are burnt or branded into the surface and take the form of an equal-armed cross pattée (<S43>, Fig 100), an incomplete semicircle (<S45>, Fig 100), an S-shaped mark burnt into the exterior surface of the base and also a faint second 'S' just above the base on the inside (<S48>, Fig 100)

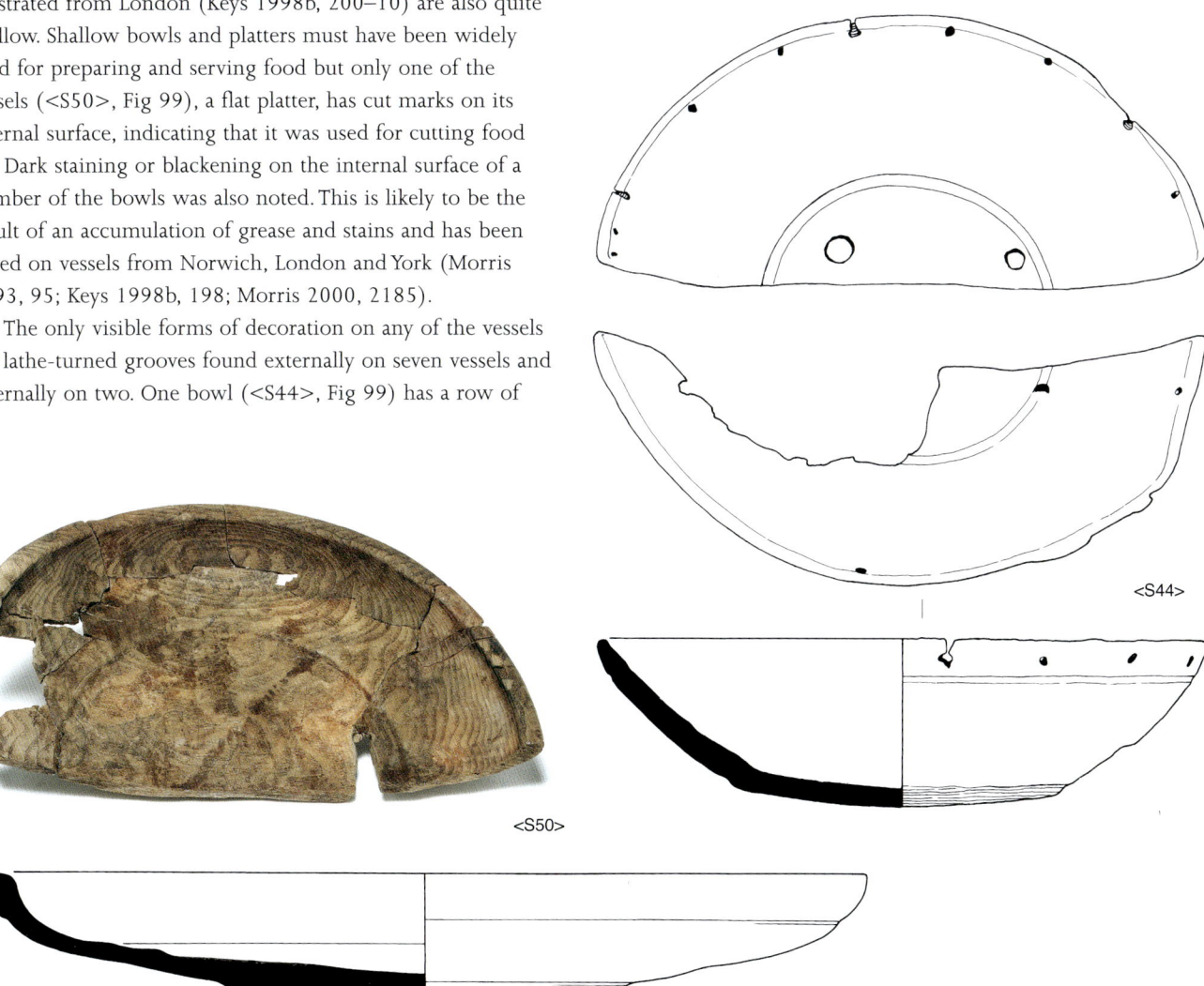

Fig 99 Flat wooden platter with cut marks on internal surface <S50> (line drawing scale 1:2), and distorted wooden bowl <S44> with series of repair holes in sides and base and 'stitch' holes near rim edge (scale 1:2)

and the imprint of a miniature human footprint (<S46>, Fig 100). The remaining three have cut or scratched marks: a linear 'M' on a rim (<S52>, Fig 100), a triangle formed of three crossing lines on the internal base (<S53>) and a shallow 'X' on an external surface (<S49>, Fig 100). The function of these marks is uncertain. Of the vessels from London discussed in *The medieval household* (Egan 1998), five were marked – three branded and two with incised lines (Keys 1998b, 197). Two of the branded vessels come from a 13th-century pit at Milk Street and have an S-like mark on their bases. The third, from 1–6 Old Bailey (LUD82, Fig 63), has a cross branded into its base and comes from a late 13th- or mid 14th-century deposit. The incised marks take the form of crosses.

COOPERED VESSELS

Two stave fragments, <1412> and <1729>, have no diagnostic features surviving, but may have come from small coopered vessels, such as buckets. A flat disc <1405>, possibly a small vessel base or lid, may also come from a coopered vessel.

WOODEN IMPLEMENTS

Wooden implements are on the whole less commonly found than vessels, although they must have been a cheap and easy alternative to metal or bone. Spoons were probably the main medieval eating and cooking utensil after the knife (Morris and Margeson 1993, 136). Given the frequency with which wooden spoons are used even today in the cooking and serving of food, their scarcity in the archaeological record must be due to poor preservation. The single spoon (<S55>, Fig 101) from the MLFC site is of particular interest as it is quite a finely made piece. Although most of the bowl is missing, it can be surmised from the remaining upper portion that it was probably oval or leaf-shaped. The interesting feature of this spoon, however, is that the tapering, slender handle is complete and includes a small conical knop terminal, reminiscent of those found on medieval metal

Fig 100 Wooden vessels with marks: bowl with cross burnt into base <S43>; bowl with burnt mark on external surface <S45>; platter or dish with 'X' on an external surface <S49>; bowl with the imprint of a miniature human footprint <S46>; bowl with S-shaped mark <S48>; and bowl or platter with 'M' scratched on rim <S52> (line drawings scale 2:1, photographs scale c 1:1 except footprint 2:1)

spoons (for example, Egan 1998, 244–52; Ruempol and van Dongen 1991, 51 and 93–4). The spoon would appear to have been made by a specialist craftworker and to have been for use as a table implement. Another finely carved spoon was found in 12th-/13th-century contexts at Coppergate, York (Morris 2000, 2267, fig 1101, no. 8899), but only the bowl survives without the handle. Examples of similar wooden spoons with knops are known from the Continent, including a 14th-century example from the Netherlands (Ruempol and van Dongen 1991, 50) and another dating to c 1500 (ibid, 94).

A small wooden spatula (<S54>, Fig 101) was also recovered from medieval deposits. This is a simple object tapering from the handle and flaring out towards the head, most of which is missing. This object is paralleled by others in London (Keys 1998a, 154, nos 430–4) and may have been used in food preparation and serving.

One of the most interesting and, at present, most enigmatic objects from the MLFC site is what appears to be the head of a wooden tool or utensil (<S56>, Fig 101). The object consists of a flat rectangular blade- or paddle-like head with the remains of a possible handle at one end and indications of wear at the other. The handle and head are carved in one piece. The upper corners of the head have been cut away where the handle meets the head, giving two concave edges at the top, and both the upper and lower surfaces of the blade have scratches from use. This may be part of a large spatula-type tool used, for example, in butter or cheese making or as a bread peel. The latter may, however, be ruled out, as there are no signs of wear or of burning on the underside as would be expected from a utensil used for placing and removing bread from an oven (Morris 2000, 2279–80; Damian Goodburn, pers comm).

Two other flat discs, <1765> and <1766>, are of interest. The former has a round central hole and is probably a pot-lid, paralleled by finds from York (Morris 2000, 2263, fig 1098). The latter disc <1766> has a series of small, randomly spaced

Fig 101 Wooden comb <S33> and wooden implements: spatula <S54>, spoon <S55> and tool <S56> (scale c 1:1 except <S56> c 1:2)

holes, not all of which completely pierce the wood. The function of this item is unknown but the holes may have formed either a source of ventilation for the contents of a container, if the disc was used as a lid, or a strainer, if the disc was used as a base. The random nature of the holes would indicate that they are a later addition to the disc.

The remaining wooden objects comprise two fragmentary double-sided combs (<S33>, Fig 101 and <1022>), as well as fragments of possible pins and pegs, from both selected and non-selected groups.

Leather finds from the phase 2 backfilling of the city ditch (OA17) and the revetment (S6) within the ditch

Jackie Keily

The waterlogged conditions in the ditch allowed a very high level of survival of leather artefacts. Due to the restrictions mentioned earlier, however, only a small portion of the leather could be studied in detail for this report. Some 24 accessioned shoes were looked at in more detail, as well as 135 strap fragments, c 24 other pieces and all 19 knife sheaths. Twenty-seven boxes of bulk material, containing many fragmentary shoes, were not available for detailed study and the notes made at the time of the assessment (Alison Nailer, MoLSS) were used. It is therefore impossible for the purposes of this report to identify the total number of shoes, waste, and so forth that came from this site.

The assemblage from the ditch fills is fairly typical for its date, consisting largely of shoes, with some waste material and a smaller quantity of sheaths and other forms. There are, however, two interesting features. Firstly, the footwear is of poor quality, both in terms of completeness and condition; most of the shoes are very fragmentary and many have been repaired or have themselves been cut up for use in the repair of other shoes. Secondly, a large number of strap fragments were recovered amounting to c 135 fragments.

FOOTWEAR

The majority of the shoe assemblage was recovered from ditch fills that produced pottery dated to c 1340–1450. All are turnshoes, the standard method of manufacturing medieval footwear until the middle of the 15th century (Grew and de Neergaard 2001, 47). The poor condition of many of the shoes and boots has affected the identification of forms. This is particularly the case with the uppers, which tend to be very fragmentary or are often missing completely. Although the full range of shoe sizes from child to large adult is present, little can be inferred about the surrounding population due to the lack of complete shoes or even complete soles. It is also interesting to note that virtually all the ditch fills produced waste material from both the manufacture and repair of shoes. Where shoe measurements are given these are pre-conservation. The vast majority of the leather came from ditch fills dating to the 14th century and mostly to the mid to late 14th century.

POINTED AND ROUNDED TOES

Footwear with both pointed and rounded toes is present throughout the assemblage, with pointed toes appearing to be rather more common. Few examples of the very elongated, sharply pointed 'poulaine' style that was common in the later 14th century were found, even from later 14th- and 15th-century deposits. Only one example, <1363>, was found =with moss stuffing in the toe and here the point of the toe is torn off and missing, making it impossible to identify how pointed it was. Moss stuffing was often used to pack pointed toe ends to keep them stiff and maintain their form (Eddy 2001, 88–9). As has already been shown, however (Grew and de Neergaard 2001, 115–17; Quita Mould, pers comm), the extremely pointed examples of the 'poulaine' shoe were probably more the exception rather than the rule, both in London and in the rest of the country. Extremely pointed shoes would not have been very practical and are thought to be associated with the upper levels of society (Grew and de Neergaard 2001, 29). This, and the overall rather plain nature of the footwear from the present site, combined with the high degree of reuse and repair, indicates that the assemblage is of a functional nature and did not originate among the higher echelons of society.

ANKLE BOOTS

Relatively few ankle boots were recorded from this assemblage, but this is probably as much due to the poor condition of the surviving uppers as it is to any style or fashion preference. Evidence for both toggle-fastened and side-laced boots was found. The earliest is a fragment of boot, <1372>, with a thong woven through three double slots and probably dating to the late 12th or 13th century. Other fills produced fragments from toggle-fastened boots but here the toggles were not threaded through multiple slots but simply laced through a row of single holes at the front. Where the toggles are complete, they have rolled ends (for example, <1300> and <1301>). A number of these pieces with fastening details have been purposefully cut from their boots, presumably so that the remainder of the boot could be reused. Another toggle-fastened boot, <1302>, appears to be child-sized; only the one-piece quarters with front fastening survive. The boot is reminiscent of another child's boot from London dated to the early to mid 14th century (Grew and de Neergaard 2001, 27, fig 38). There is less evidence for side-laced boots since many of these uppers are very fragmentary and could have come from shoes or boots. Two definite boot fragments were identified. One had a sole measuring c 248mm in length (equivalent to between a modern English size 4 and 5) and is laced up the side with 12 lace holes, with an internal reinforcement strip. Ankle-boot <1305> has a largely one-piece upper with a back seam and had a now-missing insert that extended from the back of the heel to the side of the foot; the boot is also missing any fastening detail.

TOGGLE-FASTENED SHOES

This form of shoe was common from the late 13th to around the middle of the 14th century (Grew and de Neergaard 2001, 2–3). The main fastening element is a toggle placed centrally on the instep with variations in the form of the straps that come from the quarters to slot onto it (Types 1 and 2; ibid, 20–2). One example, <1370>, is a child's size and has the thong still in situ in the instep and a fastening strap with one buttonhole remaining on one side (Type 1). Two further child-sized examples were identified, <1303> and <S97>. The latter is near complete, apart from the fastening area, although again this appears to have had a central toggle on the vamp. This example is also child-sized and measures c 142mm in length, the equivalent of between an English child's size 4 and 5.

FRONT-LACED SHOES

Front-lacing shoes were recovered from most of the deposits in the ditch. In general they are not thought to have been common until the later 14th century and, indeed, an example from a mid 14th-century dump at Baynard's Castle was identified as a forerunner of the later 14th-century styles, with a front-laced vamp and separate quarters that are cut and shaped below the ankle (Grew and de Neergaard 2001, 35, fig 52). On the MLFC site a front-laced vamp and, from a separate shoe, a one-piece quarters cut to shape around the anklebone, occur in ditch fills which produced pottery dating to the mid 13th to mid 14th centuries. This may indicate that these styles, while not as common as the toggle-fastened shoes in the mid 14th century, were more common than was previously thought (ibid, vii). Such shoes are common in the Netherlands from the early 14th century (Goubitz et al 2001, 195). All the front-laced shoes from the MLFC site have two sets of lace holes and include a child's size and two examples with the leather lace still in situ.

SIDE-LACED SHOES

This form of shoe is common in the 13th century and again in the early 15th century, but is found sporadically in between (Grew and de Neergaard 2001, 18). The earliest example came from fills that produced pottery dating to the mid to late 14th century. This is a near complete shoe <1299> with a two-part pieced sole and a virtually one-piece upper (missing a small side insert comprising part of the fastening). This may be a much earlier shoe, however, as the sole and upper both show signs of very heavy wear and the upper has also been slashed. This assemblage also contained a child's shoe <1570>, also with a virtually one-piece upper and an incomplete side seam with at least two lace holes. Ditch fills which date into the 15th century also produced fragments of side-lacing shoes.

LATCHET-FASTENING SHOES

Two examples of latchet-fastening shoes were recovered, a form common from the late 14th century (Grew and de Neergaard 2001, 28). One is part of a vamp, with a front latchet fastening of which only the side with the latchet-holes survives, and the other is a vamp with a very narrow strap with two latchet holes in its end.

BUCKLE-FASTENING SHOES

Buckle-fastening shoes became common in the later 14th century. The only example from the site is a near complete wrap-round upper from a shoe, with a small circular iron buckle fastening. The strap, which would have passed over the instep to form the other half of the fastening, was a separate insert and is now missing. Two small circular iron shoe buckles <1501> and <1502> also came from Structure 6.

PATTEN OR SANDAL

Only one piece from a leather patten or sandal was found and it is very fragmentary.

SHOEMAKING, REPAIRS AND ADDITIONS

All the contexts that produced quantities of leather footwear also produced waste material, evidence for both shoemaking (cordwaining) and shoe repairing (cobbling). Some of this comprised waste from the initial stages of shoemaking – the cutting out of the shoe parts from the hide – and included pieces of the natural hide edge. The latter would have been trimmed off as it tends to be thicker than the inner part of the hide and is, therefore, unsuitable for use. Cobbling or repairing was also evident in the many uppers and soles that had been cut up, with sections removed for reuse. In addition, most contexts produced fragmentary clump soles, repair pieces that were stitched onto the sole to cover an area of wear. They are distinguished by the tunnel stitching used to attach them. Three other probable repair soles are more unusual. The forepart of a sole (<S98>, Fig 102), has numerous small, random holes. The edges of the sole are quite angular and there are no signs of any seams along them. The holes may have been for small nails or rivets but there are no signs of any corrosion products, which would seem unusual if metal nails had been present. It is therefore likely that this sole was attached by means of small wooden pegs. A similar sole came from excavations at the Austin Friars in Leicester (Allin 1981, 146, fig 55, no. 8). Two other sole fragments (<S99>, Fig 102 and <1313>) appear to be outer, clump soles but unusually they have been nailed on, a number of the nails being still in situ. The use of nails in shoes is very unusual at this time, although an example of a leather patten or sandal from London (Grew and de Neergaard 2001, 101, fig 142) has additional nailed-on repairs.

Sometimes, if a shoe was ill fitting or the foot was deformed in some way, the shape of the shoe could be altered quite cheaply and easily by making a number of cuts or slashes in the leather. One shoe has diagonal slashes across the vamp, probably to alleviate pressure on the foot. A more extreme case is a near-complete side-laced shoe <1299> with very heavy wear on the right side of the sole's forepart and the same side of the upper. The front of the vamp has four vertical slashes, including one along the right-hand side. It would appear that these cuts were made to alleviate pressure for the wearer, but they may only have been made towards the end of the life of the shoe, as they do not appear much worn. Similarly cut shoes have been found in London (Grew and de Neergaard 2001,

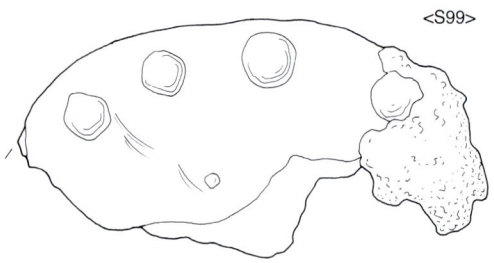

Fig 102 Forepart of shoe sole with multiple small holes <S98> (scale 1:1) and child-sized leather shoe with nailed sole <S99> (scale 1:2)

110, fig 149) and elsewhere (Goubitz et al 2001, 304).

Insufficient evidence has come from the archaeological record to identify the exact locations of leather workers in London. However, it is known that cordwainers were located in Newgate in 1305, as well as at Billingsgate and Gracechurch Street, and records of 1320 indicate that they were working in many of the wards of the City (Waterland Mander 1931, 40). Large quantities of waste material, such as offcuts, as well as shoes and other leather items, have been recovered from the Thames waterfront, where they were dumped from elsewhere in the City. Recent archaeological excavations at Hosier Lane to the west of the present site also produced both shoemaking and repairing waste in features dated to the 12th–14th centuries (Telfer 2003, 115–20). As Telfer has pointed out, the proximity of the Smithfield meat market may have provided a centre point for related industries, such as tanning, animal bone processing and leather working (ibid, 116 and 120). Given this and the evidence from the MLFC site it would seem likely that leather working was taking place in this north-western part of the City, although on what scale and how it was organised is unknown.

SHOE DISCUSSION

Overall, when compared with other leather from London, this shoe assemblage can best be described as utilitarian. There is no evidence for any form of decoration and little of any fashionable exaggeration, such as the sharply pointed 'poulaine' shoes found in more well-to-do assemblages of the later 14th century. In addition, many of the uppers and soles have been reused or repaired before being discarded. The only other published City ditch assemblage comes from the Ludgate area (LUD82). Here 26 accessioned shoes were recovered from a section of the ditch that appears to have been levelled with rubbish by about 1340 (Grew and de Neergaard 2001, 133). The material compares reasonably well with the early 14th-century groups from the MLFC site. The two assemblages are similar in having toggle-fastened shoes, although they differ in that front-laced shoes appear to be present in earlier deposits at the MLFC site than so far found elsewhere in London (ibid, 20, table 4). Comparison with the large body of material recovered from the Thames waterfront sites further underlines the utilitarian nature of the material. Footwear from the later 14th- and 15th-century deposits at the MLFC site is closer to the more functional assemblages, such as the later 14th-century group from Trig Lane rather than the 'wealthier' material from Baynard's Castle (ibid, 29, tables 6 and 7). At the MLFC site the small number of shoes with elongated toes is accompanied by a similarly small number of latchet- and buckle-fastened shoes.

The question of whether any of the footwear can be associated with the Greyfriars Friary, which was located near by, is more difficult to answer. The Grey Friars or Franciscans are traditionally associated with poverty and a lack of ostentation but the Greyfriars Friary was a particularly wealthy house. Its church was second in size only to St Paul's and during the 14th century many wealthy Londoners were buried there, most notably Queen Margaret, wife of Edward I (Schofield 1993, 70). It is also interesting to note that in *Piers Plowman* the Franciscans were particularly condemned for wearing buckled shoes and hose instead of going barefoot as their founder had desired (Grew and de Neergaard 2001, 116). The overall nature of the footwear from the ditch, however, is plain and functional, with many repaired or reused shoes and boots. None of it indicates any great social status or wealth among its owners. The lack of decoration on any of the shoes is interesting, considering how highly decorated the surviving sheaths are. Pictorial evidence indicates that decorated shoes were common among the wealthy, including churchmen (ibid, 112–22), but the waterfront sites in London only produced in the region of 13 examples of shoes decorated with openwork, tooled or incised designs from the 13th to 15th centuries (ibid, 79–86) and they are also rarely found elsewhere in Britain (Quita Mould, pers comm). It would therefore seem likely that the bulk of the population wore shoes that were plain, with little or no decoration. Excavations at the Austin Friars in Leicester produced similarly plain shoes with either central front-laced fastening with two pairs of lace holes or side-laced fastening; only one strap-fastened shoe was found (Allin 1981, 145).

SHEATHS

The site produced 19 knife sheaths and also three sheath-like containers. Where identifiable, all bar one were made for knives, the exception being <1386>, which may have been for a knife, dagger or sword but only the tip of which survives. The assemblage compares well with those already published from London (Cowgill et al 1987) and adds to the known designs in use. With the exception of <S80> (Fig 103), which is too worn for the leather type to be identified, all the sheaths are made from bovine leather. It was not possible to identify the leather more precisely, although one (<S76>, Fig 106), which has an inner and outer sheath, may be calf (both layers). Another sheath (<S75>, Fig 103) has a well worn grain surface but is probably also bovine. Calf leather was the usual hide used in sheath manufacture (ibid, 34) and it may therefore be assumed that at least some of the sheaths identified in the present assemblage only as bovine are calf. In 1350 the Guild of Furbishers forbade the use of any hide other than calf for sheaths (ibid), which may indicate that other hide types were being used. An example of a sheep/goat sheath is known from London and a number were also found at Leicester (ibid, 35).

Four leather sheath linings survived, three still in situ and one (<1382>) on its own. Two, <1382> and <S76>, are of bovine leather (the latter probably calf). Lining <S76> (Fig 106) is of particular interest as it has tooled decoration, indicating the reuse of an old sheath as a lining. The two remaining linings (<S84>, Fig 106; <S80>, Fig 103) are sheep/goat hide. Sixteen of the sheaths from London published by Cowgill et al have linings, all either poor quality calf or sheep/goat leather, as a thin supple leather was required (Cowgill et al 1987, 35).

The majority of the sheaths are decorated with designs on both the front and the back. In most cases these designs are divided into panels, corresponding to the handle and blade sections of the knife. All the main decorative techniques so far identified on medieval London sheaths (de Neergaard 1987, 40–4) are present: tooling (or engraving), stamping, embossing, pricking or stabbing, and scraping of the background to form a contrast. Often two or more of these decorative techniques are combined on the same sheath. It should also be remembered that some may have been painted and even gilded (ibid, 40). Only one had no form of decoration: this is a plain tip cut from a sheath or possibly from a lining.

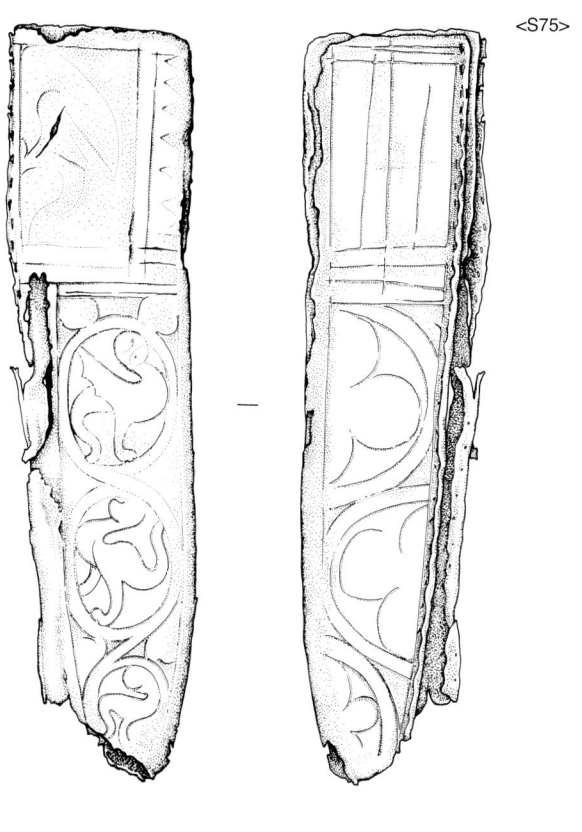

Fig 103 *Knife sheath with engraved decoration of griffins and a bird <S75> and sheath engraved with mythological beast<S80> (scale 1:2)*

SHEATHS WITH TOOLED DECORATION

Thirteen sheaths have tooled decoration, the most common technique used in the medieval period (de Neergaard 1987, 40). It is often found used with other forms of decoration: on a stamped sheath, for example, the area around the stamped panel may have simple tooled lines and chevrons. Quite a wide variety of designs were tooled. The earliest designs are interlace, although these continued to be used into the mid 14th century (ibid); one example was found from the MLFC site (<S83>, Fig 104). A more common motif in this assemblage is zoomorphic roundels, consisting of birds or animals, sometimes mythological,

The medieval archaeological sequence

within circular frames. This is often accompanied by half quatrefoils on the back and appears to have been quite a common design, with numerous variations (some of which can be seen in Cowgill et al 1987, eg nos 414, 417, 419, 421–2 and 472). This design is present on sheaths <S75> (Fig 103), <S79> and <S81> (Fig 104). On <S88> birds and foliage alternate (Fig 104). Other sheaths, such as <S80> (Fig 103),

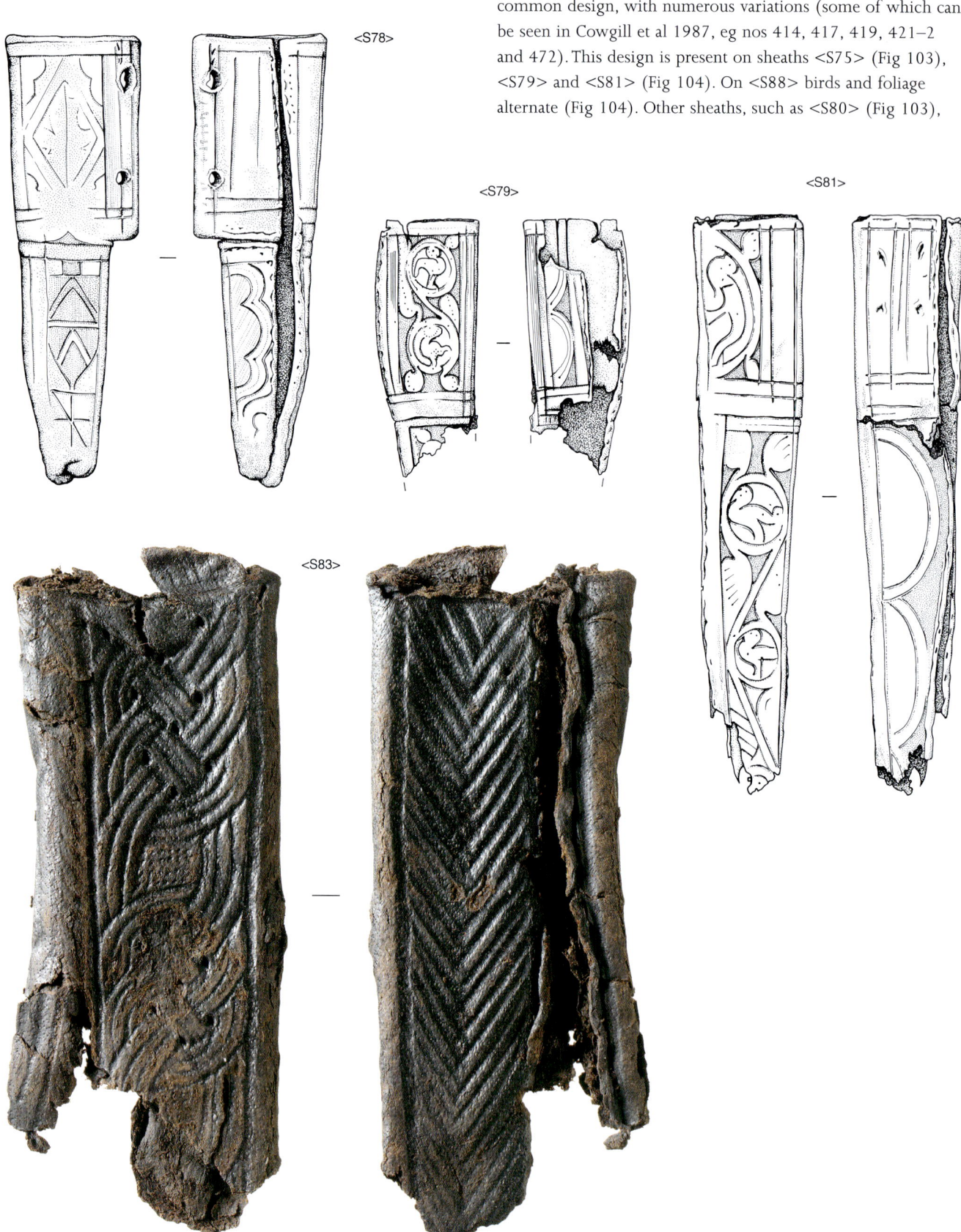

Fig 104 Knife sheaths with engraved decoration: heraldic design <S78>, zoomorphic motif within roundels <S79>, bird and zoomorphic forms within circular foliate frames <S81>, front interlace back chevron <S83>, flared top and heraldic design <S85> and alternating birds and foliage within panels <S88>; sheath-like object with heraldic decoration and holes for a suspension thong <S89>; sheath-like objects with heraldic decoration <S90>–<S91> (all scale 1:2 apart from <S83> scale 2:1; <S85> and <S91> scale 1:1)

Later medieval settlement, *c* 1300–1500 (period 5)

which has a mythological beast along the full length of its front, have less formalised designs. Heraldic devices were also very popular, particularly in the mid 14th century (de Neergaard 1987, 42) and are found on two of the tooled sheaths. In addition, the three sheath-like objects also use tooled heraldic motifs and two of the stamped sheaths use fleurs-de-lis, which may or may not have had a particular heraldic significance. In some cases the devices almost certainly had a meaning, although it is likely that others may just have been used as fashionable motifs. One knife sheath (<S78>, Fig 104) has a number of devices including one – a fess between two chevrons – that may have been associated with the Fitzwalter family (Wilmott 1987, 45); seven examples of this device, both singly and in combination with other arms, have been published from London (Cowgill et al 1987, eg nos 432 and 435). Another sheath (<S89>, Fig 104), while probably not used for a knife, has a variety of heraldic arms on the front, back and sides. A small sheath with a flared top (<S85>, Fig 104) is tooled with a lozenge containing a fleur-de-lis dimidiating a castle triple-towered, within a square with foliage. This device may have continental associations (Wilmott 1987, 47) but it is very sketchily drawn here and may not have had a particular heraldic significance. The two other sheath-like objects (<S90>–<S91>, Fig 104) both have heraldic devices. The former has concentric lozenges on its front, the innermost with a fleur-de-lis at each corner and what appears to be a central castle triple-towered. Part of the background to this has been scraped away to form a contrasting colour and texture, a technique noted on other sheaths from London (de Neergaard 1987, 41). The other (<S91>, Fig 104) has a lion/leopard passant, a symbol found on other sheaths from London (ibid, 43 and 44, fig 11, nos 447–8 and 445).

SHEATHS WITH STAMPED DECORATION

Small stamped motifs on sheaths are also quite common and could be used singly or to form an overall repeating pattern; five of the sheaths are thus decorated. Sheath <S77> (Fig 105) has panels of very small floral-like motifs stamped on its front, with additional simple tooled decoration. Sheath <S82> (Fig 105) is decorated with rows of a rosette within a lozenge stamp, again with additional tooled decoration. Small stamped fleurs-de-lis within tooled lozenges are found on both <S86> and <S87> (Fig 105). The blade area of <S86> is further decorated with small stamped birds within lozenges. Sheath <S74> (Fig 105) has a simpler motif of panels containing small stamped dots.

SHEATHS WITH EMBOSSED DECORATION

Two sheaths (<S84> and <S76>, Fig 106) are decorated with an embossed technique using small cubes of leather wedged between the sheath and the lining to raise areas of decoration on the sheath's surface. Two other 14th-century sheaths from London also have this form of decoration (Cowgill et al 1987, nos 418 and 464). Both the examples from the present assemblage have zoomorphic and foliate designs, with the bodies of the animals raised. These and the foliage are further decorated with stabbing or pricking.

FUNCTION OF SHEATHS

The majority of the sheaths were used with knives, which were mostly quite small and probably for personal use. This is reinforced by the fact that nearly all the sheaths have suspension holes in their upper ends, indicating that they were hung, probably from a belt. Some showed signs of alteration, for example <1386> which is a cut-off sheath tip, presumably removed so the original sheath could be remodelled. Both the embossed sheaths (<S84> and <S76>, Fig 106) depict animals associated with hunting and it is tempting to see these as containers for hunting knives, as has been suggested for other similarly decorated sheaths from London (de Neergaard 1987, 41).

OTHER SHEATH-LIKE OBJECTS

Three sheath-like objects are similar in design and decoration to the knife sheaths above but were probably used as other forms of containers or covers. One (<S90>, Fig 104) is short and broad (79mm x 68mm), with a cut top edge and an incomplete U-shaped end. Its tooled decoration has contrasting areas of scraped surface. The 'front' has a heraldic device (concentric lozenges, the innermost with fleurs-de-lis at each corner and what appears to be a central castle triple-towered). This surface is c 65mm wide and does not appear to have been folded; a seam runs down one side but the other side continues with a panel of linear tooled decoration which folds over part of the back and also has a seam edge. This would indicate that a missing insert would have joined the two seamed edges and that this object was not used as a knife sheath but as some other form of container or cover. There are two suspension holes on the folded edge. Another non-sheath (<S91>, Fig 104) is a rectangular piece decorated with arms containing a tooled lion or leopard, apparently passant but, given its position in the arms, possibly rampant. There is a seam down one edge and the other edge is folded back with a seam, indicating that the two were joined by an insert, as above. However, the folded side also has a seam running along its outer edge, indicating that it formed either part of a larger sheath with a 'wing' or some other form of cover, possibly for a small box or container. The final non-knife sheath (<S89>, Fig 104) may be a lid of some form. It appears to be part of a larger sheath cut down (64mm x 38mm) and has two sets of two near-central suspension holes in the front and back for a vertical thong. This also has tooled heraldic decoration, but unlike the other heraldic devices on sheaths from this site, these are upside down when the sheath is suspended. It is similar in size and decoration to another example from London (Cowgill et al 1987, no. 456), but there the heraldic devices are the right way up. It is therefore possible that this may have been used as a lid or cover, which would place the motifs the right way up when used, and may have been used with some sort of tubular container that also hung from the waist (Quita Mould, pers comm). Cut-up sheaths for later use as cases or pouches were also found at the Austin Friars in Leicester (Allin 1981, 160 and 159, fig 61, nos 42 and 43), including one that has been identified as a possible spectacle case or incomplete pen case.

Later medieval settlement, c 1300–1500 (period 5)

Fig 105 (above and over page) Knife sheaths with stamped motifs: panels with small stamped dots <S74>; small floral-like motifs stamped on front <S77> (detail scale 3:1); rows of a rosette within a lozenge stamp <S82> (details 5:1 and 2:1); small stamped fleurs-de-lis within tooled lozenges <S86> and <S87> and small stamped birds within lozenges <S86> (scale 1:1 except details and <S87> 1:2)

The medieval archaeological sequence

<S82>

Fig 105 (cont)

Later medieval settlement, c 1300–1500 (period 5)

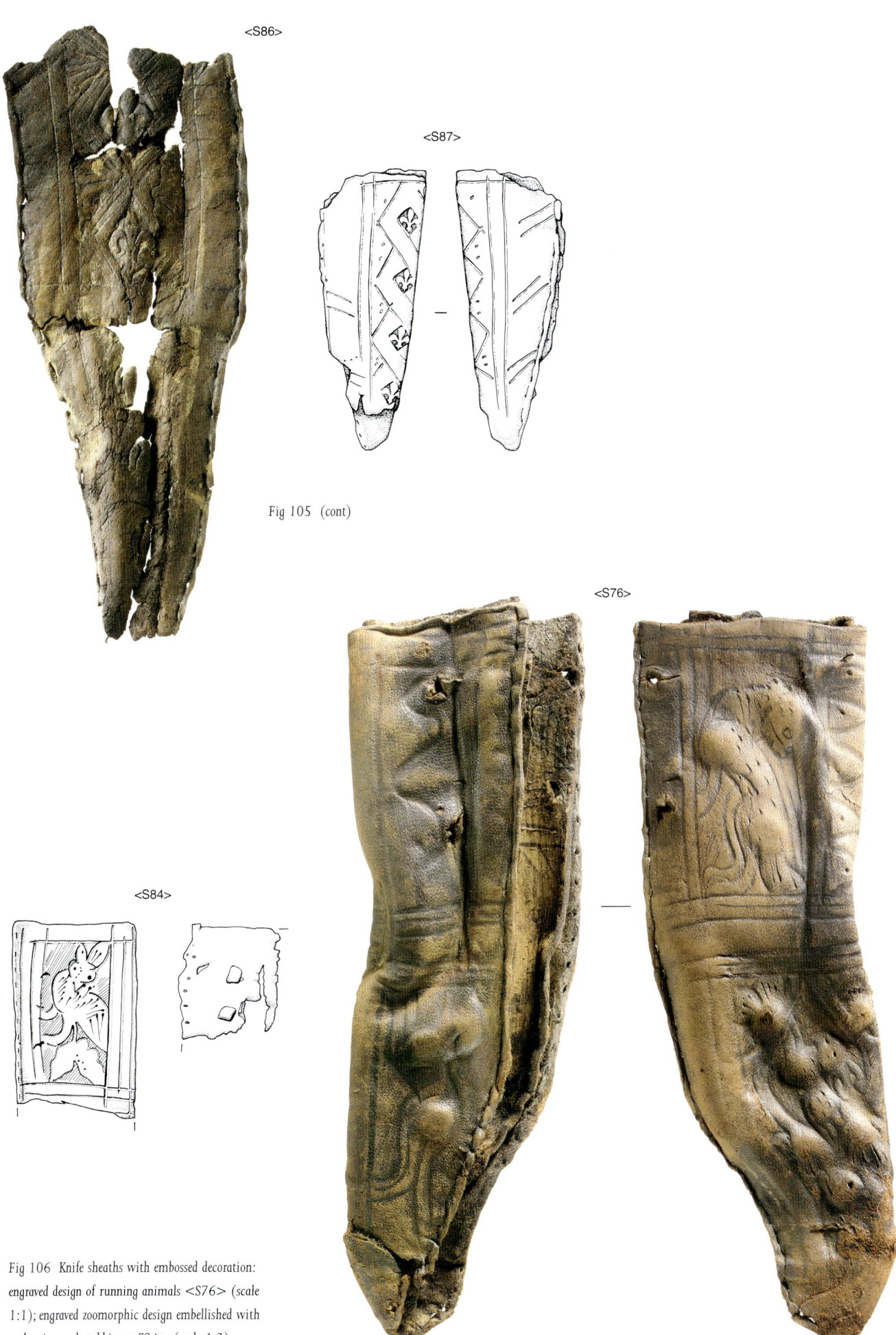

Fig 105 (cont)

Fig 106 Knife sheaths with embossed decoration: engraved design of running animals <S76> (scale 1:1); engraved zoomorphic design embellished with embossing and stabbing <S84> (scale 1:2)

STRAPS

Approximately 135 fragments of strap were recovered from the selected ditch fills and 120 of these came from a single dump layer. A number may be from the same strap but few are complete and most of the fragments are torn (eg <S112>, Fig 107) and/or cut, indicating that they may have been either repaired or used for repairing other straps. The main problem with such a large group is trying to identify what they may have been used for. Some are very narrow and are decorated with small metal studs or rivets, for example <S114> (Fig 107), which is 4mm wide, and <1287> (6mm wide). Such straps may have come from girdles worn around the waist but are also similar to spur straps (Egan 1995, 150–6), which were decorated with metal studs. Similarly, at the other end of the spectrum, the widest straps <S111> (Fig 107), which are c 45–52mm wide, could have been used for heavy-duty belts, such as sword belts, or for harnesses or other functional uses. At the Austin Friars, Leicester, similar belt fragments with a width of c 40mm and a squared end were also found (Allin 1981, 159, fig 61, no. 36). It is tempting to see the present assemblage as waste from a single workshop, for example a girdler's or a harness maker's, but it is more likely that they come from a repair workshop rather than from the primary manufacturing of belts and straps. The belts may also, however, have been associated with the friary. At the Austin Friars in Leicester a number of belt fragments were found, some of which may have belonged to the friars or their lay patrons and may even have been made in a friary workshop (ibid, 158).

The straps also include a wide variety of awl holes and stitching detail. Many have diagonal holes punched with a small diamond or rectangular-headed awl, although a few have vertical holes. In some cases these holes were used for stitching and the imprint of the thread is visible, although the actual thread survives in very few cases. Where thread impressions are visible, the holes are described as stitch holes. Some of the straps combine rows of stitching with presumably decorative rows of awl holes. Strap <1545> has a single row of small, closely spaced (6 per 10mm) diagonal awl holes along its centre and the imprint of a possible buckle plate at one end. Similar central rows of small awl holes have been noted on other straps from London, dating to not later than the mid 14th century (Egan and Pritchard 1991, 39). Three small fragments <1254> have a row of stitch holes parallel to each edge but also have plain sections with no stitching, possibly where mounts were attached. These mainly have cut ends and may have been offcuts from strap making or mending.

One of the straps from <1243> is near complete and may have been a collar for an animal, such as a dog. Both ends are incomplete but one is split and has holes for the attachment of a buckle plate, while the other end has a fastening hole and fine stitching for reinforcement. It is c 290mm in length. Two other straps also appear to have had a specific, if unknown, function. Both are quite similar. Strap <1283> is near complete, measuring c 290mm in length, while <1289> is 265mm in length. Both are quite plain with no stitching or awl holes and both taper along their length, one from 9mm to 18mm and the other from 10mm to 20mm. Both also have rivet holes at their wider ends and <1289> has a very corroded fitting at its narrower end, while <1283> has a further hole. Another of the straps from <1243> has one end cut to a point and split with a fine thong threaded through the split. Strap <1573> has both long edges folded back to form a central back flesh/edge butt seam. A similar strap also with a stitched centre back seam was found attached to a stirrup from Billingsgate, London

Fig 107 Selection of leather straps <S111>–<S114> (scale 1:2)

(Clark 1995, 71–2, no. 82), but other examples may have had other uses (Egan and Pritchard 1991, 37). Another strap <1294> comprises three layers of leather held together by a group of five iron rivets and terminating in a bifurcated end where a buckle would have been attached. The other end has been cut and the whole may have been attached to something by the rivets as part of a fastening. Two interwoven straps (<S113>, Fig 107) may have been used in harness, while a narrow strap <1787> has been slit along its central row of awl holes so that a thong can be threaded through, possibly for the suspension of accessories.

A number of fragmentary knotted thongs were also recovered, some of which may have had similar functions to the straps. One <1239> has been twisted into a circular loop and secured with a reef knot, either as a plaything or possibly used around the neck of a flask or bottle as a fastening or suspension loop. Six other knotted thongs <1236> may again be either playthings or functional items; some do appear to have been fastened for a purpose and one (<S102>, Fig 108), a single thong with a finely crafted knot in one end, may have been used as a drawstring for fastening a purse.

OTHER LEATHER ITEMS

A number of sheet or other unidentifiable fragments were recovered, some of which may have come from garments, saddles, upholstery or bags. The most impressive of these is <S92> (Fig 109), a very large, roughly rectangular piece of thick bovine leather, c 1060mm x 500mm, and probably one of the largest fragments of medieval leather to have been found in London. It has seamed edges and a small dart cut and seamed in one of the shorter sides. This would seem to indicate that it was made for a specific purpose and to fit a specific shape or form, rather than just being a rectangular panel from a larger sheet item. This is supported by the fact that one of the long sides has seven round eyelets and evidence of having had a reinforcement

Fig 108 *Thong with knot terminal, perhaps used as a drawstring for a purse* <S102> *(Diam of knot 12mm)*

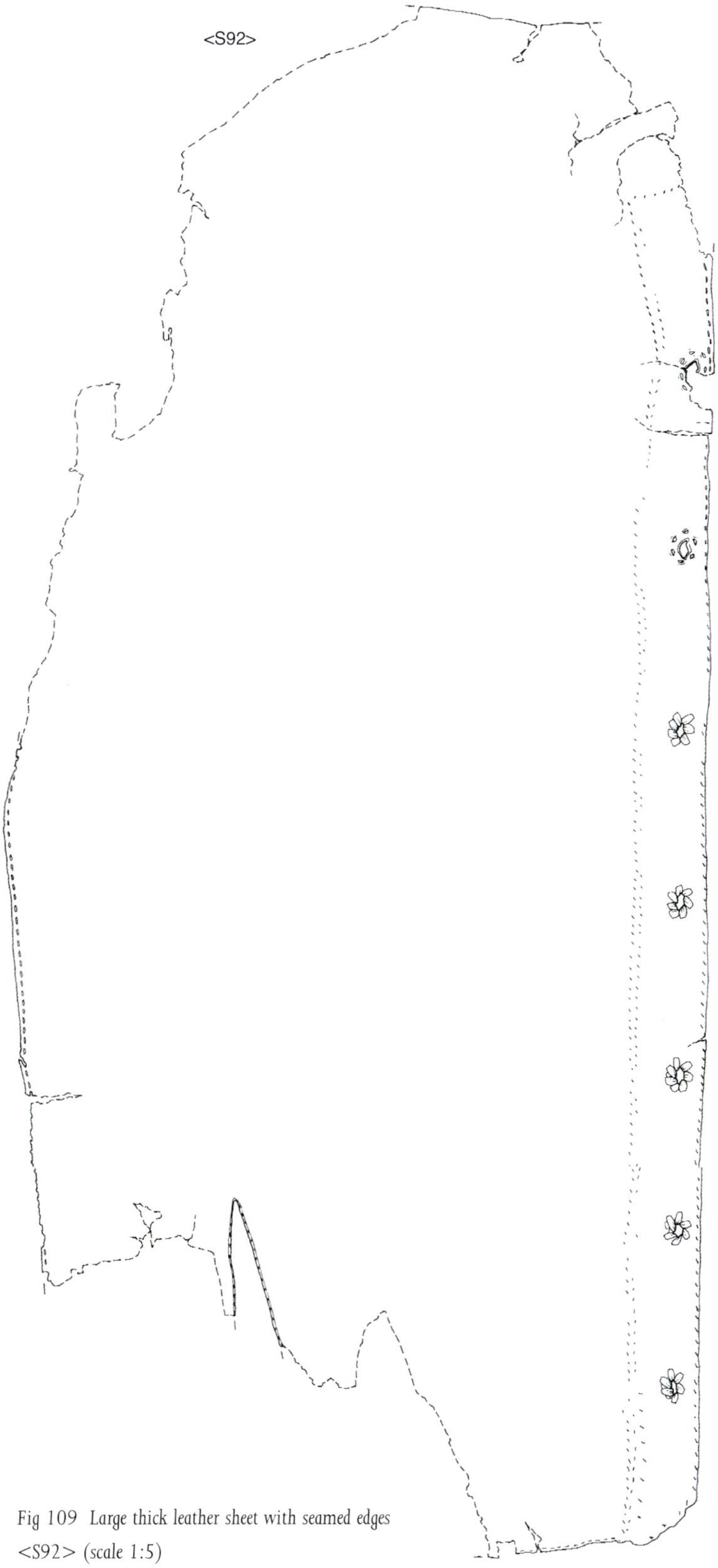

Fig 109 *Large thick leather sheet with seamed edges* <S92> *(scale 1:5)*

strip attached. Five of the eyelets have themselves been reinforced with thong whip-stitching around their edges. The overall impression is that this edge was made to take great pressure or stress, yet none of the eyelets appears to have taken any stress and indeed they appear not to have been used. The actual function of this piece is at present unknown; it may have formed part of a cover with the reinforced eyelets part of an opening.

The remainder of the leather comprises sheet fragments and smaller pieces, all with evidence of seams or hems: some, like <1238> and <S96> (Fig 110), have the impressions of

Fig 110 *Sheet leather: with the impressions of rows of studs <S96>; with fine stitching and lace hole <S107>; decorated with cut-out designs <S94>; quilted with rows of stitching <S101>; with unusual stamped decoration <S104> (scale c 1:3 except <S94> c 2:1 and detail of <S104> c 3:1)*

missing metal mounts and a small number show evidence of decoration. Two small rectangular fragments have sides with closed seams. The larger piece has a single row of fine grain/flesh stitching across the centre, while the smaller piece has a lace hole in the corner (<S107>, Fig 110). Another small fragment (<S94>, Fig 110) is decorated with openwork crosses, dots and lines; the latter are of particular note as they have been made with a finely serrated punch or tool (see similarly serrated edges on the openwork decoration of a shoe from London, probably of late 14th-century date; Grew and de Neergaard 2001, 80 and 82, fig 116b). It is possible that this fragment formed part of a decorative strap: a single medieval strap from London with openwork sexfoils is known (Egan and Pritchard 1991, 47, fig 29, no. 25), and openwork decoration is also found on a small number of medieval shoes (Grew and de Neergaard 2001, 79–83). Three very crumpled and torn fragments (<S101>, Fig 110; two fragments illustrated) have curving rows of stitch holes, perhaps evidence for a quilted garment. The most unusual decorated fragment, however, may come from upholstery or some form of cover (<S104>, Fig 110) and has stamped decoration in the form of small tri-lobed motifs and small ellipses filled with dots. Such decoration is quite common on sheaths (Cowgill et al 1987, 43) and is also found used on bookbindings (ibid). It is very rare to recover decorated sheet leather from an archaeological excavation with such decoration and few parallels have been found for this piece. A possible jerkin or garment from Exeter is decorated with an incised border pattern but may be later in date (Friendship-Taylor 1984, 327). The only other non-sheath fragment of leather to have stamped decoration (<S95>, Fig 111) is a trimmed piece covered with interlocking single and double crescents.

The majority of this leather, however, is undecorated and very fragmentary. A piece of thicker leather (<S100>, Fig 112) appears to be a reused garment with a buttonhole (possibly a later addition). A curving leather strap (<S103>, Fig 112) with nails may have been a mount. Other pieces – for example, <S109> (Fig 112) – have multiple rows of stitching, possibly part of a reinforced wrist guard. One of the fragments with mount impressions is also probably from a garment or from upholstery or a saddle (<S96>, Fig 110). It has two hemmed long sides, the hems secured by a row of now missing small circular-headed rivets/mounts. The other two sides have two central rows of four circular mounts running perpendicular to them. Again the mounts are missing but the impressions of the heads survive. Both of these edges are much damaged but one partly survives with a curving whip-stitched edge. Another unusual piece is <S105> (Fig 112), again made for a specific, now unknown, purpose. It comprises a long, tapering piece of leather seamed along one side and with small iron rivets along the other long side. One end is straight with a butt seam and the other tapers to a seamed bifurcated point. The rivets indicate that it was probably attached to another material, possibly wood, and it may have formed some sort of edging or collar, possibly in upholstery. An interesting piece (<S93>, Fig 112) is rectangular with a row of central holes, like fastening holes on a belt, but also with two groups of horizontal slashes. It is possible that this is part of a large belt or strap, cut and trimmed for reuse, possibly as some form of wrist guard. A small triangular fragment (<S106>, Fig 112) appears to be an insert from something like a garment or possibly a saddle; it is made of two layers of leather carefully stitched together, one overlapping the other on two sides to form a hem. Other fragments (<S108>, Fig 112) may be part of a bag with a base or side insert; most of these have thick folded over seams with a double row of stitch holes of varying sizes. Another possible fragment of garment, saddle or bag (<S110>, Fig 112) has a diagonal row of stitching across its centre.

Further non-shoe leather was recovered from the non-selected groups but is not discussed in detail here. Brief descriptions of these pieces and of all the unidentified leather are available in the archive report. A number of them may also come from garments and are worthy of further future study.

Fig 111 *Leather waste stamped with interlocking single and double crescents <S95> (scale 1:1)*

Later medieval settlement, c 1300–1500 (period 5)

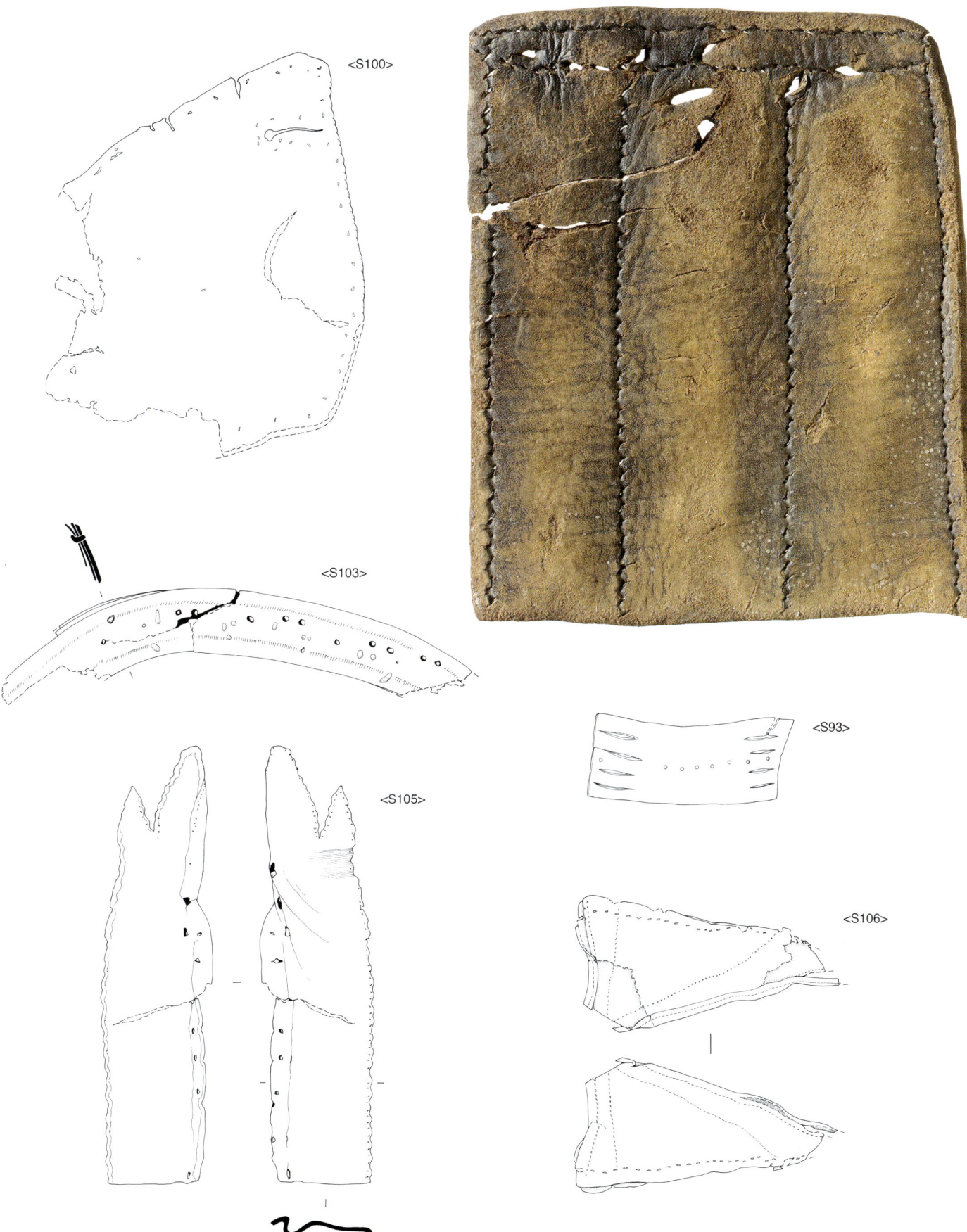

Fig 112 Leather items: ?garment with reinforced buttonhole <S100>; wrist guard with stitching <S109>; strap with nails <S103>; incomplete cover or edging <S105>; strap or wrist guard <S93>; fragment of garment or saddle insert <S106>; fragments of possible bag with diagonal row of stitching across centre <S110>; fragments from a possible bag <S108> (scale 1:3 except <S109> 2:1)

Fig 112 (cont)

Building material from the phase 2 backfilling of the city ditch (OA17) and the revetment (S6) within the ditch

Ian Betts

A wide range of different building material was present in the backfilled city ditch. The most common finds were medieval peg roofing tiles, all of standard London two round nail hole type, and plain ridge tiles. Many of these tiles have areas of splash glaze: the peg tiles have it on the bottom third of the tile and on the ridge tiles it appears as a line along the tile crest. Various different types of floor tiles were also found. These include plain and decorated 'Westminster' tiles, plain Low Countries and Eltham Palace/Lesnes Abbey group tiles and solitary Chertsey-Westminster and French decorated examples. A fragmentary decorated tile may also belong to the Eltham Palace/Lesnes Abbey group (<T2>, Fig 113). Of particular importance are a Penn tile (<T3>, Fig 113) and French tile (<T4>, Fig 113), which have previously unpublished design types. There is also a 13th-century floor tile, which displays another currently unique design. This is in a 'Westminster' fabric but it is uncertain if it was actually made by the 'Westminster' tilemakers (<T5>, Fig 113). This sort of tile was used as flooring either in churches or in other religious buildings, and could conceivably have come from the Greyfriars complex. Reigate stone ashlar and a moulding (<1780>, Fig 114), made from the same stone, may have come from the same source.

A Purbeck 'marble' column shaft was found, which

Fig 113 *Decorated floor tiles from backfilling of the city ditch (OA17): possible late 13th-/early 14th-century Eltham/Lesnes group design <T2>; mid to late 14th-century Penn design <T3>; late 14th-century/early 15th-century Dieppe (France) design <T4>; mid to late 13th-century London (?'Westminster') tile <T5> (scale 1:3)*

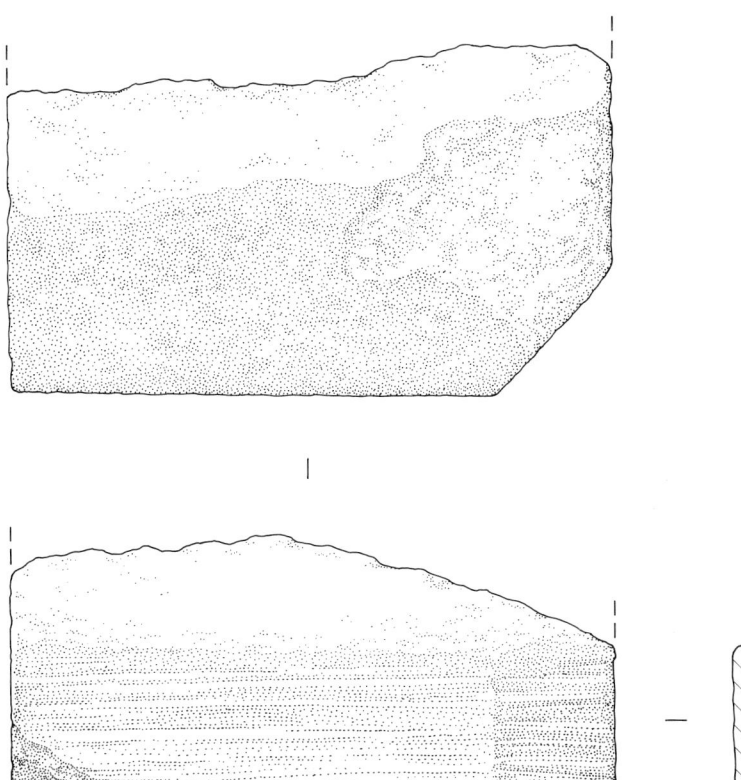

Fig 114 *Reigate stone moulding <1780> from Open Area 17 (scale 1:2)*

Fig 115 *Decorated floor tiles from Structure 6: mid to late 14th-century Penn design <T6>; mid to late 13th-century 'Westminster' design <T7>; and London (?'Westminster') tile <T8> (scale 1:3)*

measures 87mm in diameter by at least 216mm in length; it is uncertain if the full length is represented. Other materials include a fragment of Purbeck limestone paving, ashlar blocks of a light grey calcareous sandstone, Portland stone, and a small broken rectangular shaped piece of highly polished dark green stone <1083>, measuring 24–25mm in breadth by 7mm in thickness. This object may be peridot from the Red Sea island of Zebirget in Egypt. Its function is unclear, but it may be furniture inlay rather than building material (Susan Walker, pers comm).

The material from Structure 6 was similar in composition to that from the rest of the backfilled ditch (OA17). The revetment deposits produced peg roofing tile, roofing slate and a couple of plain glazed Low Countries and 14th-century decorated Penn floor tiles, of Eames design 2355 and one of three possible Eames designs (types 2837–2840, Eames 1980). Further plain glazed Low Countries and decorated Penn floor tiles were found in other Structure 6 deposits. The Penn tiles are of Eames design types 2355, 2409 and 2773, and included a previously unpublished type (<T6>, Fig 115). Also present is a decorated 'Westminster' floor tile with a previously unpublished design, now designated W164 (<T7>, Fig 115), together with another 13th-century tile, which although from London seems not have been made by the 'Westminster' tilemakers (<T8>, Fig 115).

Animal bone

Jane Liddle

ANIMAL BONE FROM THE PHASE 2 BACKFILLING OF THE CITY DITCH (OA17)

The second phase of backfilling of the city ditch (OA17) provided a large, diverse assemblage; c 1800 bone fragments were recovered in total (Table 14; Table 15). The largest single assemblage [3768] contained over 1100 bones and represents waste from a number of activities, namely butchery waste from cattle and sheep processing. Waste from cat skinning and goat-horn working was also recovered, with a lesser quantity of general household refuse including food debris from fallow deer, fish and birds. There were also remains of pet dogs and scavengers, including red kite and raven.

Large quantities of cattle and sheep head and limb bones were recovered from [3768] and [3799], with a lesser quantity of pig. At least two newborn piglets and an infant pig were recovered from [3799] and may relate to local pig husbandry. The sheep limb bones were mainly from the lower leg, shoulder, pelvis and skull. This emphasis of body parts is likely to suggest butchers' waste, with these bones removed during the first stages of carcass processing. Many of the skulls were from polled sheep and a number were split in half to extract the brain, which further indicates that the bones derived from butchers' waste. Sexing indicates that males were most prevalent and ageing suggests most were between 4 and 6 years old. This points to a primary use for wool production, possibly using wethers (castrated sheep), which produce the best fleeces (Grant 1988, 153), and a secondary use for meat. A smaller number of younger individuals were recovered and are likely to derive from sheep culled primarily for meat, after just one or at the most two fleeces (ibid).

The cattle bones from [3768] derived from the limb and head, including skull and jaw. The limb bones were heavily butchered and derived from the upper and lower limbs. The ages, with two peaks at 1–8 months and 3.5–over 4 years, indicate a twofold culling pattern with young, probably male, calves bred and culled primarily for veal meat and an older group of individuals used for a primary purpose, possibly milking (sexing showed the adult cattle were mainly female), before they were slaughtered for meat. This indicates that meat was both a primary and secondary product.

The proximity of the site to the butchers' shops and permanent stalls of St Nicholas Shambles may explain the source of the waste dumps. St Nicholas Shambles was one of the three butchers' markets within London during the medieval period and extended along much of Newgate Street. The market was also a place of slaughter with beasts being killed in the street (Archer et al 1988, 7 and 91–2), thus producing large quantities of primary slaughter and butchery waste. The city ditch would have acted as a useful dump for this waste material.

Food waste from fish, domestic birds and wild species was recovered from a number of the ditch fills (OA17). Fish from [3768] and [3799] included a number of large gadid (probably cod) vertebrae as well as cod head bones, and eel and herring family vertebrae. Larger samples from [3768] contained a small number of herring family vertebrae and herring head bones as well as eel, smelt, cyprinid and plaice/flounder vertebrae. Teal was recovered from [3763] and partridge and quail from [3768]. A small quantity of fallow deer limb bones, possibly from good quality food waste and also from [3768], was the only wild animal bone recovered. Young swan from [3799] also indicates good quality table waste, as swans were often eaten at feasts. They commanded a high price and were semi-domesticated and owned by private individuals, who marked their young swans during the annual swan-upping on the Thames (Fitter 1990, 41–2) and later sold them on the open market. Bramwell notes that a number were recovered from similarly dated deposits at Baynard's Castle (1975, 15). Chicken and goose bones were not very common. They were represented in similar numbers and were recovered from [3768], [3799] and [3763]. A number of the chickens were young, and although sexing was only possible on a small number, these were all female, indicating that hens were bred and kept for meat and eggs. Very young goose bones were recovered from [3768], possibly the remains from a single meal.

Horn working was evident from a deposit of 15 goat horncores recovered from [3768]. The size of the horncores indicates females and a single male. They were all chopped from the skull and showed cuts around the base from horn removal. An absence of goat bones, with the exception of one juvenile jaw, indicates that the horncores are likely to have been brought into the City with horns attached and sent to the horn worker, rather than being cut from the skulls of goats brought to the City. This indicates the movement of just the raw material for horn working, with cores discarded once the horn had been removed. A number of the cores showed a sawn cut around the shaft, possibly resulting from horn removal in segments. Single goat horncores were also recovered from [3799] and [3728], the sizes being comparable with the sample from [3768]. The front of a horse jawbone, sawn across, was also recovered from [3728] and is likely to represent waste from bone working, possibly to provide a flat length of bone from the shaft of the jaw.

Cats were recovered in large numbers, a minimum of ten individuals from [3768] based on the number of femurs, the most frequently occurring bone, and including two near complete skeletons. Butchery was evident on the skull and jaws of one of the articulated skeletons and on the jaws of three further individuals. The style and location of butchery marks are consistent with similar dumps of cat skinning waste recovered at Guildhall (Rielly in prep) and Northgate House, Moorgate (Drummond-Murray and Liddle 2003), although the presence of toes in these deposits may indicate a slightly different style of skinning. Butchered cat skulls and jaws were also recovered from contexts [3763] and [3799].

Scavengers included raven from [3817]. Ravens were common residents of London during the medieval period and were protected by law for their services in consuming waste and refuse in the City (Fitter 1990, 51). A barn owl from [3768] may have been a wild inhabitant of the area. A goshawk from [3768] may have been a resident scavenger or could possibly have been used for hawking. The goshawk was a common choice for falconers and generally flown by yeomen (Grant 1988, 180). A golden eagle from [3799] (Fig 116) represents the only known occurrence from an archaeological

Later medieval settlement, c 1300–1500 (period 5)

semi-articulation, were recovered from Open Area 17. They are likely to derive from pets dumped with household refuse, with most around the size of a medium to large terrier or spaniel. One dog skull of interest (Fig 117) was recovered from [3051]: its size compared favourably with modern measurements from mastiffs (Foulsham 2001). The snout was chopped off with three oblique chops from the right-hand side. It is possible that the chopped snout was associated with disarticulation for meat removal but no parallels are known in London. A very similar form of butchery was evident on a similarly sized skull from [3553] from Structure 6 (Fig 117), and the presence of skinning cuts on this skull could indicate that the butchery was a form of preparation for skinning.

Horse bones were not a very common find in the medieval ditch fills. They comprised a butchered horse metacarpal from one ditch fill [3817] and a small quantity of bones, possibly redeposited from earlier Roman deposits. An exception is the partial burial of a male horse c 8 years old from [3823]. An entire skull, with both sides of the jaw present, was recovered, together with most of the vertebrae and ribs. The skull and jawbones showed knife cuts indicative of skinning, and the absence of limb bones indicates that the horse derived from skinning and feed waste. It is unlikely that horsemeat would have been used for human consumption, due mainly to the decree from Pope Gregory III in AD 732 forbidding the consumption of horseflesh (Rixson 2000, 86–7). It is therefore much more likely that the horse would have been processed for dog feed once the skin had been removed.

A single human bone from [3799] is the only evidence of human remains from the ditch. One side of the bone shows marks from knife shaving.

ANIMAL BONE FROM THE REVETMENT (S6) WITHIN THE CITY DITCH

The bone collections associated with Structure 6 were similar in composition to the deposits within the phase 2 backfill of the ditch (OA17). Sheep/goat and cattle were recovered in the same proportion, with a lesser quantity of pig. Similar domesticate bones to the ditch fills were recovered, with emphasis on the head and lower leg bones of cattle, and skulls, mandibles, lower leg and pelvis for the sheep. A small quantity of female goat horncores chopped from the skull, probably resulting from goat horn working, was recovered from [3553] and [2982]. As suggested for the phase 2 assemblage, the absence of additional goat bones indicates that the horns were removed from the skull prior to transportation to the City.

A small quantity of good quality food waste was recovered, including fallow deer from [2982], [3168] and [3358], and a fragment of sturgeon dermal scute from [3168]. Sturgeon would have represented waste from very expensive food and venison would only have been procured by the gentry (for example Rixson 2000, 177), unless it had arrived by unscrupulous means through poaching. A small quantity of rabbit was recovered from [2982] and represents the only evidence of this species from the ditch fills. The bones may derive from the same individual and could have been

Fig 116 Distal humerus and ulna from a golden eagle from [3799] (scale 1:1)

site in London, and probably also Great Britain. Mulkeen and O'Connor (1997, 443 and 445) note that only seven archaeological records of golden eagle have ever been found, which were from medieval layers at sites in Denmark, Norway, Germany and Poland. Wing bones from both sides of the body, one with butchery cut marks, may suggest that only parts of the bird were brought in, possibly for feathers; alternatively it may have been a hunting bird, although Salvin and Brodrick (1997, 13) comment that golden eagles are 'perfectly useless' to train due to 'their powers of fasting', 'inability to turn quickly' and 'sulky disposition should it miss its quarry'.

A small number of dog bones of varying sizes, some in

Fig 117 Dog skulls from [3553] and [3051], showing evidence of skinning cuts

purchased from the local butchers' stalls, for example at the markets of St Nicholas Shambles, or from cook shops or 'piebakers' who sold ready cooked meat from shops close to the Thames or along the Shambles (Telfer 2003, 118–19; Hammond 1995, 50–1). Additional food waste was recovered, mainly from chicken and goose, with only a very small quantity of fish, namely herring and cod family.

A small quantity of dog bones, of similar size and stature to those recovered from the phase 2 backfill, was represented, including a skull from [3553] which was of mastiff size with the snout chopped obliquely from the right-hand side (Fig 117). Although only one heavy oblique chop was required to remove the snout, the skull also showed one fine knife cut on the zygomatic arch, a common place for skinning cuts. The similarity of the place and style of butchery on the skull to that from [3051], as discussed above, suggests they both derived from a common source (Fig 117).

Plant remains from the phase 2 backfilling of the city ditch (OA17) and the revetment (S6) within the ditch

Anne Davis

Most of the samples from the ditch backfill (Table 16) contained rich and diverse assemblages of waterlogged plant macrofossils, including not only fruits and seeds but also stems, buds, thorns and other plant tissue including, in some samples, leaves of bracken (*Pteridium aquilinum*), box (*Buxus sempervirens*) and holly (*Ilex aquifolium*). The majority of these remains came from wild plants, but almost all samples included an element of useful plants, mainly foodstuffs.

THE NATURAL ENVIRONMENT OF THE CITY DITCH

Seeds and fruits from a relatively small number of species were found in virtually all samples throughout the sequence, and were extremely abundant in some. These are thought to represent plants growing in and around the ditch, and their habitat preferences therefore give an indication of the local environment.

Seeds of celery-leaved crowfoot (*Ranunculus sceleratus*), which were very common in all samples, as well as the less frequent tripartite bur-marigold (*Bidens tripartita*), water pepper (*Polygonum hydropiper*) and golden dock (*Rumex maritimus*), all come from plants of muddy ditch and stream banks, with high levels of nitrogen and wet, often water-saturated soils (Ellenberg 1988). There was no evidence for fully aquatic plants in the samples, although occasional seeds of plants characteristic of semi-aquatic habitats such as stream edges and marshy ground were seen. Water-flea eggs (Cladoceran ephippia), which require a body of standing water during their development, were present in most samples. Both flora and fauna suggest that although the ditch would have contained water on a seasonal basis, it may have dried out in the summer leaving muddy banks where the plants described above would thrive. Conditions must have remained wet enough in the bottom of the ditch, however, to inhibit decomposition of the organic remains.

Other seeds that were very abundant came from plants that grow in highly nitrogenous soils, similar to the group discussed above, but prefer rather drier conditions. Stinging nettle (*Urtica dioica*), hemlock (*Conium maculatum*), white horehound (*Marrubium vulgare*) and elder (*Sambucus nigra*) are all ruderals that inhabit rubbish tips and waste places, and small nettle (*Urtica urens*), red/glaucous goosefoot (*Chenopodium* rubrum/glaucum), black nightshade (*Solanum nigrum*), orache (*Atriplex* spp), thistles (*Carduus/Cirsium* spp) and knotgrass (*Polygonum aviculare*) have similar habitat preferences, but are also found in cultivated ground, particularly gardens. These plants may have dominated the vegetation around the top of the ditch, where conditions were moist but not waterlogged. Very similar plant assemblages to those recovered here have been seen in samples from sections of the medieval city ditch excavated on other sites. These include Ludgate Hill (LUD82, Fig 63) (Wilkinson 1983), Aldersgate (Carruthers 2001) and 1 London Wall (Davis 2001).

While seeds from many other taxa were common in small numbers, those described above dominated nearly all the samples. They give a strong impression of a rather polluted ditch, supporting luxuriant vegetation on its muddy banks in the summer, most of which would die back in winter when the ditch would, for some of the time at least, be flooded. The high nitrogen levels in the soils of the ditch and its surroundings, which are indicated by these plants, would result from regular dumping and decomposition of organic materials in the ditch. Some of these are evident in the plant remains and are discussed below.

DUMPED MATERIAL

Most of the dumped material was derived from domestic waste and included a wide variety of foodstuffs. Fig (*Ficus carica*), blackberry (*Rubus* cf *fruticosus*) and elder (*Sambucus nigra*) seeds, apple (*Malus domestica/sylvestris*) endocarp (from the hard inner core), and fragments of hazelnut (*Corylus avellana*) shell were found in almost all samples. This indicates the easy availability and widespread use of these foods (although elder and blackberry are wild plants whose seeds could also have arrived in the ditch by natural means). Cereal bran, including wheat and/or rye (*Triticum/Secale* sp) and fragments of corn cockle (*Agrostemma githago*) seeds were also seen in the majority of samples. These would have come from wholemeal flour and its weed contaminants, probably in the form of bread, and, along with the small fruit seeds mentioned above, almost certainly indicate the presence of human faeces in the deposits. Grape (*Vitis vinifera*) pips, stones of sloe (*Prunus spinosa*), cherry (*P. cerasus/avium*) and plum/bullace (*P. domestica*), and fragments of walnut (*Juglans regia*) shell were less ubiquitous but found in several samples, and probably indicate waste from food preparation and meals as well as faecal material. More unusual, and found in only one or two samples, were wild strawberry (*Fragaria vesca*), mulberry (*Morus nigra*), and raspberry (*Rubus* cf *idaeus*) pips, and a single olive (*Olea europaea*) stone. Occasional finds of the spices coriander (*Coriandrum sativum*), dill (*Anethum graveolens*), alexanders (*Smyrnium olusatrum*) and black mustard (*Brassica nigra*) were also made. The find of alexanders is only the second recorded from London; the previous example came from a 10th- to 11th-century pit fill at Milk Street (Jones et al 1991). Fruits of beet (*Beta vulgaris*) and brassica (*Brassica* sp) seeds may come from plants grown as green leafy vegetables. Several other wild plants such as mallow (*Malva* cf *sylvestris*), fat hen (*Chenopodium album*) and orache (*Atriplex* sp), whose seeds were relatively common in the samples, were used as potherbs in the past and may have been either cultivated nearby or gathered from the wild.

Many, if not most, of the wild plants whose seeds were recovered here have documented medicinal uses, and it is quite possible that some of the seeds found could be the undigested remains of plants taken for health reasons. Similar plant assemblages were found at nearby stretches of the western city ditch at Aldersgate, to the north of this site, and many of the taxa described above were thought to have been used medicinally (Carruthers 2001). There is no particular concentration of medicinal plants in any of the individual samples, however, so it is likely that the seeds found here simply represent the flora of the ditch and its surroundings.

Several of the plants whose remains were found in the ditch samples are potential garden cultivars. For example, mallow, orache, brassicas and beet may have been grown for potherbs; celery, fennel, and black mustard as flavourings; wild strawberry and raspberry for their fruits; and plants such as flax and fuller's teasel for their industrial uses (Harvey 1981). Plants such as hemlock, mallow and white horehound could have been brought in from the wild and cultivated as medicinal herbs. Occasional finds of leaves and seeds from potentially ornamental plants, including box, holly, rose, poppy and greater celandine, may also indicate garden waste contributing to the material dumped in the ditch. Gardening as a commercial operation around London is well attested by the late 13th century: for example, the Earl of Lincoln's Holborn garden and that of Sir James Audley in Shoe Lane (Harvey 1981, 84) are both close to the MLFC site. Gardens of this size would have included orchards of fruit and nut trees, and perhaps vineyards, but even the smallest garden would have produced potherbs and medicinal plants for family use.

Occasional flax (*Linum usitatissimum*) seeds were seen in the majority of samples from the medieval ditch fills, and could be evidence for the production of linen, or for the consumption of linseeds or their oil. In most samples, however, small fragments of flax seed capsules were also found, suggesting that the seeds are not present merely as food waste, but that a relatively early stage in the extraction of flax products is indicated. The quantities involved are small, but they are present throughout the sequence, suggesting that flax growing or processing may have been taking place in the area for some time. A more concentrated deposit of flax seeds, stems and capsule fragments was found in the early medieval fill of a ditch, just outside the City to the north-east (Davis 1997, 18), suggesting that flax processing may have been commonplace in the areas immediately outside the City. Flax stems would be 'retted' in streams or pools before the seed capsules were removed by combing (Baines 1985, 133).

Occasional rachis fragments (chaff) of rye (*Secale cereale*) and barley (*Hordeum vulgare*), complete cereal caryopses, plant stems and grassland weed seeds could have come from animal fodder and hay, perhaps indicating that small amounts of herbivore dung or stable sweepings were included in the dumped material.

Discussion of the infilling of the medieval city ditch

The evidence from the MLFC site suggests that ditch infilling began only 100 years after it was first dug, if one accepts Stow's date of 1211. Although Stow records that the ditch was frequently cleaned – and evidence from various nearby sites confirms this – there is no evidence of wholesale clearance on the MLFC site. At 1–6 Old Bailey (LUD82, Fig 63) the ditch was also backfilled without major recutting and was substantially choked with rubbish by the first half of the 14th century.

Analysis of selected finds from the ditch finds little extant evidence for organised, progressive backfill. The pottery assemblage was very mixed, but it is clear that the main period of infilling took place between 1300 and 1400, similar to that at 1–6 Old Bailey (LUD82, Fig 63). The western part of the ditch circuit seems to have become a convenient dumping area as the medieval period progressed. At least part of the ditch was kept open for a time but was much narrower, with a revetment along the City side of the ditch on the MLFC site. The ditch was evidently polluted throughout most of the medieval period, a fact documented by Stow, and filled with all manner of rubbish, including primary butchers' waste, discarded animal carcasses and large amounts of human faecal material. It would have been a rotting, seething mass and it is difficult to imagine how the inhabitants of the friary tolerated the smell. The ditch appears to have been kept much cleaner in other areas, such as 1–6 Aldersgate Street (AES96), where it was maintained long into the post-medieval period.

The material dumped in the ditch is likely to have come from both the local area and the wider settlement. No diagnostic items whose source could be unequivocally traced were present. A wide variety of pottery vessel forms are present in the assemblage, predominantly those associated with food preparation and serving, especially vessels such as jugs. A small proportion of the vessels was highly decorated and clearly came from high status households, and it is possible that some of these high status ceramic vessels may have originated from Greyfriars Friary.

Given the nearness of the friary and the presence of several artefacts commonly found associated with religious establishments, it is likely that at least some of the objects from the ditch fill are related to the friary. A number of categories of artefact have been identified (Egan, in Thomas et al 1997, 109) as being frequently found in association with religious houses. Some are specifically religious objects but others are secular items found associated with wealthy households and which also have a recurring presence on religious sites. Only one object was recovered that could be definitely associated with a religious establishment: a copper-alloy tomb inscription letter (<S63>, Fig 118) which probably dates to the late 13th to mid 14th centuries. This letter probably came from a funerary monument associated with Greyfriars. Secular objects which may also have religious associations include items associated with literacy and writing, of which a bone stylus <S64> and two possible goose radius pens were found (<S65>–<S66>,

Fig 118 Copper-alloy tomb inscription letter <S63>: Lombardic letter A (scale c 1:1)

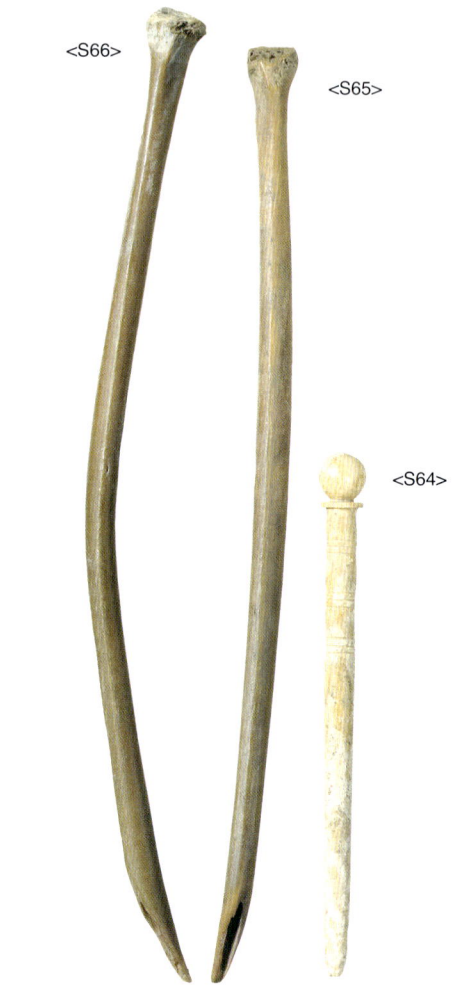

Fig 119 Bone pens <S65>–<S66> and bone stylus <S64> (scale c 1:1)

Fig 119). Another category is objects associated with music: a bone tuning peg was recovered (<S68>, Fig 97), and belongs to Lawson's type A, a type used with open frame instruments such as harps and lutes (Lawson 1985, 152 and 154). A second, contemporary tuning peg (<S67>, Fig 97) was found in the backfill of a 17th-century cellar (B27, Chapter 5.3). This one belongs to Lawson's type B, for use with instruments with a box-like frame, for example, zithers, psalteries and most keyboard instruments (ibid).

Stone lamps are another artefact type often associated with religious establishments. Three were recovered from the MLFC site, as well as a glass lamp. The wooden bowls and platters and the stone mortars may have been used at a religious establishment, although like the high status imported glassware, these may have belonged to a wealthy secular household. Other high status objects were also recovered (some from non-selected contexts) and include a copper-alloy casket mount coated with silver and two fragments of imported, high quality glass. A plain, slender gold finger-ring may not be such a high status item but is paralleled by similar finger-rings from Bermondsey Abbey, Southwark (Geoff Egan, pers comm) and St Mary Stratford Langthorne Abbey, Newham (Keily 2004, 152). These objects may have come from a wealthy secular household or equally from a wealthy religious house, such as Greyfriars.

Other materials in the ditch may have come from sources nearby. Animal bone, possibly derived from primary butchers' waste, could have been from the Shambles meat market on Newgate Street. The Shambles was a place of slaughter and processing, as well as selling, and would have generated much primary butchers' waste. A local skinning industry may be represented by large numbers of cat bones and skulls.

5
The post-medieval archaeological sequence

5.1 Introduction

The dissolution of the monasteries, which took place between 1536 and 1540, was orchestrated by King Henry VIII and generally supported by the English population, many of whom considered the monasteries to be outmoded and even degenerate institutions (Schofield 1993, 138). In London the dissolution had a major effect on the landscape of the City. The monasteries were demolished, converted into parish churches, or turned into residential housing. A large amount of space became available for new uses, spurring the City into a period of great change and redevelopment.

Migrants from the poorer rural areas of England contributed to a massive demand for housing (Milne 1986, 20), and housing for the rich, artisan and poorer classes was built in the remaining open areas of the City (ibid). This included the spaces left by the monasteries, garden areas, and land owned by City authorities. The ribbon of land occupied by the defensive circuit was common land, owned by the City of London. The bastions and gatehouses had been leased out from the early medieval period on condition that the City could repossess in times of war. Renting of City land increased in the early post-medieval period and by this time included much of the land that had previously been occupied by the city ditch (Bell et al 1937, 71). At first an attempt was made to keep some form of defensive ditch open, but the process of backfilling that had begun in the medieval period intensified and the ditch was encroached first by yards and then by buildings.

By the 17th century London was crowded with many narrow streets and squares, lined with buildings of many different styles, some dating back hundreds of years. Although brick was widely used by this time, many of the older buildings were largely timber, especially those owned by old institutions that were unwilling to modernise (Schofield 1993, 170). It was probably this great diversity in building material, along with the cluttered streets and their tall jettied buildings, which allowed the Great Fire of 1666 to cause such devastation. Post-Fire rebuilding was carried out at an erratic pace through a mixture of privately and publicly funded schemes, taking place whenever the landowners or tenants could afford to build (ibid, 175; Milne 1986, 83). Ogilby and Morgan's map of 1676 (Ogilby and Morgan 1676) (Fig 120) shows that most of the City had been rebuilt, and the streets and property boundaries set out after the fire were similar to those of the earlier medieval town, although the streets were considerably wider and buildings mainly constructed out of brick and stone (Milne 1986, 82). Development over the last 100 years or so has started to obliterate these ancient boundaries, but the medieval town plan can still be seen in many areas of the modern City.

Pre-Great Fire settlement, c 1500–1666 (period 6)

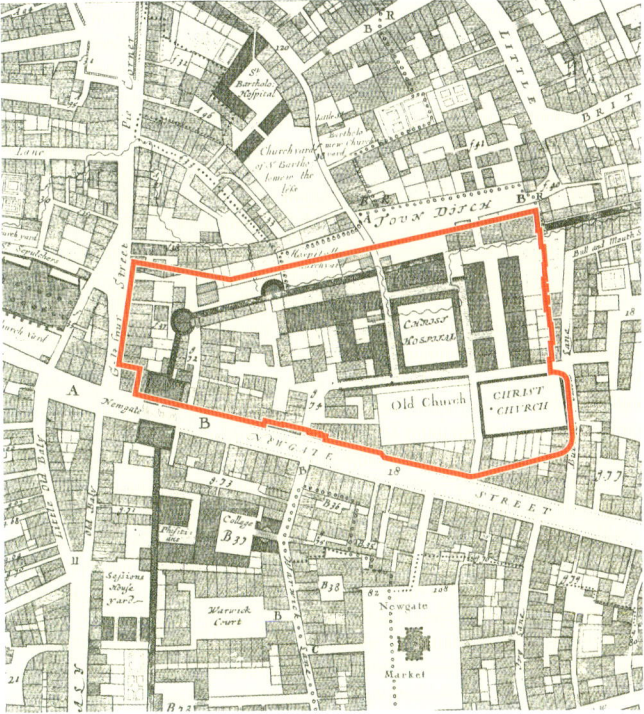

Fig 120 Detail from Ogilby and Morgan's map of 1676 (Ogilby and Morgan 1676)

5.2 Pre-Great Fire settlement, *c* 1500–1666 (period 6)

Documentary records indicate that very few changes occurred to the layout of the MLFC site in the decades leading up to the dissolution. Life at the friary also seems to have continued as normal. In 1508 a custom was established in which the mayor and aldermen (who were the friary's patrons and founders) paid an annual visit to the friary for the feast of St Francis (on 4 October). Fourteen years after the tradition was started, it was noted that the procession was followed by a dinner at which the friars 'entertained the rulers of the city' (Kingsford 1915, 23). The last main function that the friary took part in was a great religious procession in 1535.

The dissolution was not immediate: Henry VIII gradually confiscated London's monasteries between 1536 and 1540, using a number of different tactics, including threats and bribery, until the monastic buildings and lands were handed over 'voluntarily' (Schofield 1993, 140). Twenty-six friars and the warden signed the surrender of Greyfriars to Henry VIII in 1538, indicating that their numbers were far fewer than in earlier periods (*VCH* 1909, 506). The friary was not destroyed, as were many other London monasteries, but turned into a boy's orphanage and school which reopened as Christ's Hospital in 1552. It is likely that most of the land in the precinct, previously owned by Greyfriars, passed directly into the hands of Christ's Hospital. The great church was shut up and used as a storehouse for a time, before being reopened as Christ Church, following the rearrangement of the parishes in the area (Kingsford 1915, 51).

Other established medieval traditions were also wiped away with the dissolution. The many anchorites (hermits) who resided along the city walls and in 'cells' against church walls disappeared. As Bell puts it, 'They possessed no property to excite the cupidity of the Tudor collectors, and their cells can have had little value. They simply disappear' (Bell et al 1937, 69).

The demise of the city defences

Although buildings were erected close to the city wall from the 16th century onwards, documentary evidence shows that the authorities attempted to ensure that a space around the perimeter of the wall's inner face stayed free from buildings, and that the wall itself remained intact. The various laws did not always stop the defences from deteriorating, however. For instance, the stretch of wall to the north of Christ's Hospital was recorded as being in great decay by the 16th century and many repairs were carried out (CLRO, CCPR, Rep 22, fo 315, 1591). While some of this decay was undoubtedly caused by general neglect, other instances can be attributed directly to the actions of particular individuals. City Lands deeds record the following: 'View ordered of ground without London Wall beside Grey Friars in the form of the Chamber and leased by John "Tyme" salter who has carried off stones and done other hurts to common ground' (ibid, Rep 5, fo 187, 1521). The outcome of this action was: 'Instructions given to John Tymy [*sic*] to amend injuries between now and All Saints. To put ground back to condition he found it in or better on pain of £40 Re the removal of stones of the city wall, this is referred to his oath' (ibid).

Further offenders were recorded in 1543: 'Richard – late Abbot of St Albans to appear for his misdemeanour in building upon London wall at the late Grey Friars' (CLRO, CCPR, Rep 10, fo 310, 1543), and in 1549: 'Monkes brewer to be warned that he shall declare by what authority he has made a door through the City wall at Newgate at the next court' (ibid, Rep 12[i], fo 68b, 1549). Similarly, in 1561 an order was given for 'Persons to view City wall near Grey Friars and Newgate and to note the holes and damages done, their quantity and the names of the offenders' (ibid, Rep 14, fo 475, 1561). The situation did not improve, as illustrated by a report in 1578, which found the 'Wall between Newgate and Aldersgate greatly decayed' (ibid, Rep 19, fo 3206, 1578). The fact that instances of the wall being illegally built upon, breached and robbed of its stonework have been meticulously recorded indicates that City and crown still considered the wall to be an important boundary. The quantity of records detailing wilful damage and general decay, however, may reflect the fact that the authorities were unable adequately to police the wall by this time. There could have been a number of reasons for this, such as lack of finances and human resources. Another reason could be that, as the City became more built up and the city ditch began to disappear, the ribbon of land occupied by the wall became obscured from view in a number of places. The authorities may potentially have been unable to access City lands without first giving notice to, or gaining permission from, local landowners. It may therefore have been tempting for local residents to breach the wall for their own convenience, or to steal stone from it for the simple reason that it was no longer possible for the authorities to view the wall easily.

By this time the defensive wall was becoming a hindrance to the developing City, and was a major obstruction to traffic. The authorities attempted to alleviate pressure by allowing a number of new posterns to be added at various locations, including one linking Christ's Hospital with St Bartholomew's Hospital in 1552 (Fig 121). The City Letter Books record the agreement 'Mayor and alderman may pull down as much of the city wall standing on backside of Christ Church in Farringdon Within as they think fit for the making of a gate there through the same for the passage of the governors of the House of the Poor in West Smithfield and for other citizens to go to and from said house' (CLRO, CCPR, Lett Bk R, fo 204b, 1552).

The wall was considered valuable as the City's last line of defence. During the Tudor period, various riots and rebellions broke out, including the 'Evil Mayday' riots and Wyatt's rebellion of 1554. The uprisings were quelled and the perpetrators punished: for instance, after Wyatt's rebellion the city gates apparently 'bristled with heads' (Bell et al 1937, 77). In October 1569 the city gates and portcullises were repaired in anticipation of the Northern Rebellion which aimed to restore Catholicism and replace Elizabeth I with Mary Queen of Scots. The 17th century was even more troubled, with the Midlands Revolt in 1607, the Western Rising in 1628–30 and the Civil War in 1642–6 (Milne 1986, 14). A new and much larger defensive circuit was constructed during this time, which encompassed not just the City but all the London suburbs too (Sturdy 1975, 334). It is not known to what extent the city wall was refurbished as part of this work, but it is documented that in 1642 Parliament ordered 'All sheds and buildings contiguous to London Wall without be taken down, and that the city wall with its bulwarks, be not only repaired and mounted with artillery, but that likewise divers new works be added to the same at places most exposed' (Bell et al 1937, 75). There is some archaeological evidence that the northern and eastern parts of the ditch circuit may have been recut at this time. The ditch circuit as a whole, however, had ceased to act as a defensive feature by this period.

Later bastion use

It is well documented that the wall's bastions were used for many different non-military purposes over the medieval and post-medieval periods. Information on the circumstances under which the bastions were leased out in the post-medieval period is contained in the City's Land Deeds, Repertories, Journals and other records. Within these documents the bastions are referred to by various different names, including 'turrett', tower, watch tower, 'tourelle', buttress and bulwark. The latter name is the most common throughout sources from the 16th century.

Little explicit documentary information about the MLFC bastions has been uncovered, but it is likely that they were rented out to local land or property owners, who owned the adjoining land, as with other bastions (Dyson 1993). As the Greyfriars precinct backed onto the city wall throughout the medieval period, it is reasonable to assume that the friary may have had use of Bastions 17 and 18, and possibly also Bastion 19 (although this lay outside the precinct). Alternatively, Bastion 19 may have been leased to the owner of the nearby Swan Inn, whose property backed onto it. After the dissolution, Christ's Hospital may have taken over the lease of some or all of these bastions.

The proceedings of the Court of Aldermen (Repertories, from 1495 onwards) and the City Lands Grant Books have revealed further information on the use of bastions on the MLFC site. For example, the following excerpts may be relevant: on 13 February 1556: 'The Recorder to move the Master of the Words for the City's tower in London Wall near Christ Church, which Lord Henry Dudley holds of the City without any title' (CLRO, CCPR, Rep 13[ii], fo 369, 1556); in July 1567: 'Lease of old decayed tower in City adjoining tenement brewhouse where Thomas Haselwoode lives. Rent 10s. p.a., term 21 years. City to do repairs' (ibid, Rep 14, 1567); and in March 1605: 'lease of a bulwark near unto Newgate fine– Rent 20l– Term 60 years. Condition substantially build the same and maintain the same bulwark during the term. Thomas Potter, saddler' (CLRO, CL Grant Book I, fo 74v, 1604–5). The latter two leases are interesting, as the first, in 1567, states that the City will make repairs to the structure, whereas in the second lease one of the conditions of the tenancy appears to be that the tenant will repair and maintain the bastion. As there are no maps or recognisable addresses associated with the above leases, it is not possible to say with certainty that they are concerned with any of the MLFC bastions.

A plan of Christ's Hospital and surrounding tenements dated 1652–60 depicts Bastions 17 and 18, with Bastion 17 labelled as 'Wash House' (Fig 122). Bastion 18 is only marked on the plan in outline, which could suggest that Bastion 17 was leased by the school, whereas Bastion 18 was not. There is at least one other record of a bastion being used as a wash house in this period, contained in the City Lands Grant Books from 1589. An entry in 1605 has details of complaints about a bastion close to Barbersurgeons' Hall, which had been used as a wash house and suffered water damage to its walls as a result. It seems the occupants had also been illegally dumping the soil from this process into the city ditch (Dyson 1993, 12).

Disuse of the defensive ditch

In 1598, John Stow wrote of the ditch that it was 'now of late neglected and forced either to a very narrow, and the same a filthy channel, or altogether stopped up for gardens planted, and houses built thereon, even to the very wall; to what danger of the city, I leave to wiser consideration, and can but wish that reformation might be had' (1598, 50). Stow's concern about the unchecked growth of the City is clear and indeed the frequency with which the ditch was cleared out in some areas during the medieval period shows that the authorities had

Pre-Great Fire settlement, c 1500–1666 (period 6)

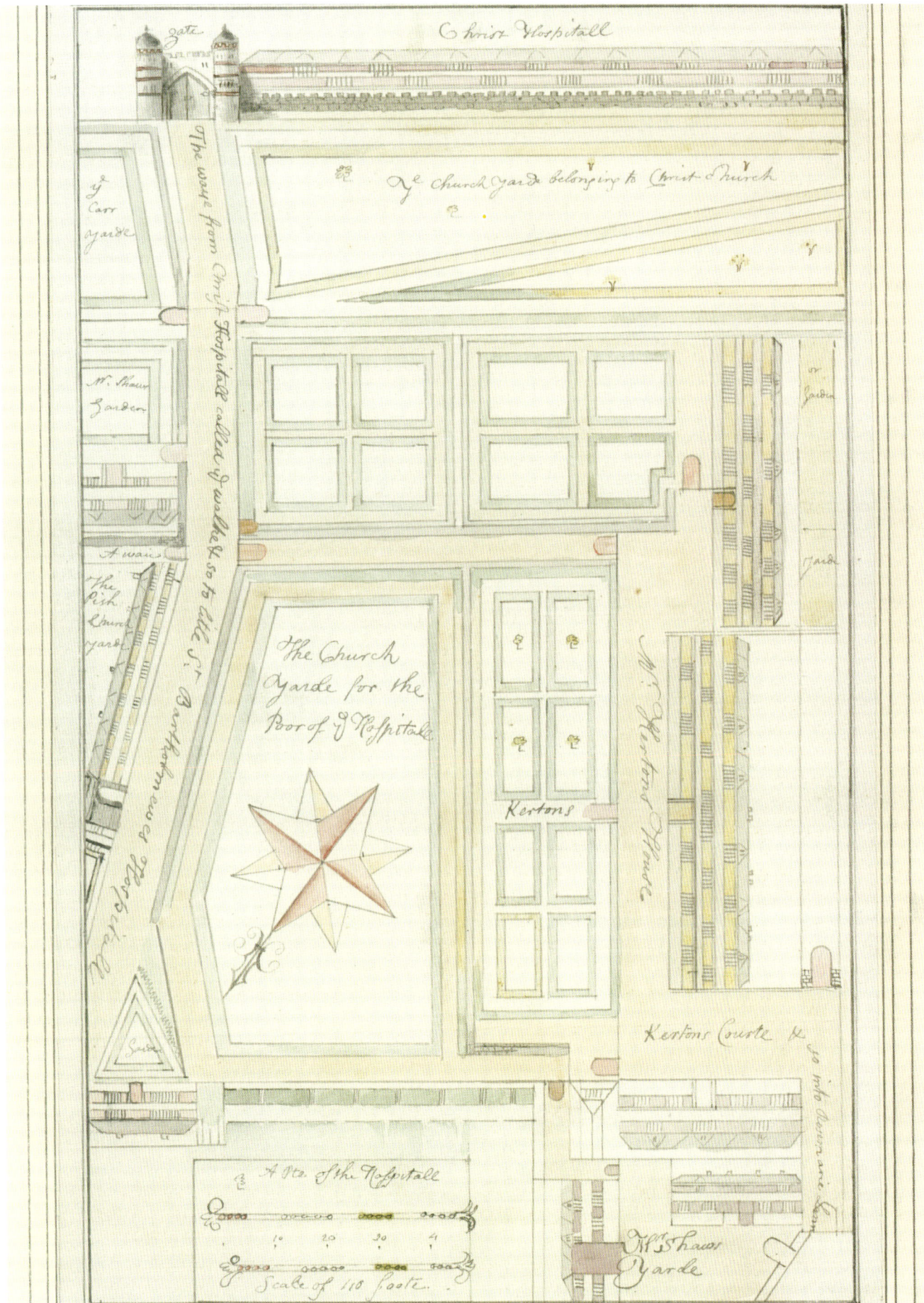

Fig 121 Plan of St Bartholomew's Hospital, showing the postern constructed in 1552 and a segment of the backfilled city ditch marked 'Ye church yard belonging to Christ Church', drawn by Ralph Treswell in 1610 (reproduced courtesy of the British Library)

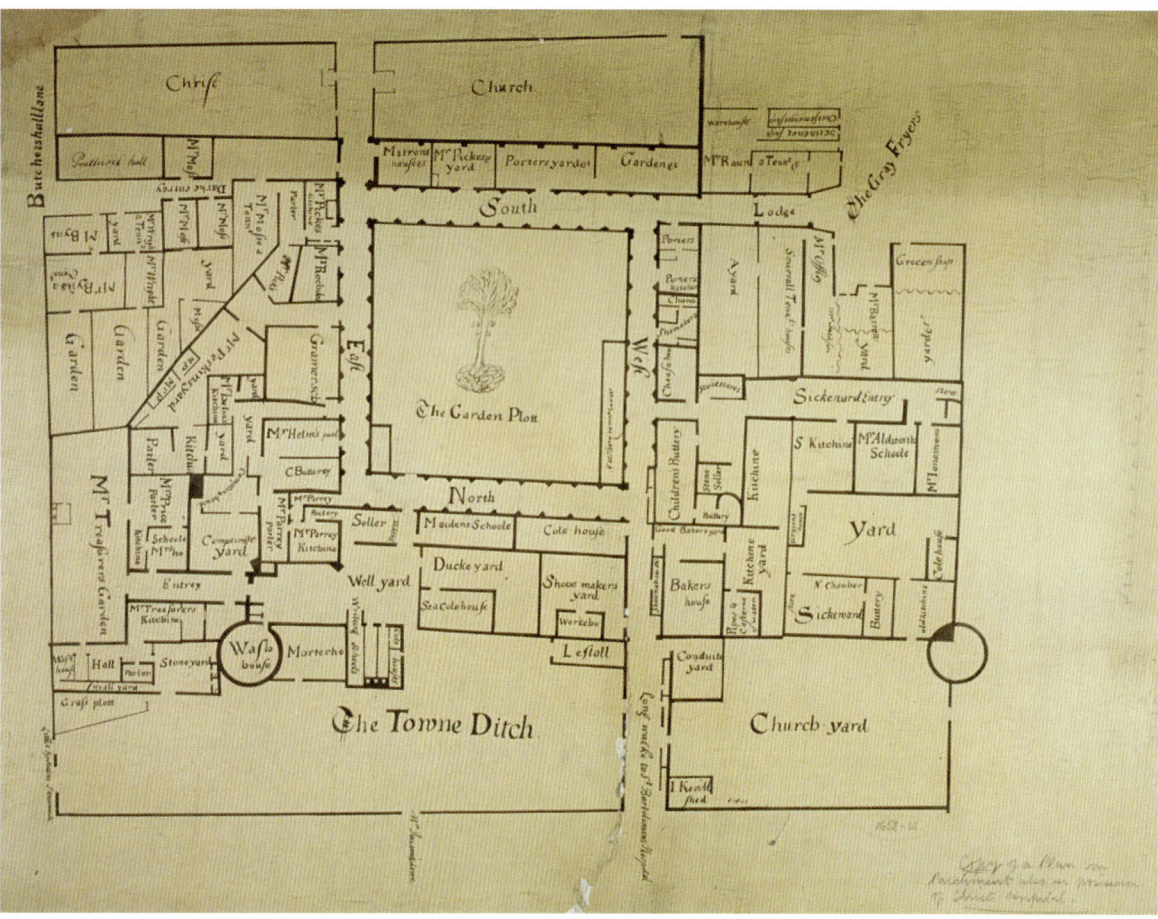

Fig 122 Plan of Christ's Hospital precinct dated 1652–60, showing Bastion 17 labelled as 'Wash House' (anon, Guildhall Library, City of London 141/CHR/1335)

waged a constant battle to keep the defensive ditch intact. By the post-medieval period, however, it seems that it was no longer possible to prevent the City from expanding over the ditch, despite the regular action taken to prevent it. For example, this excerpt from a Wardmote Inquest of the Ward of Aldersgate in 1510 is typical of the time: 'Item, we present II draughts and a hoole owte of the kechyn into the Towne Dyche of William Nycholson's House, which annoys the King's people and the Towne Dyche' (Bell et al 1937, 72).

In the western part of the City, large areas of the ditch went out of use relatively early in the medieval period, as shown by the archaeological evidence from 1–6 Old Bailey (LUD82, Fig 63). In the eastern part of the City the ditch was kept open for a much longer period. For instance, excavations on sites such as 1–6 Aldersgate Street (AES96, Fig 63), St Alphege Street (WFG17) and Dukes Place (DUK77, Fig 63) all revealed numerous post-medieval ditch recuts, some of which may have been associated with the Civil War of 1642–6 (Maloney and Harding 1979, 354; Butler 2001, 62). If this were the case, however, it is difficult to see why the whole circuit was not maintained at this time.

The archaeological evidence concurs with the evidence from contemporary maps. The 'Agas' map of c 1562 (Fig 74) indicates that the area to the west of the site was occupied by the backyard areas of tenements fronting Gilford Street (now Giltspur Street). In the area to the north, between Greyfriars and the former precinct of St Bartholomew's, an open space on the map is the only evidence that the ditch ever existed. The ditch resumes its normal course just east of Aldersgate (opposite Bastion 15), from which point it flows unbroken eastwards past Moorgate. The map does not show the eastern half of the City.

By the time St Bartholomew's and Christ's hospitals had reopened in 1555 the ditch was in such a state that John Calthorpe, Citizen and Draper, paid for it to be arched over from Newgate to Aldersgate (Bell et al 1937, 72). The information displayed on the Braun and Hogenberg map of 1572 (Fig 77) is similar to that shown on the 'Agas' map, but this map also depicts the far eastern extent of the City. The ditch is shown to continue past Bishopsgate as far as Aldgate, at which point it is open, but partially obscured by a number of structures on its western side (possibly tenter grounds). Little change is evident on the Faithorne and Newcourt map of 1658 (Faithorne and Newcourt 1658, 13) (Fig 123), apart from the fact that a graveyard is now marked in the open space which separates Greyfriars and St Bartholomew's, to the north of Bastion 17. The ditch has also largely disappeared further to the east, with the exception of the stretch between Aldersgate and Cripplegate, which is marked 'town ditch'.

CITY DITCH BACKFILLING PHASE 3 (OA17)

By the later medieval period the ditch on the MLFC site was

Pre-Great Fire settlement, c 1500–1666 (period 6)

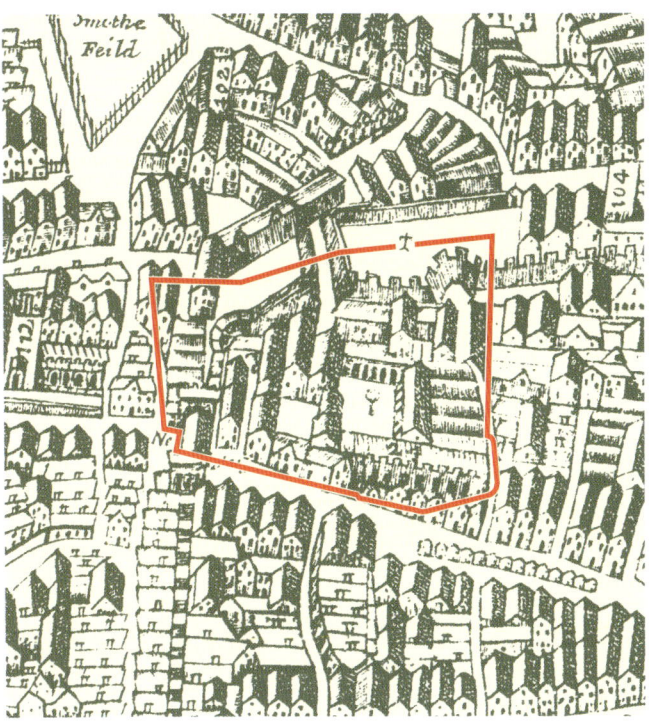

Fig 123 *Detail from the Faithorne and Newcourt map of 1658 (Faithorne and Newcourt 1658, 13)*

much narrower and had been reduced to a revetted channel, close to the city wall. The outside edges of the ditch had been backfilled and nearby properties had started to encroach on the area. By the end of the 16th century the revetted channel along the inside edge of the ditch had also gone out of use and the whole area was systematically backfilled. Again, the 'Agas' map of c 1562 (Fig 74) shows that by this time this process was complete in the western part of the ditch, adjacent to Gilford Street (now Giltspur Street). The ditch area to the north of Greyfriars, depicted on the 'Agas' map as an open area, is marked as a cemetery on the Faithorne and Newcourt map of 1658 (Fig 123) indicating that backfilling had certainly been completed by this time.

This area of the ditch was quickly occupied by tenants who leased the newly available land from the City for building on. The details of some of these transactions have survived in the records made by the Court of Aldermen (and Repertories from 1495): for instance, 'Note of lease read: land lying by city ditch leading from Newgate to Aldersgate, in length 533ft [162.4m] Rent 8s pa Term 10 years. John Hone Tallowchandler' (CLRO, CCPR, Rep 4, fo 160, 1523). Some years later, in 1560, it was agreed that Anthony Sylver, Leatherseller, could lease a plot of 'void' land to the north of Newgate: 'It is now agreed that he and assignees shall have the same ground and the new house which he has built there for a rent of 20s pa and term of 10 years' (ibid, Rep 14, fo 332b, 1560).

GILFORD STREET BUILDING (B18)
Evidence for late medieval/early post-medieval buildings encroaching into the backfilled ditch was found on the MLFC site, although only deep foundations survived, due to the truncation caused by the Giltspur Street Compter (Chapter 5.3). Building 18 consisted of a long, chalk-built foundation (Fig 124; Fig 125). The wall extended north–south for c 23m and was c 1.5m thick at top and 2m thick at base. It had three buttresses built onto its eastern face (Fig 126) but may originally have had more; the interval between the first two buttresses (from south to north) was c 6.3m, while that between the second and third was c 11.6m. This leaves room for a fourth buttress if they were spaced evenly.

The thick foundation and buttresses would have been necessary in order to prevent subsidence in the wet and unstable conditions of the backfilled city ditch. The wall was trench-built and produced no dating evidence; however, it was sealed by cellars of post-Great Fire date and so must have pre-dated 1666. The nature of construction suggests it was built in the early post-medieval period, during a boom period for the City. It is possible that Building 18 was the result of a tenancy agreement between Anthony Sylver, Leatherseller, and the City in 1560. The 'Agas' map of c 1562 (Fig 74) depicts a row of buildings fronting onto Gilford Street (now Giltspur Street), and it is probable that the foundations were associated with one or more of these properties.

GREEN DRAGON YARD BUILDING (B19) AND OTHER EVIDENCE (B13)
At the north-western extent of the excavations lay the remains of cellars belonging to a set of buildings which formed Green Dragon Yard (Fig 124). The remains, which were recorded in section and ran beyond the limit of excavation, consisted of a robbed out wall, a chalk rubble foundation and two brick foundations which may have post-dated the fire. The surviving remains of Building 13 (Fig 124) consisted of an incomplete charred wooden floor, perhaps burnt in the Great Fire.

Christ Church and Christ's Hospital

In 1547 the conventual buildings of Greyfriars Friary were granted to the City of London and adapted into a boy's orphanage and school, under the name of Christ's Hospital (Fig 127). The orphanage was officially opened in 1552 and was home to 400 boys (Kingsford 1915, 51–2). In the same year, the former friary church was renamed Christ Church and recreated as a parish church, comprising the former parishes of St Nicholas Shambles, St Edwin, and part of the Church of the Holy Sepulchre, Giltspur Street. The new parish church occupied the choir, or eastern portion, of the former friary church. The nave, or western portion, was occupied by the king's printing presses. During the conversion many of the altars and tombs within the church were stripped out (ibid, 51). Despite this destruction John Stow, writing in 1598, listed numerous tombs of aristocratic, royal and rich patrons who had been interred within the church:

> All these and five times so many more have been buried there, whose monuments are wholly defaced; for there were nine tombs of alabaster and marble, environed with strikes of

121

The post-medieval archaeological sequence

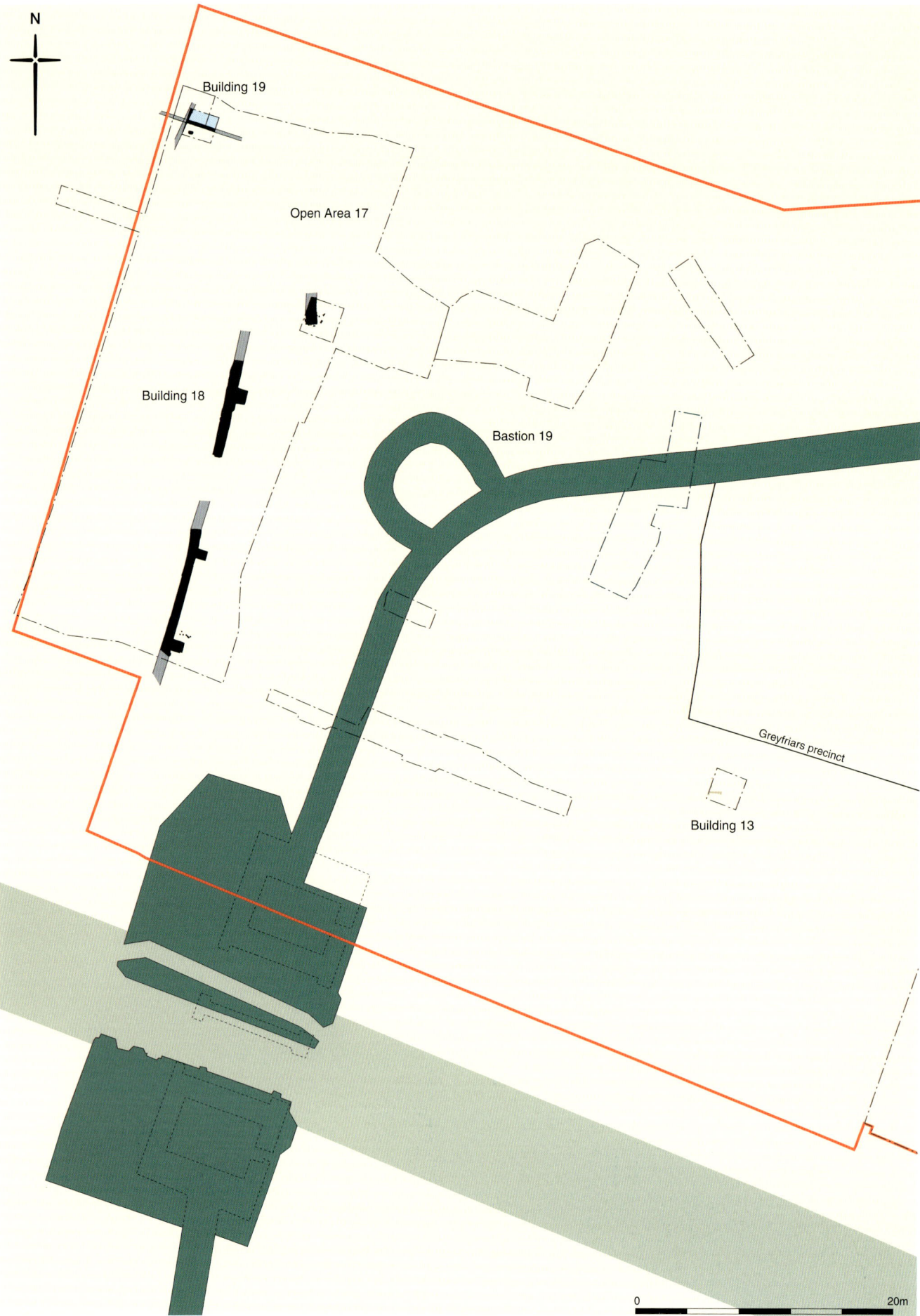

Fig 124 Pre-Great Fire of London settlement, c 1500–1666 (period 6) (scale 1:400)

Pre-Great Fire settlement, c 1500–1666 (period 6)

Fig 125 Chalk-built foundations of Building 18, looking north

Fig 126 Southernmost buttress on north–south wall of Building 18, looking south

The post-medieval archaeological sequence

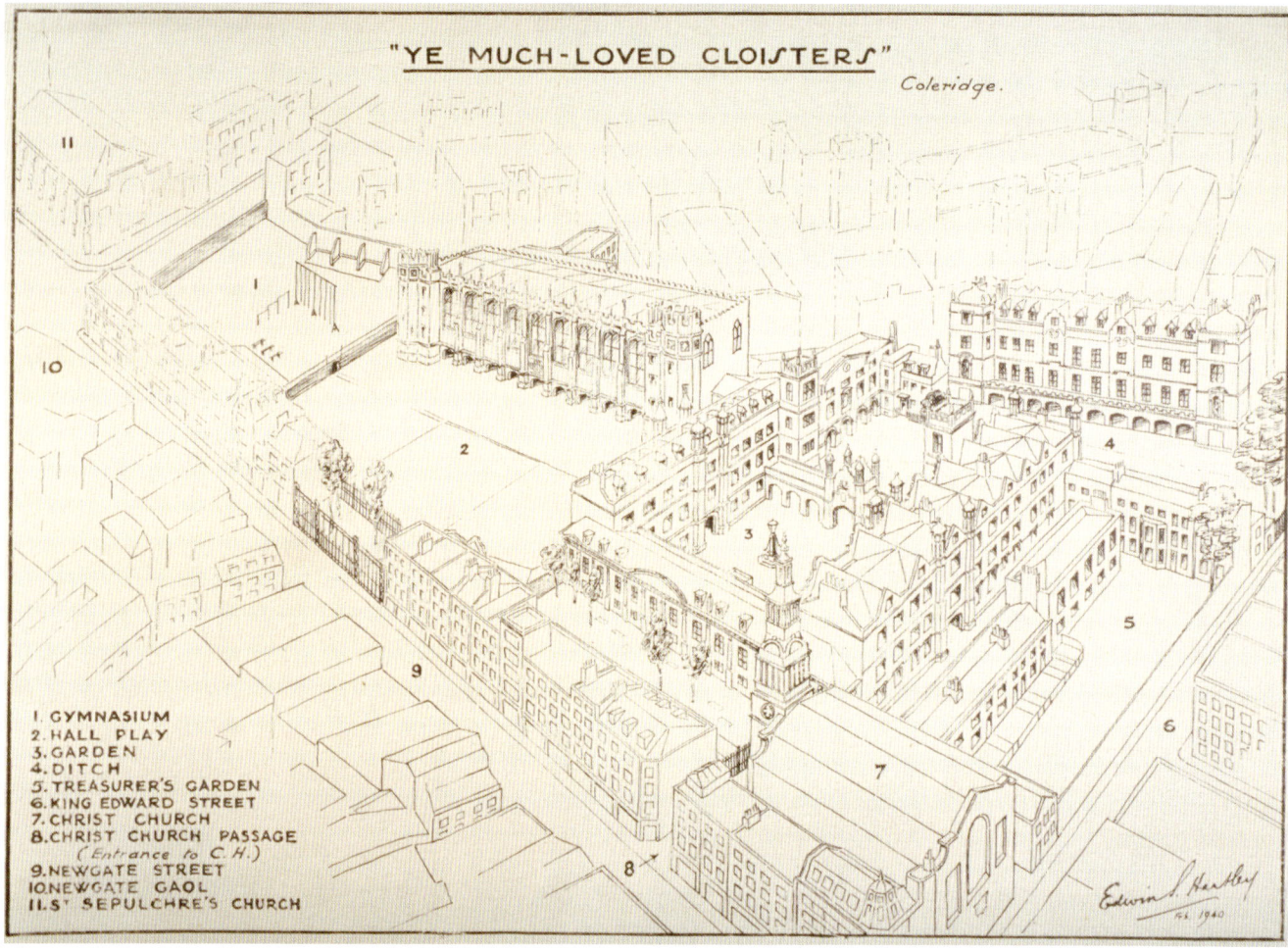

Fig 127 View of Christ's Hospital and vicinity entitled 'ye much loved cloisters', by E S Hartley, 1940 (Guildhall Library, City of London)

iron in the choir, and one tomb in the body of the church, also coped with iron, all pulled down, besides sevenscore of grave-stones of marble, all sold for fifty pounds, or thereabouts. (1598, 305)

In 1553 Queen Mary made her first visit to the City and requested that the Christ's Hospital boys play a part in her welcome. The event was attended by John Howes (clerk to the Treasurer-General of the Hospital), who described the scene. The children were presented to the queen on a stage. One boy was selected to perform an oration, but 'wan shee came nere unto them shee cast hir eie another waie and never stayed nor gave any countnunce to them'. Howes concluded: 'for nowe I knowe shee did not lyke of the blewe boyes, but if they had bene so manye Greyefryers shee would have gyven them bettwe countnunce' (Bell et al 1937, 77). In this way the queen openly showed her opinion of the reformation.

The 'blewe boys' were not deterred by this royal snub and for many years afterwards the school gave an address on the occasion of the first official entry of a new monarch to the City (Bell et al 1937, 77). Today the school remains a part of many ancient City traditions, including the lord mayor's annual parade and the St Matthew's day parade on 26 September, despite the fact that the school is no longer based in London (Fig 128).

Discussion (period 6)

The dissolution caused few physical changes to the landscape of the MLFC site, with the conventual buildings of the friary simply being converted into the Christ's Hospital school, and the great church renamed as Christ Church within the new parish. Although these were certainly major changes, they were political ones that would have had very little visible archaeological impact. New buildings are known to have been added to the Christ's Hospital complex over time, but none of these was investigated during the excavation of the site.

The land outside the precinct became more built up, with buildings extending ever closer to the city wall. The ditch had been reduced to a narrow channel during the late medieval period, and yards and buildings occupied its outside edges. The City authorities had waged a battle to keep the defensive circuit intact but illegal dumping and building encroachment could not be stopped, and the City decided to sell off or rent out large areas of the ditch. On the MLFC site, archaeological evidence shows that the western part of the ditch was finally built over during the mid 16th century. The city wall and gates were still regarded as important for defence and policing, and were retained intact. There are many documented instances of the wall being wilfully damaged, and legal thoroughfares were also

Fig 128 Interior view of Christ's Hospital showing the annual orations on St Matthew's day in 1798, by Thomas Stothard (Guildhall Library, City of London)

inserted through the wall to relieve traffic flow through the congested City.

5.3 Post-Great Fire redevelopment (period 7)

The Great Fire of London started in Thomas Faryner's bakehouse on Pudding Lane in the early hours of Sunday 2 September 1666 and lasted until Friday 7 September (Milne 1986, 24). The fire swept across London destroying virtually every building in its path and foiling the many attempts by Londoners to put it out. The City lost nearly all its residential houses along with most of its significant religious and secular buildings, including St Paul's Cathedral, the parish churches and the Company halls. The total cost of the damage may have been in the region of £10,000,000 (ibid, 77). Leake's map of 1667 (Leake 1667) (Fig 129) shows the full extent of the damage and the enormity of the rebuilding task that faced the City.

Rebuilding was funded via a mixture of public and private resources. The City that emerged was a cleaner and better-ordered place than its medieval predecessor. Almost all of London's parish churches were designed and rebuilt by Christopher Wren and his team of architects. Examples of both public and private rebuilding were identified during the excavation at the MLFC site. It was apparent that the area had been thoroughly cleared and levelled before redevelopment took place.

By the 18th century the city wall had ceased to be a significant boundary in London's landscape. Congestion was so bad that in 1760 Parliament gave the order to pull down all the gates. Newgate was the last gate to disappear in 1777 (Bell et al 1937, 93). The city wall was removed gradually over the following centuries, whenever redevelopment required it, and its removal went largely unrecorded.

Residential redevelopment

The area of the city ditch was covered with buildings during the post-Great Fire redevelopment. Earlier buildings were replaced with deep-cellared, brick buildings, which lined Newgate Street and Giltspur Street. The extent of the redevelopment can be seen on Ogilby and Morgan's map of 1676 (Fig 120). The area where the city ditch had been is almost completely covered in the western part of the site; to the east, opposite Christ's Hospital, part of the ditch is still open. The city wall and two of its bastions are still extant on this map, but by the time of Rocque's map of 1746 (Rocque 1746) (Fig 130) the city wall has completely disappeared. Some of the post-Great Fire cellared buildings excavated on the MLFC site were very well preserved, despite the truncation caused by the later Compter.

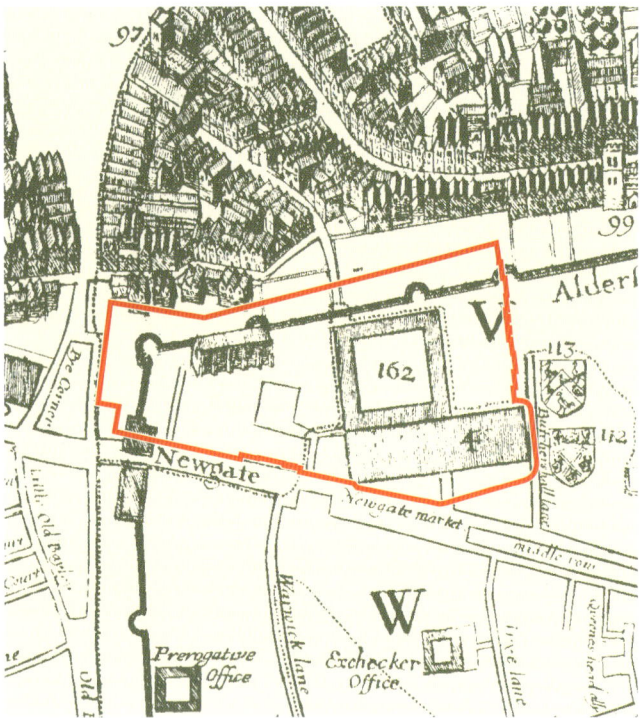

Fig 129 Detail from Leake's post-fire survey of 1667 (Leake 1667)

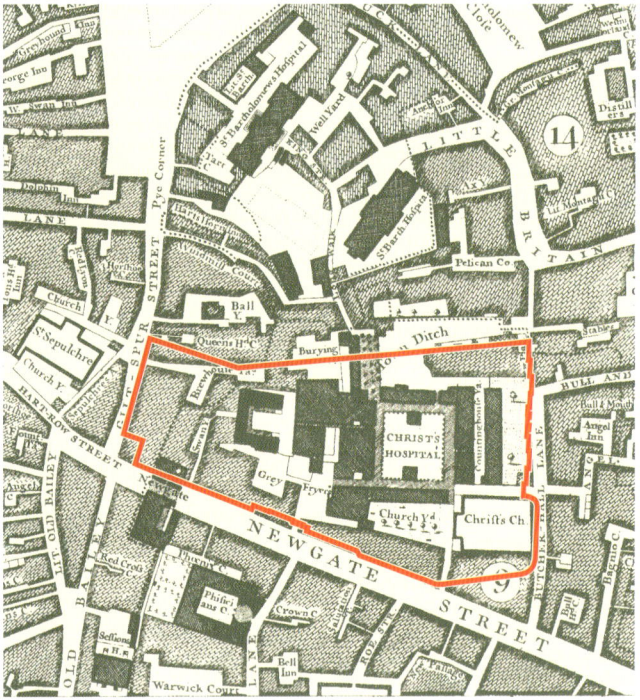

Fig 130 Detail from Rocque's map of 1746 (Rocque 1746)

BUILDINGS FRONTING NEWGATE STREET (B22–B25 AND B29)

Ephemeral remains of buildings, recorded in several small pile-probe excavation trenches, belonged to properties fronting Newgate Street (B22–B25 and B29, Fig 131). Building 25 was built over the top of the truncated remains of the city wall. A barrel-vaulted cellar was all that remained of Building 22. It was backfilled with large amounts of human bone from Greyfriars graveyard, thought to have been dumped there during the 1907–9 redevelopment of the site. The backfill of the cellar also contained a corner fragment of a green-glazed stove tile, with scallop shell decoration, dated to the 15th or 16th century (<T9>, Fig 132).

BUILDINGS FRONTING GILTSPUR STREET (B26 AND B27)

The remains of Buildings 26 and 27 can be associated with two adjacent cellared properties (Fig 131) which had partially survived truncation by the later Compter prison. The remains comprised walls standing to c 1.2m and intact brick floors (Fig 133). The southernmost of the buildings (B26) contained original internal features, including a rectangular brick feature which may have been used for storing barrels, and a semicircular brick structure. A reinforced opening was found in the cellar floor which had served as the access point to a chalk-built cesspit. The cellars of both buildings had been laid directly over the backfilled city ditch and the earlier north–south wall of Building 18 (Fig 134; Fig 135). This had caused a visible 'hump' in the surface of the floor, where the earlier wall ran. The west wall of the cesspit belonging to Building 26 had been incorporated into the earlier north–south wall of Building 18.

The rubble backfill of the cellars contained several plain and decorated residual medieval floor tiles, tin-glazed wall and floor tiles, a late 12th- to 13th-century green-glazed London-type ware (LOND) louver and an unusual fragment of curved moulded brick (<1001>, fabric 3250). The moulded brick appears to be the base of a Tudor decorative brick chimney (T Smith, pers comm.) (<T10>, Fig 136). The buildings would have originally fronted onto Giltspur Street and seem to have been built rapidly. They were demolished in 1787, when the Compter prison was constructed. Dance recorded that there were 14 properties in Giltspur Street and six in Swan Yard at the time. Some residents petitioned against the Compter's purchase order, but most were apparently content to accept the compensation sums offered for their 'rather rickety' dwellings (Stroud 1984, 129).

GREEN DRAGON YARD BUILDING (B28)

The buildings on Green Dragon Yard were also rebuilt after the Great Fire. Fragments of Building 28 were recorded in section and included external and internal walls, stone and brick floors, an intact internal pillar and column fragments (B28, Fig 131). A water cistern was also associated with this building, which had been constructed over the infilled ditch. The tank was of particular interest as it had been lined with reused 18th-century tin-glazed 'delftware' wall tiles (Figs 137–138, 162–163). The tiles form one of the largest and most diverse delftware tile assemblages excavated in London. These and the other wall tiles associated with Building 28 are listed, described and illustrated in the relevant specialist appendix (Chapter 7.1, Figs 162–164).

Christ Church and Christ's Hospital rebuilt

The whole of the friary church and most of Christ's Hospital school were destroyed in the Great Fire of 1666. The school was rebuilt by various architects including Peter Mills, Hooke

Post-Great Fire redevelopment (period 7)

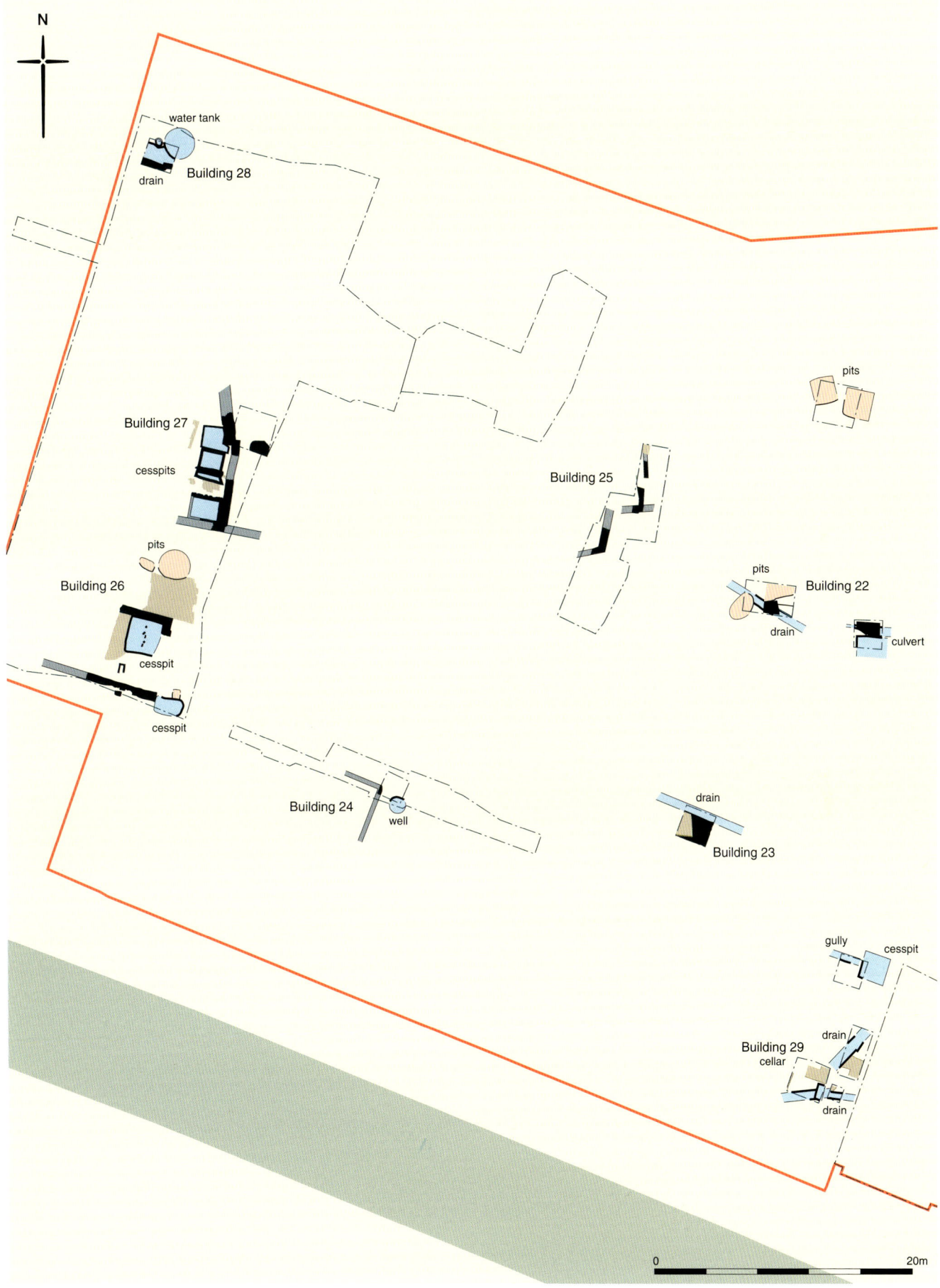

Fig 131 Post-Great Fire of London settlement, c 1666–1787 (period 7) (scale 1:400)

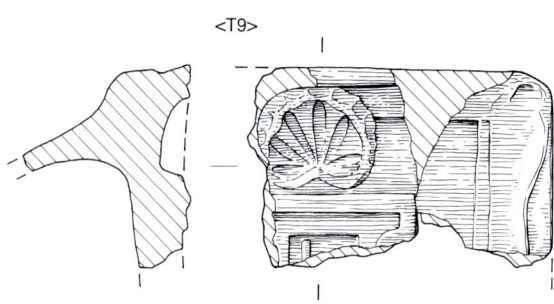

Fig 132 Decorated 15th- to 16th-century stove tile <T9> from cellar infill of Building 22 (scale 1:2)

Fig 133 Cellar floor of Building 27, looking west (scale 0.5m)

Fig 134 Rear wall of Building 27 built directly over the backfilled city ditch, looking east (scale 1m)

Post-Great Fire redevelopment (period 7)

Fig 135 Cleaning the cellar floor of Building 26, looking east

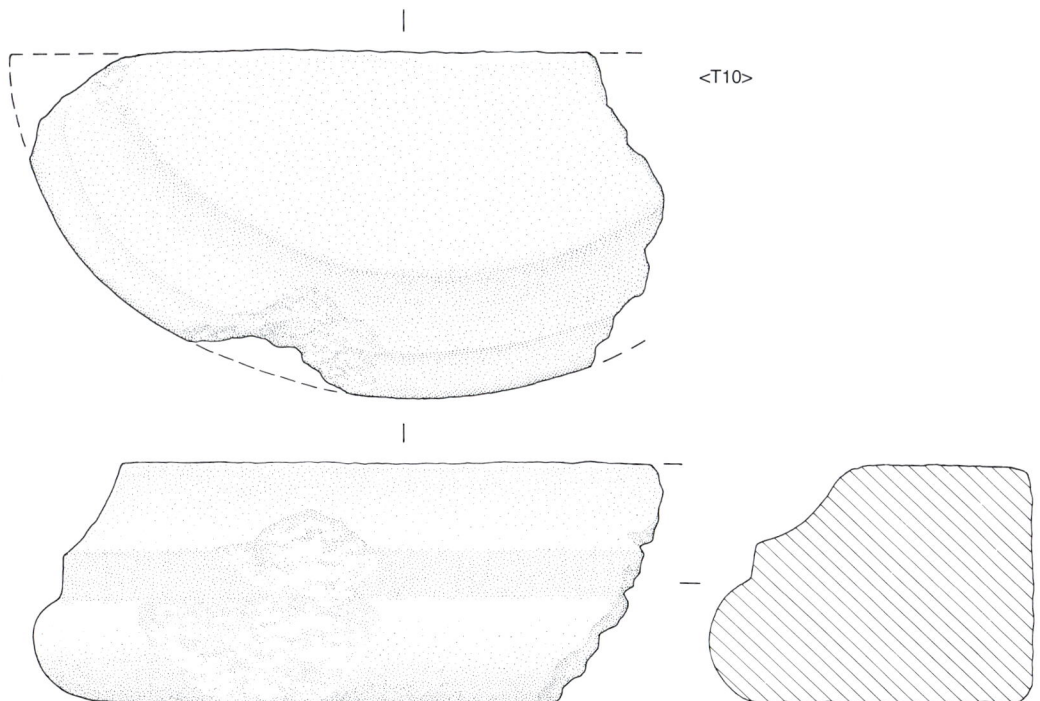

Fig 136 Tudor brick chimney fragment <T10> (scale 1:2)

and Oliver, between 1667 and 1683. Wren and Hawksmoor constructed the Sir John Moore's Writing School in 1672–5, and John Shaw senior carried out later work in 1820–32, building the gothic Great Hall (Fig 139) (Bradley and Pevsner 1997, 97).

Between 1674 and 1687 the parish church was rebuilt on the site of the choir of the friary church, under the architectural direction of Sir Christopher Wren; the steeple was added later during 1703–4 (Fig 140) (Jeffery 1996, 190). After the Great Fire the site of the former friary church nave was converted into a burial ground to serve the parish of Christ Church. Ogilby and Morgan's map of 1676 (Fig 120) shows the site of the nave as an open space, described as the 'Old Church' with a series of buildings occupying the Newgate

The post-medieval archaeological sequence

Fig 137 Building 28 showing the position of the tile-lined tank, looking west

Fig 138 The tile-lined tank in Building 28, looking east

Post-Great Fire redevelopment (period 7)

Fig 139 *Entrances of Christ's Hospital and Christ Church, 1895 (watercolour by P Norman, Norman 1905, 144, pl 35)*

Street frontage. The Vestry House, adjoining the south-west corner of the church, dates from 1760. It was destroyed during the Blitz but was rebuilt in 1981.

The new church had a fairly standard rectangular plan and was divided into two aisles and a nave. The nave was separated from its twin aisles by a series of ten pillars (five on each side). Wren's aim was to provide seating for the maximum number of people, so there were galleries above the north and south aisles. This was done so that more people could hear the sermon, which was the focal point of 17th-century church services. The box pews were arranged so as to give the congregation a good view of the pulpit, rather than the altar (Fig 141).

The adjoining burial ground remained in use as a parish cemetery until the mid 19th-century public health reforms, when the overcrowded City of London burial grounds were closed. By 1873 the site of the disused burial ground had been laid out as a public garden except for the strip of land adjoining Newgate Street, which is still occupied by a series of buildings.

During the 1907–9 redevelopment of the site the remaining buildings of Christ's Hospital were demolished, although Christ Church remained intact. Norman and Reader observed the foundations of many of these buildings during their investigation of the site in 1907–12. They described the demolition and removal of Shaw's Great Hall, the foundations of which had been built over the line of the city wall. The builders of the Great Hall clearly had similar problems with poor ground conditions to their Roman predecessors. Shaw's

Fig 140 *West view of Christ Church, with part of Christ's Hospital, drawn by Thomas Hosmer Shepherd in 1830 (Guildhall Library, City of London)*

131

Fig 141 *Interior view of Christ Church, drawn by R Randoll in 1896 (Guildhall Library, City of London)*

solution was to build the foundations on a series of massive beech piles driven through the waterlogged ground. Norman and Reader (1912, 282) record that the piles 'when uncovered were found to be in wonderful preservation and presented the appearance of a veritable forest'.

In 1940 the Blitz destroyed the Wren church (Fig 142). The steeple was restored during 1960 and the ruined church was laid out as a garden, which is now managed by the City (formerly Corporation) of London. In 1973 the east wall of the choir and the adjoining part of the church were demolished as part of a Corporation of London road widening scheme. The small excavation that preceded this work (GF73, Johnson 1974, 221) suggested that the pillar bases of the Wren church sat directly on the arcade foundations of the medieval church. A number of medieval graves were also defined within the area of the medieval high altar, but were not excavated, and a series of large post-medieval, brick-built burial vaults in the north and south aisles was located (Johnson 1974, 221–5).

The remains of Christ Church and Christ's Hospital were not formally investigated during the MLFC excavations. Christ's Hospital progressed from being a boys' orphanage and school to a private boarding school, which remained on the site until 1902. The western half of the MLFC site was not extensively redeveloped by the school and was used as a playground from 1858 until 1902. Norman and Reader uncovered 'several layers of asphalt which had formed the surface of the playground' (1912, 286). The Ordnance Survey map of 1894–6 (Fig 154) depicts the site after the demolition of the prison, but before

Post-Great Fire redevelopment (period 7)

Fig 142 Watercolour of Christ Church after the Blitz in 1941, by R G Matthews (Guildhall Library, City of London)

Christ's Hospital had disappeared. The few remains that were recorded during the MLFC excavations are described below, but do not add substantially to the understanding of the site in this period.

WREN'S CHRIST CHURCH (B20)

The foundations of the rebuilt, post-medieval Christ Church were observed during a watching brief of cable trench laying in King Edward Street in 1999. There was no sign of the foundations of the medieval church underneath the post-medieval structure, as seen by Johnson in the 1970s. It is possible that Wren considered the medieval foundations inadequate in this area and did not build on them. Another possibility is that he realigned the foundations of the eastern portion of the church, in advance of a post-Great Fire road-widening scheme. The remains were not excavated but preserved in situ.

CHRIST'S HOSPITAL SCHOOL (B21)

Fragmentary building remains relating to the post-fire rebuilding of the hospital were found in various trenches across the site. Of particular note were the foundations of the Great Hall, built by John Shaw senior in 1825 (Fig 153; Fig 143; Fig 144).

The Giltspur Street Compter (1787–1854)

Before the construction of the Giltspur Street Compter prison, the City's petty criminals were housed in the Bread Street (Wood Street after 1555) and Poultry Compters. Conditions within these prisons were appalling, and following a survey on the state of London's prisons in 1777 a decision was made to close and demolish both prisons (Stroud 1984, 127–8). The Giltspur Street Compter, constructed between 1787 and 1791 under the direction of its architect George Dance the Younger, Clerk of Works to the City authorities, was intended to replace the earlier prisons and greatly improve conditions.

The Giltspur Street site was selected out of four possible locations for the prison, and together with Newgate Prison (also by Dance), which was rebuilt in 1770–8 on the site of the modern day Old Bailey, would have formed an imposing entrance to the City from the west. Thomas Pennant, writing in 1805, described the Newgate and Giltspur Street gaols as 'a superb, but melancholy group of public buildings; and are a noble improvement of this spot' (1805, 203). The final appearance of the prison was, however, very different from Dance's original blueprints. The first plan (a copy of which exists in the Sir John Soane's Museum library), was reminiscent

133

The post-medieval archaeological sequence

Fig 143 *The Great Hall of Christ's Hospital c 1825 (Guildhall Library, City of London)*

Fig 144 *Foundation of a stairwell in the Great Hall of Christ's Hospital, looking north (scale 0.5m)*

of Bentham's 'panoptical principle', complete with quadrangle and central observation tower (Stroud 1984, 129). The design was intended for 180 prisoners at a cost of £39,000, but this was evidently too expensive, as the committee rejected it. The cost was continually revised downwards over the course of the design period, resulting in a number of different blueprints for the prison. The final plan was approved on 16 June 1787 (Fig 145) and was intended for 136 prisoners at a cost of £15,120 (ibid).

The design as originally approved was for a west-facing rectangular building fronting onto Giltspur Street, occupying the western half of the site and preserving a strip along Newgate Street for the construction of residential houses to let. The building of the prison would also involve the widening and general improvement of Giltspur Street (Fig 146; Fig 147). The facade was to be faced with rusticated Purbeck stone and topped by crenellations formed of massive ashlar blocks, although the latter were omitted during early stages of construction and replaced by three pediments (Stroud 1984, 130). The front block was three storeys high and contained the sheriff and turnkey's offices. The central buildings, housing the wards and cells, were four storeys high and accessed by three main staircases. Further cells, wards and yards were situated towards the back and edges of the prison (Fig 145).

It is now known that the plan of June 1787 (Soane, D4/3/34) was not in fact the final plan, as has been suggested by Stroud. There is another plan, dated 22 September 1787 (Fig 148), which indicates that further changes were made to the

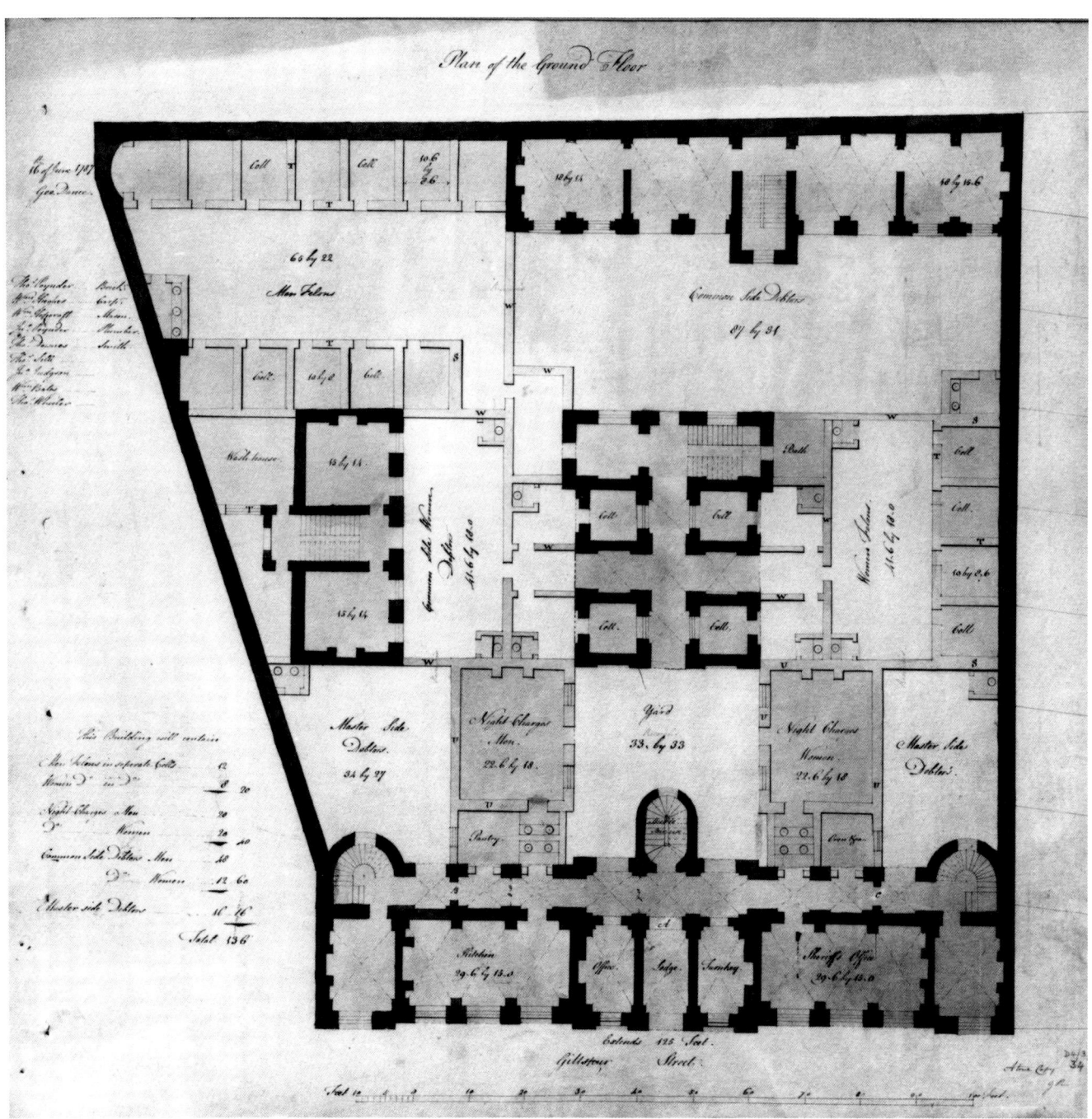

Fig 145 George Dance's approved plan of the Compter, dated 16 June 1787 (Soane, D4/3/34, reproduced courtesy of Sir John Soane's Museum)

The post-medieval archaeological sequence

Fig 146 Facade of the Compter prison, painting by G Shepherd, 1812 (Guildhall Library, City of London)

Fig 147 Giltspur Street facade, showing the Compter and Viaduct Tavern, drawn by Thomas Hosmer Shepherd, 1813 (Guildhall Library, City of London)

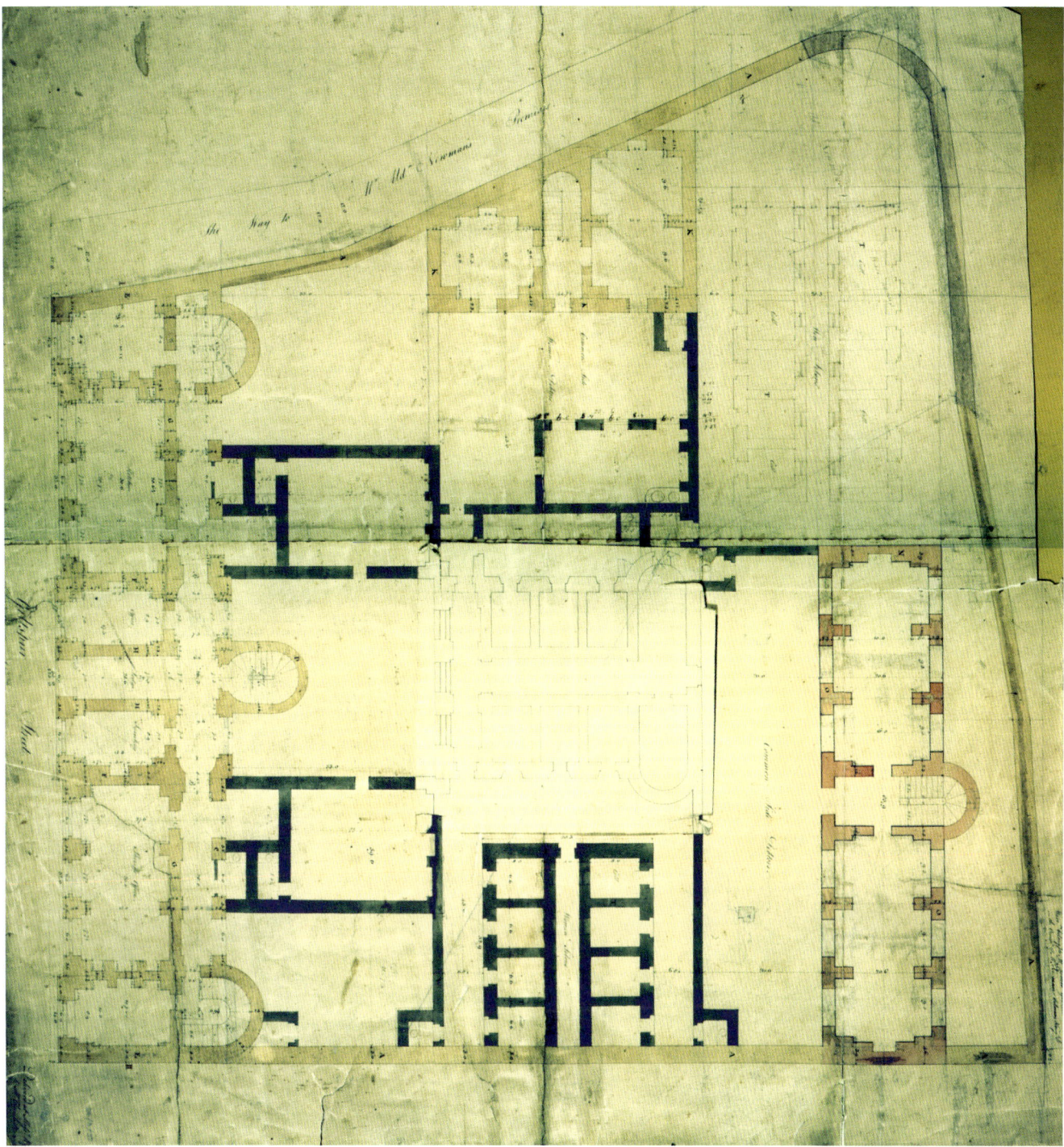

Fig 148 *George Dance's revised plan of the Giltspur Street Compter, dated 22 September 1787 (Soane, D4/3/37, reproduced courtesy of Sir John Soane's Museum)*

internal arrangement of the prison during construction, mainly to the accommodation for male/female commonside debtors and male/female commonside felons. During the 1999 excavation of the prison, it became apparent that the remains of the prison in the ground differed even from this revised plan, suggesting that further revisions were made, the plans for which must have since been lost.

This prison, with its fireplaces, toilets and even a bath (Stroud 1984, 130), was radically different from earlier prisons, where conditions were so terrible that incarceration for any amount of time was often equivalent to a death sentence.

The committee report on the prisons of the metropolis clearly shows that time and money were spent ensuring that the inmates of the City's prisons, including Giltspur Street, did not suffer needlessly from cold, illness or starvation. The internal workings of the prison are revealed in great detail in these reports, even down to descriptions of the typical cell. For example, most of the overnight cells were 8ft [2.4m] by 7ft [2.1m], containing one 7ft [2.1m] long bed, and slept two or three people: 'we have a sort of tick filled with straw, and about four rugs to each cell' (House of Commons paper 392, 81). The prison also attempted to order and separate the prisoners into different classes. Women, boys and men were kept separate from one another, and vagrants were separated from those who had committed assault or been detained for disorderly conduct (ibid).

According to the testimony of Mr John Teague, keeper of the Giltspur Street Compter and governor of the House of Correction, the Compter prisoners consisted of 'people committed for assaults, misdemeanors, prisoners for further examination, vagrants and night charges' (House of Commons paper 392, 79). Many of those who passed through the gaol were in there for one night only, following their arrest, before being sent on elsewhere. Others were kept for a few days or weeks, or were sentenced to hard labour in the House of Correction for a period of months or years. One example from the prison record books states that over 100 sailors were detained for a month in 1818, causing severe overcrowding, before being deported (ibid). The charge book of 1811–23 (CLRO, Giltspur Street Compter Charge Book PC1/23) gives a fascinating insight into the prisoners, complete with detailed physical descriptions, although little information on the actual crime committed is given. Many of the people who were detained came from London, but others originated from places like Scotland, Cornwall, Liverpool, Dublin, France, Sicily, Stockholm and even New York. Many were artisans or sailors by profession. Under the heading 'remarks' the comment 'pitted by pox' appeared very frequently. Here are two entries, by way of example, using the original headings from the report book:

Date: 1816, Name: Henry Thatcher, Age: 21, Height: 5ft 7ins, Complexion: fairish, Hair: sandy, Eyes: blue, 'Make' [presumably build]: stoutish, Profession: silver-smith, Wherever born: Back Road, Islington, Remarks: Stammers when speaking.

Date: 1820, Name: John Thompson, Age: 46, Height: 5ft 3ins, Complexion: brown, Hair: black, Eyes: blue, Make: stout, Profession: sail maker, Wherever born: Liverpool, Remarks: Long nose. Wooden leg left.

The Giltspur Street Compter was closed down and demolished in 1854, after only 63 years of use. By this time ideas on prison design had changed and other prisons had been constructed, such as Pentonville Prison in 1840–2 and Holloway. Following demolition, the space was left open and came to be used as a car park for the Royal Mail sorting office. During the excavations in 1999 extensive remains of the prison foundations were discovered.

GILTSPUR STREET COMPTER (B30)

The excavations uncovered fragments of the scalloped, eastern perimeter wall of the Giltspur Street Compter (B30), along with a large segment of the northern perimeter wall and the cellars of the entire front range, including the stairwells and water tanks (Fig 149; Fig 150; Fig 153). The main areas of the prison which fell within the excavation areas were the male/female

Fig 149 Foundations of the front range of the Compter showing the main stairwell, looking west

Post-Great Fire redevelopment (period 7)

Fig 150 *Water tank and other foundations of the Compter, looking south*

night charges' cell blocks, the male/female felons' cell block and the male/female commonside debtors' cell block. The excavation also located a number of undocumented drains, including a brick-built culvert, which followed the line of the infilled city ditch (Fig 151).

The cellar floors of the prison buildings and many of its walls had been extensively robbed during demolition. The prison's deep foundations, however, had survived virtually intact and confirmed that the stepped brickwork had been founded on a series of tangentially faced pine beams and planks, as shown on Dance's original plans (Fig 152).

The survival of so many of the prison's foundations has allowed comparison to be made between Dance's original plan of June 1787 (Fig 145), the revised plan of September 1787 (Fig 148) and the Compter foundations as built. Both Dance's plans show little change to the western perimeter but considerable revision to the eastern Compter foundations as built. Fig 153 shows Dance's original plan of June 1787 overlaid onto the foundations of the prison, using the main stairwell, the western perimeter wall and the positions of the various drains as fixing points. The figure illustrates the reason why the plan was revised, as the eastern perimeter walls shown on Dance's original plan of June 1787 overlap the Great Hall of Christ's Hospital. Furthermore, although the foundations as excavated follow the September plan closely there are still several minor discrepancies between the architect's plan, the 19th-century mapping and the physical remains of the prison as found. For instance, the Compter precinct boundary, as

Fig 151 *Brick-built culvert, cut through backfilled city ditch, looking south*

139

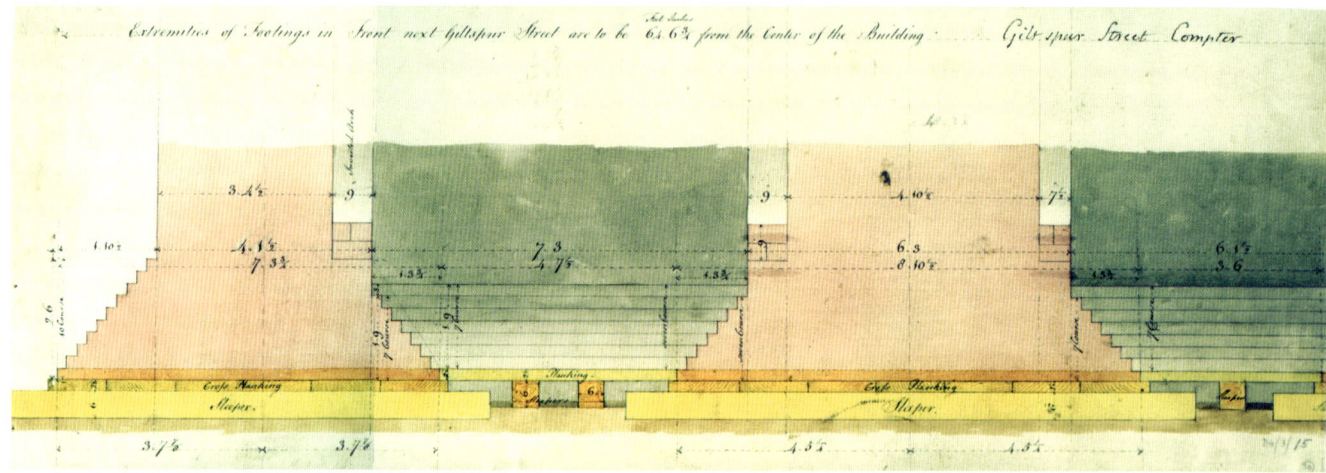

Fig 152 a – George Dance's 1787 elevation through foundations of Giltspur Street Compter, showing stepped brickwork on a raft of pine beams and planks (Soane, D4/3, reproduced courtesy of Sir John Soane's Museum); b and c – the stepped brickwork as found during the recent excavations (scale 0.2m)

depicted on the Ordnance Survey map of 1894–6 (Fig 154), but also shown on Fig 153 by way of comparison, is clearly inaccurate and suggests either that Dance's revised plan contains errors, which were rectified while the prison was being built, or that further revisions were made to the building design, the plans for which have since been lost.

Many of the materials used to build the prison were found among the demolition debris and dumped in the backfill of the robber trenches. Fragments of Purbeck limestone paving and roofing slate were found, along with tin-glazed wall tiles. One very unusual tile has a design impressed in counter-relief, picked out in blue on a white background (<T11>, Fig 155), perhaps a one-off experiment by London's tilemakers (Jonathan Horne, pers comm). There is another tile with the same design in the Museum of London collections (MoL 36.144/3).

Two green-glazed louvers were also recovered from a robber trench associated with Building 30, one with an unusual,

Post-Great Fire redevelopment (period 7)

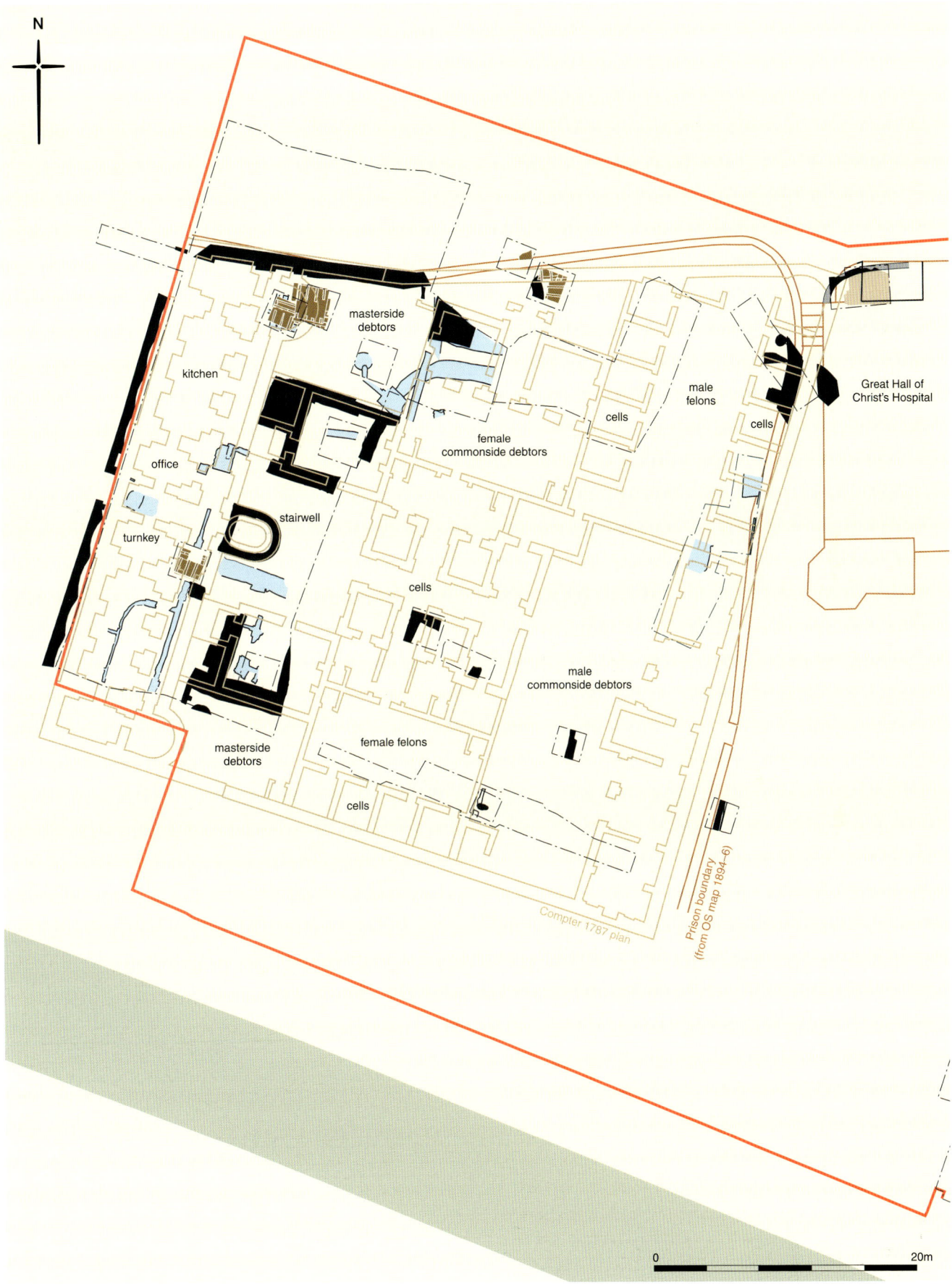

Fig 153 The remains of the Giltspur Street Compter and the Great Hall of Christ's Hospital as found during excavations 1992–2000, with Dance's original plan of June 1787 (Soane, D4/3/34) and the prison boundary from the 1894–6 Ordnance Survey map superimposed (scale 1:400)

The post-medieval archaeological sequence

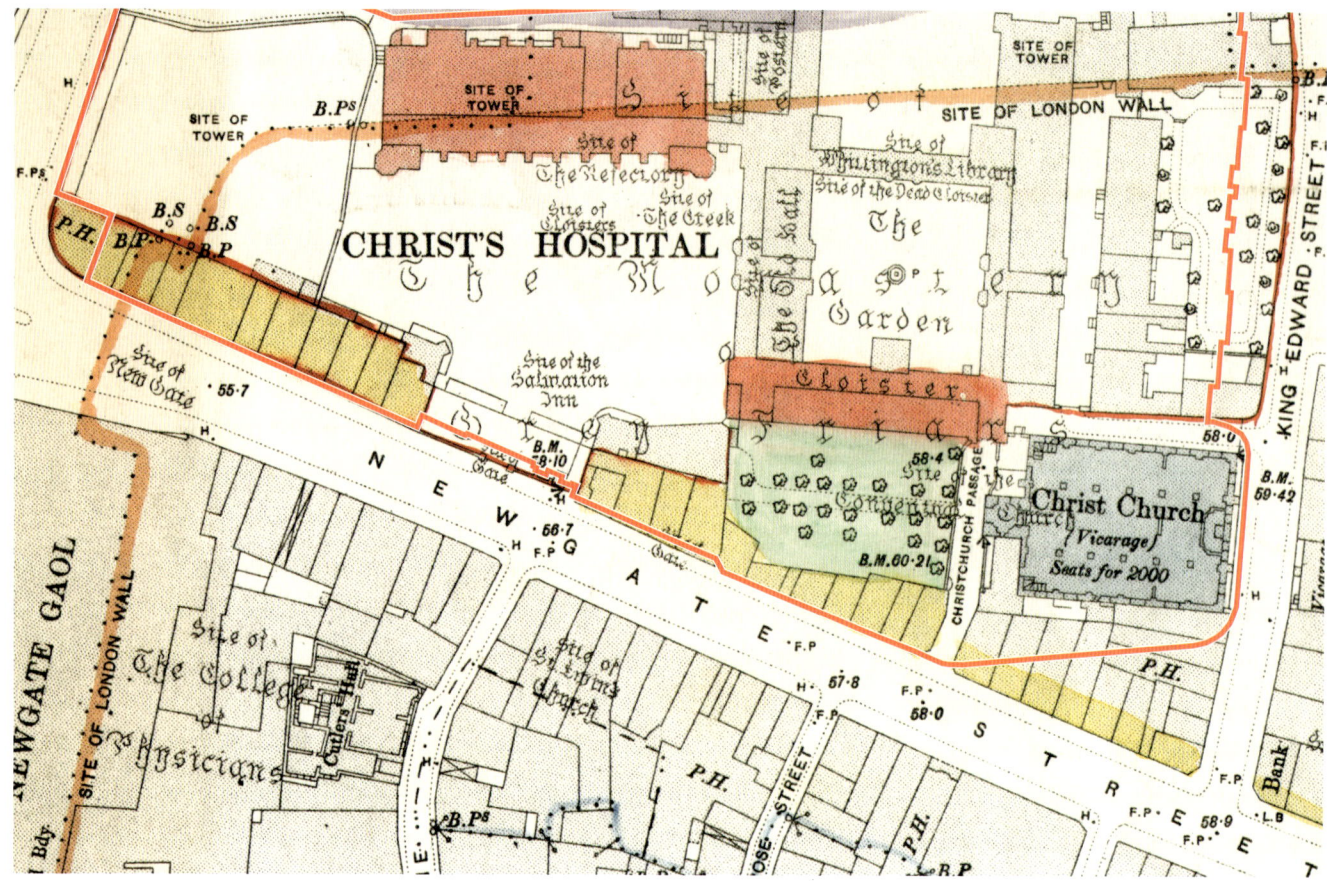

Fig 154 Detail from Ordnance Survey map of 1894–6

Fig 155 Blue on white counter-relief delftware floor tile <T11> from a drain in the Compter (B30) (scale 1:1)

scored square and dot decoration (<T12>–<T13>, Fig 156). The louvers are in Kingston-type ware (KING) and can be dated to 1230–1550; they were made by potters rather than tilers.

The General Post Office and the Merrill Lynch Financial Centre

In 1902 Christ's Hospital school moved to Horsham in Sussex, where it remains to this day. The eastern half of the site was redeveloped in 1907–9 (Fig 157) except for the site of the school buildings, where the Royal Mail sorting office was constructed (Fig 158). The western part of the site was used as a yard for Post Office vehicles (Fig 159) and also housed Norman and Reader's preserved bastion chamber. The Post Office had a member of staff whose duty was to look after the bastion (Watson and Jones 1999).

The Royal Mail sorting office occupied the site until its closure in 1997 and the Merrill Lynch redevelopment began in

142

Post-Great Fire redevelopment (period 7)

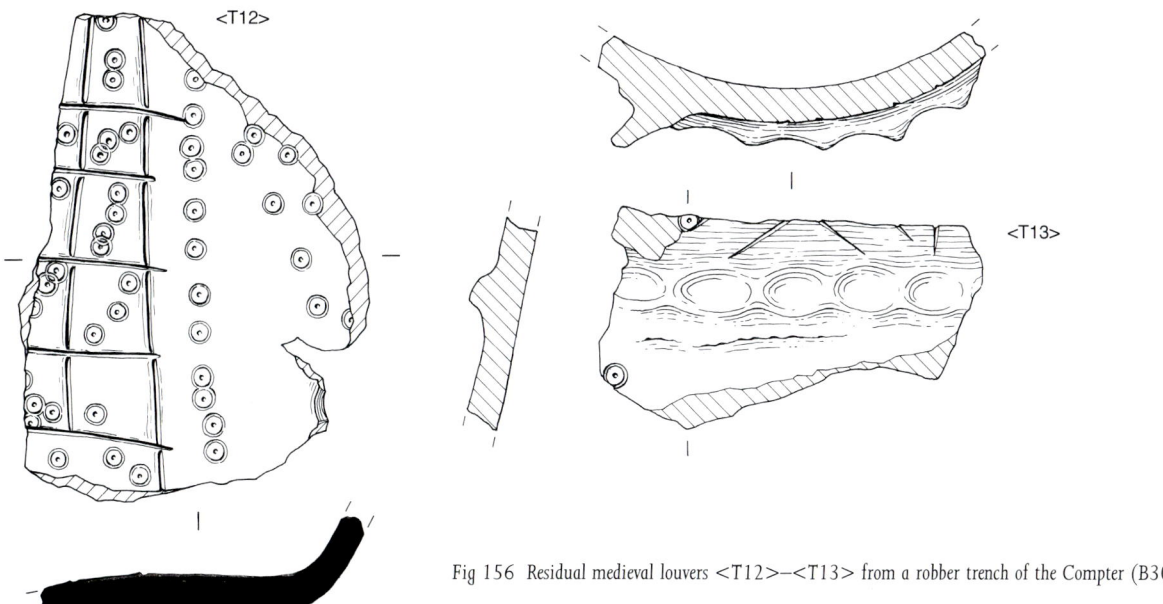

Fig 156 Residual medieval louvers <T12>–<T13> from a robber trench of the Compter (B30) (scale 1:2)

Fig 157 The site during the 1907–9 redevelopment, looking east (Norman and Reader 1912, pl XXXIX)

June 1998. The foundations of the Merrill Lynch building were designed so that little archaeological impact would occur in the western part of the site, where archaeological survival was thought to be highest. The development design incorporated reuse of the buildings along the Newgate Street frontage, keeping archaeological impact in these areas to a minimum. The new building was completed in 2003. The line of the city wall is included in the design of the building's new paving and the bastion chamber, situated inside the development area, has been redisplayed (Fig 160; Fig 161).

The post-medieval archaeological sequence

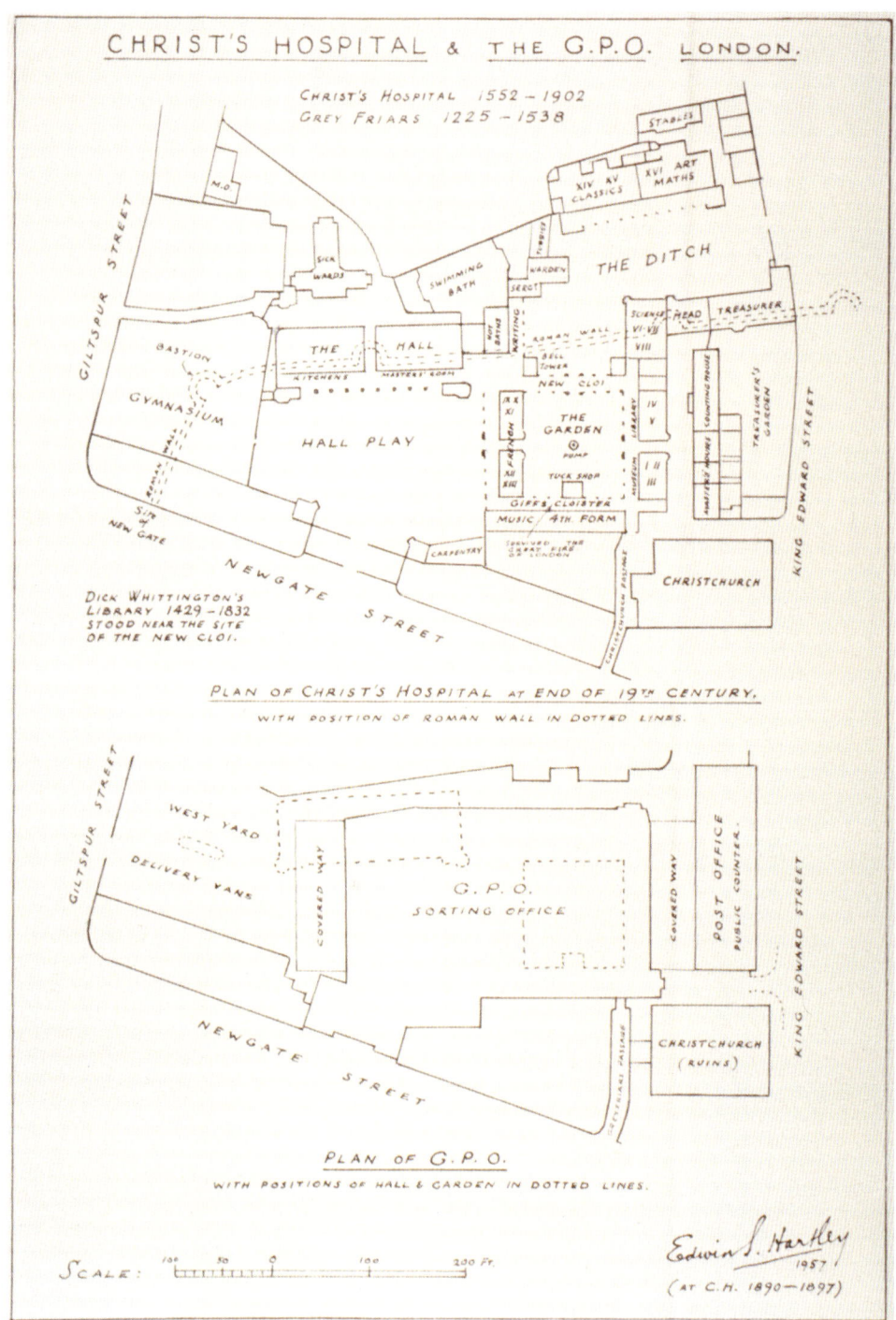

Fig 158 Plan of Christ's Hospital and the General Post Office building, by E S Hartley, 1957 (reproduced courtesy of Guildhall Library, City of London)

Discussion (period 7)

The Great Fire of 1666 damaged or destroyed all the buildings then standing on the MLFC site. The rebuilding of Christ Church was carried out by Wren, while the Christ's Hospital buildings were designed and rebuilt by a variety of people. The privately owned buildings fronting Newgate and Giltspur Street were rebuilt fairly rapidly in comparison to other areas of the City.

The city wall and its gates did not survive the redevelopment process and were gradually pulled down over the 18th and 19th centuries. On the MLFC site, cellared buildings were built over the line of the wall by the mid 18th century. The deep foundation of the Compter prison, constructed in the late 18th century, removed a large portion of the wall and most of Bastion 19. More of the wall was obliterated in 1825, along with Bastion 18, when the Great Hall of Christ's Hospital was built.

The main post-fire buildings of note were Christ's Hospital and the Giltspur Street Compter. The prison housed the common thieves, drunkards, prostitutes and debtors of the City who were previously detained at the Wood Street and Poultry Compters. Christ's Hospital developed from being a boys' orphanage and school into a well-regarded private boarding school, and one of its students was Samuel Taylor Coleridge. The hospital school survived until 1902, outliving the prison, which was demolished in 1854. The school was refounded in Horsham and the hospital and all its buildings were demolished, ending the long reign of the old monastery's buildings on the site. Christ Church was the only old public building to remain on the site after the opening years of the new century, but was destroyed in the Blitz.

Fig 159 *West yard of Royal Mail sorting office with Post Office vans, looking west*

Fig 160 *The line of the city wall marked in paving slabs (in darker stone)*

The post-medieval archaeological sequence

Fig 161 *The new bastion chamber in the MLFC building*

6 Conclusions

Analysis of the findings from the Merrill Lynch Financial Centre site, a large site in the north-western corner of the Roman and later city, has resulted in new information about the early settlement of the area and significant additions to our knowledge of the Roman and medieval defences and later activity at the site.

The archaeological potential of the site was outlined in the project design and a number of later assessment reports (Watson 1993). Revised research aims were developed during the post-excavation assessment and are set out in the updated project design (Lyon 2002) in accordance with guidance set out by the local planning authority (Corporation of London 1994) and national advisory and regulatory bodies (Department of the Environment 1990; English Heritage 1991). Although the work at the MLFC site preceded the publication of the London assessment (Museum of London 2000) and the formal setting-out of regional research priorities (Nixon et al 2002), the results address many of the important themes and research aims that have since been identified.

6.1 The Roman period

The pre-Roman topography of the study area included two stream channels which crossed the MLFC site and flowed south-west to the River Fleet (Pitt 2006, 46–7; Watson in prep). London was founded shortly after the Roman invasion of AD 43. Construction of the settlement's main east–west road, leading from Cornhill westwards across the Walbrook towards Newgate, probably took place before AD 50. Establishment of the road, which passed along the southern side of the site, was fundamental to the site's subsequent development and to both the commercial and defensive importance of Newgate.

The site's location, to the west of the main area of settlement, meant that little roadside development took place in the decade leading up to the Boudican revolt of AD 60. Post-Boudican recovery and expansion of the settlement included new properties along the main roads, and buildings were established on the site by the AD 70s. The 1st-century AD street was commercial in character and roadside development at Newgate would have been encouraged by the growth in trade. Several late 1st-century AD buildings were identified in the parts of the site investigated, but it is likely that there were far more than this originally. The finds evidence suggests that at least some of the buildings were taverns or shops.

The western and northern boundaries of the early Roman settlement are not clear, but the built up area seems to have extended further west and north than the later city defences at Newgate. The remains of early Roman buildings were recorded beneath the late defences at the MLFC site and to the north at St Bartholomew's Hospital.

In c AD 125 the Hadrianic fire devastated much of the settlement, including the Newgate area. Rebuilding was halting

Conclusions

in many areas, and there is little evidence for post-Hadrianic rebuilding at the MLFC site. Fragmentary remains of three mid 2nd-century AD buildings were found. They appear to have gone out of use by c AD 160 and there is no evidence for later roadside buildings. A similar sequence recorded at nearby sites suggests that the settlement had begun to contract. The decline of the settlement in the post-Hadrianic period was probably caused by economic change and London's less central role in the province's fortunes. Deposits of dark earth, which were dumped or formed in many parts of the settlement from the late 2nd century AD onwards, are a physical sign of these changes.

Land use at Newgate may also have changed in anticipation of the construction of the city's defensive circuit. The two stream channels that crossed the site were backfilled and diverted southwards into a new drainage scheme before the wall was constructed (Pitt 2006, 47–8; Watson in prep). A substantial north–south aligned masonry foundation, observed by Norman and Reader to run along the base of the eastern stream channel, may have been associated with the modification of the feature. The route of the city defences, constructed at about the end of the 2nd century AD, crossed the northern part of the MLFC site before turning south towards the Thames. The new city boundary defined an oblong area, between the main road and the wall, which would exert an influence on subsequent development of the area.

The siting of the city boundary was not by chance but influenced by topographic factors as well as the extent of the existing settlement. The route of the wall at Newgate follows the curve of the brickearth ground surface, which offered better ground conditions for building than the wetter area to the north. The route of the western side of the defensive circuit north of Newgate lay close to the edge of the Fleet valley. The builders were aware that there was a threat of subsidence at this point, as they levelled the ground up and deepened the wall foundations.

The building of the city wall may have been prompted by a desire for status as much as a need for defence. The first phase of the defences consisted of a landward wall, ditch and gatehouses constructed c AD 190–225. Later phases involved the building of the riverside wall by c AD 275, the addition of a series of bastions c AD 341–75 and the digging of a larger defensive ditch. It is widely believed that only the eastern side of the defensive circuit was furnished with bastions in the 4th century AD, and that the bastions on the western side of the city were constructed in the medieval period, but evidence from the MLFC site suggests that some of the western bastions could also have been built in the Roman period. Norman and Reader observed that Bastions 17 and 18 had many similar characteristics to the Roman bastions, with the exception that no reused Roman monumental stone was found in their structures. They also found evidence that the U-shaped ditch, which was built to accommodate the bastions, extended all the way around the defensive circuit in the late Roman period. A Roman date for some of the western bastions cannot therefore be ruled out.

6.2 The medieval period

Londinium was abandoned in the years following the early 5th-century AD collapse of the Roman Empire. There is no evidence for early or middle Saxon occupation in the Newgate area. The intramural area of the former Roman settlement was reoccupied in the late 9th century AD, but no direct evidence of this event or of earlier post-Roman activity was found at the MLFC site, although St Paul's Cathedral had been founded in the 7th century AD. There is some evidence that the Roman drainage ditch, which flowed southwards from the MLFC site to cross the site of Paternoster Square, was modified to form part of the St Paul's precinct boundary at about this time (Watson in prep).

The city's defensive ditches may have been redug in the Late Saxon period, perhaps in an effort to help protect St Paul's or a contemporary settlement from Viking raiders. A ditch discovered at 1–6 Old Bailey may date from the late 9th century AD. Two phases of Saxo-Norman defensive ditch were identified on the MLFC site, dating to 1000–1200 and 1150–1200 respectively.

Relatively little property development took place in the Newgate area until the 13th century, when the Grey Friars took possession of the site, although there is some evidence for earlier roadside buildings. The arrival of the Grey Friars marked the beginning of a period of great change at Newgate. The site was furnished with ornate stone buildings and the city defences renovated and restored. Work on the defences included repairing the structure of the wall, digging a much larger defensive ditch, and the addition of at least one, and possibly three, new bastions (Bastions 17–19). However, as the Greyfriars site expanded and became more built up, the city defences began to decline.

The evidence from the MLFC site shows that the city ditch began to silt up soon after its 13th-century restoration, and was soon reduced to a rubbish dump. Documentary sources record that refuse disposal was a perennial problem along the whole ditch circuit. Many attempts were made to keep the ditch clear, including physically cleaning it out, passing by-laws to make dumping illegal and fining offenders. However, there is no evidence that the ditch on the MLFC site was ever cleared out and recut on any large scale. The same is true of the southern part of the ditch, and at 1–6 Old Bailey the ditch was completely choked with rubbish by the 14th century. The proximity of this part of the ditch to Ludgate may have encouraged rubbish disposal, and the same may have been true for the MLFC segment of ditch close to Newgate.

The ditch at Newgate did not fall out of use completely but was reduced to a much narrower revetted channel by the 15th century. The jumbled nature of the material in the ditch suggests that backfilling was not ordered or systematic. Material thrown into the ditch could have been brought from across the settlement. The environmental evidence suggests that the ditch may have been treated like an open sewer in the later medieval period.

Aside from public health concerns created by the foul ditch, the friary must have considerably improved the area, especially with the completion of the great church in 1327. The Grey Friars occupied and redeveloped virtually all the land within the city wall on the MLFC site, but most of the evidence relating to the monastery buildings was destroyed in the 1907–9 redevelopment. Norman states that 'To the interest and beauty of these buildings the writer felt bound to bear witness before a committee of the House of Commons; and he will always remember with a pang of regret the time-hallowed precinct now almost utterly effaced' (Norman 1905, 148).

6.3 The post-medieval period

The buildings of the Greyfriars precinct were handed over to Christ's Hospital after the dissolution and the choir of the friary church became the parish church of Christ Church. The only archaeologically visible change recorded on the site was the final infilling of the city ditch. In the period leading up to the Great Fire of 1666 the ditch was consolidated and building encroachment along Giltspur Street saw cellars constructed over its backfill. More extensive buildings were constructed following the Great Fire, and some of the associated cellars survived remarkably well.

Documentary records indicate that the city wall persisted as a boundary until the 18th century. By this time the City's growing size and traffic congestion had made the wall unviable, and it was breached, demolished and incorporated into new buildings whenever required. On the MLFC site the construction of the Giltspur Street Compter in 1787–91 resulted in the destruction of half of Bastion 19 and a large north–south stretch of city wall. In 1825 the construction of the Great Hall of Christ's Hospital caused the demolition of Bastion 18 and adjacent segments of an east–west section of city wall. Removal of the wall presumably continued piecemeal, although it is not known precisely when the destruction of the rest of the wall occurred.

By the end of the 18th century the site was no longer defined by the presence of a city boundary. The city wall, first constructed by the Romans, had finally disappeared from public view. The two major public buildings that occupied the site throughout the post-medieval period – the Compter prison and Christ's Hospital – survived until the late 19th century, when first the prison was demolished and then Christ's Hospital school relocated. The site was completely redeveloped in 1907–9, when the General Post Office building was constructed, and again in 1998–2000 with the Merrill Lynch Financial Centre.

6.4 Informing future research

The recent post-excavation research into the findings from the Merrill Lynch Financial Centre site has resulted in the publication of this monograph and the creation of a research archive available for consultation at the LAARC. The work, though now complete, can help us to formulate future research aims for similar London sites. The experiences gained from the MLFC work should not only prove valuable when designing archaeological excavation and mitigation works along the city's Roman and medieval defences, but could also be important when analysing archives from defensive sites excavated in the past (Nixon et al 2002).

The findings from the MLFC site, coupled with those from 3–9 Newgate and Paternoster Square to the south, have changed our understanding of the pre-Roman topography of the Newgate area, its influence on Roman development, and the topographic changes which that development caused. Evidence for 1st- and 2nd-century Roman roadside building along the main east–west road, although sparse at the MLFC site, contributes to ongoing research into the nature of radial development west of the Walbrook; many other publications are now complete or in preparation (Pitt 2006; Watson in prep; Hill and Rowsome in prep; Blair and Watson in prep) and more excavations are under way. Study of the Roman and later defences at the MLFC site, including new evidence for their date and changing form and function over time, is no doubt the most important contribution that the recent work has made to our overall knowledge of London's archaeology and history.

The approach taken to the archaeological work at the MLFC site is deserving of review itself, as it included a mixture of evaluation and assessment techniques, excavation and mitigation. This allowed selective research to be carried out in parallel with the preservation of remains in situ and could be considered a qualified success, although constraints on excavation have limited the ability fully to interpret the early Roman building sequence or primary fills of the deep medieval defensive ditch. The analytical approach is also noteworthy, with a spatially selective approach used during analysis of the medieval ditch sequence. The very large finds assemblages recovered from the last infilling of the medieval ditch, apparently derived from the disposal of rubbish from across the settlement, raise particular challenges of interpretation; the way these are studied might be further refined on excavations in the future.

The recent work at and analysis of the MLFC site suggest that research issues worth pursuing at Newgate and other sites along London's defensive circuit might include: the impact of the natural terrain on the route of the defences; the process of economic change in relation to the construction and maintenance of the city's defences; and settlement-wide finds studies based on assemblages from the city ditch.

The overall experience at the MLFC site has been good, but shows that there will be a continuing need for developers, curators and archaeologists to weigh up the relative merits of excavation, preservation in situ and research when considering the approach to future redevelopment work along the city defences.

7 Specialist appendices

The catalogue entries in the specialist appendices follow the sequence: catalogue number, brief description and figure number if illustrated; then accession number, context number, period found, and land use found. Abbreviations of dimensions used in the catalogues are as follows:

L	length
W	width
H	height
Th	thickness
Diam	diameter
D	depth
Wt	weight

7.1 The tin-glazed wall tiles

Ian Betts

A water cistern associated with a post-Great Fire building (B28, period 7; Chapter 5.3, Fig 131) was lined with reused 18th-century tin-glazed 'delftware' wall tiles (Figs 137–138, 162–163). The tiles form one of the largest and most diverse delftware tile assemblages ever excavated in London, and are of crucial importance in the study of the decorative designs used on the walls of the capital's buildings during the late 17th and 18th centuries. These and the other wall tiles associated with Building 28 (period 7) are described in detail here (<T14>–<T62>), and the major design types are illustrated (Fig 164).

Analysis of the other ceramic building material (Roman and medieval/post-medieval bricks and tiles) has been integrated into the chronological narrative (Chapters 3 and 4), along with illustrated examples (<T1>–<T13>) which are detailed in Table 6.

Blue on white (or pale blue) designs

Circular border – ox-head corners

<T14> Flower vase design
(Fig 164)
<848>, [1479]
With typical Dutch style ox-head corners (for latter see Pluis 1997, 550, C.07.00.04–05). Dutch flower vase tiles with similar corners are illustrated by van Dam (1991, 70, no. 78). Dutch, 17th century.

<T15> Figures in landscape
(Fig 164)
<859>, [1479]
London, mid 18th century.

<T16> Figures in landscape
(Fig 164)
<860>, [1479]
A slightly different version of the scene shown on <T16> is illustrated in Horne (1989, 29, no. 87). London, 1740–60.

<T17> Figures in landscape
(Fig 164)
<855>, [1479]
Dutch, mid 18th century.

<T18> Figures in landscape
(Fig 164)
<856>, [1479]
The white glaze combined with the better quality of the painted scheme would suggest these are Dutch. 18th century.

Circular border – spider's-head corners

<T19> Biblical scene (Matthew 28 v.1–6) (Fig 164)
<879>, [1479]
Jonathan Horne (pers comm) believes this could be a rare example of an early English tile. Other early English blue on white biblical tiles identified by Horne are <400>, <538>, <956> and <519>. London, c 1680–1700.

Circular border – carnation head corners

<T20> Carnation head corners (Fig 164)
<534>, [1479]
Landscape tiles with carnation head corners are very rare in London. Parts of two separate tiles were found (<T20> and <1634>), which show slight differences in the style of the corner decoration. The example illustrated has a similar carnation head to that found on a Dutch tile illustrated by Pluis (1997, 567, C.17.00.06). Dutch, possibly Amsterdam, c 1720–90.

Circular border – diaper corners

Landscape (not illustrated)
<945>, [1479]
Ray 1973, 163, no. 251. English, 18th century.

Two line hexagonal border – quarter flower corners

Landscape (not illustrated)
<891>, [1479]
van Dam 1991, 94, no. 129. Dutch, 1725–75.

Two line octagonal border – fleur-de-lis corners

<T21> Fleur-de-lis corners (Fig 164)
<867>, [1479]
Landscape tile (also <567>)
with Dutch border design (see Pluis 1997, 531, B.12.00.17–18). ?Dutch, 1730–60.

Two line octagonal border – quarter flower

<T22> Figures in landscape (Fig 164)
<845>, [1479]
This stone palisade is typical of

Table 6 Details of illustrated tile and brick <T1>–<T13>

	Accession no.	Context no.	Description	Fig no.
<T1>	<1739>	[1569]	decorated tegula	37
<T2>	<838>	[2363]	floor tile	113
<T3>	<835>	[2873]	Penn floor tile	113
<T4>	<992>	[3117]	French floor tile	113
<T5>	<1219>	[3728]	London floor tile	113
<T6>	<1050>	[2982]	Penn floor tile	115
<T7>	<1774>	[3194]	'Westminster' floor tile	115
<T8>	<1150>	[3373]	London floor tile	115
<T9>	<604>	[1905]	stove tile	132
<T10>	<1001>	[2700]	moulded brick	136
<T11>	<352>	[652]	delftware floor tile; blue on white	155
<T12>	<636>	[1237]	louver	156
<T13>	<637>	[1237]	louver	156

Fig 162 Cleaning and removal of tiles, looking west

Specialist appendices

Fig 163 Detail of tiles in situ, looking east (scale 0.2m)

Dutch tiles. Pluis (1997, 381, A.03.05.05) shows a Dutch tile with the same scene. The scene was also copied by London tilemakers (see Horne 1989, 26, no. 65, with position of figures reversed), but the corner motif on <T22> is exclusively Dutch (see Pluis 1997, 559, C.12.00.10). Dutch, 1750–70.

<T23> Mounted figure in landscape (Fig 164)
<858>, [1479]
Landscape with different flower head corner motif. Dutch, c 1750–1800.

Four line octagonal border – quarter flower head corners

Landscape (not illustrated)
<138>, [38]
cf van Dam 1991, 113, no. 136. Dutch, 1730–1810.

Octagonal dash border – quarter flower head corners

Landscape (not illustrated)
<861>, [1479]
cf van Dam 1991, 104, no. 121. Dutch, 1730–c 1800.

Floral ground border

<T24> Landscape with figure (Fig 164)
<843>, [1479]
This border is exclusive to Liverpool (Horne 1989, 41, nos 185–186). Liverpool, 1750–75.

Louis XV border – diaper corners

<T25> Landscape scene (Fig 164)
<866>, [1479]
For similar tiles, see Horne 1989, 45, nos 209–217. Liverpool, 1750–80.

Louis XV border – buttercup corners

<T26> Landscape scene (Fig 164)
<555>, [1479]
For similar tiles see Horne 1989, 44, nos 205–208. Liverpool, 1750–80.

Lozenge border – fleur-de-lis corners

<T27> Tulip design in square border (Fig 164)
<844>, [1479]
Painted in a similar style to thicker mid 17th-century tiles from Rotherhithe, London (also <563>). English/Dutch, 17th century.

Floral pattern

<T28> Floral pattern (Fig 164)
<872>, [1479]
A complex floral pattern covers the whole tile. A very similar design is shown in Pluis (1997, 135, no. 49). Dutch, 1750–1800.

Other tiles with no borders

Tiles in this group can be sub-divided by corner motif, if present.

BARRED OX-HEAD CORNERS

Flower vase (not illustrated)
<534>, [1414]
?English, ?18th century.

SPIDER'S-HEAD CORNERS

<T29> Biblical scene (Fig 164)
<841>, [1479]
Similar to Dutch biblical tiles (eg van Dam 1991, 87, no. 98). Dutch, 1670–1720.

<T30> Two figures talking (Fig 164)
<562>, [1479]
One of many similar designs showing scenes from everyday life (for example van Dam 1991, 101, no. 113; van Sabben and Hollem 1987, 81, nos 284–285; Phil 1984, 109, no. 129). Dutch, 1680–1750.

<T31> Mythical sea creature (Fig 164)
<868>, [1479]
For similar tiles see Phil 1984, 151, no. 196. Dutch, 1680–1750.

<T32> Landscape tile with unusual spider's-head corner (Fig 164)
<959>, [1479]
The Philadelphia Museum (Phil 1984, 113, no. 138) has two tiles with the same corner. Dutch, 1750–c 1800.

ELABORATE SPIDER'S-HEAD CORNERS

Flower vase (not illustrated)
<928>, [1479]
cf Horne 1989, 63, nos 346–349. London, 1720–60.

QUARTER ROSE CORNERS

Plain with quarter rose corners (not illustrated)
<874>–<876>, [1479]
Ray 1973, 234, no. 586. London, 1760–80.

ELABORATED CORNERS

<T33> Flower vase decoration (Fig 164)
<936>, [1479]
The same design is in Archer (1997, 498 N347). Liverpool, c 1750–75.

<T34> Flower vase design (Fig 164)
<865>, [1479]
Horne 1989, 72, no. 418; Archer 1997, 496 N338. Liverpool, 1740–70.

NO CORNER MOTIFS

<T35>, <T36>, <T37> Landscape scenes (Fig 164)
<863>, <864>, <883>, [1479]
Painted on a pale blue background. Two show typical Liverpool landscape scenes but the third <T37> shows sailing ships, a rare Liverpool decorative design (J Horne, pers comm). For similar tiles see Horne 1989, 39, nos 167–175. Liverpool, 1750–75.

<T38> Landscape scene (Fig 164)
<566>, [1479]
A very rare design (J Horne, pers comm) showing a landscape scene with classical ruins. Liverpool, c 1760–70.

Letter panels

<T39> Letter panel (Fig 164)
<950>, [1479]

<T40> Letter panel (Fig 164)
<51>, [5]
These may be parts of a trade sign, such as that illustrated by Horne (1989, 119, no. 677). The first <T39> shows the letter R while the second <T40> shows part of what may be the letter L (or perhaps an E). ?London, mid 18th century.

Specialist appendices

Purple on white designs

Circular border - barred ox-head corners

Landscapes (none illustrated)
<106>, [38]; <850>, [1479]

Dutch/English.

Four line octagonal border – quarter flower head corners

<T41> Landscape tiles (Fig 164)
<881>, [1479]
For fairly similar Dutch tile see

Pluis 1997, 370, A.03.01.37
(also <871>, <878> and
<882>). Dutch, 1730–c 1790.

Octagonal powdered purple border – carnation head corners

<T42> Harbour scene (Fig 164)
<880>, [1479]
Horne illustrates a London tile with

a similar harbour scene (but in
blue) with the same border (1989,
23, no. 51). London, 1740–60.

Geometrical designs

<T43> Geometric design
(Fig 164)
<893>, [1479]
Also <947>. Dutch, 1740–1800.

<T44> Geometric design
(Fig 164)
<85>, [33]
Tiles with the same design are in
van Sabben and Hollem 1987,

134, no. 415 and Phil 1984, 161,
no. 214. Dutch, 1750–c 1800.

<T45> Geometric design
(Fig 164)
<935>, [1479]
Similar to Dutch tiles illustrated in
van Sabben and Hollem 1987,
134, no. 417 and Pluis 1997, 263,
A.01.12.62. Dutch, 1740–1800.

Floral pattern

<T46> Floral pattern
(Fig 164)
<884>, [1479]
Complex floral pattern
incorporating a bird. Dutch,
c 1740– c 1800.

<T47> Floral pattern (Fig 164)
<980>, [1479]

Pluis shows a Dutch tile with a
similar design, but in blue (1997,
219, A.01.05.29). Dutch, 1740–
c 1800.

Floral pattern (not illustrated)
<109>, [38]
Pluis 1997, 219, A.01.05.20.
Dutch, 1730–c 1790.

No border – spider's head corners

<T48> Soldier on horseback
(Fig 164)
<565>, [1479]
Soldier on horseback; another tile
(also <869>) shows a similar

figure but without a helmet. This
is similar to a tile with mounted
soldier illustrated by Pluis (1997,
356, A.02.07.06). Dutch,
1700–1750.

Blue and purple on white designs

Circular border – spider's head corners

<T49> Sailing ship in full sail
(Fig 164)
<954>, [1479]

The tile is 13mm thick
suggesting an early date. Dutch
tiles of this thickness showing
sailing ships (but with different
corners and no border) are
dated 1645–75 (van Dam 1991,
80, no. 89). The colour purple
was first used on Dutch tiles
from c 1650 (Pluis 1997, 103).
?Dutch, mid to late 17th
century.

Circular powdered purple border – cherub corners

Flower vase (none illustrated)
<126>–<128>, [38]

Horne 1989, 62, no. 339.
London, 1730–50.

Circular powdered purple border – carnation head corners

<60>, [5]

(not illustrated)

Octagonal powdered purple border

Landscape (not illustrated)
<68>, [5]

cf Phil 1984, 133, no. 168. Dutch,
1680–1730.

Octagonal powdered purple border – carnation head corners

Landscape (not illustrated)
<940>, [1479]

Ray 1973, 161, no. 235. London,
1760–80.

Circular powdered purple border – geometrical corners

Flower vase/fruit basket (not
illustrated)
<1623>, [1479]

Corner in van Dam 1991, 90,
no. 119. Dutch, 1680–1750.

Octagonal blue and powdered purple Louis XV-style border

Landscape (not illustrated)
<1477>, [3382]

Dutch/English, 1700–1800.

Geometrical and floral design

<45>, [5]
(not illustrated)

Similar to Horne 1989, 74, no.
434. London, 1750–70.

Purple and pale bluish-purple on white design

<T50> Biblical tile of Abraham
dismissing Hagar (Genesis 21
v.14) (Fig 164)
<59>, [5]
A rare combination of colours.

The same biblical scene, but in
more normal blue on white, is
present on a London tile (Horne
1989, 78, no. 450). ?English,
1680–1720.

Polychrome designs

<T51> Chinese figure
(Fig 164)
<569>, [1479]

Chinese figure with Michaelmas
daisy corners. Liverpool,
1750–75.

The tin-glazed wall tiles

\<T52\> Bird (Fig 164)
\<564\>, [1479]
Bird holding fruit, with fleur-de-lis corners. Dutch, mid 17th–18th century.

\<T53\> Carnation flower head (Fig 164)
\<952\>, [1479]
Carnation flower head in blue and green, barred ox-head corners. The tile thickness (9–10mm) indicates a 17th-century date. Similar to Dutch tiles in van Sabben and Hollem 1987, 38, nos 99–100. Dutch, mid to late 17th century.

Edging tiles

Purpose made rectangular edging tiles were occasionally used in London buildings but they are rare; normally it was easier to score and break square tiles to the required size.

\<T54\> Purple on white floral design with insect (Fig 164)
\<571\>, [1479]
Dutch, 1750–1800.

\<T55\> Floral design in purple on white (Fig 164)
\<520\>, [1507]
Horne shows an English edging tile with a similar design (Horne 1989, 70, no. 398) but notes that it is also a Dutch design. Dutch, mid to late 18th century.

\<T56\> Tulip floral decoration in blue on white (Fig 164)
\<1640\>, [1479]
Dutch, 1700–1800.

'Marble' tiles

These imitation marble designs in purple are probably Dutch (for similar, although not identical Dutch examples, see Phil 1984, 158, no. 208). 18th century.

Tile pictures

Tiles belonging to four separate tile pictures were found in the tile-lined tank.

\<T57\> Back and tail of a ?horse in purple on white (Fig 164)
\<939\>, [1479]
Dutch, 1700–1800.

\<T58\> Part of a floral scene in purple on white (Fig 164)
\<877\>, [1479]
Tile \<1603\> shows another part of the same panel. Dutch, 1700–1800.

\<T59\> Bottom of a standing figure showing part of two legs in blue on white (Fig 164)
\<960\>, [1479]
English/Dutch, 17th century.

?Figure/?animal in blue on pale blue (not illustrated)
\<1614\>, [1479]
English/Dutch, 1700–1800.

Woodblock print design

\<T60\> Girl and a shepherd with a crook (Fig 164)
\<827\>, [1479]
Made in Liverpool by John Sadler between 1756 and 1757 (Ray 1994, 5–6). There are two woodblock tiles (see \<852\>), both showing a girl and a shepherd with a crook (Ray 1994, 17, no. A1–6).

Copper plate designs

\<T61\> Flower vase decoration (Fig 164)
\<56\>, [5]

\<T62\> Flower vase decoration (Fig 164)
\<775\>, [2183]

Made in Liverpool between c 1770 and 1780. Two designs are present, both showing flower vase decoration (\<T61\>, Ray 1994, 56, E3–4; \<T62\>, ibid, 54, E2–4).

Blue on white (or pale blue) designs \<T14\>–\<T40\>

\<T14\>

\<T15\>

Fig 164 (above and over) Reused 18th-century tin-glazed wall tiles \<T14\>–\<T62\> from Building 28: blue on white (or pale blue) designs \<T14\>–\<T40\>; purple on white designs \<T41\>–\<T48\>; blue and purple on white design \<T49\>; purple and pale bluish-purple on white design \<T50\>; polychrome designs \<T51\>–\<T53\>; edging tiles \<T54\>–\<T56\>; tile pictures \<T57\>–\<T59\>; woodblock print design \<T60\>; copper-plate designs \<T61\>–\<T62\> (scale 1:2)

Specialist appendices

Fig 164 (cont)

<T22>   <T23>

                    <T25>

<T24>

<T26>   <T27>

Specialist appendices

Fig 164 (cont)

The tin-glazed wall tiles

<T34> <T35>

<T36> <T37>

<T38> <T39> <T40>

  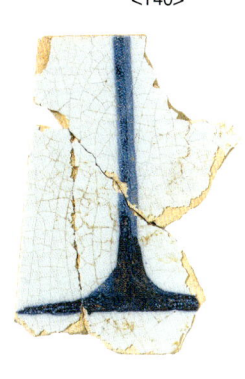

159

Specialist appendices

Purple on white designs <T41>–<T48>

<T41>

<T42>

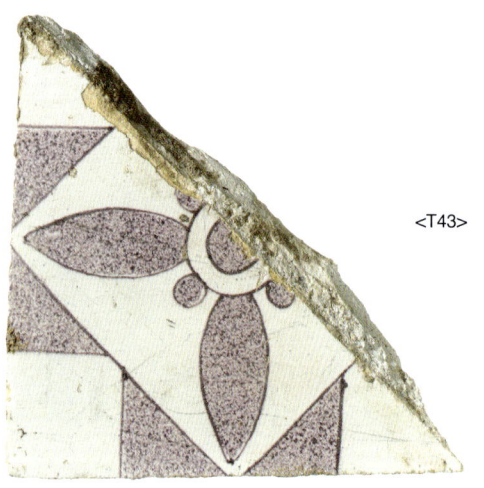
<T43>

<T44>

<T45>

<T46>

Fig 164 (cont)

160

The tin-glazed wall tiles

<T47>

<T48>

Blue and purple on white design <T49>

Purple and pale bluish-purple on white design <T50>

<T49>

<T50>

Polychrome designs <T51>–<T53>

<T51>

<T52>

<T53>

161

Specialist appendices

Edging tiles <T54>–<T56>

 <T54>

 <T55>

 <T56>

Tile pictures <T57>–<T59>

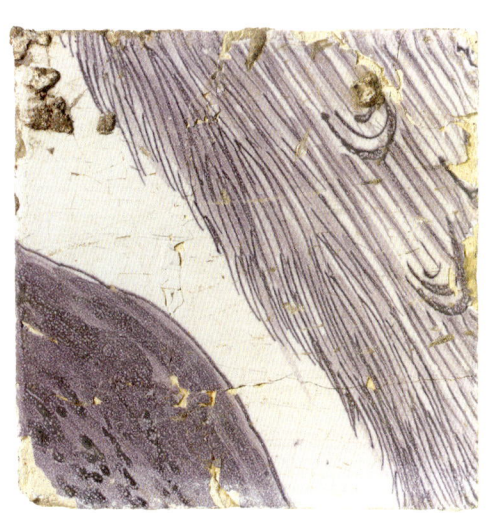 <T57>

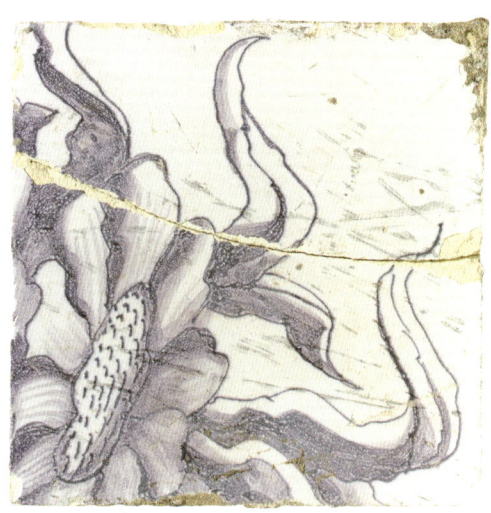 <T58>

 <T59>

Woodblock print design <T60>

 <T60>

Fig 164 (cont)

Copper-plate designs <T61>–<T62>

<T61>

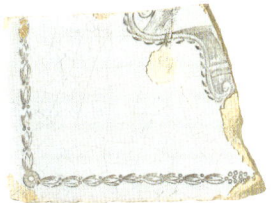

<T62>

7.2 The Roman pottery

Rupert Featherby

Methodology

The pottery was spot dated and assessed to MoLAS/MoLSS standards. The computerized spot date records are held on the Oracle database. The pottery and full paper archive have been deposited in the Museum of London Archive. The form codes used are those established by Marsh and Tyers (1978) and subsequently developed by the DUA and MoLAS/MoLSS (Davies et al 1994, 5–8) incorporating established typologies and classifications (eg Marsh 1978). Full expansions of the fabric and form codes used are in Davies et al (1994) for the early period and Symonds and Tomber (1991) for the later period.

Quantification

This assemblage has been quantified by three methods. Contexts that were spot dated for the 1992 phase of the excavation were quantified by presence, and all contexts spot dated for the 1998 phase were quantified by sherd count. However, during the analysis the opportunity arose to re-quantify contexts from the 1992 phase that were found to pertain to structures, allowing for proper comparison between phases. Additionally all contexts from the wells were quantified by weight and Estimated Vessel Equivalent (EVEs) (Orton 1975).

The results of the analysis of the Roman pottery are integrated into the chronological narrative (Chapter 3).

Principal Roman pottery fabrics, forms and decoration, giving date ranges, are listed in Table 7; this also serves as a checklist of Roman fabrics present on the site. Details of the illustrated Roman pottery are given in Table 8.

Table 7 Expansion of Roman pottery fabric codes used in this report, with their date ranges

Fabric code	Expansion	Approximate date range (AD)
AHSU	Alice Holt/Surrey ware	50–160
AMPH	unsourced amphora fabric	50–400
ARGO	Argonne samian ware	250–400
BAETE	Baetican early Dressel 20/Haltern 70 fabric	50–170
BB1	black-burnished ware 1	120–400
BB2	black-burnished ware 2	120–250
BHWS	Brockley Hill white-slipped ware	50–160
BLEG	black eggshell ware	45–75
CADIZ	Camulodunum 186 amphora fabric	50–140
CCGW	Copthall Close grey ware	70–150
CGGW	central Gaulish glazed ware	50–100
CGBL	central Gaulish/Lezoux black colour-coated ware	150–250
ECCW	Eccles ware	50–100
ERMS	early Roman micaceous sandy ware	50–100
ERSA	early Roman sandy ware A	50–70
ERSS	early Roman sandy ware with shell	50–120
FINE	unsourced fine reduced ware	50–400
FMIC	fine micaceous reduced ware	50–120
GAUL1	Pélichet 47/Dressel 30 amphora fabric	50–250
GAUL2	London 555/Haltern 70 similis amphora fabric	50–120
GROG	unsourced grog-tempered ware	40–400
HOO	Hoo Island white-slipped ware	50–100
HWB	Highgate Wood ware B	40–100
HWC	Highgate Wood ware C	70–160
LOMI	London mica-dusted ware	70–120
LOXI	London oxidised ware	90–160
LYON	Lyon colour-coated ware	50–70
NFSE	north French/south-east English oxidised ware	50–160
NKGW	north Kent grey ware	100–150
NKSH	north Kent shell-tempered ware	50–150
OXID	unsourced oxidised ware	50–400
OXIDF	unsourced fine oxidised fabric	50–400
PORD	Portchester ware D	350–400
RDBK	ring-and-dot beaker fabric	50–100
RGGW	Rhineland granular grey ware	50–80
RWS	unsourced white-slipped ware	50–300
SAMCG	central Gaulish samian	120–250
SAMEG	east Gaulish samian	150–300
SAMLG	la Graufesenque samian	50–100
SAMMV2	les Martres-de-Veyre samian fabric 2 (limestone-rich)	100–120
SAND	unsourced sand-tempered ware	50–400
SEAL	amphora seal fabric	50–400
SHEL	unsourced shell-tempered ware	40–400
SLOW	Sugar Loaf Court ware	50–80
TN	terra nigra	40–80
VCWS	Verulamium region coarse white-slipped ware	140–200
VRG	Verulamium region grey ware	50–200
VRW	Verulamium region white ware	50–160
WSEL	West Stow/Essex/London stamped ware	70–120

Specialist appendices

Table 8 Details of illustrated Roman pottery <P1>–<P53> (see Table 7 for expansion of fabric codes; M and T = Marsh and Tyers 1978)

	Context no.	Land use	Period	Form	Fabric	Decoration	Fig no.
<P1>	[3075]	OA7	2	bead-rimmed jar with high round shoulder (M and T, fig 234, nos IIA12–13)	AHSU		28
<P2>	[3075]	OA7	2	necked jar with carinated shoulder and figure 7 rim (M and T, fig 235, nos IIC1–2)	AHSU		28
<P3>	[3075]	OA7	2	miscellaneous or unidentified flagon	CGGW	barbotine figure decoration	28
<P4>	[3075]/[3078]	OA7	2	miscellaneous or unidentified dish	CGGW	barbotine dot decoration	28
<P5>	[3075]	OA7	2	necked jar with carinated shoulder and figure 7 rim (M and T, fig 235, nos IIC1–2)	ERSB		28
<P6>	[3075]	OA7	2	ovoid beaker (M and T, fig 239, no. IIIB1)	FINE	barbotine dot decoration	28
<P7>	[3075]	OA7	2	poppy-head beaker (M and T, fig 239, nos IIIF1–6)	FINE	barbotine dot decoration	28
<P8>	[3078]	OA7	2	hemispherical bowl, imitating Dragendorff form 37 (M and T, fig 241, no. IVE1)	FMIC	rouletted decoration	28
<P9>	[3075]	OA7	2	round-bodied necked jar with decorated shoulder (M and T, fig 235, no. IIE)	HWC	burnished decoration	28
<P10>	[3075]	OA7	2	bowl with constriction below folded down/undercut rim (M and T, fig 241, no. IVF4)	HWC		28
<P11>	[3075]	OA7	2	ovoid beaker (M and T, fig 239, no. IIIB1)	LOMI	embossed decoration	28
<P12>	[3075]	OA7	2	ovoid beaker (M and T, fig 239, no. IIIB1)	LOMI	elongated indentations	28
<P13>	[3075]	OA7	2	bowl with deep hooked flange (M and T, fig 241, no. IVB1)	LOMI		28
<P14>	[3075]	OA7	2	tazza	VRW		28
<P15>	[3075]	OA7	2	collared (Hofheim-type) flagon (M and T, fig 232, nos IA1–3)	NFSE		28
<P16>	[3075]	OA7	2	storage jar with rolled rim and decoration on shoulder (M and T, fig 237, no. IIM)	NKSH	elongated indentations	28
<P17>	[3075]	OA7	2	necked jar with carinated shoulder and figure 7 rim (M and T, fig 235, nos IIC1–2)	OXIDF		28
<P18>	[3078]	OA7	2	ring-necked flagon	RDBK		28
<P19>	[3075]	OA7	2	ring-necked flagon with flared mouth (M and T, fig 232, no. IB2)	RWS		28
<P20>	[3075]	OA7	2	ring-necked flagon with flared mouth (M and T, fig 232, no. IB2)	VRW		28
<P21>	[3075]	OA7	2	ring-necked flagon with flared mouth (M and T, fig 232, no. IB2)	VRW		28
<P22>	[3075]	OA7	2	ring-necked flagon with flared mouth (M and T, fig 232, no. IB2)	VRW		28
<P23>	[3075]	OA7	2	ring-necked flagon with flared mouth (M and T, fig 232, no. IB2)	VRW		28
<P24>	[3078]	OA7	2	flaring-rimmed flagon with mouldings on inner lip (M and T, fig 233, no. IF)	VRW		28
<P25>	[3078]	OA7	2	two-handled honey-pot jar (M and T, fig 237, no. IIK)	VRW		28
<P26>	[3075]	OA7	2	hook-flanged mortarium	VRW		28
<P27>	[2044]	OA9	2	necked jar with carinated shoulder and figure 7 rim (M and T, fig 235, nos IIC1–2)	AHSU		22
<P28>	[2043]	OA9	2	necked jar with carinated shoulder and figure 7 rim (M and T, fig 235, nos IIC1–2)	AHSU		22
<P29>	[2043]	OA9	2	indistinguishable necked jar	AHSU		22
<P30>	[2043]	OA9	2	'Surrey' bowl (M and T, fig 242, no. IVK)	AHSU		22
<P31>	[2044]/[2045]	OA9	2	carinated beaker with tall upright plain rim (M and T, fig 239, no. IIIG)	BLEG		22
<P32>	[2045]	OA9	2	round-bodied jar with thickened or out-turned rim (M and T, fig 235, nos IIB1–2)	ERMS		22
<P33>	[2043]/[2044]	OA9	2	round-bodied jar with thickened or out-turned rim (M and T, fig 235, nos IIB1–2)	ERMS	ungrouped vertical burnished lines	22
<P34>	[2043]	OA9	2	miscellaneous or unidentified bowl	ERMS	burnished decoration	22
<P35>	[2045]	OA9	2	indistinguishable necked jar	ERSB	burnished decoration	22
<P36>	[2045]	OA9	2	bead-rimmed jar (M and T, figs 234–5, nos IIA1–17)	ERSS		22
<P37>	[2044]	OA9	2	miscellaneous or unidentified beaker	FMIC	elongated indentations	22
<P38>	[2044]	OA9	2	ovoid beaker (M and T, fig 239, no. IIIB1)	FMIC	barbotine dot decoration	22
<P39>	[2043]	OA9	2	everted-rimmed beaker (M and T, fig 239, no. IIIC)	FMIC	compass-inscribed decoration	22
<P40>	[2044]	OA9	2	bowl with curved walls and flat, hooked or folded rim (M and T, fig 241, nos IVF1–6)	GROG		22
<P41>	[2043]	OA9	2	miscellaneous or unidentified jar	HWB		22
<P42>	[2044]/[2045]	OA9	2	bead-rimmed jar (M and T, figs 234–5, nos IIA1–17)	HWB		22
<P43>	[2043]	OA9	2	bead-rimmed jar with simple thickened rim (M and T, fig 234, nos IIA1–4)	HWB		22
<P44>	[2043]	OA9	2	lid-seated bead-rimmed jar (M and T, fig 235, no. IIA16)	HWB		22
<P45>	[2043]	OA9	2	bowl with curved walls and flat, hooked or folded rim (M and T, fig 241, nos IVF1–6)	HWB		22
<P46>	[2043]	OA9	2	dish with external moulding (M and T, fig 242, no. VB)	HWB		22
<P47>	[2044]	OA9	2	lid	HWB		22
<P48>	[2043]/[2044]	OA9	2	bowl with curved walls and flat, hooked or folded rim (M and T, fig 241, nos IVF1–6)	HWC		22
<P49>	[2043]	OA9	2	miscellaneous or unidentified jar or beaker	OXID		22
<P50>	[2043]	OA9	2	ovoid beaker (M and T, fig 239, no. IIIB1)	OXID	rouletted decoration	22
<P51>	[2044]/[2045]	OA9	2	ovoid beaker (M and T, fig 239, no. IIIB1)	RDBK	barbotine dot decoration	22
<P52>	[2043]	OA9	2	simple dish with pointed, slightly inturned wall (M and T, fig 242, no. IVJ3)	TN		22
<P53>	[2044]	OA9	2	reed-rimmed bowl (M and T, fig 240, nos IVA1–9)	VRW		22

7.3 The medieval and post-medieval pottery

Lucy Whittingham

Methodology

The medieval assemblages from phase 2 of the city ditch backfilling (OA17, period 5), including the revetment and gully (S6), have been selected for publication and are described in Chapter 4.4. Large sections of the material in this assemblage are defined and illustrated in the various volumes that cover the dated type-series of London medieval pottery, for example Mill Green ware (Pearce et al 1982), London-type ware (Pearce et al 1985) and Surrey whitewares (Pearce and Vince 1988). Vessel form terminology in this report follows that established and illustrated in these volumes. Principal medieval and post-medieval pottery fabrics, giving approximate date ranges, are listed in Table 9; this list also serves as a check of post-Roman fabrics present on the site. Details of the illustrated medieval and post-medieval pottery are given in Table 10.

Quantification

All of the medieval and post-medieval pottery from the MLFC site (10,126 sherds from 512 contexts) has been examined; the key stratigraphic contexts, containing 4256 sherds, were spot dated, recording size of assemblage by sherd count, fabric type, vessel form, ENV (estimated number of vessels), and context date. The pottery from all other contexts was scanned, recording size of assemblage as S, M or L, fabric types and context date. Full quantification of the phase 2 city ditch assemblages (OA17 and S6, period 5) has been undertaken for this publication. A total of 4991 sherds, from 1371 ENV weighing 98kg, have been recorded in standard MoLSS format and the data entered on the Oracle database. The pottery and paper archives have been deposited in the Museum of London Archive (LAARC).

Sources

This assemblage, dated c 1230–1450, can be summarised as containing four/five principal components; London-type ware (37%), coarse Surrey-Hampshire border ware (26%), Kingston-type ware (18%), Mill Green ware (13%) and Cheam whiteware (5%). This demonstrates a consumer pattern of

Table 9 Expansion of medieval and post-medieval pottery fabric codes used in this report, with their date ranges

Fabric code	Expansion	Approximate date range
CBW	coarse Surrey-Hampshire border ware	1270–1500
CBW HD	coarse Surrey-Hampshire border ware in the highly decorated style	1270–1350
CHEA	Cheam whiteware	1350–1500
KING	Kingston-type ware	1240–1400
KING ANT	Kingston-type ware with anthropomorphic/zoomorphic decoration	1240–1350
KING HD	Kingston-type ware in the highly decorated style	1240–1300
KING POLY	Kingston-type ware with polychrome decoration	1240–1300
KING SBOSS	Kingston-type ware stamped boss decoration (except wheat ear)	1270–1350
KING WSBOSS	Kingston-type ware wheat-ear stamped boss decoration	1340–1400
KINGSL	Kingston-type slipware	1250–1400
LANG	Langerwehe stoneware	1350–1500
LCGR	Low Countries greyware	1350–1500
LLON	late London-type ware	1400–1500
LLSL	late London-type slipware	1400–1500
LMHG	late medieval Hertfordshire glazed ware	1340–1450
LOND	London-type ware	1080–1350
LOND BAL	London-type ware baluster jug	1180–1350
LOND HD	London-type ware in the highly decorated style	1240–1350
LOND NFR	London-type ware with north French-style decoration	1180–1270
LOND ROU	London-type ware Rouen-style decoration	1180–1270
LOND WSD	London-type ware with white slip decoration	1240–1350
MG	Mill Green ware	1270–1350
SAIM	Saintonge ware with mottled green glaze	1250–1650
SAIN	Saintonge ware	1250–1500
SAIP	Saintonge ware with polychrome decoration	1280–1350
SHER	south Hertfordshire-type greyware	1170–1350
SIEG	Siegburg stoneware	1300–1500
SSW	shelly-sandy ware	1140–1220
TUDG	'Tudor green' ware	1350–1500

Specialist appendices

Table 10 Illustrated medieval and post-medieval pottery <P54>–<P93> (see Table 9 for expansion of codes)

	Context no.	Land use	Period	Fabric	Form	Decoration	Fig no.
<P54>	[3465]	S3	4	SSW	cooking pot		60
<P55>	[3553]	S6	6	LOND	drinking jug		78
<P56>	[3768]	OA17	6	LOND	bottle		78
<P57>	[3763]	OA17	6	KING	drinking cup	scale decoration	78
<P58>	[3790]	OA17	6	LOND BAL	baluster jug	continuous basal thumbing	79
<P59>	[3790]	OA17	6	LOND HD	jug	polychrome	80
<P60>	[3798]	OA17	6	LOND ROU	baluster jug	pellet decoration	80
<P61>	[3768]	OA17	6	LOND ROU	jug	pellet decoration	80
<P62>	[2583]	B26	8	KING ANT	anthropomorphic or face jug		81
<P63>	[3763]	OA17	6	KING ANT	anthropomorphic or face jug	anthropomorphic	81
<P64>	[3768]	OA17	6	KING SBOSS	jug		81
<P65>	[3799]	OA17	6	KING SBOSS	pear-shaped jug		81
<P66>	[3768]	OA17	6	KING SBOSS	baluster jug	stamped boss	81
<P67>	[3799]	OA17	6	KING SBOSS	jug	glazed externally	81
<P68>	[3799]	OA17	6	KING SBOSS	jug	glazed externally	81
<P69>	[1095]	OA17	6	KING HD	jug		81
<P70>	[3553]	S6	6	KING WSBOSS	baluster jug	stamped boss	81
<P71>	[3768]	OA17	6	LOND	conical jug		82
<P72>	[3768]	OA17	6	SHER	pitcher		82
<P73>	[3799]	OA17	6	CBW	cauldron		83
<P74>	[3799]	OA17	6	CBW	cooking pot		83
<P75>	[3799]	OA17	6	CBW	cauldron		83
<P76>	[3768]	OA17	6	CBW	cauldron		83
<P77>	[3709]	OA17	6	CBW	cooking pot with flat-topped rim		83
<P78>	[3768]	OA17	6	SHER	cooking pot		83
<P79>	[3768]	OA17	6	SHER	cooking pot		83
<P80>	[3768]	OA17	6	LMHG	cauldron		83
<P81>	[3763]	OA17	6	KING	frying pan	glazed internally	83
<P82>	[3553]	S6	6	CBW	frying pan		83
<P83>	[3768]	OA17	6	CBW	frying pan		83
<P84>	[3799]	OA17	6	LOND	skillet		83
<P85>	[3752]	OA17	6	KING	bowl		84
<P86>	[3768]	OA17	6	CBW	dish/saucer		84
<P87>	[3768]	OA17	6	LOND	small dish		84
<P88>	[3074]	OA17	6	CHEA	small dish	glazed internally/sooted	84
<P89>	[3768]	OA17	6	CBW	dish		84
<P90>	[3752]	OA17	6	CBW	carinated bowl		84
<P91>	[3752]	OA17	6	CBW	carinated bowl		84
<P92>	[3799]	OA17	6	CBW	dish	glazed internally/externally	84
<P93>	[3553]	S6	6	CBW	dish	glazed internally/externally	85

pottery being supplied from Essex, the Surrey-Hampshire borders and from within London, a pattern somewhat typical of mid 13th-century assemblages from the City. Comparison with other assemblages from the city ditch reveals some interesting parallels. Previous excavations by MoLAS at WAY83 (7–9 Pilgrim Street, 10–13 Ludgate Broadway, EC4), LUD82 (1–6 Old Bailey, 42–46 Ludgate Hill, EC4), PIC87 (55–66 Carter Lane, 1–3 Pilgrim Street and 29–33 Ludgate Hill) and LGA87 (41–43 Ludgate Hill, 8 Pilgrim Street, EC4) produced assemblages of medieval pottery from the backfilled city ditch.

The most useful comparative statistics are available from LUD82 (Vince and Ford 1982), which also show that the principal components of the assemblage were London-type wares, coarse Surrey-Hampshire border ware, Kingston-type ware and Mill Green ware, although at this site south Hertfordshire-type greyware (SHER) is also relatively frequent. Vince and Ford comment that the composition of this assemblage is mainly chronologically determined, as the same sequence of wares is found at many other sites, for example Trig Lane. They determine that the date of the assemblage fits into a bracket c 1240–1340. These assemblages have several factors in common, which may indicate that the pottery relates to the disposal of material from a similar source and possibly a large establishment such as Greyfriars. In general, the character of the deposited material at both LUD82 and

MLFC is of contemporary rubbish without much noticeable residual pottery. The large size of the sherds preserved at the MLFC site indicates that this material is of primary deposition and has not travelled far nor been redeposited several times. Further similarities between the LUD82 and MLFC assemblages are a very low quantity of imported or non-local pottery and a high proportion of serving vessels, including decorated jugs. The large number and variety of serving vessels in the form of highly decorated jugs in London-type ware and Kingston-type ware are notable features of the MLFC assemblage. Other rare vessels, such as the Kingston-type ware cup (<P57>, Fig 78) are also indicative of the use of high quality tableware. The quality of these vessels and the lack of a wide range of fabrics, such as European imports, suggests that this assemblage is the discarded rubbish of one particular establishment using a larger than average quantity of quality tableware. Such an establishment, Greyfriars, can be found close to this section of the city ditch. The quantity of similar types of vessel and their state of preservation suggest that they were discarded more or less at the same time, rather than over an extended period. The lack of certain forms, such as coarse Surrey-Hampshire border ware bifid cooking pots, indicates that most vessels in this assemblage were deposited before c 1380.

7.4 Roman accessioned finds

Angela Wardle

Introduction

The excavations at the MLFC site produced 276 Roman artefacts, other than ceramic vessels and building materials, which were previously examined and assessed (Wardle 2001). This report concentrates on a limited number of groups which were thought to be of greatest significance: those associated with the excellent sequence of pre-Hadrianic Roman clay and timber buildings and an interesting group from an isolated well of early 2nd-century date (OA7, period 2). The catalogue of finds from the well, which is treated as a discrete group, precedes the main catalogue, which is arranged by function.

The entire assemblage is summarised by functional category (Table 11), adapted from Crummy (1983). Categories such as agricultural tools and military equipment, which are not represented, have been omitted. The composition of the assemblage and its significance are discussed in the archaeological sequence (Chapter 3). Objects specifically mentioned in the text are described below; details of the full assemblage are held on the MoLAS database and a more detailed archive catalogue of all identified artefacts and vessel glass has also been prepared (Wardle 2003). These can be consulted on application to the Museum of London Archive (LAARC), where the full archive is deposited.

Table 11 Finds tabulated by functional category and period

Period	2	3	4	5	Total
Personal ornament	7	13	2	3	25
Toilet and cosmetic implements	4	2		1	7
Textile working	2				2
Domestic implements	4	5			9
Recreation and leisure	1				1
Tools	2				2
Fasteners and fittings	7	5	1		13
Religion	2				2
Metalworking	2				2
Shoes/leather working	2	3			5
Total	33	28	3	4	68

Selected catalogue of accessioned finds from the well north of Building 8 (OA7, period 2)

<S1> Ceramic figurine (Fig 27) <883>, [3078]; period 2, OA7 Almost complete; H 131mm, W of base 42mm x 29mm. Minerva stands on a pedestal, her right arm upraised to her shoulder, her left arm holding an oval shield supported against her left leg. The right arm may originally have held a spear. She wears an ankle length tunic, with a breast-plate on which the aegis, the head of the gorgon Medusa, can be seen. The figure is now headless but she may have worn a helmet. A low vertical ridge at the nape of her neck could be either the end of an Athenian helmet crest or hair; analogy with other representations (Rouvier-Jeanlin 1972, pl 449–451) suggests that the former is more likely. The figure is very well moulded and finely detailed. There is slight damage to the base of the rectangular pedestal which is slightly abraded, but there is a very clean (although ancient) break at the neck, where the two sections of mould have fractured in different places. The figurine has been previously published by Hall and Watson (2000). Pipe clay figurines such as this one were made in the late 1st/2nd century AD in central Gaul in what is now the Allier region.

Representations of Minerva are far less common than the ubiquitous Venus figurines or the popular mother goddess (*Dea Nutrix*) type and only three are known from London. The others are from Monument House (MFI87, <5>) and from recent excavations at Plantation House (FER97, <2559>). The Monument House example is of particular interest as the figurine, which lacks both head and feet, also came from a well. In all these imported figurines Minerva is seen in her classical form, not equated with the Celtic deity Sulis, as at Bath, where she is associated with water. There are frequent references to Minerva in Roman-British iconography (Henig 1984), both in her classical form and as a Celtic/Roman deity. As a god in the Roman pantheon she had her own festival, celebrated on 19–23 March (*Quinquatrus*), and votive figurines could have been used in both public and private worship.

<S2> Copper-alloy vessel (Fig 29) <832>, [3078]; period 2, OA7 Incomplete; Diam c 180mm, H at least 120mm, Th 1.5mm. Seven fragments of a convex vessel made of thin sheet metal with simple out-turned rim; only two fragments joining. One piece which turns inwards suggests that it had a simple flattened base. There are no mounts, attachments or handle fragments, nor is the vessel decorated.

<S3> Copper-alloy mount (Fig 29) <1168>, [3078]; period 2, OA7 Complete; Diam 45mm, W of ring 11mm. Circular mount; the ring is D-shaped in section with

decoration on one section of the visible (convex) side. This is badly corroded but consists of two opposing scrolls, cast in relief, with ring-and-dot detail, similar to Celtic motifs. The remaining surface is plain. Immediately behind the decorated zone, on the flat back, is a heavy stud projecting 17mm, suitable for insertion into a leather strap. The head of the stud is decorated with a raised collar and small central boss, similar to the heads of bell-shaped mounts. There is no trace of enamel. The object appears to be a leather mount, probably used on a harness, or possibly as a vehicle fitting. The decorated convex face was clearly intended to be visible, although the top of the stud, where it would have projected from the strap, is also decorative.

<S4> Bone counter (Fig 29)
<1006>, [3075]; period 2, OA7
Complete; Diam 17mm. Plain with lathe mark on one face.

<S5> Bone handle (Fig 29)
<1008>, [3075]; period 2, OA7
Incomplete; L 70mm. One section of a two-part handle mount; hemispherical in shape, cut from a long bone, with two holes for the securing rivets. Probably a knife handle.

Glass vessels

<S6> Cup (Fig 29)
<1020>, [3078]; period 2, OA7
7mm x 4mm. Green. Small fragment from the body of a Hofheim cup (Isings form 12) decorated with bands of horizontal abrasion. Mid 1st century AD.

<S7> Cup (Fig 29)
<1055>, [3078]; period 2, OA7
42.5mm x 19mm. Natural pale green. Fragment from the body of a Hofheim cup (Isings form 12); bands of wheel-cut abrasion and a single line.

<S8> Jug (Fig 29)
<1043>, [3075]; period 2, OA7
Curved D-section rod handle 14mm x 7mm. Natural blue/green. Decorated with pinched projections; self coloured trail at rim edge. From a jug with pinched-in spout, variant with pinched projections (Price and Cottam 1998, 157). Late 1st/2nd century AD.

<S9> Jug/jar (Fig 29)
<1052>, [3075]; period 2, OA7
Base Diam c 80mm. Natural blue/green. Concave base from a jug, eg Isings form 55a, or jar. Late 1st/2nd century AD.

<S10> Bottle (Fig 29)
<1051>, [3075]; period 2, OA7
Base Diam 130mm. Natural blue. Part of the base and lower body from a cylindrical bottle, Isings form 51. Mid 1st to mid 2nd century AD.

Selected catalogue of other Roman accessioned finds

Personal ornaments

<S11> Copper-alloy brooch (Fig 21)
<446>, [1503]; period 2, OA9
Incomplete; L 59mm. Aucissa or variant. Very heavy with an arched bow, the metal 3mm thick. Details of the head remain obscure due to corrosion, but the missing pin was hinged. The upper part of the bow is undecorated, but the central part is decorated with a rectangular design of cast crosses. The foot, with terminal knob, is very short and there is a solid catchplate. This appears to be a Germanic form. Mid 1st century AD.

<S12> Copper-alloy brooch
<440>, [1412]; period 2, OA14
Complete; Diam 30mm. Pennanular brooch with small knob terminals, complete with pin. Long-lived type (Fowler 1960, A1) common until the end of the 2nd century AD.

<S13> Glass bead (Fig 26)
<510>, [1750]; period 2, B8
Complete; Diam 25mm, H 16mm. Dark blue glass melon bead, rather poorly made, with surface voids and bubbles. Possibly manufactured locally: there is evidence for 1st-century bead-making at Gresham Street (Wardle 2002).

<S14> Glass bead (Fig 26)
<343>, [715]; period 5, OA17
Complete; Diam 15mm. Turquoise faience, rather misshapen and irregular in form.

<S15> Bone hairpin (Fig 17)
<180>, [221]; period 2, OA8
Incomplete; L 54mm. Conical head set over two grooves and cordon, with part of shaft; Crummy type 2. 1st/2nd century AD.

<S16> Bone hairpin (Fig 36)
<224>, [348]; period 3, OA12
Incomplete; L 56mm. Very roughly carved; conical head over two cordons. The shaft shows knife cuts and is almost rectangular rather than the usual circular section.

<S17> Bone hairpin (Fig 36)
<2>, [16]; period 3, OA12
Incomplete; L 65mm. Crummy type 3, with globular head and swelling shank; broken above the point.

Toilet and cosmetic implements

<S18> Copper-alloy tweezers
<619>, [2028]; period 2, OA11
Incomplete; L 36mm. Very encrusted, with plain arms, the ends missing.

<S19> Copper-alloy ligula
<606>, [1972]; period 2, OA11
Complete; L 130mm (bent). Plain ligula with flat oval spoon.

<S20> Copper-alloy medical implement
<1465>, [2043]; period 2, OA9
Incomplete; L 75mm. Handle with octagonal section, terminating in an olivary probe at one end; the other end, which may have been a spoon, spatula or hook, is lost.

<S21> Bone spatula (Fig 17)
<172>, [193]; period 2, OA8
Incomplete; L 85mm. Plain tapering handle with elongated oval spoon, V-shaped in section. This is a well-preserved example of a class of object which is infrequently identified in this material, although such artefacts were undoubtedly common.

Textile working

<S22> Bone needle
<171>, [173]; period 2, B2
Incomplete; L 102mm. Three joining fragments, broken at rectangular eye.

<S23> Ceramic spindle whorl
<598>, [1979]; period 2, OA14
Complete; Diam 33mm. Roundel cut from a potsherd, pierced with a hole. The hole is 5mm in diameter, just large enough for use as a spindle whorl, but slightly off centre. Unsourced fine reduced ware; 2nd century AD.

Domestic utensils

<S24> Ceramic lamp (Fig 26)
<600>, [2021]; period 2, OA11
Complete; L 105mm. Firmalampe, Loeschke type X; very well moulded with FORTIS stamp on base. Slight soot on nozzle. Unsourced fine oxidised fabric; late 1st/2nd century AD.

<S25> Ceramic lamp
<516>, [1596]; period 2, B8
Incomplete; L 36mm. Volute lamp, Loeschcke IV, nozzle only. Oxidised fabric. ?Central Gaul.

<S26> Stone quern
<642>, [1980]; period 2, OA14
Incomplete; L 100mm, H 60mm. Lava quern (Mayen), with faint traces of striations on one edge; all other faces broken.

Fasteners and fittings

<S27> Iron key
<437>, [1327]; period 2, OA11
?Complete; L 75mm. Tumbler lock slide key with ?L-shaped bit. The distinctive handle with circular suspension hole and narrower bit can be distinguished on the x-ray.

<S28> Copper-alloy key
<212>, [454]; period 2, B4
Complete; L 85mm. Tumbler-lock slide key, very encrusted.

Religion

<S29> Ceramic figurine
<645>, [2027]; period 2, OA11
Incomplete; L 50mm. Fragment from the edge of an unidentified figurine, on which there is a flat border and then a raised section, possibly a limb, but more probably part of an architectural structure, such as an aedicula. The border has traces of two holes on the broken edges, which from the chipped edges appear to have been drilled after firing of the object. The fabric is the normal pipe clay from the Allier district of France. See also the figurine <S1>.

Glass

Ninety-four fragments of Roman vessel glass were recovered from the site, together with five glass beads, three fragments of window glass and a fragment of tank metal. The vessel glass is summarised by colour and function in Table 12 and Table 13. All glass has been recorded on the MoLAS oracle database and a more detailed catalogue of identified forms is available in archive.

The glass covers a limited range of vessel forms, mostly dating from the late 1st and 2nd centuries. A very small amount dates from the mid 1st century AD, and comprises dark blue fragments from unidentified vessels and two Hofheim cups (Isings form 12), <1020> in a strong green colour, both from the well group (OA7). The only cast vessel is a pillar moulded bowl in blue/green glass, a common 1st-century form. Apart from small fragments, two colourless vessels can be recognised, one a good quality facet-cut beaker <S30>, from Building 2, the other a fragment of jug handle. Three rim fragments from 'standard' tubular rim bowls (Isings form 44) survive and three jug handles, one in a yellow/brown glass <430>, are typical of forms used at table in the late 1st/2nd century AD. Apart from the yellow/brown jug, these and other identified vessels, which include a phial (<476>; Isings form 8), are in naturally coloured glass. Most fragments are small, although the upper part of a square bottle (<507>; Isings form 50) is well preserved. In total there are 13 bottles from the site, and both cylindrical and square forms are represented.

One fragment of tank metal from a post-medieval context may have been redeposited from local glass-making activities (Shepherd and Heyworth 1991).

ILLUSTRATED GLASS
(See also catalogue of finds from the well)

<S30> Beaker (Fig 20)
<196>, [173]; period 2, B2
Incomplete; rim Diam 103mm.
Facet-cut colourless beaker; late 1st century AD. Rim and side present. This is a vessel of good quality and the oval facets are unusually large.

7.5 Medieval accessioned finds

Jackie Keily

Methodology

It was decided to prioritise certain stratigraphic groups and therefore to concentrate the analysis on the material from those chosen groups. The backfilling of the city ditch (OA17) in period 5 produced in the region of 248 accessioned finds (excluding leather and building materials), of which 166 came from non-selected groups; the timber revetment and an associated gully (S6) produced in the region of 72 accessioned finds (excluding leather and building materials), of which 17 came from non-selected contexts. Analysis was concentrated on the accessioned finds from the selected contexts, but certain noteworthy objects from the non-selected contexts and material that complemented or paralleled material from the selected contexts have also been included. The results of this analysis are integrated into the chronological narrative (Chapter 4.4). The following is a catalogue of the medieval accessioned finds illustrated or mentioned in the text, including the wood and leather. Full archive catalogues and a report detailing all the finds from the selected groups are available from the LAARC.

Table 12 Summary of the Roman vessel glass by colour

	Monochrome	Colourless	Blue/green	Bottle	Late green	Total
Period 2	2	4	41	8		55
Period 3		4	10	2	1	17
Period 4			6			6
Period 5	2	2	4			8
Period 7			5	3		8
Total	4	10	66	13	1	94

Table 13 Summary of the Roman vessel glass by function

	Drinking	Tableware	Storage	Bottle	Vessel	Total
Period 2	3	4	2	8	38	55
Period 3		4		2	11	17
Period 4					6	6
Period 5					8	8
Period 7		1		3	4	8
Total	3	9	2	13	67	94

Specialist appendices

Selected catalogue

Dress accessories

<S31> Gold finger-ring (Fig 86)
<1069>, [3117]; period 5, OA17
Complete; Diam c 19mm, H 1mm, W 0.5mm. Plain, very thin ring; oval/D-section; split and shape now distorted.

Objects associated with personal hygiene

<S32> Copper-alloy cosmetic tool (Fig 92)
<1090>, [3552]; period 5, S6
Incomplete; L 66mm. Long narrow rod, one end terminating in a sharp point and the other flattened to form an incomplete spatula or scoop.

<S33> Wood comb (Fig 101)
<1077>, [3110]; period 5, OA17
Incomplete; L 125mm, surviving W c 73mm, Th at middle 9–10mm. Approximately half of a double-sided comb; one set of fine teeth (c 6.5 teeth per 10mm) and one set of coarser teeth (2 teeth per 10mm). Central handle area (L c 23mm) has simple linear decoration. There is a small round hole (Diam 6mm) adjacent to the one surviving end edge. The only surviving edge appears to be concave with its edge chamfered to a point, indicating a 14th-century date (Egan and Pritchard 1991, 374). Box (*buxus sempervirens*): identified by Anne Davis.

Household objects

<S34> Stone mortar (Fig 87)
<1734>, [3763]; period 5, OA17
Incomplete; H c 134mm, rim Diam c 250mm, rim Th 31mm, external base Diam c 185mm. Base with pecked external surfaces and a very smooth internal base surface; remains of two lugs, one on each side; also a small pouring lip.

<S35> Stone mortar (Fig 87)
<358>, [754]; period 5, OA17
Incomplete; base Diam c 255mm. Complete base with a small collar around it; two lugs, one on each side. External base surface worn and pecked; other external surfaces and all internal surfaces are smooth.

<S36> Stone mortar (Fig 87)
<357>, [755]; period 5, OA17
Incomplete; base Diam c 195mm. Near complete base and part of wall; remains of two lugs, one on each side. External surface of base pecked and worn; external walls smooth with fine pecking; internal base and wall surfaces smooth.

<S37> Stone lamp (Fig 93; Fig 165)
<1146>, [3553]; period 5, S6
Complete; L 54mm, W 50mm, H 28–34mm, Th of wall 6–14mm. Roughly square with a rounded flat base. The outer surfaces and inner base are roughened and pecked; the inner sides and edges are smoothed. A fragment of a larger but very similarly shaped lamp was found at Milk Street in the City (Pritchard 1991, 160, fig 3.44, no. 149) in a late 11th- to early 12th-century deposit.

<S38> Stone lamp (Fig 88; Fig 165)
<1044>, [3044]; period 5, OA17
Incomplete; L 49mm, W 46mm, H 27mm. The corner of a square or rectangular lamp, possibly part of a multiple reservoir form. The internal sides slope and the object is well-made with smooth inner and outer surfaces. This lamp is very similar to an example from Bedern, York (Ottaway and Rogers 2002, 2858, fig 1435, no. 13475), a rectangular lamp of at least two reservoirs, which appears to date to the 14th to early 15th centuries (ibid, 2859–60).

<S39> Stone lamp (Fig 88; Fig 165)
<359>, [906]; period 5, OA17
Incomplete; external Diam 140mm, H 95mm, Th of wall c 24mm. Approximately half of a round lamp with a flat base and straight walls. The outer surfaces of the walls and base are smooth, while the inner surfaces and the rim have been left rough. The inner surface of the wall and rim is blackened with soot from use.

<S40> Glass lid (Fig 93)
<1040>, [2897]; period 5, S6
Incomplete; Diam c 93mm. Colourless, decorated with a colourless applied pinched trail and two applied blue trails connected by zig-zagging blue trails; knop missing; belongs to Tyson's type A18 (2000, 70); imported, probably from Italy (Venice) or France; dated to the 13th to 14th centuries.

Lids for goblets were high status objects; Tyson has described the lidded cup as 'a vessel of special distinction' (2000, 26) as the lid enhanced the already high status of the goblet. It is interesting to note that glass lids found in pre-15th-century contexts are concentrated in London (ibid, 50–1). Only two examples in colourless glass with blue trails are known, both from London: one from St Swithin's Lane and the other from Threadneedle Street (ibid, 70).

<S41> Glass drinking cup (Fig 89)
<1041>, [2964]; period 5, OA17
Incomplete; rim Diam c 110mm. Part of the body of a colourless stemmed drinking glass with a plain rim. The rounded body is decorated with applied and marvered thin opaque white glass trails. This probably came from southern France and dates from the 14th or 15th centuries. Fragments of a similar vessel with the same decoration were found at Gateway House (CAO96 <134>).

<S42> Copper-alloy loop-handle (Fig 93)
<1091>, [3552]; period 5, S6
Complete; L 45mm, W 58mm, Th 8mm x 3mm. T-shaped loop handle, of a type used on chafing dishes (Lewis 1973, 59–70); similar examples from Norwich date to the late medieval to early post-medieval period (Margeson 1993, 78–9 and fig 45, nos 489–91). Appears to be unused.

<S43> Turned wooden bowl (Fig 98; Fig 100)
<1209>, [3763]; period 5, OA17
Incomplete; rim Diam c 170mm, distorted base 62mm x 70mm. Face-turned; plain shallow bowl with rounded profile and flat base. Internal and external turning lines; groove c 7mm below rim on part of external surface; blackened internal surface with a good grain pattern. Base has a cross (c 25mm x 22mm) burnt into its external surface. Ash (*fraxinus excelsior*): identified by Anne Davis.

<S44> Turned wooden bowl (Fig 98; Fig 99)
<1410> and <1411>, [3763]; period 5, OA17
Incomplete; rim Diam c 180mm, base Diam c 80mm, H c 40mm, wall Th 5–7mm, base Th 4.5mm. Face-turned; part of wall and base of a footed bowl, distorted but originally had a rounded profile; very good grain pattern. Grooves on external surface, one just above foot and another c 9mm below rim.

A series of very small holes (Diam c 1mm) has been punched through the wood just below the rim: the holes are approximately 25mm apart, perhaps for the attachment of an edging strip around the rim, possibly a silver rim, although no trace of metal is discernible around the holes or on the wood. In addition, there are the remains of a number of larger round holes (Diam c 4mm), three in the base and three in the sides, apparently drilled through the wall of the bowl to fix breaks. All these fragments are assumed to come from the same vessel, although no joins could be found between <1410> and <1411>. Ash (*fraxinus excelsior*): identified by Anne Davis.

<S45> Turned wooden bowl (Fig 98, Fig 100)
<1728>, [3817]; period 5, OA17
Incomplete; rim Diam c 180mm, base Diam 63mm, H c 40mm, wall Th 5mm, base Th 5mm. Face-turned; almost half of a small shallow bowl with a slight foot and a complete profile; internal surface blackened. Faint internal and external turning lines, and a groove around the internal surface, just below the rim edge. A semicircle (Diam 25mm, Th of line c 4mm), part of a symbol or

Medieval accessioned finds

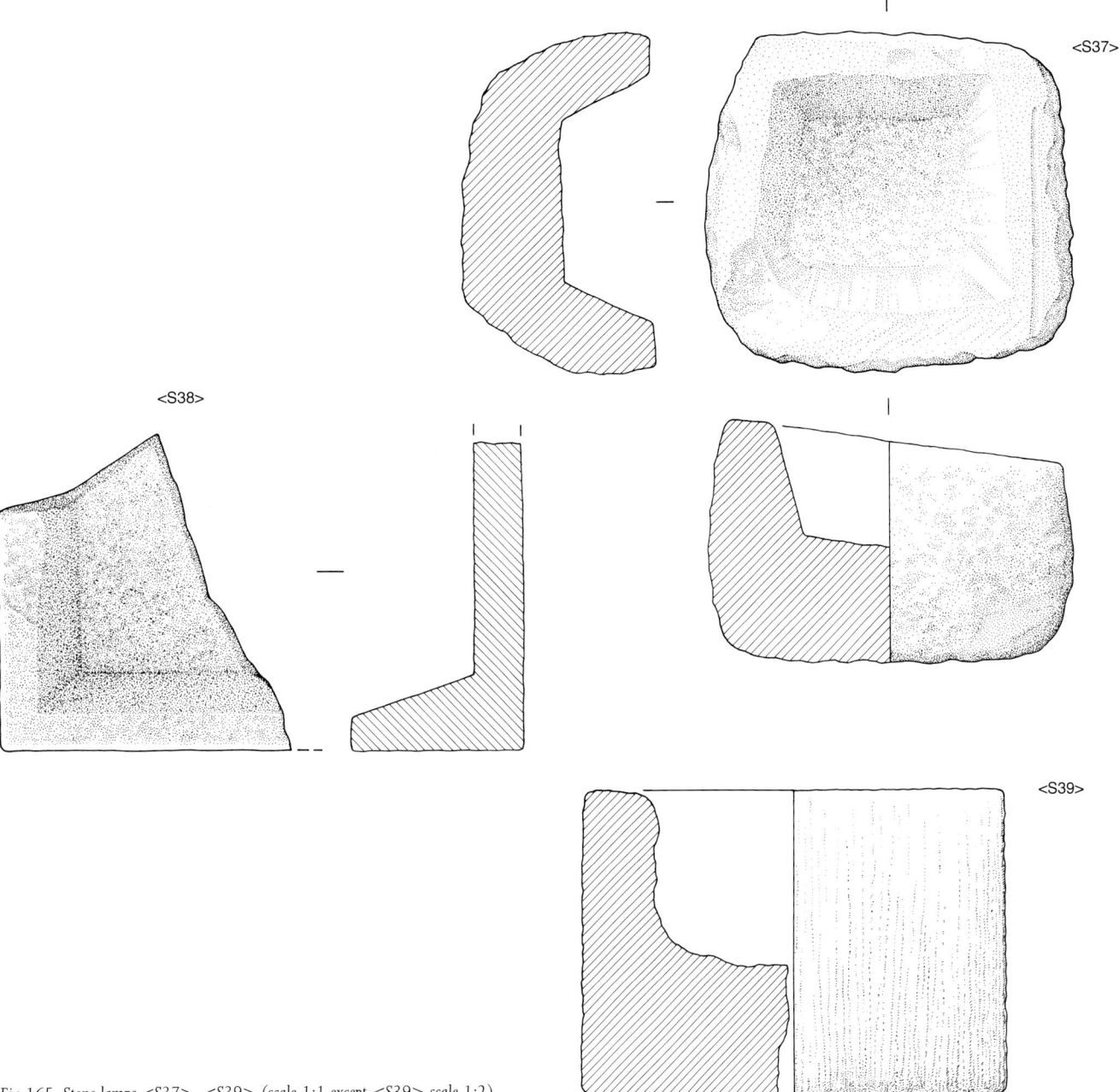

Fig 165 Stone lamps <S37>–<S39> (scale 1:1 except <S39> scale 1:2)

letter, has been burnt into the external surface of the wall. Cf Ash (fraxinus excelsior): identified by Anne Davis.

<S46> Turned wooden bowl (Fig 100)
<1726>, [3817]; period 5, OA17
Near complete; rim Diam c 230mm, base Diam 60–68mm, H c 45mm. Face-turned; plain shallow bowl with rounded profile and flattened base; shape now distorted and oval; internal and external turning lines; internal surface blackened. A small naked human footprint has been burnt into the outer surface of base. Cf Ash (fraxinus excelsior):

identified by Anne Davis.

<S47> Turned wooden bowl/platter (Fig 98)
<1409>, [3763]; period 5, OA17
Incomplete; rim Diam c 160–170mm, base Diam 66mm, wall Th 6mm. Face-turned; shallow bowl/platter now squashed and its shape distorted. There are faint internal and external turning lines, as well as two grooves on the external surface near the base and a groove around the base.

<S48> Turned wooden bowl (Fig 100)
<360>, [1003]; period 5, OA17
Incomplete; base Diam c 65mm.

Face-turned; rim and base fragments from a small shallow bowl; flat base; internal and external turning lines with some deeper grooves on external surface near base. An S-shaped mark has been burnt into external surface of base and also a faint second 'S' on inside wall just above base. Ash (fraxinus excelsior): identified by Anne Davis.

<S49> Turned wooden platter (Fig 100)
<1210>, [3763]; period 5, OA17
Incomplete; rim Diam c 210mm, wall Th 4mm. Face-turned; rim fragments from a shallow dish or platter. The inner edge of the rim

has been chamfered or flattened to give the appearance of a plain flat, flanged rim (W 13mm). The external surface is blackened and there is patchy blackening on internal surface. There is a shallow scored 'X' on external surface of rim edge.

<S50> Turned wooden platter (Fig 99)
<1727>, [3817]; period 5, OA17
Incomplete; rim Diam c 260mm, base Diam 110mm, H c 30mm, rim edge Th 9.5mm, wall Th c 5mm, base Th 6.5mm. Face-turned; approximately half of a flat platter with an upright squared rim, a shallow foot and a

171

stepped internal surface. There are three grooves on the external surface at point where the rim starts to curve upwards, and also a groove around the base on the exterior and an internal groove on the base (Diam c 145mm). There are shallow blade cut marks on the internal surface from use. Good grain pattern. Ash (fraxinus excelsior): identified by Anne Davis.

<S51> Turned wooden platter (Fig 98)
<1420>, [3796]; period 5, OA17
Incomplete; rim Diam 180mm, base Diam c 73mm, H c 32mm, wall Th 6.5mm, base Th c 3.5mm. Face-turned; near complete, shallow platter with a rounded profile and flat base. The foot is marked by a deeply cut groove. There are internal and external turning lines.

<S52> Turned wooden platter/bowl (Fig 100)
<1421>, [3799]; period 5, OA17
Incomplete; rim Diam 130mm, rim Th c 4mm. Face-turned; part of a flat everted rim (W 18mm) from a small platter or bowl; faint 'M' scratched on rim.

<S53> Turned wooden platter/bowl (not illustrated)
<1422>, [3799]; period 5, OA17
Near complete; rim Diam c 150–160mm, base Diam c 67mm, H c 40mm. Face-turned; small, shallow, rounded platter or bowl; flat base; very faint triangle formed of three crossing lines scratched on internal surface of base; knot inside near rim; internal and external turning lines; groove on external surface below rim; blackened internal surface.

<S54> Wood spatula (Fig 101)
<1416>, [3768]; period 5, OA17
Incomplete; L 132mm, Diam 3.5–4mm widening to 7mm. Tapers from end of handle before flaring out into the spatula head; most of the latter is broken off and missing.

<S55> Wood spoon (Fig 101)
<1024>, [3123]; period 5, OA17
Incomplete; L 133mm, handle Diam 4–6mm (oval section). Long thin handle with a small conical terminal (W c 7mm); virtually all the bowl is missing. The form is similar to medieval metal spoons with straight handles and knop terminals (for example, Egan 1998, 244–52; Ruempol and van Dongen 1991, 51 and 93–4). Examples of similar wooden spoons are more unusual but are known from elsewhere in Britain – for example, a finely carved spoon was found in 12th-/13th-century contexts at Coppergate, York (Morris 2000, 2267, fig 1101, no. 8899), where only the bowl survives without the handle – and on the Continent, including a 14th-century example from the Netherlands (Ruempol and van Dongen 1991, 50) and another dating to c 1500 (ibid, 94).

Tools and knives

<S56> Wood tool (Fig 101)
<1208>, [3799]; period 5, OA17
Incomplete; overall L 350mm, maximum W of blade c 115mm tapering to 65mm near base, blade Th 20mm, handle c 18mm x 30mm. Four joining fragments; a tool with a flat, rectangular blade or spade-type head and the remains of a round section handle; blade and handle carved in one piece.
The upper corners have been cut away where the handle meets the head, giving two concave edges at the top. Below this the edges taper and become quite worn, ending in a rounded edge. This was possibly a large spatula-type tool used, for example, in butter or cheese making. The lower edge is worn through use; the upper edges and the handle are unworn with quite sharp edges. Both surfaces of the blade have scratches from use. Ash (fraxinus excelsior): identified by Anne Davis.

<S57> Iron shears (Fig 90)
<1193>, [3752]; period 5, OA17
Incomplete; L 71mm, Diam of loop 12mm; maximum W of blade 8mm. One arm surviving but missing tip of blade; junction of blade and handle has a single semicircular recess. No maker's mark.

<S58> Antler rake or tool (Fig 90)
<1110>, [3209]; period 5, OA17
Incomplete; L 210mm. Antler branch with three upper tines, two broken off and the third incomplete. A small rectangular hole pierces the beam below two of the tines and there is also an iron nail or rivet driven through the beam further from the tines; this end of the beam is also broken and incomplete.
This object is similar to those described by MacGregor as rakes (1985, 178–9), although all of those date to the Roman period. The present example was found in a medieval deposit, suggesting either that this is a residual Roman object or the possibility that such simple tools continued in use.

Weapons

<S61> Copper-alloy dagger (Fig 94)
<662>, [2183]; period 7, Building 30
Incomplete; Diam 23mm. Dagger hilt with triangular aperture.

Horse equipment

<S62> Iron spur (Fig 94)
<1166>, [3374]; period 5, S6
Incomplete; Diam 41mm, Diam of central hole 5mm. Spur rowel with eight points; traces of tinning.

Religious items

<S63> Copper-alloy tomb inscription letter (Fig 118)
<813>, [2926]; period 5, OA17
Complete; H 35–37mm, W 33.5mm, Th 2.5–3mm. Lombardic letter A belonging to 'Main Group Size III', the smallest of the three size groups (Blair 1987, 140) and probably dating to the late 13th to mid 14th centuries.
This letter probably comes from a funerary monument associated with the Greyfriars monastic house. In the 14th century the church attracted many wealthy donors, who were also buried there (Schofield 1993, 70).

Writing equipment

<S64> Bone stylus (Fig 119)
<667>, [2600]; period 7, B26
Near complete; L 69mm, head Diam 6.5mm. Spherical head on a collar; tapering shaft decorated with three groups of three grooves; metal point missing.

<S65> Bone pen (Fig 119)
<1756>, [3183]; period 5, OA17
Complete; L 123mm. Goose radius; nib cut obliquely at the distal end; nib area worn and smooth. Similar objects have been found on many sites including Norwich (Margeson 1993, 68–9) and York, where six were found associated with the area around The Bedern, the College of the Vicars Choral of York Minster (MacGregor et al 1999, 1976).

<S59> Iron knife (Fig 90)
<1102>, [3109]; period 5, OA17
Incomplete; L 93mm, W 20mm, Th 2.5mm. Blade fragment; tip and tang missing; angled back; maker's mark; trefoil shaped.

<S60> Iron, copper-alloy and wood knife (Fig 90)
<1000>, [3074]; period 5, OA17
Near complete; overall L 174mm, blade L 100mm, blade W 13mm, Th 2.5mm. Scale tang knife with iron blade and tang; wooden scales; three copper-alloy tubular rivets along the handle; copper-alloy end cap with tapering terminal and copper-alloy shoulder plates. Very clear maker's mark on the well-preserved blade, indecipherable although possibly zoomorphic.

<S66> Bone pen (Fig 119)
<1750>, [3183]; period 5, OA17
Complete; L 130mm. Goose radius; nib cut obliquely at the

distal end; nib shows no signs of wear and the object many not have been much used. This may have been because of the distinct curvature of the bone, which took place post-mortem (Jane Liddle, pers comm), possibly during manufacture or use.

Items associated with music

<S67> Bone tuning peg (Fig 97)
<1009>, [2675]; period 7, B27
Complete; L 55mm, head W 5.5mm x 3mm, shaft Diam 3–5.5mm. Tapering shaft with a flattened head of rectangular section; unusually the hole is in the head end (Lawson type B; Lawson 1985, 152) and is very small (Diam 1.5mm), possibly indicating it was used with metal wire (Angela Wardle, pers comm). The hole appears to have been unused. Type B pegs appear to have been used with instruments with a box-like frame, for example, zithers, psalteries and most keyboard instruments (Lawson 1985, 154).

<S68> Bone tuning peg (Fig 97)
<1494>, [1002]; period 5, S6
Complete; L 54mm, head W 7mm x 6mm, shaft Diam 4–6mm. Roughly rectangular head (slightly distorted by presence of cancellous tissue); tapering shaft pierced by a round hole near its end; Lawson type A (Lawson 1985, 152). Lathe marks are visible on the flat surfaces of either end. Type A pegs were used with open frame instruments, such as harps and lutes (Lawson 1985, 154).

Bone working

<S69> Bone bead-making waste (Fig 95)
<1034>, [3168]; period 5, S6
Incomplete; L 58mm, W 26mm, Th 5mm, hole Diam 7mm. Cattle-size long bone fragment; knife-trimmed with two rows of seven round holes drilled out. Also remains of one part-made bead still in situ with a central hole.

Fasteners and fittings

<S70> Copper-alloy cap or ferrule (Fig 94)
<1084>, [3552]; period 5, S6
Complete; L 16mm, Diam 15mm. Small tubular mount or cap; presumably used as an end cap on a scale tang knife handle. There are two slits, one up each side (for the knife tang) and a rivet hole on each other side for attachment. The outer surfaces are decorated with simple linear engraving, with a linear star on the end.

<S71> Copper-alloy/silver mount (Fig 91)
<821>, [2896]; period 5, OA17
Incomplete; L 38mm, W of main part of mount 6mm, maximum W 17mm. Part of a narrow strap mount widening at one end which has broken off; other end terminates in a pointed terminal with a circular rivet hole; the strap section is D-section and has a moulded ridge at either end and one along its length. The surface has been coated with silver. This was probably for use on a casket.

<S72> Copper-alloy mount (Fig 91)
<379>, [938]; period 5, OA17
Incomplete; L 37mm, W 16mm. Part of a strip mount, possibly a buckle plate, with part of the shaft of a small iron rivet in situ near one end and a large round hole (Diam 5mm) about halfway along its length. The surface is decorated with linear engraving, although the form of the design is not identifiable.

<S73> Iron mount (Fig 96)
<1532>, [3194]; period 5, S6
Incomplete; L 114mm, W 43mm, Th 0.5mm. Rectangular sheet mount; one corner missing, but the other three all have a nail/rivet hole. There is also a ?copper-alloy rivet at one end. The surface is tinned and is decorated with a punched dot design in the form of three rectangles, each divided into eight triangles. The decoration stops short of the nail hole at each end and is only on one side of a ridge that runs lengthways along the mount. This ridge may have traces of textile on and near it. This was possibly part of sheet armour, but is probably too thin.

Leather sheaths

<S74> Knife sheath (Fig 105)
<1076>, [3209]; period 5, OA17
Incomplete; L 130mm, W 40mm. Bovine. Side seam, top edge cut, no suspension holes, back torn away. Decoration engraved and stamped. Front: engraved lines creating two panels filled with small stamped dots; back: mostly missing but appears same as front.

<S75> Knife sheath (Fig 103)
<1153>, [3728]; period 5, OA17
Incomplete; L 198mm, W 50mm. Worn; probably bovine. Side seam, top edge cut. Decoration engraved. Front: handle unclear, blade three zoomorphic roundels (two griffins and a ?bird). Back: handle vertical linear, blade three half quatrefoils.

<S76> Knife sheath (Fig 106)
<1205>, [3768]; period 5, OA17
Complete; L 142mm, W 46mm. Both outer and inner bovine. Short knife; side seam; cut top edge. Decoration engraved, embossed (supported by small cubes of leather) and pricked. Front: handle, zoomorphic with vertical row of zig-zags; body of animal has pricked/stabbed spots; blade, rabbit within scrolling foliage (both foliage and animal decorated with pricking). Back: handle, curving and straight linear; blade, hunting dog. Two holes in back and two near seamed side on front for suspension. Lined with inner scabbard (flesh to flesh); traces of linear engraved decoration. One of the cubes of leather used in the embossing is still in situ. This sheath was possibly for a hunting knife (Cowgill et al 1987, 41).

<S77> Knife sheath (Fig 105)
<1206>, [3763]; period 5, OA17
Incomplete; L 180mm, W 40mm. Bovine. Top end cut; other end torn; centre back edge/grain butt seam with two suspension holes either side. Decoration stamped and engraved. Back: handle, engraved linear (groups of diagonal lines); blade, engraved linear (chevrons). Front: handle and blade, panels of very small stamped ?floral motifs; handle and blade areas separated by engraved lines.

<S78> Knife sheath (Fig 104)
<1222>, [3768]; period 5, OA17
Near complete; L 160mm, W 50mm. Bovine. Centre back split seam; cut top edge, very tip torn. Decoration engraved. Front: handle, worn, diamond with foliage, blade, heraldic; back: handle, linear, blade, half quatrefoil. The heraldic device comprises a shield bearing a fess between two chevrons, above another shield (only part of which survives) bearing a gyronny of six or eight. The former device may be associated with the Fitzwalter family (Wilmott 1987, 45). Two suspension slots on the side are pierced all the way through.

<S79> Knife sheath (Fig 104)
<1384>, [3519]; period 5, B27
Incomplete; L 93mm, W 38mm. Bovine. Side back seam; cut top edge; no suspension holes. Engraved decoration. Front: handle, two roundels with foliage containing birds, background scraped away for contrast; blade: torn-off and missing. Back: handle, hemispheres and linear.

<S80> Knife sheath (Fig 103)
<1390>, [3768]; period 5, OA17
Incomplete; L 181mm, W 43mm. Outer worn; inner sheep/goat. Torn; centre back seam, cut and stitched top edge; no separation between handle and blade. Decoration engraved with contrasting areas blackened by scraping the leather. Front: zoomorphic mythical ?dragon along full length with parallel blank area; back: one side of opening is missing, other has ovolo row along length. Part of possible lining remains inside.

<S81> Knife sheath (Fig 104)
<1391>, [3768]; period 5, OA17
Incomplete; L 210mm, W 40mm.
Bovine. Side seam; torn end, cut top. Decoration engraved; front: handle, zoomorphic and linear, blade, bird/zoomorphic in circular frames and foliage; back: handle linear, blade linear semicircles. Four holes for belt in back (handle).

<S82> Knife sheath (Fig 105)
<1394>, [3790]; period 5, OA17
Incomplete; L 185mm, W 45mm.
Bovine. Side seam; flesh/grain stitches; cut top edge. Decoration stamped and engraved. Front: handle, vertical row of four stamped rosettes within lozenges, engraved linear decoration and zig-zag line; blade, stamped rosettes within lozenges partitioned by engraved lines. Back: handle, a single stamped rosette within lozenge and engraved linear decoration; blade, central vertical row of stamped rosettes within lozenges with linear engraved decoration. No suspension slots.

<S83> Knife sheath (Fig 104)
<1555>, [882]; period 5, OA17
Incomplete; L 62mm, W 24mm.
Bovine. Side back seam. Engraved decoration. Front: blade, interlace; back: fine chevron. Three smaller fragments with linear decoration. Seam worn, possibly grain/flesh seam.

<S84> Knife sheath (Fig 106)
<1075>, [3149]; period 5, OA17
Incomplete; L 75mm, W 48mm.
Outer: Bovine. Lining: sheep/goat. Possible side seam; small section cut from a larger scabbard. Engraved, embossed and stabbed decoration. Front: seated rabbit with foliage with stabbed dot detail and embossed body. Small cubes of leather placed at back and held in place by remains of lining.

<S85> Knife sheath (Fig 104)
<655>, [2117]; period 5, OA17
Incomplete; L 175mm, W 76mm.
Bovine. Flared top. Section and one seam edge cut from back. Side seam; two suspension holes near remaining seam edge; top edge cut. Engraved decoration. Front: handle, lozenge containing a fleur-de-lis dimidiating a castle triple-towered, within a square with foliage; blade, loosely braided design. Back: part linear; most missing.

<S86> Knife sheath (Fig 105)
<1567>, [1043]; period 5, OA17
Incomplete; L 120mm, W c 23mm.
Bovine. Possible side seam (possibly refolded centre back). Stamped and engraved decoration; no separation between front and back. Handle: engraved lozenges containing small stamped fleurs-de-lis; blade: vertical row of small stamped birds within lozenges.

<S87> Knife sheath (Fig 105)
<1743>, [3110]; period 5, OA17
Incomplete; L 110mm, W 45mm.
Bovine. Torn top and tip. Centre back seam. Grain/edge butt seam. Only blade section remains. Engraved and stamped decoration. Blade: front, three interlace lozenges each with a central fleur-de-lis stamp; back, linear chevron.

<S88> Knife sheath (Fig 104)
<1564>, [1043]; period 5, OA17
Incomplete; L 163mm, W 34mm.
Bovine. Side back seam, cut top edge; four suspension holes, two either side of opening. Engraved decoration. Front: split into handle and blade but overall alternating panels containing roughly sketched birds and foliage. Back: handle, vertical lines; blade, wide chevrons.

Sheath-like objects

<S89> Leather sheath-like object (Fig 104)
<1387>, [3765]; period 5, OA17
?Complete; L 64mm, W 38mm.
Bovine. Sheath-like object; top edge cut; side edge/grain butt seam continuing along rounded base. Two suspension holes on front and back for vertical thongs. Decoration tooled. Front: heraldic (quarterly, two and three fesses, overall a bend, a bordure); side panel: heraldic, elongated arms (three chevrons); back: heraldic (gyronny of eight); vertical engraved lines at base of front and back.

This appears to be a larger sheath cut down for reuse; interestingly the heraldic devices would all be upside down if the object were hung vertically from a belt (as a sheath). See Cowgill et al 1987, 152 and 154, no. 456.

<S90> Leather sheath-like object (Fig 104)
<1388>, [3768]; period 5, OA17
Incomplete; L 79mm, W 68mm.
Bovine. Sheath-like object; centre back edge/grain butt seam. Two suspension holes through both layers of leather on the folded side. Decoration tooled. Front: lozenge (concentric), innermost lozenge has fleurs-de-lis at each corner and contains a ?castle triple-towered at centre, parts of background scraped away to show darker contrast; back: linear.

<S91> Leather sheath-like object (Fig 104)
<1383>, [3194]; period 5, OA17
Incomplete; L 82mm, W 61mm.
Rectangular panel, folded, seams suggest second piece inserted to form back. One end cut; other seamed. There is a seam down one edge and the other edge is folded back with a seam, indicating that the two were joined by an insert. However, the folded side also has a seam running along its outer edge, indicating either that it formed part of a larger sheath with a 'wing' or that it formed some other form of cover, possibly for a small box or container. There is tooled zoomorphic decoration of a lion/leopard passant, a symbol found on other sheaths from London (de Neergaard 1987, 43 and 44, fig 11, nos 447, 448 and 445), but possibly rampant, given its position in the arms.

Other leather artefacts

<S92> Leather sheet (Fig 109)
<1231>, [3768]; period 5, OA17
Near complete; L 1060mm, W 500mm. Large roughly rectangular piece of thick bovine leather. Two parallel straight seamed edges (grain/flesh stitch). Longest edge has seven eyelets (five with thong reinforcement in situ; thong whip-stitched around edges and then neatly folded through a slot) and stitching for reinforcement strip along edge. Possible nail/stitch holes scattered near eyelets. One side is cut; one side has flesh/edge butt seam, a dart with flesh/edge seams and flesh/edge seam below dart; last side has flesh/grain seam and slightly curved up edge.

<S93> Leather strap or wrist guard (Fig 112)
<1237>, [3768]; period 5, OA17
Incomplete; L 115mm, W 45mm.
Quite thick leather; worn grain surface but probably bovine; cut edges. Rectangular fragment with four slashes at each end, eight holes along its length and one at the very end. Possibly some form of wrist guard or a cut-down fragment from a large strap.

<S94> Leather (Fig 110)
<1241>, [3768]; period 5, OA17
Incomplete; W 55mm. Small fragment; bovine; elaborate openwork decoration with round, diamond and cross-shaped cut-outs, as well as diagonal linear cut-outs made with a serrated bladed implement. No signs of any stitching.

<S95> Leather waste (Fig 111)
<1295>, [3768]; period 5, OA17
Complete. Trimmed fragment of stamped leather, covered with interlocking single and double crescents.

<S96> Leather (Fig 110)
<1296>, [3768]; period 5, OA17
Incomplete; L 410mm, W 330mm. Sheep/goat, but very thin and possibly deer. Torn. The two long edges have been folded back onto the flesh surface and secured with a row of small round-headed rivets/mounts (head Diam 4mm); these are now missing but the imprints of the heads remain. One of the other two edges curves and has been whip-stitched; two short parallel rows of four holes, each with a circular mount impression (head Diam 8mm), extend from this curved edge. The fourth edge is torn but there are the remains of a further (worn) row of four holes with circular impressions and probably a parallel one,

indicating that it mirrors the other edge. This was possibly part of a garment or something like a saddle.

<S97> Leather shoe
<1304>, [3768]; period 5, OA17
Near complete, apart from the fastening area, although this appears to have had a central toggle on the vamp. This example is child-sized and measures c 142mm in length (maximum W 48mm, maximum H 75–80mm), the equivalent of between an English child's size 4 and 5.

<S98> Leather shoe (Fig 102)
<1368>, [3763]; period 5, OA17
L 120mm, W 75mm. Forepart of a shoe sole with multiple small holes; purpose unknown.

<S99> Leather shoe (Fig 102)
<1312>, [3768]; period 5 OA17
L 130mm, W 62mm. Nailed sole, possible repair.

<S100> Leather ?garment (Fig 112)
<1309>, [3768]; period 5, OA17, group 96, 221
Incomplete; L 220mm, W 165mm. Worn grain surface but probably sheep/goat; cut and torn; original edges whip-stitched; coarse, irregular stitch holes (c 10–15mm apart) remain along original edges, with more for a repair or reinforcement around a large buttonhole in one corner; uncertain if the buttonhole is an original feature or not.

<S101> Leather ?garment (Fig 110)
<1310>, [3768]; period 5, OA17
Incomplete; largest fragment L 255mm, W 175mm. Worn grain surface, probably sheep/goat. Three fragments of very thin, badly crumpled and torn leather with fine stitch holes in parallel rows forming a swirling pattern; appear to have been quilted.

<S102> Large knot (Fig 108)
<1338>, [3717]; period 5, OA17
Diam of knot 12mm. Possibly used on a drawstring purse.

<S103> Strap with nails (Fig 112)
<1343>, [3763]; period 5, OA17
Incomplete; L c 280mm, W 36mm. Bovine; three fragments; curving strap made up of two layers joined by small iron nails (mainly along the centre but some also near one edge) and leather thongs (one still in situ, the others inferred by a number of holes). Each layer has a row of fine diagonal awl holes parallel to each edge. This was possibly used as a mount or frame around an edge.

<S104> Leather sheet (Fig 110)
<1377>, [3728]; period 5, OA17
Incomplete; two fragments L c 240mm, W 240mm and L 111mm, W 150mm. Bovine. The smaller fragment is plain, tapering and roughly rectangular. Three sides have over stitching or whip-stitched seams, while the fourth is torn. The larger fragment is obviously part of the same item. It has two adjoining seamed edges, the same as on the smaller fragment, but with a pointed corner and one incomplete curving edge. All the rest of it is torn and the further in from the seam the poorer the condition of the leather. The seam areas, in fact, appear hardly worn, whereas the interior is very worn and fragmentary. This worn, incomplete area also has stamped decoration in the form of rows of small tri-lobed motifs, and the same motifs mixed with small elliptical shapes filled with circles. These fragments are probably upholstery or possibly a garment.

<S105> Leather ?edging/cover (Fig 112)
<1393>, [3768]; period 5, OA17
Incomplete; L 255mm, W 60mm. Bovine; long, tapering object; one end bifurcated, the other straight with butt seam. The bifurcated end and one side have fine grain/flesh stitch holes (?closed seam). The other side has numerous rivet holes, some with iron rivets in situ. This was part of an edging or cover, possibly for upholstery.

<S106> Leather insert (Fig 112)
<1572>, [3768]; period 5, OA17
Incomplete; L 155mm, W 72mm. Both pieces bovine; triangular fragment made from two layers of leather placed flesh-to-flesh. On two sides one edge overlaps the other to form a hem; the third appears to have had a binding. This is possibly an insert from a garment or saddle.

<S107> Leather sheet (Fig 110)
<1580>, [3560]; period 5, S6
Incomplete; maximum L 240mm, maximum W 150mm. Two fragments; rectangular; closed seam on three sides of larger fragment and two sides of smaller. Single row of very fine grain/flesh stitching across centre of larger piece; lace hole in corner of small fragment; both torn.

<S108> Leather (Fig 112)
<1781>, [3799]; period 5, OA17
Incomplete; largest fragment L 137mm, W 95mm; sheet fragments; cut and torn; four fragments have folded seams with grain/flesh stitch holes, rows of finer stitches and angled corners. Fifth fragment has a flat seam with fine grain/flesh stitch holes. These pieces may come from some form of bag or container with part of an inserted base or side panel.

<S109> Wrist guard with stitching (Fig 112)
<1577>, [3711]; period 5, OA17
Incomplete; L 58mm, W 49mm. Bovine; small rectangular fragment with fine stitching around three edges and two parallel rows along centre. Fourth edge cut. Coarser stitch holes (anchor point?) at one end. Possibly part of a wrist guard or other reinforced object.

<S110> Leather sheet (Fig 112)
<1308>, [3768]; period 5, OA17
Incomplete; L 225mm, W 166mm. Sheep/goat; roughly rectangular, torn. All edges have been whip-stitched; diagonal line of small tacking stitches extends from one corner across full width and another across one corner. One part of the leather has worn through completely, suggesting that this area came under heavy use or abrasion; part of a garment, saddle or bag.

<S111>–<S114> Leather: selection of straps (Fig 107)
<1284>, <1250>, <1240>, <1291>; all [3768]; period 5, OA17
Incomplete; torn or cut strap fragments with a variety of awl holes and stitching.

7.6 Animal bone

Jane Liddle

Summary statistics and methodology

A total of 2711 animal bone fragments (Table 14) were analysed from hand-collection contexts deriving from a Roman well and backfill layers from the medieval city ditch. In addition, a further 135 fragments (Table 15) were recorded from seven samples taken from these features. All bones were recorded onto the MoLAS/MoLSS Oracle database on a bone-by-bone basis. Each bone was recorded in terms of species, element, part and proportion of bone, side and fusion and sex where appropriate. Instances of foetal/neonate, infant and juvenile bones were also recorded. To maximise the number of contexts analysed, ribs were not recorded and all vertebrae were recorded as 'vertebrae' rather than broken down by bone, with the exception of atlas, axis and sacrum. For the purpose of this publication some information has been summarised, but detailed records, analytical notes and tables are available as part of the site archive.

Identifications were carried out using the MoLSS reference

Table 14 Hand-collected animal bone from selected land uses

Period	2	5		Total
Land use	OA7	OA17	S6	
Species				
Cattle (Bos taurus)	27	572	246	845
Horse (Equus caballus)		43	3	46
Fallow deer (Dama dama)		4	4	8
Cattle-sized	2	64	42	108
Sheep (Ovis aries)	4	164	63	231
Goat (Capra hircus)		19	4	23
Sheep/goat (O aries/C hircus)	15	243	176	434
Pig (Sus scrofa)	12	153	105	270
Sheep-sized	1	9	12	22
Dog (Canis familiaris)		38	23	61
Cat (Felis catus)	1	336	36	373
Rabbit (Oryctolagus cuniculus)			5	5
Small mammal		1		1
Chicken (Gallus gallus)	4	65	39	108
Chicken-sized		1		1
Swan species (Cygnus sp)	1	1		2
Goose (Anser anser)		63	30	93
Goose-sized		1	1	2
Teal (Anas crecca)		1		1
Duck species (Anas sp)		1		1
Goshawk (Accipiter gentilis)		1		1
Golden eagle (Aquila chrysaetos)		2		2
Partridge (Perdix perdix)		1		1
Quail (Coturnix coturnix)		1		1
Barn owl (Tyto alba)		1		1
Large thrush (cf Turdus merula)	2			2
Raven (Corvus corax)		4	1	5
Unidentified bird			1	1
Sturgeon (Acipenser sturio)			1	1
Cod (Gadus morhua)		17		17
Haddock (Melanogrammus aeglefinus)		2		2
Large gadids		33	2	35
Gadid species		1	3	4
Plaice/flounder (Pleuronectidae)		1		1
Total	69	1842	798	2709

Table 15 Wet-sieved animal bone from selected land uses

Period	2	5		Total
Land use	OA7	OA17	S6	
Species				
Cattle (Bos taurus)	2	3		5
Sheep/goat (Ovis aries/Capra hircus)	1	1		2
Pig (Sus scrofa)	1	6		7
Cat (Felis catus)		1	2	3
Rat species (Rattus sp)		2		2
Small mammal		1		1
Chicken (Gallus gallus)	3	5		8
Chicken-sized	1			1
Woodcock (Scolopax rusticola)	1			1
Unidentified bird		1		1
Eel (Anguilla anguilla)	2	4		6
Herring (Clupea harengus)		6	1	7
Herring family (Clupeidae)	1	46	1	48
Smelt (Osmerus eperlanus)		4		4
Carp family (Cyprinidae)		1		1
Cod (Gadus morhua)		1		1
Large gadids		6		6
Gadid species		17		17
Gurnard (Triglidae)		1		1
Plaice/flounder (Pleuronectidae)	6	5		11
Frog/toad (Rana sp/Bufo sp)		2		2
Total	18	113	4	135

collection with wild bird bones identified at the Natural History Museum's bird collection at Tring, Hertfordshire. Distinction between sheep and goat was made by horncores and, where possible, using criteria from Boessneck (1969), Payne (1985) and Prummel and Frisch (1986).

Sexing of cattle and sheep pelves and pig canines was carried out where appropriate. Chickens were sexed by the presence or absence of spurs on metatarsals (see West 1982) and medullary bone in long bones was recorded as indicating laying hens (see Driver 1982). Horses were sexed by the presence of maxillary incisors for males.

Toothwear stages were recorded using Grant (1982) for cattle and pig, and Payne (1973) for sheep/goat. Age ranges were allocated using Halstead (1985) for cattle, Payne (1973) for sheep/goat and Bull and Payne (1982) for pigs. Age ranges from the epiphysial fusion of long bones were calculated using Schmid (1972). A horse skull was aged using maxillary incisor wear patterns defined by Goody (1983).

Measurements were limited to greatest length and epiphysial and shaft diameter of adult fused bones and followed the conventions of von den Driesch (1976). Withers (shoulder) heights were calculated using von den Driesch and Boessneck (1974).

Modification from butchery, gnawing, burning, pathology and working was recorded where evident on each bone, with a description of location and severity. Gnawing by rodents was only evident on two bones and dog gnawing affected only 5% of the assemblage. Burning was also present on only a small quantity of bones; the distribution of most of these indicates no definite episode of burning, but single incidences of overcooking or heating. A concentration of nearly 20 sheep/goat mandibles from period 5 ditch fills with scorching on the basal diastema is the only evidence of localised heating, although the cause is not clear.

7.7 Plant remains

Anne Davis

Introduction

One hundred and two samples were taken for environmental analysis from Roman, medieval and post-medieval features at KEW98. Nearly half the samples came from fills of the medieval city ditch, but a variety of other deposits were sampled including pit, well and drain fills, dumps and middens, and dark earth deposits. Sample sizes ranged from 10 to 20 litres. After assessment, 22 samples from the Roman and medieval key contexts were selected for further study. Six samples from the early Roman period (period 2) were selected for study from Open Areas 7, 8, and 9, and one from Building 10. All the selected post-Roman samples come from successive Saxo-Norman and medieval fills of the city ditch (periods 4 and 5), including three fills of pits cut into these fills during period 4.

Methodology

All samples were processed by flotation, using a Siraf flotation tank, and meshes of 0.25mm and 1.00mm to catch the flot and residue respectively. The residues were dried, and sorted for artefacts and environmental material. Flots that appeared to contain organic material were stored in industrial methylated spirits, and the remainder were dried. Flots were studied with a low-powered binocular microscope, and any charred plant remains were sorted, identified and counted. Organic flots were scanned, and the abundance of waterlogged and mineralised plant remains estimated. Identifications were made using the MoLSS botanical reference collection and standard identification reference manuals (Beijerinck 1947, Berggren 1981, Anderberg 1994). The results were recorded on the MoLAS ORACLE database, and all plant taxa identified from each sample from the medieval city ditch are shown in Table 16. Analysis included grouping the plant taxa according to the habitats in which they are most commonly found, and any uses the plants may have had.

Results

Preservation of both charred and waterlogged plant remains from the Roman (period 2) samples was patchy. Only one sample, from a rubbish dump (OA9), contained a moderate-sized assemblage of charred remains. This consisted of semi-cleaned barley (*Hordeum vulgare*), perhaps intended for use in brewing or for animal feed, but accidentally burnt during processing. Waterlogged plant assemblages from all the period 2 samples were broadly similar, and give quite a clear picture of the use of the site in the early Roman period. Parts of the site were clearly prone to flooding, but the soil also seems to have had a high input of manure or other nitrogen-rich organic matter, either deliberately added to enrich it for gardens or other horticultural use, or from use of the area for dumping rubbish. In contrast to some other Roman sites in London, a rather narrow range of plant foods was recovered, but this may be a result of the preservation conditions rather than a reflection of diet on the site. Full descriptions of these assemblages can be found in the MoLAS archive report (Davis 2003).

The plant remains from fills of the medieval ditch are described together (Chapter 4.4), because of the general similarity of these assemblages. Most of the samples contained rich and diverse assemblages of waterlogged plant macrofossils including not only fruits and seeds, but also stems, buds, thorns and other plant tissue including, in some samples, leaves of bracken (*Pteridium aquilinum*), box (*Buxus sempervirens*) and holly (*Ilex aquifolium*). The majority of these remains come from wild plants, but almost all samples included an element of useful plants, mainly foodstuffs.

Conclusions

Evidence from the plant remains suggests that conditions in and around the medieval ditch were similar throughout the period represented by the samples. The ditch was used for the dumping of all sorts of refuse including domestic waste, human excrement, probably stable sweepings, possibly garden weeds and prunings, and waste from industrial activities taking place in the area, such as flax growing or processing and leather working. In winter the ditch would have contained water, which may have become stagnant, but this would have receded in summer, allowing abundant vegetation to grow in the rich soil of the banks, and almost certainly producing a very unpleasant stench in hot weather.

Table 16 Plant remains from fills of the medieval ditch

	Period	4	4	4	4	5	5	5	5	5	5	5	5	5	5	5
	Land use	S3	S3	S3	S3	OA17	OA17	OA17	OA17	OA17	OA17	OA17	OA17	OA17	OA17	S6	S6
	Context no.	[3579]	[3579]	[3486]	[3465]	[3790]	[3772]	[3697]	[3763]	[3817]	[3768]	[3799]	[953]	[882]	[3752]	[3168]	[3552]
	Sample no.	{339}	{338}	{333}	{331}	{385}	{383}	{381}	{384}	{391}	{386}	{389}	{120}	{115}	{382}	{325}	{337}
Latin name	**English name**																
Charred remains																	
Triticum spelta L	spelt wheat glume base			1													
Triticum cf *aestivum* sl	bread/club wheat		1			1				1		4		2		1	
Triticum sp	wheat								2						1		
cf *Triticum* sp	wheat							1									
Secale cereale L	rye							1			3						
Triticum/Secale sp	wheat/rye							1									
Hordeum vulgare (L)	barley rachis												1				

Specialist appendices

Table 16 (cont)

Latin name	English name	Period	4	4	4	4	5	5	5	5	5	5	5	5	5	5	5
		Land use	S3	S3	S3	S3	OA17	OA17	OA17	OA17	OA17	OA17	OA17	OA17	OA17	S6	S6
		Context no.	[3579]	[3579]	[3486]	[3465]	[3790]	[3772]	[3697]	[3763]	[3817]	[3768]	[3799]	[953]	[882]	[3752]	[3168]	[3552]
		Sample no.	{339}	{338}	{333}	{331}	{385}	{383}	{381}	{384}	{391}	{386}	{389}	{120}	{115}	{382}	{325}	{337}
cf *Hordeum vulgare*	barley				1													
Avena sativa L	cultivated oat floret													1				
Avena sp	oat								1			1		1			1	
Cerealia	indet. cereal												1	2				
Vicia/Lathyrus sp	vetch/tare				1													
Vicia/Lathyrus/Pisum sp	vetch/tare/pea												1					
Lapsana communis L	nipplewort				1													
Bromus spp	brome grasses												2					
indeterminate	charcoal fragments		++	+	+	++	++	+	++	++	+	+	++	+	+	+++	++	+++
Waterlogged remains																		
Bryophyta indet.	mosses		++	++++		+	++	++	+++	++++	++		+++	+++	++	+	++	++++ ++
Pteridium aquilinum (L) Kuhn	bracken, leaf					+			+		+	+			+	+	+	
Ranunculus acris/repens/ bulbosus	buttercups		++	+		++	+		+	+	++		++	+	+	+	++	+
Ranunculus sardous Crantz	hairy buttercup		+		+	++	+	+			+		+		+		+	
Ranunculus flammula L	lesser spearwort		+			+												
Ranunculus sceleratus L	celery-leaved crowfoot		+++	++	+	++	++++	+++	+++	+++	++++	+++	+++	+++	+++	++	++++	+
Papaver sp	poppy																+	+
Chelidonium majus L	greater celandine		+							+								+
Fumaria sp	fumitory								+			+						
Brassica cf *nigra*	black mustard				+					+						+	+	
Brassica sp	wild cabbage etc		+	+	+		+	+	+		+			+	+	+	+	+
Raphanus raphanistrum L	wild radish, capsule						+	+		+	+	+		+				+
Capsella bursa-pastoris (L) Medic	shepherd's purse		++		+	++	+	+	+	+	+	+	++		+	+		
Reseda luteola L	weld													+	+			
Silene spp	campions			++		+		+				+	+	+	+	+		++
Agrostemma githago L	corn cockle		++	+++	+	++	+	+	++	++	++	++	++	+	++	++	++	++
Cerastium sp	mouse-ear chickweed						+										+	
Stellaria media (L) Vill	common chickweed		+			+	++	+			+		+	+	+	+	+	+
Stellaria graminea L	lesser stitchwort						+			+						+		
Scleranthus annuus L	annual knawel		+									+						
Chenopodium album L	fat hen			+	+	++	+	+	++	+	+	+	++	+	++	++	++	+
Chenopodium murale L	nettle-leaved goosefoot		+			++	+	+	+		++			+		+	+	
Chenopodium rubrum/ glaucum	red/glaucous goosefoot			+++	+		++	++	++++	+		+	+++	++	+	+++	++++	++
Beta vulgaris L	beet, fruit																+	++
cf *Beta vulgaris* L	beet, fruit						+											
Atriplex spp	orache		+	+	+	++	++	++	++++		++	+	+	+	+	++	++	++++
Malva cf *sylvestris*	common mallow, capsule						+		+	+	+	+	+		+	+		++
Malva sp	mallow									+			++					+
Linum usitatissimum L	cultivated flax		+	+			+	+	+		+	+	+	+	+			
Linum usitatissimum L	cultivated flax, capsule		++				+	+	+		++	+	++	+	+			
cf *Linum* sp	flax															+		
Ilex aquifolium L	holly, leaf													+				
Buxus sempervirens L	box, leaf								+									
cf *Buxus sempervirens* L	box, leaf									+								
Vitis vinifera L	grape			+			+			+	+	+	+	+				+
Medicago cf *arabica* (L) Huds	spotted medick, legume								+								+	
Filipendula ulmaria (L) Maxim	meadow-sweet											+						
Rubus cf *fruticosus* agg	blackberry			+	+	++	+			+			++	+	+	+		
Rubus fruticosus/idaeus	blackberry/raspberry		+										++					
Rubus cf *idaeus*	raspberry																	++
Potentilla cf *erecta*	tormentil													+				
Potentilla sp	cinquefoil/tormentil									+							+	
Fragaria vesca L	wild strawberry				+							+						
Rosa sp	rose													+				

Table 16 (cont)

Latin name	English name	Period 4	4	4	4	5	5	5	5	5	5	5	5	5	5	5	5
	Land use	S3	S3	S3	S3	OA17	OA17	OA17	OA17	OA17	OA17	OA17	OA17	OA17	OA17	S6	S6
	Context no.	[3579]	[3579]	[3486]	[3465]	[3790]	[3772]	[3697]	[3763]	[3817]	[3768]	[3799]	[953]	[882]	[3752]	[3168]	[3552]
	Sample no.	{339}	{338}	{333}	{331}	{385}	{383}	{381}	{384}	{391}	{386}	{389}	{120}	{115}	{382}	{325}	{337}
Prunus spinosa L	sloe, blackthorn		+++		+	+				+	+	+	+	+			
Prunus domestica L	plum/bullace		+++		+		+		+	+	+		+	+			+
Prunus avium/cerasus	cherry		+++	+	+					+							
Prunus sp	-			+				+	+		+						
cf *Prunus* sp	fruit		+														
Malus domestica/sylvestris	apple/crab apple		+	+	+		+					+	+				
Malus domestica/sylvestris	apple/crab apple, endocarp		+++	+	++	+		+	+		+	++		+	++	+	
cf *Chaerophyllum aureum*	golden chervil		+									+	+				
Chaerophyllum sp	chervil							+									+
cf *Chaerophyllum* sp	chervil															+	
cf *Anthriscus caucalis*	bur chervil	+	+				+			+	+			+	+	+	
Coriandrum sativum L	coriander															+	
cf *Smyrnium olusatrum* L	alexanders									+							
Aethusa cynapium L	fool's parsley			+													
cf *Anethum graveolens*	dill			+													
Conium maculatum L	hemlock			+	+	+++	+	+	++	+++	++	++++	++	+	++	+++	++
cf *Bupleurum* sp	-														+		
Apium graveolens L	celery										+				+		
Apium cf *graveolens*	celery																+
Apium nodiflorum (L) Lag	fool's watercress				+												
Apiaceae indeterminate	-							+		+		+			+		
Bryonia dioica Jacq	bryony																+
Polygonum aviculare agg	knotgrass		++	+	+	+	++	++	++	++	++	++	+++	+	++	++	++	+
Persicaria lapathifolia (L) Gray	pale persicaria											+				+	
Persicaria hydropiper (L) Spach	water pepper		+		+					++					+		
Rumex acetosella agg	sheep's sorrel		+	+		+		+	+			+	+			+	+
Rumex maritimus L	golden dock		++				+++										
Rumex spp	docks	+	+	+		+	+	+				+	+	+	+	+	+
Urtica urens L	small nettle	+	+	+		+	++	+++	++		+	+	+	+	+++	+	+
Urtica dioica L	stinging nettle	+		+	+	++++	++++	++	++	+++	+++	+++	+	++	++	++++	++
Ficus carica L	fig		+++	+	+	++		++	+	++	++	+++	+	++	++	++	+++
Morus nigra L	mulberry										+						
Juglans regia L	walnut, nutshell						+			+	+						
cf *Juglans regia*	walnut, nutshell													+			
Corylus avellana L	hazel, nutshell		+	+	+		+		+		+		+		+	+	+
cf *Corylus avellana*	hazel, nutshell										++						
cf *Salix* sp	willow						+										
cf *Salix* sp	willow, capsule						+				+						
cf *Olea europaea*	olive														+		
Hyoscyamus niger L	henbane		+		+	+	+								+	+	+
cf *Solanum dulcamara*	woody nightshade															+	
Solanum nigrum L	black nightshade		++	+	+	+++	+	+	+	++	+++	++	++++	+++	++	+++	+++	++
Verbena officinalis L	vervain										+		++				
cf *Mentha* sp	mint										+						
Lycopus europaeus L	gipsy-wort	+			+	+		+		+		+					
Prunella vulgaris L	self-heal	+	+						+		+	+					
Lamium sp	dead-nettle																++
Galeopsis tetrahit L	common hemp-nettle					+		+						+	+		
Marrubium vulgare L	white horehound	+	+	+	+	++	++++	++	++++	++	++++	++	++++	++++	+++	++++	++++
Plantago major L	great plantain						+						+				
Sambucus nigra L	elder	+		+	+	+++	+	++	+++	++++	+++	+++	+++	++	+++	++
Valeriana cf *officinalis*	common valerian										+						
Dipsacus cf *sativus* (L) Honckeny	fuller's teasel																+
Knautia arvensis (L) Coulter	field scabious		+				+		+		+				+	+	
cf *Knautia arvensis*	field scabious					+				+		+	+	+			
Bidens tripartita L	tripartite bur-marigold							+	++		+		+	+			
Bidens sp	bur-marigold					+				+		+			+		

Specialist appendices

Table 16 (cont)

Latin name	English name	Period	4	4	4	4	5	5	5	5	5	5	5	5	5	5	5	5
		Land use	S3	S3	S3	S3	OA17	OA17	OA17	OA17	OA17	OA17	OA17	OA17	OA17	OA17	S6	S6
		Context no.	[3579]	[3579]	[3486]	[3465]	[3790]	[3772]	[3697]	[3763]	[3817]	[3768]	[3799]	[953]	[882]	[3752]	[3168]	[3552]
		Sample no.	{339}	{338}	{333}	{331}	{385}	{383}	{381}	{384}	{391}	{386}	{389}	{120}	{115}	{382}	{325}	{337}
cf *Senecio* sp	ragwort											+			+			
Anthemis cotula L	stinking mayweed		+		+	+		+	+	+	+	+	+		+	++	+	+
Chrysanthemum segetum L	corn marigold			+	+	+	+			+			++	+	++	+	+	
Arctium sp	burdock										+	+						
cf *Arctium* sp	burdock						+											
Carduus sp	thistles				+			+++	+	+			+		+			
Carduus/Cirsium spp	thistles				+	+	+	++		+	+++	+	+	+	+	+	++	+
Centaurea cf *cyanus*	cornflower		+	+			+	+	+	+	+	+	+	+	+	+	+	
Centaurea sp	knapweed/thistle														+			
Lapsana communis L	nipplewort		+	+	+	+	+		+	+	+	+	+		+	+	+	++
Hypochoeris radicata L	cat's ear										+						+	
Leontodon autumnalis L	autumnal hawkbit														+			
Leontodon autumnalis/ hispidus	hawkbit										+	+	+	+	+	+		
Leontodon sp	hawkbit		+			+												
Picris hieracioides L	hawkweed							+					+					
Sonchus oleraceus L	milk-thistle		+				+		+	+	+	+	+	+	+		+	++
Sonchus asper (L) Hill	spiny milk-thistle		+					+	+	+	+				+	+	+	
Taraxacum sp	dandelion						+		+		+		+		+			
Triglochin maritima L	sea arrow-head												+					
Juncus spp	rushes		++		+		+		+					+				+
Eleocharis palustris/ uniglumis	spike-rush			+	+	++			+	+	+	+	+	+		+		
cf *Schoenoplectus lacustris*	bulrush		+															
Carex spp	sedges		+		+	+	+		+	+	+	+	+	+	+	+	+	+
cf *Secale cereale*	rye, rachis														+			
Hordeum sativum L	barley, rachis											+						
Cerealia	indeterminate cereal			+	+			+		+					+	+		
Cerealia	indeterminate cereal bran		++++			++++	+++	+++	++	++	++	+++	+++	++		+++	+++	
Poaceae indeterminate	grasses					+	+	+				+	++		+	+	+	+

FRENCH AND GERMAN SUMMARIES

Résumé

Les fouilles archéologiques conduites au Centre Financier Merrill Lynch entre 1992 et 2001 ont fourni de nouvelles informations de premier choix sur l'occupation antique et ultérieure dans la partie nord-ouest de la Cité de Londres. Les données matérielles provenant du site ont été complétées par une recherche documentaire et par l'exploitation de données anciennes comme de découvertes récentes faites à proximité.

La topographie naturelle du site était rendue complexe par la présence de cours d'eau sur le côté oriental de la vallée de la rivière Fleet. L'occupation romaine précoce fut installée le long de la voie est-ouest, qui est immédiatement au sud du site, le long de Newgate Street et qui conduit à l'ouest vers Silchester. L'occupation s'étendit à la fin du Ier siècle et au début du IIe siècle alors que la zone fut aménagée et que des bâtiments furent construits le long de la voie. Parmi ces établissements, des boutiques et des tavernes profitaient du passage de voyageurs ainsi que d'habitants locals.

La construction de l'enceinte urbaine vers la fin du IIe siècle eut un impact décisif sur l'utilisation du sol à Newgate et a pu précipiter l'abandon et le comblement d'au moins deux des cours d'eau. Le tracé des défenses fut déterminé par des facteurs topographiques comme par la taille de l'habitat existant et sur le site du Centre Financier Merrill Lynch l'emplacement du mur fut influencé par la présence de la vallée de la rivière Fleet et l'étendue limitée de la terrasse de graviers et des niveaux supérieurs d'argile, la ligne de l'enceinte suivant le rebord de ce terrain plus élevé et plus sec. Les fondations de l'enceinte et de ses bastions ultérieurs au nord de Newgate n'étaient pas d'un type uniforme mais variaient pour s'adapter aux contraintes topographiques locales.

L'enceinte antique continua à délimiter la Cité pendant tout le Moyen Age et le début de l'époque moderne. La configuration et l'emplacement du site, pris entre Newgate Street au sud et la courbure de la muraille à l'ouest et au nord, eurent une influence forte sur les transformations de l'usage du sol à partir de la fin de l'Antiquité. Pour le Moyen Age, les études documentaires, cartographiques et archéologiques prouvent que la taille du terrain et sa forme ont conduit à le choisir pour l'édification du couvent des Greyfriars en 1225. Pendant le Moyen Age, l'enclos conventuel occupa la plus grande partie du secteur fouillé.

Le fossé défensif au nord de Newgate fut recreusé à la fin de l'époque saxonne et dans le courant du Moyen Age. Sur le site, le comblement du fossé médiéval le réduisit à un petit chenal après seulement une centaine d'années d'utilisation. L'expansion des zones bâties au XVIe siècle fut une raison supplémentaire de gagner du terrain sur le fossé qui, au milieu du XVIe siècle, avait été complètement remblayé dans le secteur de Newgate, le terrain étant loué ou vendu pour de nouvelles constructions. Le couvent fut supprimé pendant la dissolution des monastères entre 1536 et 1540 et converti en une école pour orphelins connue comme Christ's Hospital. Des portions du site extérieures à l'établissement furent transformées en lieux d'habitation. Le chevet de l'église conventuelle fut utilisé

comme église paroissiale, sous le nom de Christ Church ;
détruite dans le Grand Incendie de 1666, elle fut reconstruite
par Christopher Wren en 1674-1687. L'emprise de la nef reçut
quant à elle le cimetière paroissial jusque dans les années 1850.

Au milieu du XVIIIe siècle, il n'était plus possible de
conserver l'enceinte urbaine intacte et elle fut progressivement
démolie. Des plans historiques montrent qu'en 1746 le mur
n'existait plus en élévation sur le site du Centre Financier
Merrill Lynch. Des bâtiments sur caves furent établis à cheval
sur l'enceinte vers la fin du XVIIIe siècle. La partie occidentale
du mur ainsi que le bastion 19 furent aussi détruits et la
construction de la prison Compter dans Giltspur Street par
l'architecte George Dance fils fut réalisée en 1787-1791. Le
reste de l'enceinte disparut à la faveur de programmes de
construction lancés par l'hôpital Saint-Barthélémy et Christ's
Hospital au XIXe siècle. La prison Compter fut démolie en
1854 ; Christ's Hospital acheta le terrain mais ne l'aménagea
jamais et au début du XXe siècle le long usage scolaire du site
prit fin, l'école étant déplacée hors de Londres.

Pendant l'essentiel du XXe siècle, le terrain fut occupé par le
bâtiment de la Poste Centrale, dont les profonds soubassements
détruisirent la plus grande partie des niveaux archéologiques. Le
nouveau bâtiment du Centre Financier Merrill Lynch reçut des
fondations conçues pour préserver in situ la plupart des niveaux
restants. L'église Christ Church de Wren fut incendiée pendant
le Blitz et jamais reconstruite, mais le clocher et la maison du
conseil paroissial ont tous les deux été restaurés. Aujourd'hui
le secteur de l'église d'époque moderne et celui du cimetière
adjacent sont devenus un jardin public et font partie du
« London Greyfriars Scheduled Ancient Monument ».

L'importance du site en tant que relique du paysage urbain
fut réaffirmée en 2005 lors de la remise du prix « Award for
Building in Context » attribué au Centre Financier Merrill
Lynch par l'Institut royal d'Urbanisme. Les juges ont ainsi
commenté cette réalisation :

« Un grand soin fut pris pour protéger les vestiges classés
au titre des Monuments historiques, en particulier ceux des
enceintes antique et médiévale. A travers la construction
d'une pièce d'observation, le public est en mesure de voir
une partie de ces impressionnantes structures. Le Centre est
un exemple parfait de la transformation de contraintes
apparentes en défis créatifs. Une profonde compréhension
des caractéristiques du site et de son potentiel a permis de
profiter d'occasions que des concepteurs moins talentueux
auraient manquées. De vieux bâtiments de haute qualité et
d'aspect harmonieux ont été ramenés à la vie. Des vestiges
archéologiques jusqu'ici dissimulés ont même été utilisés
pour renforcer l'intérêt du hall d'accueil. Par leur sobriété
et leur dignité, les nouvelles constructions ne font pas
concurrence à leur environnement si fragile ni le domine. »

Zusammenfassung

Archäologische Ausgrabungen im Bereich des Merrill Lynch
Financial Centre haben zwischen 1992 und 2001 wichtige neue
Informationen zu römischen und späteren Aktivitäten im
Nordwestteil der City of London erbracht. Der archäologische
Befund wird ergänzt durch das Studium der schriftlichen
Quellen, die antiquarische Analyse und die Auswertung von
benachbarten Ausgrabungen der letzten Jahre.

Bachläufe östlich des Fleet-Tales geben der natürlichen
Topographie des Fundplatzes eine komplexe Gestalt. Die
frührömische Bebauung folgte der Ost-West verlaufenden
Hauptstraße, die unmittelbar südlich des Fundplatzes entlang
der Newgate Street verlief und in westlicher Richtung nach
Silchester führte. Die Besiedlung geht zurück auf das späte 1.
und frühe 2. Jh. n.Chr., als das Gebiet zu Baugelände gemacht
wurde und Straßenhäuser entstanden. Letztere enthielten auch
Läden und Tavernen, die sowohl von den Durchreisenden wie
von der Einwohnerschaft profitierten.

Der Bau der landeinwärts gerichteten Stadtbefestigung
gegen Ende des 2. Jhs wirkte sich stark auf die Bodennutzung
in Newgate aus und mag dazu geführt haben, dass zwei
Bachläufe nicht mehr genutzt und verfüllt wurden. Der Verlauf
der Stadtbefestigung wurde durch topographische Gegebenheiten
und die Größe der Ansiedlung bestimmt. Im Bereich vom
Merrill Lynch Financial Centre nahm die Stadtmauer Rücksicht
auf das Fleet-Tal und das Ausmaß der Kiesterrassen und darüber
liegenden natürlichen Ziegelerde, so dass sie der Kante dieses
höheren und trockneren Grundes folgte. Die Fundamente der
Verteidigungsmauer und ihrer späteren Bastionen nördlich von
Newgate besaßen keine einheitliche Gestalt, sondern waren
durch unterschiedliche Konstruktion den lokalen
topographischen Verhältnissen angepasst.

Die römische Stadtbefestigung blieb die Stadtgrenze auch
im Mittelalter und in der frühen Neuzeit. Gestalt und Lage des
Platzes vom Merrill Lynch Financial Centre zwischen Newgate
Street im Süden und dem Bogen der Stadtmauer im Westen und
Norden hatte starken Einfluss auf die Landnutzung von der
spätrömischen Periode an. Für das Mittelalter zeigen
Schriftquellen, Karten und archäologischer Befund, dass Größe
und Gestalt des Platzes dazu führten, diese Stelle 1225 für die
Anlage des Greyfriars Mönchsklosters auszuwählen. Während
des Mittelalters bedeckte das Anwesen des Klosters den Großteil
des Untersuchungsgebietes.

In der spätangelsächsischen und mittelalterlichen Zeit
wurde der Verteidigungsgraben nördlich von Newgate erneuert.
Am Fundplatz Merrill Lynch Financial Centre war der
mittelalterliche Graben nach nur ca. 100 Jahren durch Verfüllen
zu einem kleinen Kanal verkommen. Der Bedarf der
expandierenden Stadt des 16. Jhs an Baugelände war ein Grund
für das weitere Heranrücken der Häuser an den Graben. Um
die Mitte des 16. Jhs war der Graben im Bereich von Newgate
vollständig zugeschüttet und der Boden zur Bebauung vermietet
oder verkauft. Während der Auflösung der Klöster zwischen
1536 und 1540 wurde das Greyfriars-Kloster geschlossen und
in eine Schule für Waisenkinder verwandelt, die unter dem
Namen Christ's Hospital bekannt ist. Die Teile des Gebietes, die
das Schulgelände nicht einnahm, wurden zu Wohngebiet. Der
Chor der Klosterkirche blieb als Gemeindekirche mit dem
Namen Christ Church in Gebrauch; sie wurde während des
Großen Feuers von 1666 zerstört und von Christopher Wren

zwischen 1674 und 1687 wieder aufgebaut. Der Bereich des Kirchenschiffes wurde bis in die 1850er als Gemeindefriedhof genutzt.

Zu Mitte des 18. Jhs war es nicht länger möglich, die Stadtmauer zu erhalten, und sie wurde langsam abgerissen. Historische Karten zeigen, dass im Untersuchungsgebiet die Mauer im Jahre 1746 oberirdisch nicht mehr existierte. Am Ende des 18. Jhs waren unterkellerte Gebäude über den ehemaligen Verlauf der Mauer hinweg errichtet worden. Der westliche Mauerteil und Bastion 19 wurden ebenfalls abgerissen, und die Erbauung des Gefängnisses Compter in Giltspur Street durch den Architekten George Dance d. J. fand von 1787 bis 1791 statt. Der Rest der Mauer musste für Bauprojekte Platz machen, die durch die Krankenhäuser von St Bartholomew und Christ's Hospital im 19. Jh. veranlasst wurden. Das Compter-Gefängnis wurde 1854 abgerissen. Christ's Hospital erwarb den Grund, baute aber nie etwas dort. Im frühen 20. Jh. kam es zum Ende der Nutzung des Geländes durch die lange bestehende Schule, die von London auszog.

Während des größten Teils des 20. Jhs wurde der Fundplatz vom General Post Office-Gebäude bedeckt, dessen tiefe Kellergeschosse die meisten archäologischen Schichten zerstörten. Das neue Merrill Lynch Financial Centre besitzt Fundamente, die so angelegt sind, dass die Mehrheit der noch bestehenden archäologischen Befunde *in situ* konserviert werden konnte. Die von Wren erbaute Christ Church wurde während des „Blitz" zerstört und nie mehr aufgebaut; Kirchturm und Gemeinderatshaus sind allerdings beide restauriert worden.

Heute dient das Gebiet der neuzeitlichen Kirche und der daran anschließende Friedhof als öffentlicher Park und bildet einen Bestandteil des „London Greyfriars Scheduled Ancient Monument".

Die Kraft der überlebenden städtischen Landschaft des Fundplatzes wurde 2005 durch den „Award for Building in Context" bestätigt, der dem Merrill Lynch Financial Centre durch das königliche Stadtplanungsinstitut bestätigt. Die Juroren gaben folgenden Kommentar ab:

„Große Sorgfalt hat gewaltet, um die denkmalgeschützten Monumente, besonders die Reste der römischen und mittelalterlichen Mauer zu erhalten. Durch die Einrichtung eines Besichtigungsraumes kann die Öffentlichkeit diese eindrucksvollen alten Strukturen sehen. Das Merrill Lynch Financial Centre ist ein perfektes Beispiel dafür, wie sogenannte Sachzwänge in kreative Herausforderungen verwandelt werden können. Aus einem gründlichen Verständnis der individuellen Charakteristiken und des Potenzials des Fundplatzes resultierten Möglichkeiten, die weniger begabte Planer nicht erkannt hätten. Feine und harmonisch aussehende alte Gebäude sind wieder zum Leben erweckt worden. Sogar bislang verborgene archäologische Reste wurden dafür benutzt, einem Empfangsbereich einen interessanteren Charakter zu verleihen. Durch ihre Bescheidenheit und Würde versuchen schließlich die errichteten Neubauten nicht in Konkurrenz mit der empfindlichen historischen Umgebung zu treten und sie nicht zu dominieren."

BIBLIOGRAPHY

Manuscript sources

City of London Records Office (CLRO) (now part of the London Metropolitan Archives)

CARD CALENDAR TO PROPERTY REFERENCES (CCPR)
References in the Journals, Repertories and unpublished Letter Books up to 1595
CCPR, Rep 4, fo 160, 1523
CCPR, Rep 5, fo 187, 1521
CCPR, Rep 10, fo 310, 1543
CCPR, Rep 12(i), fo 68b, 1549
CCPR, Rep 13(ii), fo 369, 1556
CCPR, Rep 14, fo 332b, 1560
CCPR, Rep 14, fo 475, 1561
CCPR, Rep 19, fo 3206, 1578
CCPR, Rep 22, fo 315, 1591

CITY LANDS GRANT BOOKS
CL Grant Book I, fo 74v, 1604–5

LETTER BOOKS
Books A to L are in published calendar form and contain a large amount of information, especially structural and topographical detail about the city wall and bastions.
CCPR, Lett Bk R, fo 204b, 1552
CCPR, Lett Bk 5 Oct 1434

PRIVATE RECORDS
Giltspur Street Compter Charge Book PC1/23, 1811–23

REPERTORIES
The Repertories date from 1495 onwards and record the business of the Court of Aldermen. The card calendar property references which were consulted to obtain information on the structure and condition of the city wall are above.

PRIVATE RECORDS
Giltspur Street Compter Charge Book PC1/23, 1811–23

Sir John Soane's Museum, London (Soane)

1–16, 19–39 LONDON: Giltspur Street Compter
Contract drawings, designs and record drawings, 1787 (37): D4/3

Printed and other secondary works

Agas, R, c 1562 'Civitas Londinum', reproduced in Margary 1981
Allin, C E, 1981 The leather, in Mellor, J E, and Pearce, T, The Austin Friars, Leicester, CBA Res Rep 35, 145–68, London
Anderberg, A-L, 1994 Atlas of seeds and small fruits of north-west European plant species (Sweden, Norway, Denmark, East Fennoscandia, and Iceland): with morphological descriptions: Part 4, Resedaceae – Umbelliferae, Stockholm

Archer, M, 1997 Delftware: the tin-glazed earthenware of the British Isles: a catalogue of the collection in the Victoria and Albert Museum, London

Archer, I, Barron, C, and Harding, V (eds), 1988 Hugh Alley's caveat; the markets of London in 1598: Folger MS Va 318, London Topogr Soc Publ 137, London

Ayre, J, and Wroe-Brown, R, in prep Queenhithe: excavations at Thames Court, City of London, 1989–97, MoLAS epublication Ser

Baines, P, 1985 Flax and linen, Shire Albums 133, London

Beijerinck, W, 1947 Zadenatlas der Nederlandsche Flora I–II, Veenman and Zonen, Wageningen

Bell, W G, Cottrill, F, and Spon, C 1937 London Wall through eighteen centuries, London and Wisbech

Bennett, P, 1989 Canterbury, in The Saxon Shore: a handbook (ed V A Maxfield), Exeter Stud Hist 25, 118–29, Exeter

Bentley, D, 1985 Roman London: a 1st-century boundary, London Archaeol 5, 124–9

Bentley, D, 1987 Western stream reconsidered: an enigma in the landscape, London Archaeol 5, 328–34

Bentley, D, and Pritchard, F, 1982 The Roman cemetery of St Bartholomew's Hospital, London, Trans London Middlesex Archaeol Soc 33, 134–72

Berggren, G, 1981 Atlas of seeds and small fruits of north-west European plant species: Part 3, Salicaceae-Cruciferae, Stockholm

Blair, I, and Watson, B, with Taylor, J, in prep Excavations at 30 Gresham Street London, City of London, MoLAS Monogr Ser

Blair, J, 1987 English monumental brasses before 1350: types, patterns and workshops, in The earliest English brasses: patronage, style and workshops, 1270–1350 (ed J Coales), 133–74, London

Boessneck, J, 1969 Osteological differences between sheep (ovis aries Linné) and goat (capra hircus Linné), in Science in archaeology (eds D Brothwell and E Higgs), 331–58, London

Bond, C J, 2002 London Tower Postern Report, unpub MoL rep

Bowsher, D, Dyson, T, Holder, N, and Howell, I, in prep The London Guildhall: archaeology and history of the site from the early medieval period to the 20th century, MoLAS Monogr Ser

Bradley, S, and Pevsner, N, 1997 London: Vol 1, The City of London, Buildings of England, London

Bramwell, D, 1975 Bird remains from medieval London, London Naturalist 54, 15–20

Braun and Hogenberg 1572 'A map of London, Westminster and Southwark', reproduced in Margary 1981

Brenan, J, 1998 Furnishings, in Egan 1998, 64–87

Bridgland, D R, 1994 Quaternary of the Thames, Geol Cons Review Ser 7, London

Brigham, T, and Watson, B, in prep Excavations at Regis House, City of London, MoLAS epublication Ser

British Geological Survey, 1982, Sheet TQ38SW solid and drift geology, 1:10,000, Nottingham

Bull, G, and Payne, S, 1982 Tooth eruption and epiphyseal fusion in pig and wild boar, in Ageing and sexing animal bones from archaeological sites (eds B Wilson, C Grigson and S Payne), BAR Brit Ser 109, 51–71, Oxford

Burch, M, and Treveil, P, with Keene, D, in prep The development of medieval and later Poultry and Cheapside: excavations at 1 Poultry and vicinity, City of London, MoLAS Monogr Ser

Butler, J, 2001 The city defences at Aldersgate, Trans London Middlesex Archaeol Soc 52, 41–112

Carruthers, W, 2001 The charred plant remains, in Butler 2001, 99–106

Clark, J (ed), 1995 The medieval horse and its equipment, c 1150–c 1450, HMSO Medieval Finds Excav London 5, London

Clay, P, 1981 The small finds – non-structural, in Mellor, J E, and Pearce, T, The Austin Friars, Leicester, CBA Res Rep 35, 130–45, London

Corcoran, J, 2002 Assessment of the auger holes through the western stream at Juxon House, unpub MoL rep

Corder, P, 1955 The reorganisation of the defences of Romano-British towns in the fourth century, Archaeol J, 112, 20–42

Corporation of London, 1994 City of London Unitary Development Plan, London

Cowgill, J, de Neergaard, M, and Griffiths, N, 1987 Medieval finds from excavations in London: 1 Knives and scabbards, London

Crummy, N, 1983 The Roman small finds from excavations in Colchester 1971–9, Colchester Archaeol Rep 2, Colchester

Dam, J D van, 1991 (1988) Nederlandse Tegels, 2 edn, Amsterdam

Davies, B J, Richardson, B, and Tomber, R S, 1994 The archaeology of Roman London: Vol 5, A dated corpus of early Roman pottery from the City of London, CBA Res Rep 98, London

Davis, A, 1997 The plant remains, in Thomas et al 1997, 18

Davis, A, 2001 Assessment of the plant macrofossils from 1 London Wall (LDN01), unpub MoL rep

Davis, A, 2003 Roman and medieval plant remains from King Edward's Buildings (KEW98), unpub MoL rep

Davis, A, Rielly, K, and Rowsome, P, in prep The faunal and botanical remains from a 1st-century AD well at Fish Street Hill, Monument, City of London (MFI87)

Dawson, G J, 1976 Kennington Palace, BAR Brit Ser 26, Oxford

Department of the Environment, 1990 Planning policy guidance note 16: archaeology and planning (PPG16), London

Driesch, A von den, 1976 A guide to the measurement of animal bones from archaeological sites, Peabody Mus Bull 1, Cambridge, Mass

Driesch, A von den, and Boessneck, J A, 1974 Kritische Anmerkungen zur Widerristhöhenberechnung aus Längenmassen vor- und frühgeschichtlicher Tierknochen, Säugetierkundliche Mitteilungen 22, 325–48

Driver, J C, 1982 Medullary bone as an indicator of sex in bird remains from archaeological sites, in Ageing and sexing animal bones from archaeological sites (eds B Wilson, C Grigson and S Payne), BAR Brit Ser 109, 251–4, Oxford

Drummond-Murray, J, and Liddle, J, 2003 Medieval industry in the Walbrook valley, London Archaeol 10(4), 87–94

Dunning, G C, 1977 Mortars, in Clarke, H, and Carter, A, Excavations in King's Lynn 1963–1970, 320–47, London

Dunwoodie, L, Harward, C, and Pitt, K, in prep Excavations at Plantation Place, City of London, MoLAS Monogr Ser

Dyson, T, 1993 London's city wall: an assessment of documentary sources, unpub MoL rep

Eames, E S, 1980 Catalogue of medieval lead-glazed earthenware tiles in the Department of Medieval and Later Antiquities, British Museum, London

Eddy, M R, 2001 in Grew and de Neergaard 2001, 88–9

Egan, G, 1985 7–12 Aldersgate Street, unpub MoL rep

Egan, G, 1995 Spur straps, in Clark 1995, 150–6

Egan, G, 1998 *The medieval household: daily living c 1150–c 1450*, HMSO Medieval Finds Excav London 6, London

Egan, G, 2002 Copper-alloy founding, in Howe 2002, 48–61

Egan, G, and Pritchard, F, 1991 *Dress accessories c 1150–c 1450*, HMSO Medieval Finds Excav London 3, London

Egan, G, Maloney, J, and Maloney, C, 1981 Excavations at Crosswall, London EC3, 1979–80, unpub MoL rep

Ellenberg, H, 1988 (1963) *Vegetation ecology of central Europe*, 4 edn, Cambridge

English Heritage, 1991 *Management of archaeological projects (MAP2)*, London

Faithorne and Newcourt, 1658 'An Exact Delineation of the Cities of London and Westminster and the suburbs thereof together with the Borough of Southwark', reproduced in Margary 1981

Fitter, R S R, 1990 (1945) *London's natural history*, revised, London

Foulsham, L, 2001 *An analysis of dog breeds in the medieval and post-medieval periods*, unpub BSc dissertation, Univ London

Fowler, E, 1960 The origins and development of the penannular brooch in Europe, *Proc Prehist Soc* 26, 149–77

Frere, S S (ed), 1983 *Verulamium excavations: Vol 2*, Rep Res Comm Soc Antiq London 41, London

Friendship-Taylor, D E, 1984 The leather, in *Medieval and post-medieval finds from Exeter, 1971–80* (ed J P Allan), Exeter Archaeol Rep 3, 323–33, Exeter

Gibbard, P L, 1994 *Pleistocene history of the lower Thames valley*, Cambridge

Gibson, S, 1995 Watching brief and evaluation at 71–76 Little Britain, 10 King Edward Street, unpub MoL rep

Goodall, I H, Rigold, S E, and Christie, P M, 1980 Appendix 6: metalwork and bone objects, in Christie, P M, and Coad, J G, Excavations at Denny Abbey, *Archaeol J* 137, 138–279

Goody, P C, 1983 *Horse anatomy: a pictorial approach to equine structure*, London

Goubitz, O, Driel-Murray, C van, and Groenman-van Waateringe, W, 2001 *Stepping through time: archaeological footwear from prehistoric times until 1800*, Zwolle

Grant, A, 1982 The use of toothwear as a guide to the age of domestic ungulates, in *Ageing and sexing animal bones from archaeological sites* (eds B Wilson, C Grigson and S Payne), BAR Brit Ser 109, 91–108, Oxford

Grant, A, 1988 Animal resources, in *The countryside of medieval England* (eds G Astill and A Grant), 149–87, Oxford

Grew, F, and Neergaard, M de, 2001, *Shoes and pattens*, HMSO Medieval Finds Excav London 7, London

Grimes, W F, 1968 *The excavation of Roman and medieval London*, London

Groves, J, 1993 Analysis of the pottery assemblages, in Milne, G, and Wardle, A, Early Roman development at Leadenhall Court, London, and related research, *Trans London Middlesex Archaeol Soc* 44, 122–7

Hall, J, 1996 The cemeteries of Roman London: a review, in *Interpreting Roman London: papers in memory of Hugh Chapman* (eds J Bird, M Hassall and H Sheldon), Oxbow Monogr Ser 58, 57–84, Oxford

Hall, J, and Watson, B, 2000 A figurine of Minerva from London, *Minerva* 11 (2), 4–5

Halstead, P, 1985 A study of mandibular teeth from Romano-British contexts at Maxey, in Pryor, F, and French, C, *The Fenland Project No. 1: archaeology and environment in the lower Welland valley*, E Anglian Archaeol Rep 27 (2 vols), 219–24, Cambridge

Hammond, P W, 1995 (1993) *Food and feast in medieval England*, 2 edn with corrections, Stroud

Hartley, K F, 1984 The mortarium stamps, in *Verulamium excavations: Vol 3* (ed S S Frere), Oxford Univ Comm Archaeol Monogr 1, 280–91, Oxford

Harvey, J, 1981 *Medieval gardens*, London

Henig, M, 1984 *Religion in Roman Britain*, London

Herbert, P, 1979 Excavations at Christchurch Greyfriars, 1976, *London Archaeol* 3, 327–32

Hill, C, 1977 Excavation in the City of London: first interim report 1974–5, *Antiq J* 57, 31–66

Hill, J, and Rowsome, P, in prep *Roman London and the Walbrook stream crossing: excavations at 1 Poultry and vicinity 1985–96*, MoLAS Monogr Ser

Hill, J, and Woodger, A, 1999 *Excavations at 72–75 Cheapside/83–93 Queen Street, City of London*, MoLAS Archaeol Stud Ser 2, London

Hill, M, 1958 *Roman Colchester*, Rep Res Comm Soc Antiq London 20, Oxford

Hillam, J, and Morgan, R, 1986 Tree-ring analysis of the Roman timbers, in Miller, L, Schofield, J, and Rhodes, M, *The Roman quay at St Magnus House, London: excavations at New Fresh Wharf, Lower Thames Street, London, 1974–8* (ed T Dyson), London Middlesex Archaeol Soc Spec Pap 8, 75–86, London

Hist MSS Comm St Paul's *Historical manuscripts commission report 9*, 1883–4, London

Hobley, B, 1981 The archaeology of London Wall, *London J* 7(1), 9

Honeybourne, M A, 1932 The precinct of the Greyfriars, *London Topogr Rec* 16, 9–51

Horne, J, 1989 *English tin-glazed tiles*, London

House of Commons paper 392, Committee on prisons within the City of London and the borough of Southwark, 1813–1822, *Prisons of the metropolis: reports and returns* 77

Howe, E, 2002 *Roman defences and medieval industry: excavations at Baltic House, City of London*, MoLAS Monogr Ser 7, London

Howe, E, and Lakin, D, 2004 *Roman and medieval Cripplegate, City of London: archaeological excavations 1992–8*, MoLAS Monogr Ser 21, London

Jamieson, D, 2002 An assessment of the feasibility of the modelling of sub surface deposits beneath the City of London, through the creation of deposit surfaces using deposit survival form data, unpub MSc dissertation, Univ College London

Jeffery, P, 1996 *The City churches of Sir Christopher Wren*, London

Johnson, T, 1974 Excavations at Christ Church, Newgate Street, 1973, *Trans London Middlesex Archaeol Soc* 25, 220–34

Jones, G, Straker, V, and Davis, A, 1991 Early medieval plant use and ecology, in *Aspects of Saxon and Norman London 2: finds and environmental evidence* (ed A G Vince), London Middlesex Archaeol Soc Spec Pap 12, 347–79, London

Keily, J, 2004 Non-ceramic finds, in Barber, B, Chew, S, Dyson, T, and White, W, *The Cistercian abbey of St Mary Stratford Langthorne, Essex*, MoLAS Monogr Ser 18, 149–56, London

Keily, J, and Shepherd, J, 2004 Glass, in Barber, B, Chew, S, Dyson, T, and White, W, *The Cistercian abbey of St Mary Stratford Langthorne, Essex*, MoLAS Monogr Ser 18, 148–9, London

Kent, J, 1978 The London area in the Late Iron Age: an interpretation of the earliest coins, in *Collectanea Londiniensia: studies in London archaeology and history presented to Ralph Merrifield* (eds J Bird, H Chapman and J Clark), London Middlesex Archaeol Soc Spec Pap 2, 53–8, London

Keys, L, 1998a Wooden spatulate implements, in Egan 1998, 154

Keys, L, 1998b Wooden vessels, in Egan 1998, 196–217

Kingsford, C L, 1915 *The Grey Friars of London*, Aberdeen

Lawson, G, 1985 Musical instrument pegs, in Hare, J N, *Battle Abbey: the eastern range and the excavations of 1978–80*, HBMCE Archaeol Rep 2, 151–4, London

Leake, J, 1667 'A map of the City of London showing the extent of the damage caused by the Great Fire of 1665', reproduced in Margary 1981

Leland, J, 1715 *Collectanea* (ed T Hearne), London

Lewis, J, 1973 Some types of metal chafing-dish *Antiq J* 53, 59–70

Lobel, M D (ed), 1989 *The British atlas of historic towns: Vol 3, The City of London, from prehistoric times to c 1520*, Oxford

Luttwack, E N, 1976 *The grand strategy of the Roman Empire from the first century AD to the third*, London

Lyon, J, 2002 Merrill Lynch Financial Centre, 2 King Edward Street, London EC1: an archaeological post-excavation assessment and updated project design, unpub MoL rep

McCann, B (ed), 1993 Fleet Valley Project: interim report, unpub MoL rep

MacGregor, A, 1985 *Bone, antler, horn and ivory: the technology of skeletal materials*, 178–9, London

MacGregor, A, Mainman, A J, and Rogers, N S H, 1999 *Craft, industry and everyday life: bone, antler, ivory and horn from Anglo-Scandinavian and medieval York*, The Archaeology of York 17/12, York

Macphail, R I, and Cruise, G M, 1993, King Edward Buildings: assessment of soils and pollen (KEB92), unpub MoL rep

Maloney, J, 1980 The discovery of Bastion 4A in the city of London and its implications, *Trans London Middlesex Archaeol Soc* 31, 68–76

Maloney, J, 1983 Recent work on London's defences, in *Roman urban defences in the west* (eds J Maloney and B Hobley), CBA Res Rep 51, 96–117, London

Maloney, J, and Harding, C, 1979 Duke's Place and Houndsditch: the medieval defences, *London Archaeol* 3, 347–54

Margary, H, 1971 'A Plan of the Cities of London Westminster and Southwark' by John Rocque, 1746, Margary in assoc Guildhall Library, Kent

Margary, H, 1981 *A collection of early maps of London 1553–1667*, Margary in assoc Guildhall Library, Kent

Margeson, S, 1993 *Norwich households: medieval and post-medieval finds from Norwich survey excavations 1971–78*, East Anglian Archaeol Rep 58, Norwich

Marsden, P, 1965 Archaeological finds in the City of London, 1961, *Trans London Middlesex Archaeol Soc* 21, 135–9

Marsden, P, 1968 Archaeological finds in the City of London, 1965–6, *Trans London Middlesex Archaeol Soc* 22(1), 1–17

Marsden, P, 1970 Archaeological finds in the City of London, 1966–9, *Trans London Middlesex Archaeol Soc* 22(3), 1–9

Marsden, P, 1980 *Roman London*, London

Marsh, G, 1978 Early 2nd-century fine wares in the London area, in *Early fine wares in Roman Britain* (eds P Arthur and G Marsh), BAR Brit Ser 57, 119–223, Oxford

Marsh, G, 1981 London's samian supply and its relationship to the development of the Gallic samian industry, in *Roman pottery research and north-western Europe: papers presented to Graham Webster* (eds A C Anderson and A S Anderson), BAR Int Ser 13, 173–238, Oxford

Marsh, G, and Tyers, P A, 1978 The Roman pottery from Southwark, in *Southwark excavations 1972–74* (eds J Bird, A H Graham, H L Sheldon and P Townend), London Middlesex Archaeol Soc/Surrey Archaeol Soc Joint Publ 1, London

Merrifield, R, 1965 *The Roman city of London*, London

Millett, M, 1990 *The Romanization of Britain: an essay in archaeological interpretation*, Cambridge

Milne, G, 1986 *The Great Fire of London*, London

Morris, C A, 1993 Wooden vessels, in Margeson 1993, 95–6

Morris, C A, 2000 *Craft, industry and everyday life: wood and woodworking in Anglo-Scandinavian and medieval York*, The Archaeology of York 17/13, York

Morris, C, A, and Margeson, S, 1993 Spoons, in Margeson 1993, 136

Morris, J, 1982 *Londinium: London in the Roman Empire*, London

Mulkeen, S, and O'Connor, T P, 1997 Raptors in towns: towards an ecological model, *Int J Osteoarchaeol* 7, 440–9

Museum of London Archaeology Service, 2000 *The archaeology of Greater London: an assessment of archaeological evidence for human presence in the area covered by Greater London*, Surveys and Handbooks, London

Neergaard, M de, 1987 The decoration of medieval scabbards, in Cowgill et al 1987, 40–4

Nixon, T, McAdam, E, Tomber, R, and Swain, H, with Rowsome, P, 2002 *A research framework for London archaeology 2002*, London

Norman, P, 1904 Roman and later remains found during the excavations on the site of Newgate Prison, 1903–4, *Archaeologia* 59, 125–42

Norman, P, 1905 *London vanished and vanishing*, London

Norman, P, and Reader, F, 1912 Further discoveries relating to Roman London, 1906–13, *Archaeologia* 63, 277–344

Ogilby, J, and Morgan, W, 1676 'Large and accurate map of the City of London', reproduced in Margary, H, 1976 'Large and accurate map of the City of London' by John Ogilby and William Morgan, 1676, Margary in assoc Guildhall Library, Kent

Orton, C, 1975 Quantitative pottery studies: some progress, problems and prospects, *Sci Archaeol* 16, 30–5

Ottaway, P, and Rogers, N, 2002 *Craft, industry and everyday life: finds from medieval York*, The Archaeology of York 17/15, York

Parnell, G, 1993 *The Tower of London*, London

Payne, S, 1973 Kill-off patterns in sheep and goats: the mandibles from Asvan Kale, *Anatolian Stud* 23, 281–303

Payne, S, 1985 Morphological distinctions between the mandibular teeth of young sheep, *Ovis*, and goats, *Capra*, *J Archaeol Sci* 12, 139–47

Pearce, J, and Vince, A, 1988 *A dated type-series of London medieval pottery: Part 4, Surrey whitewares*, London Middlesex Archaeol Soc Spec Pap 10, London

Pearce, J E, Vince, A G, and Jenner, M A, 1985 *A dated type series of London medieval pottery: Part 2, London-type ware*, London Middlesex Archaeol Soc Spec Pap 6, London

Pearce, J E, Vince, A G, White, R, and Cunningham, C M, 1982 A dated type-series of London medieval pottery: Part 1, Mill Green ware, *Trans London Middlesex Archaeol Soc* 33, 266–98

Pennant, T, 1805 *Some account of London*, 4 edn, London

Perring, D, 1991 *Roman London*, London

Perring, D, and Roskams, S P, with Allen, P, 1991 *The archaeology of Roman London: Vol 2, Early development of Roman London west of the Walbrook*, CBA Res Rep 70, London

Phil, 1984 Philadelphia Museum of Art, *Dutch tiles in the Philadelphia Museum of Art*, Philadelphia

Pitt, K, 2006 *Roman and medieval development south of Newgate: excavations at 3–9 Newgate Street and 16–17 Old Bailey, City of London*, MoLAS Archaeol Stud Ser 14, London

Pluis, J, 1997 *The Dutch tile: designs and names*, Leiden

Price, J, and Cottam, S, 1998 *Romano-British glass vessels: a handbook*, CBA Practical Handbook in Archaeology 14, York

Pritchard, F, 1991 Small finds, in *Aspects of Saxo-Norman London: Vol 2, Finds and environmental evidence* (ed A G Vince), London Middlesex Archaeol Soc Spec Pap 12, 120–278, London

Prummel, W, and Frisch, H J, 1986 A guide for the distinction of species, sex and body side in bones of sheep and goat, *J Archaeol Sci* 13, 567–77

Pye, B, 1985 A watching brief opposite 57 London Wall at junction with Blomfield Street (LON82), unpub MoL rep

Ray, A, 1994 *Liverpool printed tiles*, London

RCHME, 1928 Roy Comm Hist Monuments (Engl), *An inventory of the historical monuments in London: Vol 3, Roman London*, London

Rielly, K, 2005 Animal remains, in Yule, B, *A prestigious Roman building complex on the Southwark waterfront: excavations at Winchester Palace, London, 1983–90*, MoLAS Monogr Ser 23, 158–66, London

Rielly, K, in prep The animal bones, in Bowsher et al in prep

Rixson, D, 2000 *The history of meat trading*, Nottingham

Robins, F W, 1939 *The story of the lamp (and the candle)* London

Rocque, J, 1746 'A Plan of the Cities of London Westminster and Southwark with contiguous buildings from an actual survey' by John Rocque, reproduced in Margary 1971

Rouvier-Jeanlin, M, 1972 *Les figurines gallo-romaines en terre cuite au Musée des Antiquités Nationales*, Gallia Suppl 24, Paris

Rowsome, P, 1984 Excavations at 1–6 Old Bailey (LUD82), unpub MoL rep

Ruempol, A P E, and Dongen, A G A van, 1991 *Pre-industriële Gebruiksvoorwerpen/Pre-industrial utensils, 1150–1800*, Museum Boymans-van Beuningen, Rotterdam

Sabben, C van, and Hollem, J, 1987, *Antieke tegels*, Haarlem

Salvin, F H, and Brodrick, W, 1997 (1855) *Falconry in the British Isles*, repr facsimile, Midhurst

Salway, 1981 *Roman Britain*, Oxford

Sankey, D, and Stephenson, A, 1991 Recent work on London's defences, in *Roman frontier studies 1989: proceedings of the 15th international congress of Roman frontier studies* (eds V A Maxfield and M J Dobson), Exeter, 117–24

Schmid, E, 1972 *Atlas of animal bones*, London

Schofield, J, 1993 (1984) *The building of London from the Conquest to the Great Fire*, rev edn, London

Schofield, J, with Maloney, C (eds), 1998 *Archaeology in the City of London, 1907–91: a guide to records of excavations by the Museum of London and its predecessors*, MoL Archaeol Gazetteer Ser 1, London

Sharpe, R (ed), 1899–1912 *Calendar of Letter-Books A–L*, London

Shepherd, J D, 1988 The Roman occupation in the area of Paternoster Square, City of London, *Trans London Middlesex Archaeol Soc* 39, 1–30

Shepherd, J D, 1998 *Post-war archaeology in the City of London, 1946–72: a guide to records of excavations by Professor W F Grimes held by the Museum of London*, MoL Archaeol Gazetteer Ser 3, London

Shepherd, J D, and Heyworth, M, 1991 Le travail du verre dans Londres romain (Londinium): un état de la question, in *Ateliers de verriers de l'antiquité à la période pré-industrielle. Actes des 4èmes Rencontres, Rouen 24–25 Novembre 1989* (eds D Foy and G Sennequier), 13–22, Rouen

Stenton, F M, 1971 *Anglo-Saxon England*, 3 edn, Oxford

Stow, J, 1598 *A survey of London* (ed H Morley, 1902), London

Stroud, D, 1984 The Giltspur Street Compter, *Architectural Hist* 27, 127–31

Sturdy, D, 1975 The Civil War defences of London, *London Archaeol* 2, 334–8

Symonds, R P, and Tomber, R S, 1991 Late Roman London: an assessment of the ceramic evidence from the City of London, *Trans London Middlesex Archaeol Soc* 42, 59–99

Telfer, A, 2003 Medieval drainage near Smithfield Market: excavations near Hosier Lane, EC1, *London Archaeol* 10, 115–20

Thomas, C, Sloane, B, and Phillpotts, C, 1997 *Excavations at the priory and hospital of St Mary Spital, London*, MoLAS Monogr Ser 1, London

Tyler, K, 1991 Excavations at the GPO75 site, post-Roman levels, unpub MoL rep

Tyler, K, 2000 The 'western stream' reconsidered: excavations at the medieval Great Wardrobe, Wardrobe Place, City of London, *Trans London Middlesex Archaeol Soc* 51, 21–44

Tyson, R, 2000 *Medieval glass vessels found in England c AD 1200–1500*, CBA Res Rep 121, York

VCH, 1909 *The Victoria History of London: Vol 1* (ed W Page), London

Vince, A, 1990 *Saxon London: an archaeological investigation*, London

Vince, A, and Ford, B, 1982 Ludgate Hill pottery report, unpub MoL rep

Wacher, J, 1995 (1974) *The towns of Roman Britain*, rev 2 edn, London

Wardle, A, 2001 Assessment of the accessioned finds from King Edward Buildings (KEW98), unpub MoL rep

Wardle, A, 2002 10 Gresham Street assessment, unpub MoL rep

Wardle, A, 2003 Catalogue of the Roman finds from King

Edward Buildings (KEW98), unpub MoL rep

Ward-Perkins, J B, 1940 *London Museum medieval catalogue*, London

Waterland Mander, C H, 1931 *A descriptive and historical account of the Guild of Cordwainers of the City of London*, London

Watson, B, 1993 King Edward Buildings, GPO West Yard, Newgate Street, London EC1: post-excavation assessment report, unpub MoL rep

Watson, B, 1998 'Dark earth' and urban decline in late Roman London, in *Roman London: recent archaeological work* (ed B Watson), J Roman Archaeol Suppl Ser 24, 100–6, Portsmouth, RI

Watson, B, 2000a An interim report on the 1998–1999 archaeological investigations at the new Merrill Lynch Regional Headquarters, King Edward Street and Newgate Street, London EC1, unpub MoL rep

Watson, B, 2000b Christ Church Greyfriars, Giltspur Street, King Edward Street, Newgate Street and Warwick Lane, London EC1: an assessment of the archaeological impact of new cable trenches, unpub MoL rep

Watson, B, and Jones, S, 1999 New Merrill Lynch Regional Headquarters, London EC1: a standing building survey, unpub MoL rep

Watson, S, with Heard, K, in prep *Development on Roman London's western hill: excavations at Paternoster Square, City of London*, MoLAS Monogr Ser

West, B, 1982 Spur development: recognising caponised fowl in archaeological material, in *Ageing and sexing animal bones from archaeological sites* (eds B Wilson, C Grigson and S Payne), BAR Brit Ser 109, 225–61, Oxford

Westman, A, 1987 The church of St Alphege, *Archaeol Today* 8(11), 7–22

Whitelock, D (ed), 1955 *English historical documents c 500–1042: Vol 1*, London

Wilkinson, T, 1983 Report on the analysis of environmental samples taken from the medieval ditch at Ludgate Hill, City of London, unpub MoL rep

Williams, T, 1993 *The archaeology of Roman London: Vol 3, Public buildings in the south-west quarter of Roman London*, CBA Res Rep 88, London

Wilmott, T, 1987 A note on the heraldic decoration of the scabbards, in Cowgill et al 1987, 45–50

Yule, B, 1990 The 'dark earth' and late Roman London, *Antiq J* 64, 620–8

INDEX

Compiled by Susanne Atkin

Page numbers in **bold** indicate illustrations.
All street names and locations are in London unless specified otherwise.
County names within parentheses refer to historic counties.

B   Building
OA Open Area
R   Road
S   Structure

'Agas' map (1562) 71, 72, **72**, 120, 121
Albinus, Clodius, governor 40, 46
Alder Castle (AES96) 7
Aldermanbury, postern gate 39
Aldersgate, gatehouse 38–9
1–6 Aldersgate Street (AES96) 7
  city wall 45
  late Saxon ditch 54, **60**
  medieval ditch **60**, 61, 74, 113, 114
  medieval pottery and tile 47
  post-medieval ditch recuts 120
  pre-wall ditch 31, **38**, 40
7–12 Aldersgate Street (ALG84) 7, 54, **60**
Aldersgate Ward 120
Aldgate 120
  gatehouse 38, 59
Alfred, King 54, 56
All Hallows (Church), bastions 48, 50
12–16 America Square (ASQ87) 7, **38**, 39
animal bone 29, 94, 109–12, 114, 115, 175–6
animal collar(?), leather 102
animal feed 113, 177
antler, offcuts 85; see also rake/tool
Audley, Sir James 113
Augustinians 57
Austin Friars, Leicester (Leics) 83, 93, 95, 98, 102

bags, leather 103, 106, **107–8**, 175
bakehouse 65, 71
Baltic Exchange, pre-wall ditch 31
Baltic House 85
banks, Roman 29, 35, 37, 38, 39, 40, **40–1**, 41, 42
  S4 (MLFC site) **40–1**, 45, **48–9**
bar mount manufacture 85
Barber-Surgeons' Hall garden (WFG3 and WFG4) 7, 118; see also Bastion 14; Windsor Court
Barbican Lakeside (WFG1A) see Bastion 11A
Bastion 1: **46**, 47, 52
Bastion 4A (8–10 Crosswall) **46**, 47, 48, 52
Bastion 6 (Duke's Place) 7, **46**, 47, 48, 52
Bastion 7 (Duke's Place) 7, **46**, 47
Bastions 8–9: **46**, 47
Bastion 11: **46**, 47, 48, 52, 60
Bastion 11A (Barbican Lakeside) 7, **46**, 47, 59
Bastion 12 and 13: 59
Bastion 14 (Barber-Surgeons' Hall garden) 7, **46**, 47, 59
Bastion 15 (Noble Street), medieval 7, **46**, 47, 59
Bastion 16: 47, 59
Bastion 17 (S2) 4, 10, 41, **46**, 47, **48–52**, **48–9**, **50**, 52, 60, 65, 72, 118, **120**, 148
Bastion 18 (S2) 4, 10, 12, **46**, 47, **48–52**, **48–9**, **50**, **51**, 52, 60, 65, 72, 118, 144, 148, 149
Bastion 19 (S2), medieval (Giltspur Street, GM146) 4–5, **5**, 7, 42–3, **46**, 47, 48–52, 59, **59–62**, 60, 65, 72, 75, 118, 144, 148, 149
  chamber preserved 1, **6**, 42–3, 142, 143, **146**
  stream channel 10, 42

Bastion 20: 47
Bastion 21: 47, 59–60, 61
bastions 7
  Roman 37, 46–52, **46**, 148
  hermits' cells in 53, 60
  medieval(?) 46, 47, 50, 51, 52, 148
  medieval repairs and rebuilding 53, 59–60, 72
  post-medieval 116, 118, 125
Baynard's Castle 57, 93, 94, 110
bead-making 168
  bone waste 85, 87, **87**, 173
beads
  faience, Roman 25, **25**
  glass, Roman 25, **25**, 35, 168, 169
  glass, medieval 85
bell and vessel casting waste, medieval 85
berm (S5), Roman 40, **40–1**, 45, **48–9**
Bermondsey Abbey, Southwark (Surrey) 82, 115
Billingsgate 94, 102
bird bone 29, 110–11, **111**, 112, 176
Bishopsgate 120
  gatehouse 38
Blackfriars Friary 57
Blomfield House, London Wall/New Broad Street (BLM87) 7, **38**, 41
bone artefacts see counter; knife handle; pegs; pens; stylus; toggle
bone working 87
  bead-working waste 85, 87, **87**, 173
bookbindings 106
Boudican revolt 16–17, 147
boundaries
  pre-Boudican settlement 15–16
  early Roman settlement boundary pre-wall ditches 31, 33, 40, 147
  Roman boundary ditch (S1) **32–3**, 33, **35**
  Roman city 13, 37–8, 148
  Late Saxon 53
  post-medieval 116
  St Paul's precinct 57
bowls/platters, wood, medieval 82, 83, 88–90, **88**, **89**, **90**, 114–15, 170–2
Braun and Hogenberg map (1572) 72, **74**, 120
bread peel 91
Bread Street Compter 133
brewhouse 65, 71
brewing 177
brick 73, 116, 125, 126, **129**, 150, 151
brickearth deposits (OA3) 9–10, **11**
brickfield 16
Bridge House Rents (B17) 65, **66–7**, 71, **71**, 72
brooches, copper-alloy, Roman 20, **21**, 35, 36, 168
buckets(?) see stave fragments
buckles, medieval 85, 93
Building 1 (B1) Roman 17–18, **18**, 19, **20**, 21, 29
Building 2 (B2) Roman 19–20, 21, **21**, 29, 168, 169
Building 3 (B3) Roman 21, 23, **23**, 29
Building 4 (B4) Roman 23, 29, 169
Building 5 (B5) Roman 23–4, **24**, 29
Building 6 (B6) **18–19**, 23, 29
  well adjacent to 20–1
Building 7 (B7) Roman 18–19, **18**, 29, 45
Building 8 (B8) Roman 24–5, **24**
  Roman finds 25, **25**, 29, 168
  temple or shrine? 29
Building 9 (B9) 31, **32–3**, 33, 35

Building 10 (B10) 31, **32–3**, 33, 35
  plant remains 31, 177
Building 11 (B11) 31, **32–3**, 33, **34**, 35
Building 12 see Greyfriars Friary, church (B12)
Building 13 (B13) 121, **122**
Building 14 (B14), cesspit **66–7**, 71, 72
Building 15 (B15), cesspits of Goldsmiths Rents **66–7**, 71, 72
Building 16 (B16) **66–7**, 71
Building 17 (B17) Bridge House Rents 65, **66–7**, 71, **71**, 72
Building 18 (B18) Gilford Street 121, **122**, **123**
Building 19 (B19) Green Dragon Yard cellars 121, **122**
Building 20 (B20), Wren's church (Christ Church) 133
Building 21 (B21) Christ's Hospital 133
Building 22 (B22) Newgate Street 126, **127**
  human bone in cellar 72, **74**, 126
  stove tile 126, **128**
Buildings 23–25 (B23–B25) Newgate Street 126, **127**
Building 26 (B26) Giltspur Street 126, **127**, 166, 172
Building 27 (B27), medieval 87, **88**, 114, 173, post-Great Fire 126, **127**, **128**
Building 28 (B28) Green Dragon Yard **127**, **130**
  water cistern (tank) 126, **127**, **130**, 150–63
  see also tin-glazed wall tiles
Building 29 (B29) Newgate Street 126, **127**
Building 30 (B30) Compter prison 138–42, 172
  louvers 140, 142, **143**, 151
Building 31 (B31), Saxo-Norman sunken-floored 55–6
building material
  OA12, Roman 36, **37**
  OA17 108–9, **108**, **109**
  Roman 30
  S6 109, **109**
Burghal Hidage 54
burial grounds, post-medieval 129, 131
burials, pre-Boudican 15, 16
butchers' shops (and markets and waste) 110, 114, 115
butter or cheese making 85, 91, 172

Calthorpe, John 120
candlestick, mould for casting 85
Canterbury (Kent), town wall 39
cap or ferrule, copper-alloy, medieval 86, **87**, 173
casket(?) mount, copper-alloy/silver 85, 115, 173
cats and cat skinning 110, 115
'cells' see Greyfriars Friary
cemetery, early Roman 16
Central Criminal Court, Old Bailey/Warwick Square (GM131) **2**, 7, **38**, 40
cesspits
  B14 **66–7**, 71, 72
  B15, of Goldsmiths Rents **66–7**, 71, 72
  B26 126, **127**
chafing dish handle, copper-alloy, medieval 85, 86, **86**, 170
chalk stand/support 85
Chamberlain Gate 59
Chatsworth House, Houndsditch/St Mary Axe (HOU78) 7
Chaucer, Geoffrey 59
Cheapside 14, 53, 54
72–75 Cheapside (CID90), Roman ditch 14–15
chimney brick, moulded 126, **129**
Christ Church Greyfriars, Newgate Street (CHR76, GCC98, GF73) (formerly friary church) 1, **2**, 7, 117, 118, **119**, 121, 124, 144, 145, 149
  rebuilt by Wren 63, 72, 126, 129, 131–3, **131**, **132**, **133**
  B20 (Wren's) **3**, 133

Christ's Hospital (orphanage and school) 4, 117, 118, 120, **120**, 121, 124, **124**, **125**, 142, 144–5, 149
  B21 133
  bastion 50
  rebuilt 126, 131–3, **131**, **144**
  records 5
  Shaw's Great Hall 41, 129, 131, 133, **134**, 139, **141**, 144, 149
Christ's Hospital, Horsham (Sussex) 72
churches 116, 121, 124, 125, 131, 132
  B12 see Greyfriars Friary
  B20 see Christ Church Greyfriars
  Saxon 54
  see also Greyfriars Friary
city defences
  dating evidence 40–1
  documentary sources 5
  Roman construction 1, **2**, 4, 37–46, **40–1**, 148
  Roman additions to 46–52, 59
  Saxon (period 4) 53, 54, 56–7, **56**, **58**, 148
  medieval (period 5) 4, 57, **58**, 59–63, 148
  later medieval 72–115
  pre-Great Fire (period 6), demise 117–21
  see also banks; bastions; berm; city ditches; city gates; city wall; gatehouses; posterns; river wall
city ditches 7
  Roman (V-shaped) 37, 38, **38**, 39–40, 41, 42, 50
  Roman V-shaped (S3, period 3) 10, **40–1**, 41, 42, 45, 46, 47, 48, **49**, 50, **50**, 52, 54
  late Roman U-shaped (S3, period 3) 45, 46, **46**, 47, 48, **48–9**, 52, 54, 148
  Saxo-Norman ditches 53, 54, 56–7, **60**
  S3 (period 4) 55–7, **56**
  medieval 11, 55, 61, 65, 73–4, 75, 148–9
  S3 (period 5) 48, **58**, 62–3, **63**, 65
  backfilling phase 1 (primary fill) 62–3
  backfilling phase 2 (OA12) **66–7**, 75–115
  backfilling phase 3 (OA17) **119**, 120–1, 124
  post-Great Fire (period 7) 125, 126, 139, **139**
  post-medieval 116, 117, 118, 120–1, 124, 149
  brickearth deposits 10
  finds from backfilling 82–7, 114–15, **114**
  plant remains 55, 112–13, 176–80
  pottery 55, 63, 75–82, 114, 166
  revetted channel 121, 124, 148
  see also Open Area 17
city gates
  medieval rebuilding 59
  pre-Great Fire (period 6) 118, 124
  post-Great Fire (period 7) 125, 144
  as prisons 59
  see also gatehouses
City Lands Deeds 5, 117, 118
City Lands Grant Books 5, 118
city wall, Roman 1, **2**, 4, 5, 29, 31, 33, 35, 36, 37–8, **40–1**, 47, 48, 50, 51, **59**, 60, 148
  brickearth deposits 10
  original height 39
  parapet walkway 39
  S2 (MLFC site) 7, **40–1**, 41–6, 47, **48–9**
  stream channel 42, culverted 12–13
  subsidence 42–3, 45, 51, 52, 148
city wall, medieval (periods 4–5) 53, 54, 57, 59, 60, 65, 73, 75
  Saxon 54
  pre-Great Fire (period 6) 117–18, 124–5
  post-Great Fire (period 7) 125, 126, 131, 143, 144, **145**, 149
Civil War 118, 120
cobbling (shoe repairing) 93–4
coins
  forger's 40–1

Index

Roman 18, 36, 40, 47
  unidentified 23
column shaft, Purbeck 'marble' 108–9
combs, wood, medieval 82, 88, **91**, 92, 170
Commonalty records 5
Compter prison, Giltspur Street 43, 121, 125, 126, 132, 133, 135–42, 144, 149
  B30 138–42
coopered vessels 85, 88, 90
15 Cooper's Row (ASQ87) 7, 53
copper-alloy working residues 85
copper working, Roman 29
cordwaining and cordwainers 93–4
Cornhill 9, 14, 29, 147
cosmetic implement, copper-alloy, medieval 85, **86**, 170
counter, bone, Roman 28, **28**, 168
Court of Aldermen 118, 121
cremations, Roman 16, 33
Cripplegate
  fort 31, 39, 45
  later Saxon buildings 54
  town ditch 120
8–10 Crosswall (XWL79) 7, 31; *see also* Bastion 4A
15–17 Crosswall (ASQ87) 7
Croydon, Hugh 72
crucibles
  Roman 29
  medieval, ceramic 85
Crutched Friars 7, 31
customs frontier 46

dagger, copper-alloy 172
dagger hilt 86, **87**
Dance the Younger, George 133, **135**, **137**, 139–40, **140**, **141**
dark earth 33, 35, 36, **37**, 45, 55, 148, 177
dendrochronology, timber drain 14
dissolution of the monasteries 4, 116, 117, 124
ditches *see* boundaries; city ditches
documentary sources 5, 148, 149
dogs (pets) 102, 110, 111, 112, **112**
Dominicans *see* Blackfriars Friary
drainage system, Roman 12, **12**, 13, 57, 148
drinking vessels
  glass 83, **84**
  wood 89
Dudley, Lord Henry 118
Duke's Place
  bastion 6 site (GM55) 7, **46**, 47, 48, 52
  bastion 7 site (GM242) 7, **46**, 47
  ditch 31, 33, 61
  post-medieval ditch recuts 120
  St James Passage subway (DUK77) 7, **38**, 40, 61, 120

Edward III 64, 74
Eocene 9

Faithorne and Newcourt map (1658) 120, 121, **121**
Falcon House (AES96) 7
Falconer, Thomas, mayor 74
falconry 110
feast of St Francis 117
ferrules, medieval 86, **87**
figurines, pipe clay, Roman 31, 169
  Minerva 25, **26**, 29, 167
finds (accessioned)
  Roman 167–9
  medieval 169–75
finger-ring, gold, medieval 82, **82**, 115, 170
fires, Boudican revolt 16; *see also* Hadrianic fire
fish bone 29, 110, 111, 112, 176
Fish Hill Street (MFI87) 29
Fitz Piers, Joce 63
FitzStephen, William 59
Fitzwalter family 98, 173
flax growing 113, 177

Fleet, River 9, 11, **11**, 12, 13, 45, 52, 147
Fleet valley 10, 11, 45, 47, 148
flooding 10, 29, 55, 113, 177
floor tiles, medieval 126
  Chertsey-Westminster 108
  Eltham Palace/Lesnes Abbey 108, **108**
  French 108, **108**, 151
  Low Countries 108, 109
  OA17/S6 108, **108**, 109, **109**, 151
  Penn 108, **108**, 109, 151
  tin-glazed 126, 140, **142**
  'Westminster' 108, **108**, 109, **109**, 151
footwear (leather), ankle boots and shoes 55, 92–5, 105, 175
Fore Street/St Alphege Garden (WFG17) 7
forger's coins, Roman 40–1
fort or defended enclosure 17
Franciscans 57, 94
fuller's teasel 113
furniture inlay 109

gardens and gardening 36, 45, 63, 65, 113, 116, 131, 132, 177
garments, leather 103, **104–5**, 105, 106, **107**, 175
gatehouses
  Roman 4, 38–9, 42, 45, 148
  medieval 4, 53
  post-medieval 116
  renovated 46, 52
gates *see* city gates
General Post Office (GPO) building 1, **3**, 4, 7, 10, 11, 72, 142–3, **144**, **145**, 149
  city wall 42
  dark earth 33, 36
  medieval buildings **60**, 63
  post-Hadrianic buildings 31
  pre-Boudican occupation 16
  strip buildings 17, 29
geology 9–13, **10**, 45
Gilford Street 120, 121; *see also* Building 18
Giltspur Street 1, **2**, 55, 125, 126, 135, 144, 149
  sunken-floored building (B31) 56
  see also Building 26; Building 27; Compter prison; Gilford Street
glass (vessels)
  Roman 18, 20, 21, **21**, 23, 28, **28**, 168, 169
  medieval 170
  see also beads; goblet lid; lamps; tank metal; window glass
goblet lid, glass, medieval 85, 86, **86**, 170
gold *see* finger-ring
golden eagle 110–11, **111**
Goldsmiths Rents **66–7**, 71, 72
Gracechurch Street 94
graphical conventions 7, **8**
gravel terraces 9, 45
grazing 36
Great Fire (1666) 72, 116, 121, 125, 126, 144, 149
Green Dragon Yard
  B19 cellars 121, **122**
  B28 126, **127**, **130**
Gregory III, Pope 111
30 Gresham Street (GHT00) 16
Grey Friars (Franciscans) 63–4, 65, 94, 148
Greyfriars Friary 4, 53, 57, **58**, 148–9
  bastions used by 118
  'cells' for hermits 60, 117
  church, medieval 64, 65, 126, 129, 132, 149
  B12 (MLFC site) 65, **66–7**, **70**, 71, 72, 117, 121
  B20 rebuilt by Wren *see* Christ Church Greyfriars
  finds 114–15
  floor tile 108
  footwear 94
  foundation 63–4, 65
  Great Cloister (cloisters) 65, **66–7**, 71, 72
  human bone from cemetery (in cellar B22) 72, **74**, 126

later medieval 65–72, **66–7**, **68–9**, **70**
  leather straps 102
  pottery from(?) 114, 166–7
  pre-Great Fire (period 6) 117, 120, 121, 124
  rosary beads 85, 87
  Scheduled Ancient Monument (SAM 129) 1, **2**, 4
  stream channel 13, 17
  surrender of 117
  tomb inscription letter 114, 172
Guildhall, London
  cat skinning waste 110
  later Saxon buildings 54
Guildhall Museum sites 7
Guy of Amiens 54

Hackney gravel terraces 9, 13
Hadrianic fire 29–31, 33–5, 147
  OA11 fire debris 20, 30–1, **34**
hairpins, bone, Roman 17, **20**, 36, **37**, 168
harness, leather straps **102**, 103
Hartley, E S 124, **144**
Haselwoode, Thomas 118
hawking 110
Hawksmoor, architect 129
hearths, Roman 29, 31
Henry VIII 116, 117
hermits (anchorites) 53, 60, 117
Holocene 9–13
Hone, John 121
hones, stone 83–4, 86
Honeybourne's reconstructed map 65, **70**
Hooke and Oliver, architects 126, 129
horn working (goat horn) 110, 111
horseshoes 86–7
horticulture 29, 36, 177
Hosier Lane 94
47–56 Houndsditch (HOU78), ditch 54, **60**, 61, 74
Howes, John 124
human bone
  in cellar B22 72, **74**, 126
  from ditch 111
human footprint, on wooden vessel 90, **90**, 171
huts, pre-Boudican 16

industrial activity
  Roman 29
  medieval 85, 177
inhumation burials, Roman 16
Iron Age settlements 14
Isabella de Valois 64
Iwyn, John 63, 64

John, King 59
Josselyn, Ralph 73, 74
Joyner, William, mayor 64
Juxon House, St Paul's Churchyard (SLY00) 7, 12, **12**

keys
  copper-alloy, Roman 23, 169
  iron, Roman 31, 169
kiln, Roman 19, 29
King Edward Buildings (KEW98) 1, **4**, 7, 176
King Edward Street 1
  B20 Wren's Christ Church 133
  city wall 41
  medieval buildings 63, 65
King Edward Street (GCC98) 4
King Edward Street (SAM 26T) 1, **2**, 4
knife handle, bone, Roman 28, **28**, 168
knives, medieval 84–5, **84**, 86, 172; *see also* sheaths
knots, leather 103, **103**

lacechapes, medieval 85
lamps
  ceramic, Roman 25, **25**, 168
  glass 114
  stone, medieval 82–3, **83**, 85, 86, **86**, 114, 170, **171**
land uses 7

Langley Silt Complex (brickearth) 9
Late Saxon settlement (period 4) 53, 54–7, **55**
lead, sheet, medieval 87
Leake's map (1667) 125, **126**
leather artefacts 92–108, 174–5; *see also* bags; footwear; garments; knots; saddles; sheaths; straps; upholstery
leatherworking 93–4, 177
Letter Books 5, 72, 118
lids, leather **96–7**, 98
lids (bases?), wooden discs 83, 88, 91–2
ligula, copper-alloy, Roman 31, 168
Lincoln, Earl of 113
Little Britain (LBT86) 7, 54, **60**
Lobel's reconstruction map (1520) 64, **64**
Lombard Street 53
London Clay 9, **11**
London to Silchester Road 14–15, **15**
1 London Wall 113
57 London Wall (LON82) 7
  city wall 45
  pre-wall ditch 31
85 London Wall (BLM87) 7
  city ditch **38**, 39–40
  metalling **38**, 39
  pre-wall ditch 31
  Roman timber buildings 45
loop fitting, iron double spiked 21
loop-handle *see* chafing dish handle
louvers
  in B26 and B27 126
  in B30 140, 142, **143**, 151
Ludgate 61
  gatehouse 38, 53, 59
Ludgate Hill
  ditches 54, 57, 148
  geology 9
42–46 Ludgate Hill (LUD82) 7, **60**, 94, 113
Lundenwic 53, **54**

makers' marks, on knives 84, **84**, 86, 172
Margaret, Queen 64, 94
marshes 10, 42, 52
Mary, Queen 124
Matthews, R G **133**
medical/surgical implement, copper-alloy, Roman 21, 168
medicines 82, 113
Merrill Lynch Financial Centre (MLFC site) 1, 142–3, 149
metalworking, medieval 85, 87
7–10 Milk Street (MIL72) 7, 36, 86, 90, 113
Mills, Peter, architect 126
Minerva 25, **26**, 29, 167
monastic buildings 53, 57
  dissolution 4, 116, 117, 124
  see also Greyfriars Friary
Montfichet's Tower 57
Moorgate 120
  postern gate 39
mortars, stone, medieval 82, **83**, 86, 115, 170
moss stuffing 92
moulding, Reigate stone 108, **109**
moulds
  for casting candlesticks 85
  ceramic for copper-alloy cast vessels 85, 87
mounts
  copper-alloy, medieval 85, **85**, 115, 173
  iron, medieval 85, 173
  Roman copper-alloy 28, **28**, 167–8
  tinned iron (sheet), medieval 87, **87**, 173
murage tax 59

nails, iron, Roman 31
needle 82
  bone, Roman 20, 168
Newgate Street (and Newgate area) 1, **2**, 63, 64–5, **73**
  butchers 110, 115
  cordwainers 94

191

Index

earlier medieval settlement 64–5
friary and gatehouse 65, 71
gate pulled down 125
medieval gatehouse 4, **43**, 59, **73**
prison 59, 72, 133
redevelopment post-Great Fire 125, 126, **127**, 144
Roman gatehouse 4, 38, **39**, **40–1**, 42, **43**, 45, 51, 53, 59
Shambles meat market 63, 115
stream channel 12
see also Bridge House Rents (B17); Building 14; Christ Church Greyfriars; Swan Inn
Newgate Street (GCC98) 4
Newgate Street (SAM 26U) 1, **2**, 4
3–9 Newgate Street (NEG98) 7, 12, **12**, 13
post-Hadrianic buildings 31, 33, 35
roadside buildings 29
Roman road and ditch 14, 15, **15**
10–15 Newgate Street (SHN97) 7
81 Newgate Street *see* General Post Office (GPO) building
114 Newgate Street (KEW98) 4
Noble Street (WFG8) *see* Bastion 15
Norman, Philip 4–5
Northgate House, Moorgate 110
Norwich (Norfolk), finds 88

OA1 gravel terraces 9
OA2 stream channels 12–13
OA3 brickearth deposits 9–10
OA4 silting and recutting of stream channels 17
OA5 early Roman landscaping 15
OA6 roadside ditch 15, **15**
OA7
 finds 25, **26**, 28–9, **28**, 29, 167–8
 plant remains 177
 pottery 25–6, **26–7**, 29, 164
 Roman well 25–9, 167–8, 175–6
OA8
 plant remains 177
 quarry pits and drain 17, 18
 Roman finds 17, **20**, 168
OA9 courtyard with wells, Roman 19, 20–1, **21**
 plant remains 177
 pottery 20–1, **22–3**, 164
 Roman finds 21, 168
 wall plaster 20, 30
OA10 well, Roman 24
OA11 Hadrianic fire debris 30–1
 glassware 31
 pottery 30–1
 Roman finds 31, 168, 169
 wall plaster 20, 30, **30**
 waster tiles 30
OA12 55
 external dark earth deposits 36, **37**, 55
 pottery 36, 55
 Roman finds 36, **37**, 168
 Saxo-Norman wells 55
OA13 9, *and see* stream channels
OA14/15 31
 finds 35–6, 168
 glass 36
 gravel surface (road) 35, **40–1**, 45, **48–9**
 gullies 35, 36
 pits 35–6, **40–1**, **48–9**
 pottery 35, 36
OA17
 animal bone 109–11, 115, 175–6
 building material 108–9, **108**, **109**
 ditch backfilling (phase 2) **66–7**, 75–115
 ditch backfilling (phase 3) **119**, 120–1, 124
 finds 82–5, **88**, **89**, 114–15, 169, 170–3
 leather artefacts 92–108, 173–5
 plant remains 112–13, 177–80
 pottery 75–81, 165–7
 Roman finds 168
 wooden artefacts 88–92
 see also bowls/platters; sheaths
Ogilby and Morgan's map (1676) 116, **117**, 125, 129

1–6 Old Bailey (LUD82) 7, **38**, 45, 54, 55, **60**, 61, 74, 75, 90, 114, 120, 148
pottery 166–7
orchards 113
Otterley (Oteley), Robert and Katharine 72
oysters 29

palaeochannels 9, 10–13, *and see* stream channels
Paternoster Square, Paternoster Row (NGT00) 7, **15**, 16, 31, 34
Paternoster Square development (GM136) 7, 12, **12**, 13, 16, 29, 45, 148
paving, sandstone, Roman 36
peg roof tiles, medieval 108, 109
pegs
 bone 87
 wood 87, 92
pendant, bronze, 9th-century AD 47
pens, bone 85, 114, **114**, 172–3
peridot 109
period 1 Pleistocene and Holocene geology 9–13
period 2 early Roman settlement 14–35
period 3 later Roman activity 35–52
period 4 Late Saxon settlement 53, 54–7, **55**
period 5 medieval settlement 57–65
 later medieval settlement 65–115
period 6 pre-Great Fire settlement 117–25
period 7 post-Great Fire 125–46
Philippa, Queen 64
Philpot, John, mayor 74
pins
 copper-alloy 82, 85
 wood 85, 92
plant remains 112–13, 176–80
 Roman 29, 31, 36
 medieval 55
 in stream channels 12, 13, 29
Plantation Place 16–17
plaster/wall plaster, Roman
 B1 18
 OA9 20, 30
 OA11 20, 30, **30**
Pleistocene 9
pollen 36
pomerium 31
portcullises 118
postern gates 39, 118, **119**
Postman's Park 1, **2**
Potter, Thomas, saddler 118
pottery
 Roman 10, 40, 163–4
 Alice Holt/Surrey ware (AHSU) 20, **22–3**, 25, **26–7**
 Argonne ware (ARGO) 36
 Baetican amphora (BAETE) 31
 black eggshell ware (BLEG) 20, **22–3**
 black-burnished wares 20, 24, 31
 central Gaulish glazed ware (CGGW) **26–7**
 central Gaulish/Lezoux black colour-coated ware (CGBL) 36
 central Gaulish samian (SAMCG) 20, 31
 early Roman micaceous sandy ware (ERMS) 20, **22–3**
 early Roman sandy ware B (ERSB) **26–7**
 early Roman sandy wares (ERS) 20, **22–3**
 east Gaulish samian (SAMEG) 33
 fine micaceous reduced ware (FMIC) 19, 20, **26–7**
 Highgate Wood red-slipped ware B (HWBR) 23
 Highgate Wood ware B (HWB) 20, **22–3**, 25
 Highgate Wood ware C (HWC) 18, 20, 21, **22–3**, 23, 25, **26–7**
 Hoo ware (HOO) 19
 London mica-dusted ware (LOMI) **26–7**, 31
 Lyon ware (LYON) 24
 north French/south-east England oxidised ware (NFSE) 20, **26–7**
 north Kent shell-tempered ware (NKSH) **26–7**
Rhineland granular grey ware (RGGW) 23
 ring-and-dot beaker ware (RDBK) 19, 21, **22–3**, 25, 26, **26–7**
 samian 29
 south Gaulish samian (SAMLG) 18, 19, 20, 23, 25
 Sugar Loaf Court ware (SLOW) 24
 terra nigra (TN) 20, **22–3**, 23
 unsourced fine oxidised fabric (OXIDF) **26–7**
 unsourced fine reduced ware (FINE) **26–7**
 unsourced grog-tempered ware (GROG) 21, **22–3**
 unsourced oxidised ware (OXID) 21, **22–3**
 unsourced sand-tempered ware (SAND) 23
 unsourced white slip ware (RWS) 26, **26–7**
 Verulamium region white ware (VRW) 19, 20, **22–3**, 23, 25, 26, **26–7**
 medieval 47, 54, 55, **57**, 75–82, 114, 165–7
 9th–10th century AD 54
 Cheam whiteware (CHEA) 75, 77, 81, **81**, 82, 165
 coarse Surrey-Hampshire border ware (CBW) 75, 76, 77, 80–1, **80**, **81**, 82, **82**, 165
 Kingston-type ware (KING) 75, 76–7, **76**, **78**, 80, **80**, **81**, **81**, 82, 142, 165
 Kingston-type ware, white slip painted (KINGSL) 76
 Langerwehe (LANG) 82
 late London-type slipware (LLSL) 75
 late London-type ware (LLON) 82
 late medieval Hertfordshire glazed ware (LMHG) 75, **80**, 81
 London-type wares (LOND) 55, 75, 76, **76**, 77, **78**, **79**, 80, **80**, **81**, **81**, 82, 165
 Low Countries greyware (LCGR) 82
 Mill Green ware (MG) 75, 76, 77, 82, 165
 Raeren 75
 Saintonge 77
 Saintonge mottled green (SAIM) 75
 Saintonge polychrome (SAIP) 75, 82
 Saxo-Norman 55
 shelly-sandy ware (SSW) 55, **57**
 Siegburg (SIEG) 75, 82
 south Hertfordshire-type greyware (SHER) 75, 77, **79**, **80**, 81, 82
 'Tudor green' ware (TUDG) 82
post-medieval 165–7
 see also crucible; louvers; moulds
Poultry Compter 133, 144
1 Poultry (ONE94) 7, 14, 36
prisons 53, 59, 72, 133, 135–42, 144;
 see also Compter prison; Newgate
purse, leather knot from drawstring 103, **103**, 175

quarrying **15**, 16
146 Queen Victoria Street (BHO86) 7
Queenhithe, Saxon dock 54
querns 36, 82, 168

rake/tool, antler, Roman(?) **84**, 85, 172
Randoll, R **132**
Reader, Francis 4–5
Regis House 16, 29
Reigate stone 108, **109**
revetment and gully (S6), medieval **66–7**, 75
 animal bone 111–12, 176
 building material 108, **109**
 finds 83, 85–7, 93, 169, 170, 172, 173, 175
 floor tiles 109, **109**
 leather 175
 plant remains 112–13, 177–80
 pottery 81–2, 165, 166, 167
 tuning peg 87, **88**, 114, 173

Richard II 74
Richard, Abbot of St Albans 117
ridge tiles, medieval 108
ritual activities, Roman 29
river wall, late Roman 46, **46**, 52, 148
Road 1 (R1) London to Silchester road 14–16, **15**, 17, 35, **40–1**
roads *see* streets and roads
roadside buildings, Roman 14, 17–29, 31, 36, 45, 148, 149
roadside ditch (OA6) 14–15, **16**
Rocque's map (1746) 125, **126**
rod, copper-alloy, medieval 87
Roman Wall House, Crutched Friars (GM247) 7
roofing
 Roman slip-decorated tegula 36, **37**
 slate 109, 140
 stone, Roman 36
rosary beads 85, 87

saddles, leather 103, **104–5**, 106, **107–8**, 175
Sadler, John, tilemaker 155
St Alphege churchyard 53, 59
St Alphege Street (WFG17) 7, 120
St Bartholomew's Hospital 1, **2**, 57, 118, **119**, 120
 BAR79 (Medical School site) 7, 10, **15**, 16, 29
 Roman buildings 33, 45, 147
 Roman cremations 33
St Mary le Bow church 14
St Mary in Southwark 59
St Mary Spital 83, 88
St Mary Stratford Langthorne Abbey, Newham (Essex) 82, 86, 115
St Matthew's day 124, **125**
St Nicholas Shambles 64, 110, 112, 121
St Paul's 54, **55**, 56, 57, 59
 Cathedral 125, 148
 precinct boundary 12, 57, 148
St Paul's Churchyard, Juxon House (SLY00) 7
1–3 St Paul's Churchyard (PCH85) 7
St Swithin's Lane, glass lid 86, 170
Saxon/Saxo-Norman
 buildings 54
 channel (ditch) 12, 13, 148
 dock 54
 ground surface 36
 Late Saxon settlement (period 4) 53, 54–7, **55**, 148
 shore raids 46, 52
 sunken buildings (and B31) 54, 55–6
Scheduled Ancient Monuments (SAM) 1, **2**, 4
Seman, Bartholomew 72
Severus, Septimus 40, 46
Shambles 63, 115
Shaw, John, architect 129, 133
shears, iron **84**, 85, 172
sheaths (and sheath-like), leather, medieval 92, 95–101, **95**, **96–7**, **99–100**, **101**, 173–4
Shepherd, G **136**
Shepherd, Thomas Hosmer **131**, **136**
shoe buckles, iron, medieval 85, 93
shoemaking and repairing 93–4
shoes *see* footwear
shops
 Roman 14, 29, 147
 medieval 112
shrines, Roman 29, 31
Simon the Ankar 60
Sir John Moore's Writing School 129
skinning industry 110, 111, 112, **112**, 115
Smithfield Market 56, 94
spatulas
 bone, Roman 17, **20**, 168
 wood 82, 83, 86, 88, 91, **91**, 172
spindle whorl, ceramic, Roman 36, 168
split-pin, copper-alloy, medieval 85
spoons, wood 83, 88, 90–1, **91**, 172
spur, iron 172
spur rowel, iron 86–7, **87**
stable sweepings 113, 177

stave fragments (coopered vessels, buckets?), wood 85, 88, 90
Stinking Lane 63, 64
stone building material, medieval 108–9, **109**
stone objects *see* hones; lamps; mortars
stone roofing, Roman 36
store rooms, Roman 18
Stothard, Thomas **125**
stove tile 126, **128**, 151
Stow, John 5, 47, 53, 59, 61, 63, 65, 73, 74, 114, 118, 121
strap-ends, copper-alloy 82
straps, leather 92, 102–3, **102**, 175
stream channels 10–13, 24, 42, 45, 51, 52, 55, 147, 148
   canalisation (OA4) 17
   eastern (OA2) 13, 17
   Holocene palaeochannels 10–13, **11**
   masonry structure (wall) and Roman finds 11–12, 17, **18–19**, 148
   in north-west of site 10–11, 13
   Pleistocene palaeochannels (OA13) 9
   western (OA2) 12–13, 16, 17, 29, 52
   'western stream' (Roman drains/later boundary ditches) 11, 12, **12**, 13, 57, 148
streets (roads)
   Roman 29, 35, 38, 39, 45
   Late Saxon 53
   post-medieval 116
   see also Road 1
Structure 1 *see* boundary ditch (S1)
Structure 2 city wall phases 7, *and see* Bastions 17 to 19; city wall
Structure 3 defensive ditch 7, *and see* city ditch
Structure 4 *see* banks, S4
Structure 5 *see* berm (S5)
Structure 6 *see* revetment and gully (S6)
stylus, bone 114, **114**, 172
Sudbury House (former), Christchurch Court/Newgate St (SHN97) 7
sunken buildings 54
   B31 Saxo-Norman 55–6
le Swan 72, 73
Swan Inn, Newgate Street 65, 118
Swan Yard 65, 126
swans 29, 110
Swereford, Alexander 59
Sylver, Anthony 121

tank metal glass, post-medieval 169
tanning 94
Taplow gravel terraces 9, 13
taverns, Roman 28–9, 147
Teague, John 138
tegula, Roman 36, **37**, 151
temple(?), Roman 29
textual conventions 7
Thames, River 9
thimble, copper-alloy 82
Threadneedle Street, glass lid 86, 170
tile manufacture, Roman 30
tiles
   (T1–T13) 150, 151
   Low Countries 108, 109
   medieval 47, 108–9, **108**, **109**
   peg roof 108, 109
   ridge 108
   waster 30
   see also floor tiles; tegula; tin-glazed wall tiles
tin-glazed floor tiles 126, 140, **142**
tin-glazed wall tiles
   B26 and B27 126

B28 water cistern 126, **127**, **130**, 150–63
Compter (B30) 140
tinned artefacts 85, 87, **87**, 173
tinned sheet iron (mount), medieval 87, **87**, 173
toggle, bone 85
tomb inscription letter 85, 114, **114**, 172
tombstones, reused 47
tool (utensil), wood 85, 88, 91, **91**, 172
topography 9–13, 40, 45, 52, 147, 148, 149
Tower Hill
   city wall 53
   postern gate 39
Treswell, Ralph 65, **68–9**, 71, **119**
Trig Lane 94, 166
triumphal arches 42
tuning pegs 87, **88**, 114, 173
tweezers, copper-alloy, Roman 31, 168
'Tyme', John, salter 117

upholstery, leather 103, **104–5**, 105–6, 175
urinal base, glass 83
uroscopy 83

vessel glass
   Roman 168, 169
   medieval 82, 83, **84**, 85, 86, **86**, 115, 168, 170
vessels
   copper-alloy, Roman 28, **28**, 167
   mould for copper-alloy cast vessels 85, 87
   wooden base/lid, medieval 83, 86, 88
Viaduct Tavern **136**
Vikings
   garrison in London 54

raids 53, 54, 56, 148

Walbrook stream 9, 14, 40, 45, **46**, 147
Walbrook valley 9, 35
wall tiles *see* tin-glazed wall tiles
Walworth, William 72
Wardmote Inquest 120
Wardrobe Court and Wardrobe Place (WAP88, WDC97) 7
Warwick Lane 4
wash houses 118, **120**
water cistern *see under* Building 28
water conduit 17
water-flea eggs 112
water supply, Roman 16
wattle-lined pits, Saxo-Norman 55, **56**, **57**
wells
   as *favissa*? 29
   Roman (OA7) 25–9, 167–8, 175–6
   Roman (OA9) 20–1, **21**, **22–3**
   Roman (OA10) 24
   Saxo-Norman (OA12) 55
Whittington, Richard 65, 72
Winchester Palace, Southwark 29
window glass, Roman 23, 31, 169
Windsor Court (WFG3) 7, **38**, 40
wire, copper-alloy, medieval 87
wire production waste(?) 85
100 Wood Street 31
Wood Street Compter 144
wooden artefacts 88–92, *and see* bowls/platters; combs; lids; pegs; pins; spatulas; spoon; stave fragments; tool; vessels
Wren, Christopher **3**, 14, 125, 133, 144
wristguards, leather 106, **107–8**, 174, 175

York (Yorks) 83, 91